Wirtschaft und Politik

Reihe herausgegeben von
G. Wegner, Erfurt, Deutschland
G. Mehlkop, Erfurt, Deutschland
A. Brodocz, Erfurt, Deutschland

Die Schriftenreihe „Wirtschaft und Politik" vereint empirisch wie theoretisch orientierte Forschungsarbeiten aus der Volkswirtschaftslehre, Politikwissenschaft und politischen Soziologie, die Fragen der Wirtschaftspolitik und Institutionenökonomie sowie der Konstitution und dem Wandel ökonomischer und politischer Ordnungen thematisieren. Darunter fällt insbesondere die Behandlung politischer Themen mittels ökonomischer Erklärungsansätze und umgekehrt die Auseinandersetzung mit ökonomischen Phänomenen aus Sicht der Politikwissenschaft oder der Soziologie.

The series "Economy and Politics" combines empirically and theoretically oriented research from the fields of economics, political science and political sociology, which analyzes issues of economic policy and institutional economics as well as the constitution and the change of economic and political orders. This includes, in particular, the treatment of political issues by means of economic approaches and, conversely, the examination of economic phenomena from the perspective of political science or sociology.

Weitere Bände in der Reihe http://www.springer.com/series/16152

Christoph Michael Hindermann

The Impact of Economic Freedom on State Legitimacy

An Empirical Investigation

With a preface by Prof. Dr. Gerhard Wegner

Springer Gabler

Christoph Michael Hindermann
Erfurt, Germany

Dissertation der Universität Erfurt, 2018

ISSN 2524-5945 ISSN 2524-5953 (electronic)
Wirtschaft und Politik
ISBN 978-3-658-23194-1 ISBN 978-3-658-23195-8 (eBook)
https://doi.org/10.1007/978-3-658-23195-8

Library of Congress Control Number: 2018951592

Springer Gabler

This Springer Gabler imprint is published by the registered company Springer Fachmedien Wiesbaden GmbH part of Springer Nature
The registered company address is: Abraham-Lincoln-Str. 46, 65189 Wiesbaden, Germany

To Amalia

Acknowledgments

This thesis was written at the University of Erfurt during the years 2014 to 2017. My deep gratitude goes first to my supervisor Professor Dr. Gerhard Wegner who provided me not only with the opportunity to work at his chair, I also greatly benefited from his expertise and his highly valuable comments for completing this thesis. My appreciation also extends to my colleagues at the faculty. This refers to Robert Fritzsch who inspired me with his deep knowledge about political economy and his readiness to discuss matters and to Professor Dr. Guido Mehlkop and Dr. Fabian Kleine who offered me statistical advice. In addition, I also want to thank the Röpke Institute which has always been a forum to present and to discuss this thesis in front of distinguished experts. Thanks to my mother, my father, my brother, and my sister.

Christoph M. Hindermann

Preface

The present study opens the new series "Economy and Politics" which combines empirically and theoretically oriented research from the fields of economics, political science, and political sociology. This includes, in particular, the treatment of political issues by means of economic approaches and, conversely, the examination of economic phenomena from the perspective of political science or sociology. The dissertation by Christoph Hindermann is, in a sense, exemplary for the new series, as it examines a topic that was previously reserved for qualitative sociological reflections. In his study, the author applies methods that are used primarily in economic theory and empirical social research. He enters new scientific territory by analyzing the influence of economic freedom on the legitimacy of states. Empirical research on the legitimacy of states is by itself still an emerging branch of research within political science and sociology, which has so far been reluctant to penetrate the disciplines. The author builds on this empirical research and extends it to the question of the influence of economic freedom, thereby abandoning speculative considerations of normative political theory that have long dominated social philosophy or political theory. These qualitative reflections include, for example, the question of whether democracies promote the legitimacy of political orders or whether capitalism undermines or reinforces their legitimacy. Typically, such analyses are characterized by overall considerations, in which the question of legitimacy is discussed from the perspective of a representative citizen. The scientific value of the present study is based on the fact that the author undertakes a well-founded empirical analysis, which aims at explaining state legitimacy based on the characteristics of countries and their individuals. Such an approach already promises a high yield of knowledge. Since data for the measurement of economic freedom are available and the measuring methods have matured in the meantime, the author can combine two strands of empirical research: Surveys to measure economic freedom and surveys to measure the legitimacy of states. Instead of examining the impact of economic freedom on legitimacy directly, the author chooses an indirect approach by first measuring determinants of the legitimacy of a political order and then, in a second step, examining whether indicators or sub-indicators of economic freedom exert an additional causal influence. While some results of the work confirm previous research, the author also comes to surprising and unexpected new findings, such as the negative influence of the Human Development Index on state legitimacy. It is desirable that the result of the present work resonate both in empirical social theory as well as in qualitative political theory.

Gerhard Wegner

Contents

List of Figures

List of Tables

Abbreviations

AIC	Akaike Information Criterion
BIC	Bayesian Information Criterion
BMA	Bayesian Model Averaging
CPI	Consumer Price Index
CSES	Comparative Study of Electoral Systems
EFW	Economic Freedom of the World Index (by Fraser Institute)
ESS	European Social Survey
EVS	European Values Study
FH	Freedom House
GDP	Gross Domestic Product
GDR	German Democratic Republic
GNI	Gross National Income
HDI	Human Development Index
ICC	Intraclass Correlation Coefficient
IEF	Index of Economic Freedom (by Heritage Foundation)
IMF	International Monetary Fund
OECD	Organization for Economic Cooperation and Development
OLS	Ordinary Least Squares
PCA	Principal Component Analysis
PIP	Posterior Inclusion Probability
PPP	Power Purchasing Parity
QoG	Quality of Government
REML	Restricted Maximum Likelihood
SED	Socialist Unity Party of Germany
SPSS	Statistical Package for the Social Sciences
TI	Transparency International
TTIP	Transatlantic Trade and Investment Partnership
USSR	Union of Soviet Socialist Republics
VIF	Variance Inflation Factor
WDI	World Development Indicators
WVS	World Values Survey

1 Introduction

Throughout history, there has been a relation between those in power and their subordinates in a variety of different settings. Among those, one of the most fascinating power relations is that between the state and its citizens. Although the existence of such a relation seems trivial at a first glance, it becomes more interesting when asking "why do people voluntarily follow and obey" the state, in particular its rules, authorities, and institutions (Dogan, 2003, 116). In short, the answer is: They do, whenever they perceive the state to be legitimate. Since legitimate states do not need to use coercion, repression, or other forms of brutal power to ensure obedience, they can profit from a variety of advantages (to give an example, the German Democratic Republic (GDR) was an illegitimate state since the SED-regime "was clearly repressive"; Jarausch, 2012, 249). Besides the fact that legitimate states have to spend fewer resources on repressing their citizens due to citizen compliance, legitimacy serves as an important pillar (among others) to maintain the stability of the whole political order (Easton, 1965, 1975; Gerschewski, 2013; Hurd, 1990; Lipset, 1959).[1] Furthermore, scholars show that the presence of state legitimacy reduces the probability of a civil war onset (Møller, 2016), increases the ability for (authoritarian) regimes to cope with external pressure such as sanctions (Grauvogel & Soest, 2013), decreases the likelihood that populism arises (Doyle, 2011; Seligson, 2007), and may lower the amount of homicides in a country (Chamlin & Cochran, 2006; Nivette & Eisner, 2013). Due to the various benefits of legitimacy, it is reasonable to ask how to achieve a high degree of state legitimacy. This thesis approaches this research question from an empirical point of view, particularly investigating to what extent state legitimacy is affected by economic institutions.

Scholars typically apply statistical methods to extract the determinants of state legitimacy either based on theoretical considerations or using extrapolative approaches. A review of the existing literature shows that a variety of theoretical reasoning has been put forward (for example Hechter, 2009; Levi et al., 2009; Lipset, 1959; Rothstein, 2009; Scharpf, 1970, 1999) that has been investigated in various empirical studies (for example Booth & Seligson, 2009a; Domański, 2005; Gilley, 2006b, 2009, 2012; Gjefsen, 2012; Levi & Sacks, 2009; Norris, 2011; Power & Cyr, 2009). A general finding of these studies is that the degree of democracy, the welfare level of a country, and the degree of general governance (in terms of fighting corruption, providing a high quality of public goods, and preserving the rule of law) are the core determinants of state legitimacy. Furthermore, other important determinants are the degree of ethnic fractionalization, the change of the welfare level, the unemployment rate, the degree of inequality, and regime tradition. As the

1 In short, Easton (1965, 1975) states that overall system support depends on diffuse and specific support, whereas legitimacy belongs to diffuse support. In the same vein, Lipset (1959) argues that system stability depends on legitimacy and on government effectiveness. Hurd (1990) notes that a system's stability depends on coercion, self-interest, and legitimacy (which are the three ideal types of social control). Finally, Gerschewski (2013) also notes that legitimacy, repression, and co-optation are the three main pillars of system stability, in particular in autocracies. A more detailed review of how legitimacy is related to system stability – according to Easton (1965, 1975), Lipset (1959), Hurd (1990), and Gerschewski (2013) – is given in Appendix A.

C. M. Hindermann, *The Impact of Economic Freedom on State Legitimacy*,
Wirtschaft und Politik, https://doi.org/10.1007/978-3-658-23195-8_1

enumeration shows, most of the extracted determinants refer to political institutions or to services that the state has to provide (the state's "output"; Scharpf, 1970, 1999). At the same time, this enumeration also reveals that one important aspect has largely been neglected in legitimacy research, namely to what degree the economic institutions affect legitimacy.[2]

The economic sphere may play a role for state legitimacy. On the one hand, it impacts the services that the state can provide. For example, if the economic institutions are well developed, citizens – that are protected by property rights – are free to choose an education, to find a profession, and to start their own business. This can increase the growth rate of an economy in the long-run, allowing the state to collect more taxes to provide better public goods. This also raises the general welfare standard of the citizens. On the other hand, economic institutions may also be responsible for adverse effects such as inequality (Berggren, 1999). In this vein, Chamlin and Cochran (2006, 238) note that "an unfair system of economic stratification can readily undermine the legitimacy of the larger social and political order". Since the potential consequences of different economic institutions are already largely reflected in the existing literature, this thesis focuses on whether the economic institutions themselves affect legitimacy. In short, economic freedom means – following liberal scholars such as Hayek (1944, 1960) or Friedman (1969) – such economic institutions that allow individuals to follow their own ends.

To answer that question, the literature provides two methodological strands. On the one hand, scholars try to measure the legitimacy of economic freedom (or the market) directly. For example, Roller (1994) uses a variety of different items to measure the support for the market economy in East and West Germany, assuming that more support for the market indicates a higher degree of market legitimacy.[3] Alternatively, Chamlin and Cochran (2006, 239) "measure perceived economic illegitimacy by the percentage of respondents who state that people in their country are poor because society treats them unfairly." Although those approaches are suitable to measure the support for the market (or economic freedom), they do not contribute to examining whether market institutions affect the legitimacy of the state. To solve this problem, on the other hand, one could measure state legitimacy at first and analyze, in a second step, whether economic freedom is a determinant of legitimacy. If that is the case, there is evidence that the degree of economic freedom (or the given set of economic institutions) affects state legitimacy.

This thesis follows the latter approach. In consequence, it is first necessary to understand the concept of state legitimacy in greater detail (chapter 2). I spend a whole chapter on the conceptualization of legitimacy since it is both a latent and a multidimensional variable. Since a latent variable is not directly observable, a proper (theoretical) concept is needed to make it visible. In addition to this, scholars claim

2 In fact, Gilley (2006a) investigates the correlations between economic freedom and legitimacy. He (2006a) finds a positive correlation and argues that more economic freedom leads to more legitimacy. However, since Gilley (2006a) does not control for other variables, this result may be spurious.

3 In greater detail, Roller (1994) uses items that reflect citizens' support for different distribution principles (achievement principle, equality principle, need principle), citizens' expectations regarding the role of government, and citizens' party preference.

that legitimacy is a multidimensional variable, which requires defining these dimensions. Based on these challenges, a proper legitimacy concept has to clarify (a) who or what is the object of legitimacy, (b) who are the subjects of legitimacy, (c) from which perspective legitimacy is evaluated (micro or macro perspective), and (d) what are the dimensions of legitimacy (Lamb, 2005; Weatherford, 1992). In this thesis, the state is the object of legitimacy that is evaluated by the citizens, assuming a micro perspective. Referring to the dimensions of legitimacy, scholars derive them applying theory-driven (in particular, Beetham, 1991, 1993; Gilley, 2006a, 2009a) or correlation-based approaches (in particular, Norris, 1999, 2011). In short, correlation-based approaches use statistical methods (such as factor analysis) to derive the dimensions of legitimacy (see chapter 3.3.2). Throughout the thesis, I use two different legitimacy concepts, namely the theoretical concept of Beetham (1991) and a correlation-based concept that I borrow from Norris (1999, 2011), which bases on Easton (1965).

Based on this conceptualization, chapter 3 focuses on the measurement of legitimacy. I first present general strategies to measure legitimacy, namely analyzing citizens' attitudes, citizens' behaviors, or public discourses. In a second sub-chapter, I display an overview of different data sources used for legitimacy research. After that, I review how scholars measure legitimacy. That shows that scholars apply either unidimensional (single items or simple indices) or multidimensional measurement approaches.[4] Regarding the latter, I extensively analyze and discuss Gilley's (2006a, 2009a, 2012) theory-driven as well as Norris' (1999, 2011) correlation-based approach. Eventually, I compare Gilley's and Norris' approaches to investigate whether both methods measure the same underlying concept. The results show that Gilley's approach is comparable to two (out of five) dimensions of Norris' approach. In addition, that chapter also provides an update on Gilley's legitimacy scores based on the most recent wave (wave six) of the World Values Survey.

In sum, chapters 2 and 3 serve to properly define and measure the dependent variable (which are two, namely Gilley's and what I call Norris' legitimacy scores). In a next step, I review the literature on the determinants of legitimacy (chapter 4). It becomes apparent that one has to distinguish between country-level and individual-level determinants. Regarding the country level, various scholars already provide classifications for legitimacy's determinants (Gilley, 2006b, 2009a; Hechter, 2009; Levi et al., 2009; Rothstein, 2009; Scharpf, 1970, 1999). In consequence, I use Scharpf's (1970, 1999) input-output scheme in an extended version (adding throughput legitimacy) as the basis to classify legitimacy's determinants. To this classification, I assign all determinants that have been found to be statistically significant in the existing literature. In particular, the input channel subsumes variables that measure the degree of democracy, a regime's tradition, or the degree of ethnic fractionalization, whereas the throughput channel contains variables that measure the level of corruption, the presence of the rule of law, or the degree of impartiality. Finally, the output channel reflects variables such as the absolute or the change of the welfare level, income inequality, the degree of general governance, or the

4 One should note that unidimensional measurement approaches violate the theoretical consideration of treating legitimacy as a multidimensional concept.

unemployment rate. Notably, the review already shows that economic institutions have barely been investigated as determinants of legitimacy.

In the next section (chapter 5), I use the extracted determinants to set up a basic model which serves as a control model for the later investigations of economic freedom's relationship to legitimacy. Since the simultaneous usage of all determinants as independent variables leads to an overspecified model, I use both the backward regression technique and the Bayesian model averaging (BMA) procedure to extract the most relevant variables. Those are the degree of democracy, an interaction term between democracy and democratic history, general governance, the absolute welfare level (HDI), and the unemployment rate. The results are largely the same, irrespective of applying Gilley's or Norris' legitimacy scores or using different methods (OLS, ordered logit models, multi-level analysis). In addition, the results also challenge the findings of Gilley (2006b, 2009a) since I find, for example, that the role of democracy is likely to depend on a country's democratic history but also remains puzzling and that the welfare level has a negative impact on legitimacy (which contrasts Gilley's findings).

Next, chapter 6 deals with the relationship between economic freedom and legitimacy. Before adding economic institutions to the regression equations, chapters 6.1 and 6.2 provide a theoretical discussion on the link between legitimacy and economic freedom referring to the works of Hayek (1944, 1960) and Friedman (1969). In short, the main argument is that legitimacy should be higher if more economic freedom exists since it allows the individuals to follow their own ends. Of course, a variety of counter-arguments exists, which I also discuss. In this vein, I stick to the Economic Freedom of the World Index of Gwartney et al. (2015) who distinguish economic freedom into five different areas, namely 'government size', 'legal system and property rights', 'sound money', 'freedom to trade internationally', and 'regulation'. In consequence, I also discuss the relation of each area to legitimacy. The theoretical arguments already reveal that the relationship is not necessarily positive but could also be negative, implying that each area of economic freedom should be analyzed separately. In addition to the theoretical discussion, I also present in an extensive manner how Gwartney et al. (2015) measure the EFW Index (and its areas).

Based on the theoretical considerations, chapter 6.3 analyzes the impact of economic freedom on legitimacy empirically at the country level. In fact, I abstain from using the overall EFW Index as an independent variable since the EFW Index turns out to be insignificant. Instead, focusing on the areas of economic freedom, the investigations show that the area 'legal system and property rights' – reflecting the rule of law – has a strong positive relation to legitimacy and, thus, also drives the correlation between the EFW Index and legitimacy. For the most part, the other four areas have no explanatory power for legitimacy. Since the results are robust irrespective of using Gilley's or Norris' legitimacy scores, it remains the question why the other four areas have no explanatory power. A potential explanation is that all of those areas have explanatory power for an individual, but – since different people have different interests (preference heterogeneity) – the net effect averages to zero at the country level.

In consequence, chapter 6.4 provides some individual-level analyses to investigate whether individual legitimacy beliefs are affected by economic institutions. Here, I assume that – referring to Scharpf's (1970, 1999) output channel – a person's legitimacy belief becomes maximized if the economic institutions are in line with its interests. Based on four items of the WVS, it is possible to capture an individual's attitude toward competition as well as an individual's satisfaction with the current situation regarding the degree of inequality, the degree of government ownership of businesses, and the degree of government responsibility. On the one hand, I use an individual's attitude toward competition as a proxy for its pro-market attitude. If the pro-market attitude equals the degree of economic freedom, legitimacy will be maximized. The empirical results support this assumption. And, on the other hand, I use the other three items (perceived inequality, government ownership, and government responsibility) to investigate whether individuals show higher legitimacy beliefs if they do not want a change in the current situation. Again, the empirical results confirm that individuals show lower legitimacy beliefs if they want more inequality, government ownership, or government responsibility or less. Hence, the results indicate that the other four areas of economic freedom (those that are found to be statistically irrelevant in the previous chapter) also impact legitimacy at the individual level but that the net effect at the country level is zero. And further, the results also suggest that an increase of economic freedom only leads to more legitimacy if the gap between an individual's pro-market attitude and economic freedom narrows.

Finally, chapter 7 offers a conclusion. Altogether, this thesis ends up with a variety of insights. These are

- an update of Gilley's (2006a, 2009a, 2012) legitimacy scores based on the sixth wave of the World Values Survey (representing the scores for ca. 2012),
- the fact that my results regarding the determinants of legitimacy challenge Gilley's (2006b, 2009a) results, in particular reassessing of the role of democracy and the role of the welfare level,
- the finding that – among the five areas of economic freedom – the area 'legal system and property rights' (i.e. the rule of law) is most important for legitimacy at the country level,
- the result that the economic institutions affect individual legitimacy beliefs (in terms of the gap between pro-market attitude and the objective degree of economic freedom) and,
- the finding that people show higher legitimacy beliefs when the current situation (concerning inequality, government responsibility, and government ownership of businesses) is in line with their preferences.

2 The Concept of Legitimacy

To investigate whether economic freedom impacts the state's legitimacy, it is first necessary to clarify the concept of legitimacy. Since the focus of legitimacy research lies in political science and sociology, it is reasonable to borrow the legitimacy concept from these scientific disciplines. However, concerning the research question, this also means that I combine political and social science (as sources for the legitimacy concept) with economics (since the concept of economic freedom stems from this literature). That is necessary since – to the best of my knowledge – no economic legitimacy concept exists that I could adopt for the research question.

When reviewing the legitimacy literature, scholars claim that legitimacy is a 'complex' concept that is difficult to conceptualize since it is a latent variable, i.e. it cannot be observed or measured directly (Gilley, 2006a, 500; O'Sullivan et al., 2014, 548). Thus, a proper (theoretical) concept and corresponding methods (such as factor analysis or other tools of index creation) are necessary to make state legitimacy visible and measurable.

This chapter is devoted to the conceptualization of legitimacy. This is important since (i) without a proper legitimacy concept it is hardly possible to measure legitimacy accurately (chapter 3) and (ii) the results of any empirical analysis can only be interpreted correctly when the conceptual basis of legitimacy is taken into consideration (chapters 5 and 6).

The concept of legitimacy depends on its definition.[5] For example, Weber (1968, qt. in Bensman, 1979, 360) defines legitimacy as "the belief in a political or social order". Somewhat different, Lipset (1959, 86) notes that legitimacy is "the belief that existing political institutions are most appropriate or proper ones for the society." As a third example, Gilley (2006a, 500) writes that "a state is more legitimate the more that it is treated by its citizens as rightfully holding and exercising political power." I apply the latter definition of legitimacy in the further thesis. Of course, a variety of further definitions exist as presented in Appendix B (Beetham, 1991, 42; Booth & Seligson, 2009b, 1; Easton, 1965, 278; Gilley, 2012, 694; Hurd, 1999, 381; Keman, 2014, 310; Levi et al., 2009, 354; Linz, 1988, 65; Tyler, 2006, 375).[6]

Although all authors define legitimacy, each definition seems to be unique. In consequence, a proper legitimacy definition is typically split up into several elements. According to Lamb (2005), a definition needs to clarify what is legitimated by whom from what perspective, i.e. what is the *object*, the *subject*, and the *perspective* of legitimacy (chapters 2.1, 2.2, 2.3). In addition, scholars also discuss the *dimensionality* of legitimacy since it "is too unwieldy and complex a concept to be grappled in a frontal assault, and virtually all the empirical literature follows the tactic of breaking it into component parts" (Weatherford, 1992, 149) (chapter 2.4).

5 The Cambridge Online Dictionary (2015) gives an initial starting point. There, *legitimacy* is defined as "the quality of being legal" and as "the quality of being reasonable and acceptable".

6 One should note that the terms *legitimacy* and *legitimation* (or *legitimization* in American English) are closely related. Legitimacy refers to "a static property of a regime or institution", whereas the term (de-)legitimation describes "the more active process by which legitimacy is created and maintained or eroded and lost" (Ansell, 2001, 8706).

C. M. Hindermann, *The Impact of Economic Freedom on State Legitimacy*,
Wirtschaft und Politik, https://doi.org/10.1007/978-3-658-23195-8_2

Based on those four elements (object, subject, perspective, and dimensionality of legitimacy), it is possible to classify different concepts of legitimacy both descriptively and formally. In this vein, I introduce and make use of the *legitimacy function L* which is a formalized image of a legitimacy concept.

2.1 The Object of Legitimacy

The object of legitimacy addresses the question what or who is legitimate. The definitions above (see also Appendix B) show that most authors define the object of legitimacy in a political sense comprising institutions, authorities, and the regime as a whole. For example, Weber (1968) speaks about the *political or social order*; Lipset (1959), Linz (1978) and Hurd (1999) refer to *political institutions*; Easton (1965) names *authorities* and *the regime;* Beetham (1991) names *political power*; and Gilley (2012) refers to *the state*. Moreover, Tyler (2006) and Booth and Seligson (2009a) speak about the *government* (governmental legitimacy) and Keman (2014) addresses the *democratic performance* (democratic legitimacy).[7]

In this thesis, I adopt the label of Gilley (2006a, 2006b, 2009a, 2012) and define the state as the object under study. Further, I use the phrases *legitimacy of the state*, *state legitimacy*, *political legitimacy*, or just *legitimacy* interchangeably throughout this thesis. The state is defined as "the basic *institutional* and *ideological* structure of a political community" (Gilley, 2006a, 501). This definition implies that I am interested in the legitimacy of the whole political system but not in the legitimacy of a particular power holder, although both types overlap to some extent.[8]

To be more precise, Gilley (2006a, 501) originally notices that the government is not part of the *state* definition, arguing that citizens in democratic countries clearly distinguish between views of the state and views of politicians, parties, and governments. Similarly, Beetham (1993, 489) also writes that the legitimacy of a government and the legitimacy of a political system are two different concepts.[9] This distinction reflects the idea that "the performance failure of a government is often irrelevant to the legitimacy of a political system, since one purpose of that latter's appointment rules is to ensure the removal of failures and to allow their replacement by new people and new policies" (for example, through elections) (Beetham, 1993, 489). At the same time, the argument also shows that the legitimacy of a government and the legitimacy of a political system are related if the political system provides no

7 Of course, the object of legitimacy depends on the research question (Lamb, 2005, 6). To name two examples, Costa-Lopes et al. (2013) investigate the legitimacy of social inequality and Schoon (2014) analyzes the legitimacy of violence.

8 Thus, one has to decide between the legitimacy of the state (representing the legitimacy of the whole political system), the legitimacy of the government (asking whether the government in place is legitimate; see Booth & Seligson, 2009a), and the legitimacy of democracy (referring to whether the democratic form of government is legitimate, see Keman, 2014).

9 Beetham (1993, 489) expresses the difference between the legitimacy of a government and the legitimacy of a political system in more descriptive manner. In detail, he (1993, 489) distinguishes between "the legitimacy of an individual power-holder and the legitimacy of the rules under which he or she holds power: between the legitimacy of a government and the legitimacy of a political system".

mechanism to correct government failures. Here, Beetham (1993, 489) notes that "[i]t is only when the system proves incapable of removing failures, or when failure becomes chronic, that the legitimacy of the political system itself is eroded." Hence, the degree to which government activities have an impact on legitimacy strongly depends on the particular political system and on the form of government (for example, is there a democratic or a totalitarian system?). Gilley (2006a, 501) also follows this line of reasoning: He writes that the government and the political system are dependent "when the government has 'captured' the state" which is typically the case in non-democratic states where the leaders, parties, and governments are not separable from the state.[10] This may be the reason why he changes his understanding of the state in his later book (2009a, 8); there, he notes that the institutional structure of the state "cover the organizations, agencies, departments, and processes of a political community, as well as the particular holders of state power ('the government')."

In sum, one can discuss whether the government (those people who hold the power of a state) should be a part of the state definition. Ideally, one could – when measuring legitimacy – control for the form of the political system. For example, one could give a high (small) weight to the government in an autocratic (democratic) regime.[11] This procedure considers that a democracy typically reflects a set of political institutions that allows for open access to the political system (for example elections or the possibility to found a party), whereas autocracies are a set of political institutions that limit or even entirely abandon the access to the political system. In this thesis, it depends on the concrete measurement approach of legitimacy whether the government is part of the state or not (chapter 3).[12]

2.2 The Subject of Legitimacy

In a next step, one needs to specify the subject of legitimacy, clarifying "who is offering or withholding support (population)" (Lamb, 2005, 5). However, not all legitimacy definitions contain an explicit statement about the subject of legitimacy. For example, Lipset (1959) and Linz (1988) write about a belief in an object of legitimacy but do not explicitly state *who* believes. Is it a person, a group of persons, or even the whole society? This becomes clearer when analyzing other legitimacy definitions. For example, Easton (1965) is interested in the "way [*a person*, author's note] sees these objects", which is similar to Hurd's (1999) understanding who refers to *an actor*. Similarly, Keman (2014) uses the word *popular*, and Tyler (2006) speaks about *those*

10 Originally, Gilley (2006a, 501) writes that "[t]he exception to this is when the government has 'captured' the state – that is, where it has overstepped the bounds of holding office to actually define that office. A better term for this would be 'state-embedded polity', which covers those cases where leaders, parties or governments are indistinguishable from the state."

11 According to this procedure, both governmental and democratic legitimacy as proposed by Booth and Seligson (2009a) and Keman (2014) can be subsumed under the concept of political legitimacy.

12 As it turns out, Gilley (2006a, 2009a, 2012) does not use items that correspond to the government (such as "Confidence in the government") to measure legitimacy. In contrast, I also compile an alternative legitimacy measure (which I call Norris' legitimacy scores) that contains items that refer to the government.

connected to the object of legitimacy. In sum, single persons or actors are the subjects of legitimacy (empirical citizens). Since the state affects all citizens of a country, this thesis defines them as the subjects of legitimacy (Gilley, 2012; Levi et al., 2009; Booth & Seligson, 2009a).[13]

2.3 The Perspectives of Legitimacy

Legitimacy can be analyzed from two perspectives (figure 1). Both focus on the question *who evaluates* political legitimacy. Weatherford (1992) and Lamb (2005) distinguish between the micro and the macro perspective.[14] The micro perspective states that the *citizens evaluate* political legitimacy such that their beliefs, attitudes, or actions matter. In contrast, in the macro perspective, the *researcher* evaluates political legitimacy according to (normative) criteria.[15] This thesis follows the micro perspective.

Figure 1: The Perspectives of Legitimacy

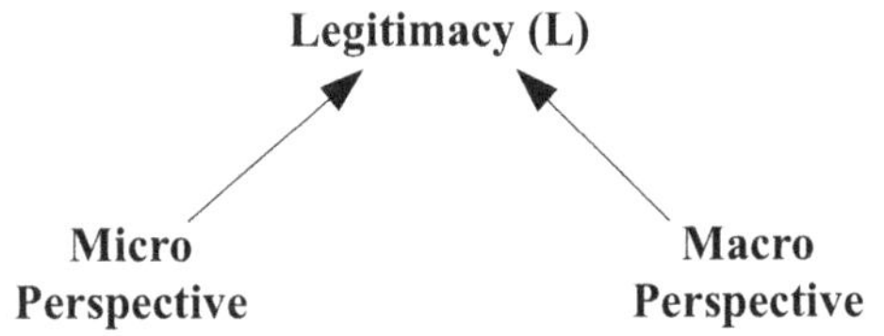

Source: Own representation

2.3.1 The Macro Perspective

According to the macro perspective, a researcher defines "both the object under study and the normative criteria for its legitimacy, then proceeds by measuring the degree to which the object meets the criteria" (Lamb, 2005, 10).[16] Thus, the researcher evaluates – based on normative criteria which specify how a legitimate political system ought to

13 Of course, the subject of legitimacy can differ, depending on the research question. For example, in an organizational context, the subject of legitimacy are the employees since they offer or withhold legitimacy toward the manager (Suchman, 1995); in an educational context, the subjects are pupils who legitimize the teacher (O'Sullivan, 1989).

14 Other scholars distinguish between a normative and a subjective view (O'Sullivan et al., 2014).

15 In addition to the micro and the macro perspective, one could also introduce a third perspective that unites both the micro and the macro perspective: The *combined perspective*. The idea is that a researcher proposes normative criteria (as in the macro perspective) that are evaluated by the citizens (as in the micro perspective).

16 However, this requires the assumption "that an outside observer, relying on fairly gross aggregate evidence, can measure the legitimacy of a political system and rank it in comparison with other systems" (Weatherford, 1992, 150).

be – whether the state is legitimate or not. That also means that citizens' attitudes are not relevant or, as Weatherford (1992, 150) puts it, "the beliefs of citizens at any given time are not essential information for determining the system's legitimacy". That can also be considered as a shortcoming of the macro approach since subjective opinions have no weight in the judgment whether the state is legitimate or not (Weatherford, 1992, 150).

Based on these considerations, the following legitimacy function represents the macro perspective. First of all, state legitimacy depends on the judgment of the researcher R (equation [1]).[17]

$$L = L(R) \qquad [1]$$

It is further assumed that legitimacy L increases in R (equation [2]).

$$\frac{\partial L}{\partial R} > 0 \qquad [2]$$

Further, the researcher's judgment depends on a normative criterion C or a vector of normative criteria **C**. To formalize this, one can write that the researcher's judgment R depends on the degree to which a criterion C_i is met (equation [3]).

$$R = R(C_i) \qquad [3]$$

In the last step, one can insert equation [3] into equation [1]. Assuming that n different normative criteria exist, the complete legitimacy function of the macro perspective reads as follows (equation [4]).

$$L = L((R)C_1, \ldots, R(C_n)) = L(R(\mathbf{C})) \qquad [4]$$

The legitimacy of the state L depends on the judgment of the researcher to what degree n different normative criteria C_i are fulfilled. Various theories and contributions exist that propose normative criteria for legitimacy. To get an overview, Zelditsch (2001) provides a comprehensive list of the theoretical legitimacy literature published since *Thucydides History of the Peloponnesian War* in 423 b.c.[18] Alternatively, in a more condensed fashion, Weatherford (1992) summarizes that important normative legitimacy criteria are accountability, efficiency, procedural fairness, and distributive fairness. In greater detail, accountability refers to the question whether there is a process that allows wide and effective participation that make rulers accountable to the governed, for example by regular and frequent elections. Efficiency refers to the question whether the system with its institutions is efficient or whether it wastes resources. Next, procedural fairness means that rights exist that guarantee open and

17 Here and in the following, any formula symbols that are **bold** represent a vector of arguments.

18 To offer selected examples, those theories range from scholars that represent social contract theory (such as Hobbes, Locke, or Rousseau) over scholars that relate or equate legitimacy to justice (such as Rawls) to scholars that have a more sociological background and stress the importance of procedures (Luhmann) and the discourse (Habermas).

equal access to the decision areas. And eventually, distributive fairness is given when some equality principle is anchored in the institutions that ensures a fair distribution of output.

2.3.2 The Micro Perspective

In contrast to the macro perspective, the micro perspective "relies instead on reported opinions about political support and the legitimacy of the object under study, and it works to identify the population's own criteria for that object's legitimacy" (Weatherford, 1992, 150-151). Thus, if one analyzes political legitimacy from a micro perspective, the beliefs (Easton, 1965, 278; Weber, 1968), the convictions (Easton, 1965, 278), or the perceptions (Tyler, 2006, 377) of the citizens matter. In consequence, it could be the case that citizens perceive the state as legitimate (since they form their beliefs according to their own individual normative criteria) although the state does not meet the criteria of legitimacy from a normative view (i.e. marco perspective) and vice versa.

The micro perspective can also be represented by the legitimacy function. As argued, political legitimacy depends on the beliefs, the convictions, or the perceptions of the citizens. Those represent an attitude A or the vector of attitudes $\boldsymbol{A}$ that the citizens have toward the state. Assuming that the beliefs lead to actions, actual behavior B or the vector of actual behaviors $\boldsymbol{B}$ of the citizens can also be used to address legitimacy from the micro perspective. The following legitimacy function (equation [5]) expresses these considerations.

$$L=L(A_1,\ldots,A_n;B_1,\ldots,B_m)=L(\boldsymbol{A};\boldsymbol{B}) \qquad [5]$$

Again, the legitimacy function L increases in affirmative attitudes $\boldsymbol{A}$ and affirmative behaviors $\boldsymbol{B}$ of the citizens toward the state (equation [6] and equation [7]).

$$\frac{\partial L}{\partial A_i}>0 \quad \forall \; i=1,\ldots,n \qquad [6]$$

$$\frac{\partial L}{\partial B_j}>0 \quad \forall \; j=1,\ldots,m \qquad [7]$$

Thus, legitimacy depends on the attitudes and the actions of the citizens. In contrast to the macro perspective, the legitimacy function contains no normative criteria.

The belief in legitimacy, which has its origin in the contributions of Weber (1922), is the very foundation of the micro perspective. Since I refer to Weber later in the thesis, I shall shortly introduce Weber's (1922) belief in legitimacy and show afterwards why scholars do not apply Weber in modern legitimacy research:

- *Weber's Belief in Legitimacy.* The belief in legitimacy strongly refers to Max Weber (1922). He not only coined the expression *Legitimitätsglauben* (belief in legitimacy) but also developed a non-normative, rather descriptive sociological theory on legitimacy. To start with, Weber (1972, 122, 549) defines legitimacy as the belief in a given '*Herrschaft*'. The belief itself refers to relevant actors (the citizens) rather than to the normative judgment of a neutral observer (Weber, 1972, 122; Beetham, 1991, 35).[19] Weber (1972, 29; Beetham, 1991, 35) defines '*Herrschaft*' as the relation between command and obedience in which subordinates unconditionally follow the instructions of the authorities (those in control of the '*Herrschaft*'). Following this, '*Herrschaft*' can also exist without legitimacy since the principle of command and obedience can also be enforced through mere coercion.

Further, Weber (1972, 549) argues that any '*Herrschaft*' is typically accompanied by the belief in legitimacy due to two reasons (Beetham, 1991, 35). One the one hand, those in control of the '*Herrschaft*' have a psychological need for self-justification such that they see their "advantage as deserved or legitimate, and not arbitrary" (Beetham, 1991, 35; Weber, 1972, 549). On the other hand, legitimacy maintains and even enhances the stability of the system or the given '*Herrschaft*'. As long as the subordinates believe in a legitimate '*Herrschaft*', they obey the authorities and comply with those in control of the '*Herrschaft*' (Beetham, 1991, 35-36).

For Weber, there exists not merely one belief in legitimacy but rather several types, depending on the organization of '*Herrschaft*' in place. Thus, a different form of '*Herrschaft*' also has a different source of the belief in legitimacy. Weber suggests three ideal forms of a legitimate '*Herrschaft*', which are based on tradition, charisma, and legal procedures (bureaucracy) (Weber, 1922, see also Beetham, 1991, 36):

> *Traditional Legitimacy.* Traditional legitimacy refers to the belief in the value of tradition. This means that subordinates obey an authority because of traditional norms and obligations.
>
> *Charismatic Legitimacy.* Charismatic legitimacy is the result of the belief in extraordinary characteristics and abilities of an individual. Subordinates obey the leader, "whose authority stands outside any rule or precedent", because of "the continued demonstration of charismatic qualities".
>
> *Legal Legitimacy.* Legal legitimacy is the result of the common belief in the authority of rules that "have been established by formally correct procedures". Thus, legal legitimacy hinges on the processes of rule creation and the interpretation of the rules. Subordinates do not obey the authorities but the rules.

As noticed, traditional, charismatic, and legal legitimacy are ideal types of a legitimate '*Herrschaft*'. Of course, one has to stress that "in practice there exist all kinds of admixture between them, and forms of transitions from one to the

19 Here, I keep German word '*Herrschaft*' as also done by Beetham (1991). He (1991, 35) also gives some reasons why the English translation of '*Herrschaft*' is problematic.

next" (Beetham, 1991, 36). To give one example, charismatic *'Herrschaft'* is typically perceived as extraordinary and may transform over time to traditional *'Herrschaft'* (Kim, 2003, 18).

- *Discussing Weber's Belief in Legitimacy.* Although Weber's contribution to legitimacy is fundamental, scholars point to four major points of critique. First, various scholars argue that Weber's typology has become obsolete and anachronistic (Dogan, 2009), is fundamentally flawed (Beetham, 1991), or "is basically unsound and should be discarded" (Friedrich, 1961, 16). For example, Dogan (2009) argues that both traditional and charismatic legitimacy hardly exist any longer in the modern world or have become obsolete.[20] According to him (2009, 202-203), only legal legitimacy remains but consists itself of at least three types: Advanced pluralist democracies, authoritarian regimes, and totalitarian regimes. In the same vein, Beetham (1991, 37) argues that Weber's typology fails to account for the legitimacy of the modern state and different political contemporary systems. To support this critique, Beetham (1991, 37) refers to several modern political systems of the twentieth century – communist regimes, liberal democracies, and military dictatorships – that can barely be addressed by the typology of Weber.[21] However, although some scholars conclude that Weber's typology is obsolete, it is still used as a basis for modifications. For example, Zhao (2009, 418) applies Weber's typology but (a) replaces traditional legitimacy with ideological legitimacy, (b) drops charismatic legitimacy (since it tends to be an extreme form of ideological legitimacy), (c) adds performance legitimacy, and (d) keeps legal-electoral legitimacy for analyzing the legitimacy of historical and contemporary China.

  Second, Weber's belief in legitimacy is not appropriate for practical or empirical applications. The argument is that the simple belief in legitimacy is not informative since it may only express the state's ability to generate consensual beliefs (Zhao, 2009, 417). Strong beliefs in legitimacy could just be a result of false consciousness of the people caused by indoctrination techniques (Zhao, 2009, 417). Schaar (1989, 20-21) puts this in a similar fashion and writes that the simple belief in legitimacy may be just "a function of a system's ability to persuade members of its own appropriateness."

20 First, Dogan (2009, 196-198) gives a variety of historical examples why traditional legitimacy has been 'desacralized'. Then, he (2009, 198-202) discusses why charismatic legitimacy is obsolete.

21 Regarding the communist regime, Beetham (1991) refers to a variety of studies that try to attribute the communist model to one of the three types of legitimacy. The results show that there is little consensus among scholars. For example, Gill (1982) ends up arguing that the communist model was primarily based on charismatic leadership. In contrast, Lane (1984) refers to the importance of longer-standing national traditions. Rigby (1982), finally, discovers a fourth Weberian type of legitimacy (goal rational) that aims at the ideal communist society. Also, with respect to liberal democracies, Beetham (1991, 37) argues that Weber's typology misses to fully explain political legitimacy. In detail, he notes that "it soon becomes evident that no amount of commitment to legality and procedural correctness can explain just what it is that gives electoral rules of appointment to office their validity [...] and that the charisma of leadership is quite insufficient to fill this gap in account of legitimation." Finally, Weber's typology also fails to explain the *'Herrschaft'* in military dictatorships. The reason is that not legitimacy but rather the absence of legitimacy characterizes this form of governance (Beetham, 1991, 37).

Third, the simple belief in legitimacy is inadequately founded from a normative or theoretical perspective. For example, Schaar (1981, 20-21) notices that the definitions of Weber and most others (see Appendix B) "all dissolve legitimacy into belief or opinion. If a people hold the belief that existing institutions are 'appropriate' or 'morally proper', then those institutions are legitimate. [...] the older concept has been trimmed of its cumbersome 'normative' and 'philosophical' parts."

And fourth, scholars criticize that the belief in legitimacy is unidimensional. For example, Beetham (1991, 42) argues that the oversimplification of "a complex of different elements" into a single dimension (the belief in legitimacy) is misleading. In particular, he (1991, 42) writes that "legitimacy is a multi-layered concept, and the legitimation of power occurs at a number of different levels, which need to be carefully distinguished."[22]

Figure 2: Summarizing the Perspectives of Legitimacy

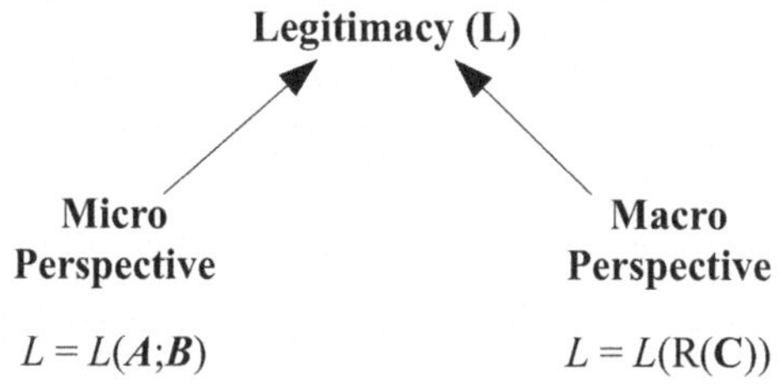

Source: Own representation

2.4 The Dimensions of Legitimacy

One critique of Weber's belief in legitimacy is its *unidimensionality*. Instead, a variety of scholars argue that legitimacy is a *multi-layered* or *multidimensional* concept (Beetham, 1991, 1993; Dalton, 2004; Easton, 1975; Gilley, 2006a, 2006b, 2009a, 2012; Møller, 2016; Norris, 1999). To determine legitimacy's dimensions, two derivation strategies exist, namely (i) one that is based on (normative) theory and (ii) another that is based on statistical methods (chapter 2.4.1). Irrespective of the applied derivation procedure, one can analyze the resulting dimensions from a micro and/or a macro perspective. To evaluate overall legitimacy, one finally needs to aggregate the dimensions. The aggregation procedure depends on the assumption whether all dimensions are necessary for legitimacy (*Beethamian legitimacy function*) or not (*Weberian legitimacy function*) (chapter 2.4.2). If one treats legitimacy as

22 In detail, Beetham (1991, 40-42) distinguishes between the juridical level of legitimacy (*the rightful source of rules or laws*), the normative-substantive level of legitimate power (*rightful source of authority for political power*), and the behavioral level of legitimacy (*actions that express consent to authority*). See chapter 2.4 for further details.

unidimensional, this represents a special case of the multidimensional conception (amount of dimensions is one). Figure 3 offers an initial overview.

Figure 3: The Dimensions of Legitimacy

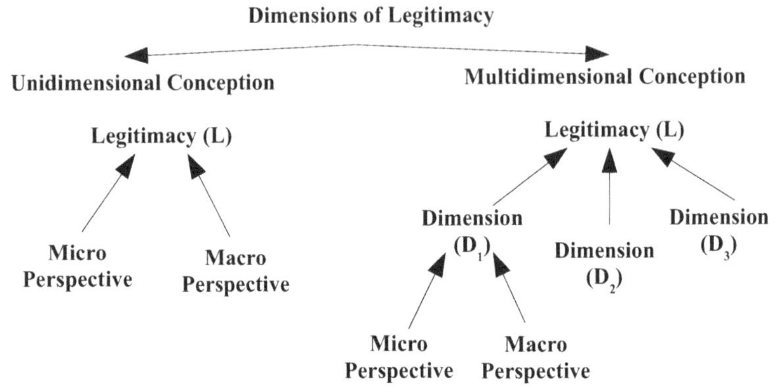

Source: Own representation

2.4.1 Derivation of the Dimensions of State Legitimacy

Across the literature, a variety of scholars recognize that legitimacy is a multi-layered concept (Beetham, 1991, 1993; Dalton, 2004; Easton, 1975; Gilley, 2006a, 2006b, 2009a, 2012; Møller, 2016; Norris, 1999). That means that legitimacy consists of several dimensions that all contribute to overall legitimacy (equation [8]).

$$L = L(D_1, D_2, \dots, D_n) = L(\boldsymbol{D}) \quad [8]$$

Again, *L* is the abbreviation for legitimacy and *D* stands for a dimension of legitimacy. The index of *D* signals that *n* dimensions exist. Thus, legitimacy *L* is a function of the vector of its dimensions ***D***. The amount of dimensions is not given in advance and depends on the method to determine the dimensions.
Further, I assume that each dimension positively contributes to overall legitimacy. Thus, the first derivative with respect to any dimension D_i is positive (equation [9]).

$$\frac{\partial L}{\partial D_i} > 0 \quad \forall \; i = 1, \dots, n \quad [9]$$

Moreover, each dimension depends on the arguments and the properties of the underlying perspective. In the case of the micro perspective, the dimension D_i depends on the vector of attitudes $\boldsymbol{A}$ and the behaviors $\boldsymbol{B}$ of the citizens (equation [10]). In the case of the macro perspective, a researcher R evaluates each dimension D_i based on the existence of specific normative criteria $\boldsymbol{C}$ (equation [11]).

(micro perspective) $$D_i = D_i(\boldsymbol{A}; \boldsymbol{B}) \qquad [10]$$

(macro perspective) $$D_i = D_i(R(\boldsymbol{C})) \qquad [11]$$

Since the number of dimensions depends on the derivation procedure, I shed some light on this issue. Again, a researcher can use either (i) *theory-driven approaches* or (ii) *statistical methods* (also called correlation-based approaches; Gilley, 2012, 693-694).

Theory-Driven Derivation

Tautologically, theory-driven approaches derive legitimacy's dimensions theoretically. Various scholars propose different (normative) theories (for example Easton (1965, 1975); but also other scholars such as Hobbes, Locke, Rousseau, Rawls, Habermas, and Luhman). In this thesis, I focus on the contribution of Beetham (1991, 1993) since his theoretical approach (i) represents the conceptual basis for the legitimacy measure in the upcoming chapters and (ii) is the basis of a variety of quantitative legitimacy studies (Gilley, 2006a, 2006b, 2009a, 2012; Nivette & Eisner, 2013; Power & Cyr, 2009).

Beetham's (1991) approach belongs neither only to the macro perspective nor only to the micro perspective. Rather, he understands legitimacy as a multidimensional concept that combines both micro and macro perspective. He (1993, 490) writes that "the purpose of my claim was to underline the focal position which the concept of legitimacy occupies between normative political philosophy and explanatory political science, and the necessity of clarifying the relationship between the two if the concept is to be used effectively in either."

Repeatedly, Beetham (1991) starts by criticizing Weber (1972). He stresses (i) that Weber's (1922) typology of legitimacy is misleading and (ii) that Weber's belief in legitimacy (*Legitimitätsglauben*) is a too simple concept to grasp the state's legitimacy appropriately. In particular, Beetham (1991, 34) writes that the "typology of Weber is a misleading tool for the analysis of the modern state; especially for the comparative analysis of political systems" (see also chapter 2.3.2). In contrast to Weber, Beetham (1991, 42) understands legitimacy as a multi-layered concept, arguing that "the legitimation of power occurs at a number of different levels, which need to be carefully distinguished." In this vein, Beetham (1991, 42) proposes that legitimacy consists of three distinct dimensions, namely '*legality*', '*normative justifiability*', and '*express consent*'. In detail,

- *Legality* refers to the extent political power "is acquired and exercised in accordance with the rules or the laws";
- *Normative justifiability* refers to the extent that "rules or laws embody an acknowledged principle of political authority, in terms of which they can be justified"; and
- *Express consent* means that there is "evidence of express consent to authority on the part of those qualified to give it."

All three dimensions – 'legality', 'normative justifiably', and 'express consent' – are essential for legitimacy. In addition, a closer look at the three dimensions shows (i) that they are non-normative, (ii) that the dimensions 'legality' and 'normative justifiability' can be related to the *rule of law*, and (iii) that they (still) have some similarities with Weber's ideal types of a legitimate '*Herrschaft*':

- *Non-Normative Dimensions.* At first, it turns out that the dimensions are free of normative statements. This allows using the dimensions to analyze different political systems (Beetham, 1991, 43). Regarding the first dimension ('legality'), every country not only has its own procedures to determine the law but also has a different juridical framework that regulates what the state is allowed to do and what not (Beetham, 1991, 43). For example, in a modern (democratic) state, political power can be achieved through elections, whereas in a traditional state, political power is acquired through heritage. To give a second example, some modern states have the right to conscript people into the basic military service, whereas other states do not have this right. Thus, to achieve legality, a state needs to act within the framework determined by the rules and the laws.
  When it comes to the second dimension ('normative justifiability'), the label of this dimension seems to indicate a normative character. However, Beetham (1991, 43) writes that "rules or laws embody an acknowledged principle of political authority, in terms of which they can be justified". Similar to the first dimension, that means that every country may have a different "source of political authority that is acknowledged as valid within the society" (Beetham, 1991, 43). In other words, 'normative justifiability' means that there is a "common framework of belief" between the political authorities (the state) and the citizens (Beetham 1991, 69; Gilley, 2006a, 502). If this dimension were normative, one would expect criteria that define when the source of political authority is justifiable (for example that rules and laws are based on human rights or come into force through a democratic process). The same argument is also put forward by Gilley (2006a, 502-503). He stresses that 'normative justifiability' is given if the state and the citizens share the same ideas, values, and principles.
  The last dimension ('express consent') is per definition positive. This dimension "refers to the positive actions that express a citizen's recognition of the state's right to hold political authority and an acceptance, at least in general, to be bound to obey the decisions that result" (Gilley, 2006a, 503). Hence,

'express consent' reflects a control dimension. For example, if the first two dimensions indicate legitimacy, but citizens protested against the state, the state is likely not to be legitimate. Then, the first two dimensions do, for whatever reason, not accurately determine political legitimacy.[23] Similar to the other dimensions, people in different countries may also have different ways to express consent. Beetham (1991, 43) notices that countries "will differ according to who is qualified to give consent, and how that consent is organized and mobilised."

To summarize the first aspect, Beetham (1991, 43) defines three dimensions of legitimacy. The combination of these determines the legitimacy of the state. In addition, it is important to notice that the dimensions are non-normative in advance. However, a researcher always has the possibility to analyze each dimension from a macro perspective. Then, the researcher has to define normative criteria for each dimension.

- *Legality, Normative Justifiability, and the Rule of Law.* Second, the dimensions 'legality' and 'normative justifiability' are related to the rule of law. In detail, 'legality' – defined as the extent to which political power "is acquired and exercised in accordance with the rules or the laws" – expresses the formal rule of law which is "characterized by their focus on the form of so-called rule of law-compliant legal rules, rather than on the content of such rules or on the values they pursue" (Hachez & Wouters, 2013, 7).[24] Thus, the formal rule of law requires that the state acts in accordance with the legal system. The actual content of the legal system is irrelevant to the formal dimension. Obviously, 'legality' and the formal rule of law are congruent. Gilley (2006a) also comes to this conclusion. Further, he (2006a, 502) notes that as long as political power is exercised in accordance with the rules and laws, it is predictable and general. As a consequence, social life becomes predictable since ordinary citizens can anticipate the benefits and consequences of their actions in political but also social and economic life (see also Hayek, 1944).[25] 'Legality' (or the formal rule of law), however, says nothing about how 'good' or 'bad' are the rules in place. For example, the police may have rights that are legal or respect the formal rule of law, but these rights may be undesired by the citizens (e.g. monitoring

23 I discuss this issue in greater detail in chapter 2.4.2 when it comes to the aggregation of the dimensions.

24 In fact, the formal rule of law depends on constituting criteria. For example, Fuller (1969, 41-90 qt. in Hachez & Wouters, 2013, 7) proposes the following eight elements: (i) the law should be general; (ii) the law must be promulgated; (iii) the law should not be retroactive; (iv) the law must be clear; (v) the law should not be self-contradictory; (vi) the law must not require the impossible; (vii) the law should be reasonably constant through time; and (viii) there should be congruence between the declared rule and official action.

25 Predictability, generality, and also publicity are the key issues of the formal rule of law since they ensure legal certainty (Hachez & Wouters, 2013, 7). Thus, the rule of law is also important in economics. For example, Hayek (1944, 76) notes that people are more likely to invest under the rule of law; the reason is that "under the Rule of Law the government is prevented from stultifying individual efforts by *ad hoc* action. Within the known rules of the game the individual is free to pursue his personal ends and desires, certain that the powers of government will not be used deliberately to frustrate his efforts." See chapter 6 for more details.

rights). To give another example, one could think about laws that discriminate certain groups of citizens. In that case, the law is legal, but it is not normatively justifiable from the point of view of the discriminated group.

Hence, also the second dimension ('normative justifiability') needs to be considered since it asks whether the "rules or laws embody an acknowledged principle of political authority, in terms of which they can be justified." In fact, the substantive (or material) rule of law expresses the same idea, which focuses more on (normative) values of the law and how they can be achieved, promoted, or embodied (Hachez & Wouters, 2013, 9). Thus, 'normative justifiability' and the substantive rule of law are widely congruent.

In total, Beetham's first two dimensions of legitimacy reflect the rule of law. This indicates that the rule of law could be the underlying (implicit) normative criterion of his legitimacy concept; at least regarding the first and second dimension (implying that a legitimate state should act in accordance with the formal and substantial rule of law).[26]

- *Similarities with Weber's Ideal Types.* Beetham's dimensions also show some similarities with Weber's three ideal types of a legitimate '*Herrschaft*'. Beetham (1991, 44-45) himself writes that:

> *It also has to do with the fact that each of Weber's types does contain, concealed within it and in a misleading manner, a different element necessary to legitimacy; so that, if they are combined together, the typology appears to have some credibility as an analytical instrument. Thus the legal type, as its name implies, focuses attention on the element of legal validity. The traditional type can serve in turn to characterise the beliefs established within a given society about the rightful source of political authority. And the charismatic type can, if attention is directed towards the actions of followers rather than the assumed qualities of leaders, serve to identify the element of consent that is necessary to legitimacy. However, in Weber's typology each of these appears in a distorted form, since what I have argued to be necessary elements of legitimacy as such become transposed into an independent and self-sufficient type of legitimacy. I hope I have not only convincingly shown where Weber was mistaken; but also have demonstrated that a multi-layered conception provides us with the only satisfactory way of elucidating the complexity of legitimacy, and in particular the legitimacy of the modern state.*

Thus, Beetham (1991, 44-45) argues that one can compare his dimensions of legitimacy ('legality', 'normative justifiability', and 'express consent') with Weber's three types of a legitimate '*Herrschaft*' (legal, traditional, and charismatic legitimacy). Furthermore, Beetham (1991, 44-45) even acknowledges that Weber's ideal types have "some credibility as an analytical

26 Above, I argue that Beetham's dimensions are non-normative since he does not claim that specific normative criteria (for example the presence of elections) need to be fulfilled. However, the analysis suggests that Beetham's dimensions have an implicit underlying normative criterion, namely the rule of law.

instrument" when combined. Thus, it remains to clarify the difference between Weber's and Beetham's understanding of legitimacy.

According to Weber, in the ideal case, '*Herrschaft*' can be legitimate if it is built on one type of legitimacy (for example, if '*Herrschaft*' is solely built on tradition, it is legitimate even without legal or charismatic legitimacy). That means that not all dimension are necessary for overall legitimacy. To be precise, Beetham (1991, 44-45) writes that each of the Weberian dimensions "appears in a distorted form; necessary elements of legitimacy transposed into an independent and self-sufficient type of legitimacy". The important point is that Weber sees in *each of the ideal types* "*an independent and self-sufficient type* of legitimacy". Formally, this means that the legitimacy function is positive (L>0) if only one dimension is positive (for example, tradition).

$$L_W(D_1,\dots,D_n)>0 \text{ if } \exists D_i>0;\ i=1,\dots,n \qquad [12]$$

In other words, the legitimacy function is only zero (L=0) if all dimensions are zero (**D** = **0**).

$$L_W(D_1,\dots,D_n)=L_W(\boldsymbol{D})=L_W(0,\dots,0)=L_W(\boldsymbol{0})=0 \qquad [13]$$

In contrast, Beetham (1991, 44-45) argues that all dimensions are necessary to legitimacy. The decisive difference is that overall legitimacy is zero (L=0) if at least one dimension is zero (D=0).

$$L_B(D_1,\dots,D_3)=0 \text{ if } \exists D_i=0;\ i=1,\dots,n \qquad [14]$$

In other words, the legitimacy function is only positive (L>0) if all dimensions are positive (***D*** > **0**).

$$L_B(D_i,\dots,D_n)=L_B(\boldsymbol{D})>0 \text{ if } D_i>0\ \forall\ i=1,\dots,n \qquad [15]$$

The difference between both the Weberian and the Beethamian legitimacy functions seems to be minor but has a theoretical impact on how the dimensions should be aggregated (which also affects the measurement). Furthermore, one should also consider that Weber's three ideal types of legitimate '*Herrschaft*' can be reinterpreted as dimensions of legitimacy. More general, this again shows that (since one could derive the dimensions of legitimacy based on Weber's ideal types) one could also use the theoretical framework of any other political philosopher or political theorist to determine legitimacy's dimensions.[27]

27 For example, in accordance with Rawls (1993, 227), the state is legitimate if political power is exercised in line with the constitutional essentials. Those are (a) fundamental principles that generally structure the government and the political process (such as the powers of the legislature, executive, and the judiciary or the scope of the majority rule) and (b) equal basic rights and liberties of citizenship (such as the right to vote and to participate in politics, liberty of conscience,

Derivation Based on Statistical Methods

The dimensions of legitimacy can also be derived based on statistical methods (correlation-based approach). The most widely applied procedure is to use factor analysis (based on an item battery of survey questions). In practice, depending on the context, a researcher has two different possibilities to apply factor analysis.

The first alternative is to use *exploratory factor analysis*. A researcher typically applies exploratory factor analysis when he or she has no theory or idea in mind how many dimensions legitimacy could have. However, the researcher needs to have some theoretical reasoning what (survey) items are related to legitimacy. Thus, the pre-selection of the (survey) items may alter the result of the factor analysis. In other words, the amount and the quality of (survey) items that are pre-selected may impact the number of extractable dimensions.

The second alternative is to use *confirmatory factor analysis*. Here, the researcher wants to confirm theoretically derived dimensions with the help of factor analysis. Thus, confirmatory factor analysis forces the researcher to think in models. If the analysis leads to the same results as the theoretical framework, the researcher has evidence to confirm the underlying theory. Otherwise, the results could indicate a theoretical misconception or that the (survey) items are wrongly chosen.

Throughout the legitimacy literature, the contributions of Norris (1999) and Dalton (1999) are widely acknowledged. In Norris' (1999) seminal book "Critical Citizens", she (1991, 1) elaborates a five-dimensional classification of political support "because factor analysis strongly suggests that the public makes these distinctions." Before I present the five dimensions in greater detail, the reader should notice two important aspects.

First, although I judge Norris' (1999) approach as a statistical one, the five-dimensional classification is not developed from scratch. Rather, it is an advancement of the Eastonian (1975) concept of political support. In short, Easton (1975) distinguishes between diffuse and specific support. Specific support reflects "a response to the authorities"; in contrast, diffuse support "underlies the regime as a whole and the political community" (Easton, 1975, 437 & 445).[28] Thus, Easton (1975) already makes the distinction between authorities, the regime as a whole, and the political community. Norris (1999, 7) expands this concept, arguing that the regime as a whole consists of different dimensions since there are "divergent trends in support for regime principles and institutions."

Second, Norris (1999) speaks about political support rather than legitimacy. Since one can argue that legitimacy is the more basic concept than political support (for example, Hurd (1999) argues that political support is determined not only by legitimacy but also by coercion and self-interest), Norris' (1999) approach aims, in a narrow sense, not at

freedom of thought and of association, as well as the protections of the rule of law). Thus, a first dimension could refer to *fundamental governmental and political principles* and the second dimension could account for *rights and liberties*.

Another recent approach to derive legitimacy's dimensions is made by Møller (2016). She does not derive legitimacy's dimensions based on a single theory; instead, she refers to theories of different scholars. See Møller (2016) for further details.

28 See Appendix A for a review of the Eastonian (1956, 1975) concept.

measuring legitimacy but rather at measuring the broader concept of political support.[29] Nonetheless, Norris' dimensions of political support can be related to legitimacy (Booth & Seligson, 2005, 2009a; Gjefsen, 2012; Seligson, 2007) since, as it will turn out in chapter 3, one can measure legitimacy when using not all but a subset of Norris' dimensions.
According to Norris (1999) and Dalton (1999), the five dimensions of political support are:

- *Political Community.* This dimension refers to citizens' "basic attachment to the nation beyond the present institutions of government and a general willingness to cooperate together politically" (Norris, 1999, 6). The underlying items refer to the extent citizens feel attached to a particular community in terms of national pride or national identity.[30]
- *Regime Principles.* This dimension refers to the core values of the political system. For example, a democratic political system is supported if it guarantees basic democratic principles such as "freedom, participation, tolerance and moderation, respect for legal institutional rights, and the rule of law" (Norris, 1999, 6).[31]
- *Regime Performance.* This dimension reflects the performance of a political system (for example democracy or autocracy) from the citizens' view. It is measured by items such as "Satisfaction with the performance of democracy" (Norris, 1999, 6).
- *Regime Institutions.* This dimension captures the support for the basic institutions of the state. These basic institutions are the government, the parliament, the parties, the legal system (courts), the police, the military, and the state bureaucracy (civil service) (Gilley, 2006a, 505; Norris, 1999, 7). Attitudes toward these basic institutions are typically measured by citizens' confidence in the particular institution.

29 Other scholars also follow the view that legitimacy is a dimension of political support more or less explicitly (Hurd, 1999; Klingemann, 1999; Lamb, 2005; Møller, 2016). For example, Klingemann (1999) adopts a taxonomy where political support subsumes identification, legitimacy, and effectiveness of actors (community, regime, and authorities). Having in mind the mechanisms of social control, Hurd (1999, 391) also stresses that legitimacy is only one pillar of (political) support. Besides legitimacy, other potential causes for overall political support are coercion and self-interest. Finally, Lamb (2005, 19) also divides political support into different parts. On the one hand, he supposes that political support can be derived from the criteria of "structural legitimacy" (consent, law, tradition, leadership, effectiveness, and norms; legitimacy in the narrow sense). On the other hand, political support may stem from "contingent legitimacy" (patronage, power, and personal preferences; legitimacy is the wider sense).

30 For example, indicators of this dimension are the citizens' responses to the questions "How proud are you to be a [nationality]?" or "Would you be willing to fight for your country?" (WVS 5 Codebook, 2005, 7, 17).

31 In general, this dimension reflects citizens' responses to survey questions such as "How important is it for you to live in a country that is governed [form of government]?", "Is a [form of governing] a very good, fairly good, fairly bad or very bad way of governing this country?", or "Would you agree that [type of government] is the best type of government? If not, which type of government do you prefer?" (WVS 5 Codebook, 2005,12).

- *Political Actors.* Finally, this dimension refers to the political actors or the incumbents in office. The support for political actors depends on the evaluation of the political actors and their perceived performance (Norris, 1999, 7).[32]

To sum up, Norris' (1999) five-dimensional concept of political support is widely used by scholars across the literature (Dalton, 1999; Gjefsen, 2012; Norris, 2011; O'Sullivan et al., 2014; Seligson, 2002). Other scholars also use exploratory or confirmatory factor analysis to confirm the dimensions of political support. However, not all of them argue for five dimensions; some apply confirmatory factor analysis and find fewer dimensions (Klingemann, 1999; Kornberg & Clarke, 1992; Weatherford, 1992); some use exploratory factor analysis and extract even more (Booth & Seligson, 2005; Booth & Seligson, 2009b) (for a review, see also Booth & Seligson, 2005, 538-539). This has two reasons.

At first, the dimensionality of legitimacy depends on the survey items available. Logically, if the survey item battery does not contain questions on authorities (e.g. feelings toward political leaders, party identification, or evaluation of politicians), factor analysis simply cannot find a corresponding dimension. That is the case in the study of Klingemann (1999) where only one item is available that could be part of the dimension 'authorities' (performance of people in national office). In the end, the confirmatory factor analysis suggests that this item (performance of people in national office) is part of the dimension 'regime performance' (rather than of the dimension 'authorities'). The same considerations apply to Booth and Seligson (2009b) who find six dimensions of political support but apply exploratory factor analysis. Their additional dimension ('support for local government') simply emerges because they add further items that reflect support for the local government.[33]

Second, the sole fact that exploratory factor analysis finds, for example, six dimensions does not necessarily mean that legitimacy also consists of six dimensions. For example, Booth and Seligson (2009b) find that political legitimacy has six dimensions ('existence of a political community', 'support for core regime principles', 'regime performance', 'support for regime institutions', 'support for local government', and 'support for political actors or authorities'). However, Gilley (2012, 694) understands political legitimacy in a more narrow sense, arguing that the dimensions 'political community' and 'economic performance' (as part of 'regime

32 The 'support of political actors' can be measured by items such as "[a]greement that the government of [president or chancellor] did well fighting poverty, promoting economic development, combating government corruption, fighting crime, protecting the environment, and promoting democratic principles" (Booth & Seligson, 2005, 548).

33 Booth and Seligson (2009b, 40) add the following items that measure the support for the local government: "How much trust do you have in the municipality?", "Would you say that the services that the municipality is providing the people of your canton (county) are very good (100), good (75), neither good nor bad (50), bad (25), very bad (1)?", "Do you think that the mayor and municipal council respond to the people's demands much of the time (100), some of the time (67), seldom(33), never (1)?", and "If you had a complaint about a local problem and took it to a member of the municipal council, how much attention would be paid? Much (100), some (67), little (33), never (1)?".

performance') should not be part of legitimacy but rather considered as determinants of legitimacy.[34]

2.4.2 Aggregation Strategy

As shown above, legitimacy is a multidimensional concept. Thus, one needs to aggregate the dimensions to obtain an overall legitimacy score. The aggregation procedure depends on the following questions:

- Are all dimensions necessary for political legitimacy?
- What is the (mathematically) correct procedure to aggregate the dimensions?
- Do all dimensions have the same weight?

Drawing on the idea that legitimacy depends on several dimensions that are positively related to legitimacy (see equations [8] & [9]), one has to assume whether all dimensions are necessary for legitimacy or not. If one assumes that every dimension is necessary (Beethamian legitimacy function, see chapter 2.4.1), the legitimacy function is zero if at least one dimension is also equal to zero. To satisfy the properties of the Beethamian legitimacy function, a researcher could apply the (weighted) geometric mean to combine the dimensions to an overall legitimacy score (as done by Møller, 2016).[35] Assuming three dimensions, the concrete Beethamian legitimacy function could have the following structure (equation [16]).

$$L_B(D_1, D_2, D_3) = D_1^{\alpha} D_2^{\beta} D_3^{\gamma} \quad 0 < \alpha, \beta, \gamma < 1; \alpha + \beta + \gamma = 1 \qquad [16]$$

The parameters α, β, and γ represent the weight of each dimension. The advantage of such a function becomes apparent when analyzing Beetham's dimensions of legitimacy. Let us assume that a state is fully legitimate according to the dimensions 'legality' and 'normative justifiability'. However, at the same time, there are no 'acts of consent' (e.g. there are daily demonstrations against the regime, massive state expenditures for police, and a high rate of murdered political opponents). Then, two dimensions ('legality' and 'normative justifiability') would be positive, but the last dimension ('acts of consent') would be zero. As a consequence, the overall legitimacy score would also be zero, even though the citizens answered in surveys that the state is legitimate. In this case, the legitimacy function implicitly considers that citizens may not answer freely in opinion polls or that surveys may be manipulated by the regime.
In contrast, the same situation leads to a different result if one assumes that not all dimensions are necessary for legitimacy (Weberian legitimacy function, see chapter chapter 2.4.1). Then, the legitimacy function is only zero if all dimensions are also zero. This can be represented by a legitimacy function that applies the (weighted)

---

34 In detail, Gilley (2012, 694) writes that "[t]hey [Booth & Seligson, (2009), author's note] also argued that 'political legitimacy' should address a wider object than only the state, and included 'political community' and 'economic performance' in their measure."

35 An alternative strategy to model the Beethamian legitimacy function is using the min-function. Here, the overall legitimacy score equals the smallest value of the n dimensions.

arithmetic mean (as done by Gilley, 2006a, 2009a, 2012). Assuming again three dimensions, the Weberian legitimacy function may have the following structure (equation [17]).

$$L_W(D_1, D_2, D_3) = \alpha D_1 + \beta D_2 + \gamma D_3 \quad 0 < \alpha, \beta, \gamma < 1; \alpha + \beta + \gamma = 1 \qquad [17]$$

Again, the parameters α, β, and γ represent the weight of each dimension. If one analyzes Beetham's dimensions of legitimacy, the result of the overall legitimacy score depends on the applied legitimacy function (Weberian or Beethamian). Again, let us assume that the state has full scores in both 'legality' and 'normative justifiability', but there are no 'acts of consent'. Again, two dimensions ('legality' and 'normative justifiability') would be positive, but the last dimension ('acts of consent') would be zero. Then, according to the Weberian legitimacy function, the resulting overall legitimacy score is not zero but still positive.

If one applies a Weberian legitimacy function, the overall legitimacy score is always equal or larger than the overall legitimacy score that results from a Beethamian legitimacy function.[36]

$$L_B(D_1, D_2, D_3) = D_1^{\alpha} D_2^{\beta} D_3^{\gamma} \leq \alpha D_1 + \beta D_2 + \gamma D_3 = L_W(D_1, D_2, D_3) \qquad [18]$$

$$0 < \alpha, \beta, \gamma < 1; \alpha + \beta + \gamma = 1$$

The following example helps us to understand this. First, let us assume that three dimensions of legitimacy exist (D_1, D_2, D_3). Each dimension is measured on a 0 to 10 scale, where 0 means 'not legitimate at all' and 10 means 'fully legitimate'. Let us further assume that the first (D_1) and the second (D_2) dimension of legitimacy are fully legitimate (score 10). Finally, all three weights have value one-third ($\alpha=\beta=\gamma=1/3$). Considering both the Weberian and the Beethamian legitimacy function, figure 4 below shows that the overall legitimacy scores depend on the third dimension (D_3).

As figure 4 shows, the overall legitimacy scores of the Weberian legitimacy function lie at all points (except for $D_3=10$) above the overall legitimacy scores of the Beethamian legitimacy function. That result is independent of the starting values of D_1 and D_2 (referring to the AM-GM inequality, see footnote 36).That has several implications. First, if one applies the Weberian legitimacy function, overall legitimacy scores are always higher than or equal to those that are based on the Beethamian legitimacy function. This does not necessarily mean that the Weberian legitimacy function is upwardly biased or that the Beethamian legitimacy function is downwardly biased. Rather, it shows that the aggregation strategy has an impact on the numerical value of the legitimacy score.

36 For a proof, check the inequality of arithmetic and geometric means (AM-GM inequality) (Chauchy, 1821).

Figure 4: The Impact of Different Aggregation Strategies

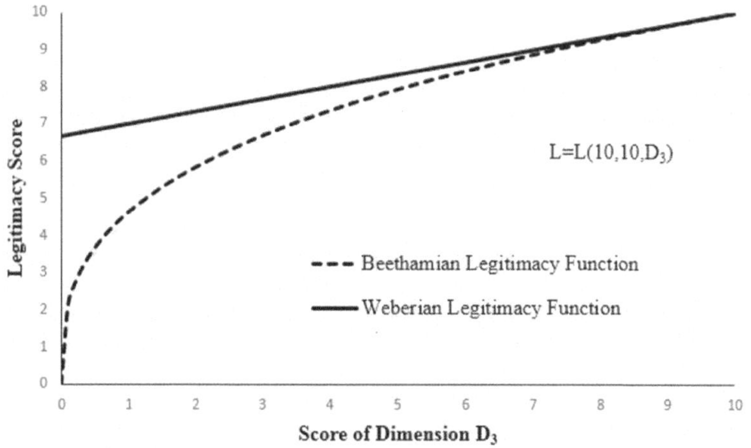

Source: Own representation

If one treats the overall legitimacy score as an ordinal variable, the change in the numerical value is not problematic as long as the relative rank between observations does not change. Unfortunately, this may happen as the following example shows. Let us assume two observations (two different states). Again, the legitimacy function has three dimensions. The first state has value five in each dimension (5,5,5). The second state has value zero in the first dimension but value nine in the other two dimensions (0,9,9). Applying the legitimacy functions with all three weights being equal to one-third ($\alpha=\beta=\gamma=1/3$), the following results can be obtained (table 1).

Table 1: Aggregation and Relative Rank

	State 1		State 2
	$D_1 = 5$ $D_2 = 5$ $D_3 = 5$		$D_1 = 0$ $D_2 = 9$ $D_3 = 9$
Overall Legitimacy Score L_W	5 (rank 2)	<	6 (rank 1)
Overall Legitimacy Score L_B	5 (rank 1)	>	0 (rank 2)

In the scenario with the Weberian legitimacy function being applied, the overall legitimacy scores suggest that state two is more legitimate than state one (5<6). In contrast, when applying the Beethamian legitimacy function, the overall legitimacy scores suggest that state one is more legitimate than state two (5>0). That shows that a different aggregation strategy may change the relative ranks. As a consequence, overall legitimacy scores of different researchers can only be compared appropriately if the same aggregation strategy is applied. In other words, if different researchers come to different results regarding the legitimacy scores, one potential reason is the application of different aggregation strategies.

If one treats the overall legitimacy score as a metric (or quasi-metric) variable, the impact of the different legitimacy functions becomes even more severe. According to the numerical specifications of the dimensions of each state, there is no difference in the overall legitimacy score in state one. In contrast, the overall legitimacy score of state two is highly dependent on the legitimacy function. The application of the Weberian legitimacy functions leads to value six, which could be interpreted as being moderately legitimate. In contrast, the application of the Beethamian legitimacy function yields value zero, which can be interpreted as being not legitimate at all. As this example shows, it may be difficult to evaluate whether state two is illegitimate or moderately legitimate since the overall legitimacy score depends on the legitimacy function.

In a scenario with three dimensions, the assumption is made that the weights of all dimensions are equal to one-third. Actually, most scholars apply this strategy (Gilley, 2006a; Møller, 2016; Power & Cyr, 2009). However, in slight contrast, Gilley (2009a) as well as Power and Cyr (2009) weight one dimension with one-half and the other two dimensions with one-quarter each (here, the weights are derived from theoretical considerations). Since legitimacy is a latent variable, an estimation of the weights via statistical methods is hardly possible.[37] Thus, the weighting of the dimensions depends on the researcher's choice. As long as no strong theoretical argument exists to weight some dimensions more heavily than others, a proper strategy is to use equal weights.

2.5 Summary

This chapter deals with the concept of legitimacy. It has a strong propaedeutic character since (i) the understanding of legitimacy's conceptualization is helpful to classify the concrete measurement strategies (chapter 3) and (ii) the results of empirical analyses can only be interpreted correctly when taking into account the conceptual basis of legitimacy (chapters 5 and 6).

The reason to deal with the conceptualization of legitimacy in such an extensive manner lies in its latent nature. In contrast to directly observable variables, the strategies to conceptualize a latent variable like legitimacy are almost infinite. This becomes apparent when comparing different definitions of legitimacy. At a fist glance, every scholar seems to have a different definition of legitimacy. However, each definition consists of the object, the subject, the perspective, and the dimensionality of legitimacy (see also figure 5). All those elements can be represented with the help of the legitimacy function L in a formalized manner.

Again, any legitimacy concept needs to define the object of legitimacy (chapter 2.1). In this thesis, the object of interest is the state. The state is defined as "the basic *institutional* and *ideological* structure of a political community" (Gilley, 2006a, 501).

37 An estimation of weights would be possible if there were a directly observable variable that proxies legitimacy (one could think of the World Bank's measure for 'political stability'; Gilley, 2006a). In this case, one could regress the dimensions on the directly observable variable to determine the weight of each dimension.

In a next step, the subject and the perspective of legitimacy need to be defined (chapters 2.2 and 2.3). In this thesis, the citizens are the subjects of legitimacy. And further, I follow a micro perspective. Eventually, legitimacy can also be classified according to its dimensionality (chapter 2.4). One can distinguish between unidimensional and multidimensional legitimacy concepts. In the case of the multidimensional approaches, the dimensions of legitimacy can be derived via theory (see Beetham, 1999) or via statistical methods (see Norris, 1999). Based on this propedeutic thoughts, the following chapter gives a literature overview of concrete measurement strategies.

Figure 5: Summarizing the Concept of Legitimacy

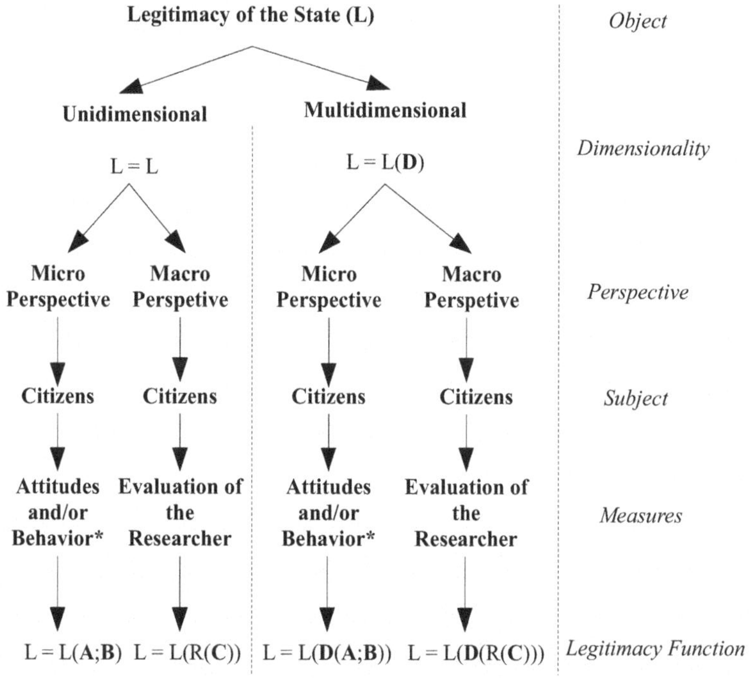

Source: Own compilation

3 Legitimacy and its Measurement: A Literature Overview

Since different legitimacy concepts exist, the possibilities to measure legitimacy are manifold. As a consequence, this chapter offers a literature overview of various strategies to measure legitimacy. The overview has two purposes. First and most important, a precise empirical measurement of legitimacy is a necessary precondition to analyze appropriately whether a relationship between economic freedom and political legitimacy exists. Thus, it is indispensable to understand the measurement approaches and their strengths and weaknesses in detail. Second, the literature overview is also designed to elaborate a 'toolkit' of different approaches. That shall sensitize the reader that no standard approach for measuring legitimacy exist. In fact, I use just two out of several measurement approaches throughout the thesis.

The first sub-chapter deals with the approaches to measure legitimacy at a very general level, namely the attitudinal, the behavioral, and the discourse analytic approaches and discusses their strengths and weaknesses (chapter 3.1). The next sub-chapter (chapter 3.2) deals with the data sources of legitimacy. That is of particular importance since there is "no existing cross-national data set on the legitimacy of states" (Gilley, 2006a, 500). As a consequence, researchers draw on already existing data sources (such as, for example, the World Values Survey) even though these are not designed to measure legitimacy. Thus, the choice of a particular data source often leads to various problems (such as missing items across several waves or the need to nest several data sources) that are hard to overcome. To illustrate this, I review the data sources that scholars typically choose for empirical legitimacy studies. In particular, I focus on the World Values Survey (WVS) since I use this data source in my later empirical analyses. In the third sub-chapter (chapter 3.3), I review existing approaches to measure legitimacy. At first, I focus on so-called unidimensional measurement approaches (chapter 3.3.1). Here, I distinguish between single items and simple indices. In the next part, I deal with multidimensional measurement approaches that can be classified into theory-driven and correlation-based measurement approaches (chapter 3.3.2). In particular, I review the theory-driven approach of Gilley (2006a, 2009a, 2012) and compare it to the correlation-based approach of Norris (1999, 2011). A comparison of the resulting legitimacy scores shows that both approaches are largely comparable. Finally, sub-chapter four (chapter 3.4) offers a summary and a conclusion.

3.1 The Measures of Legitimacy

Depending on the perspective, a researcher can use different measures to operationalize legitimacy. Repeatedly, according to the macro perspective, the measure is a researcher's judgment to what extent normative criteria are met. Second, according to the micro perspective, scholars have the possibility to measure legitimacy and its dimensions based on attitudes, beliefs, convictions, and/or observable behaviors of the citizens. Since this thesis follows the latter perspective, it is sufficient to discuss those approaches that refer to the subjective views of citizens. According to the literature, these are the attitudinal, the behavioral, and the discourse-analytic approaches (Gaus, 2011, 9-10; Schmidtke & Schneider, 2012, 229-238).

C. M. Hindermann, *The Impact of Economic Freedom on State Legitimacy*,
Wirtschaft und Politik, https://doi.org/10.1007/978-3-658-23195-8_3

Attitudinal Approach. The attitudinal approach relies on public opinion that is typically measured by opinion polls or surveys. This approach assumes that citizens' attitudes are appropriate to measure the underlying concept of legitimacy; it also measures legitimacy in a very narrow sense since it explicitly understands legitimacy as a belief or conviction. However, critics argue that the studying of individuals' attitudes may be biased or that attitude items may be used incorrectly. The following five arguments are typically put forward.

First, attitude items may be normatively biased. To show this with an example, Gilley (2006a) uses, among others, the item "How do you rate the current political system?" to measure legitimacy. Obviously, this item is non-normative since it does not refer to a specific type of political system. In contrast, the item "How democratically is your country being governed today?" is strongly normative since the underlying assumption is that a higher degree of democracy indicates legitimacy (see Gilley, 2012a and Møller, 2016). This is problematic since it neglects that other forms of government may also be legitimate from the citizens' view.

Second, it is often not clearly identifiable which attitudes belong to legitimacy or to other spheres of support. For example, Beetham (1993, 489) asks what beliefs "are relevant to the moral authority or legitimacy of governments?" and responds "two different kinds: beliefs about the rightful source of political authority, and beliefs about the appropriate ends or purposes that government should serve".[38] Although he gives a precise answer, there is still a risk that specific survey items do not measure legitimacy but rather political support. This becomes obvious when considering the survey item "Would you be willing to fight for your country?" Although this survey item belongs to the dimension "political community" (which is a dimension of political support; see Norris, 1999), it may be inappropriate to measure state legitimacy since it may refer to a different object (not to the state but to the nation).

Third, some surveys do not contain relevant items such that legitimacy can be measured only with a loss of reliability and/or validity. For example, the World Values Surveys contain the question "How do you rate the current political system?" in the third and the fourth but not in the fifth and sixth wave. This implies that one can hardly follow legitimacy over time based on a consistent construct.

Fourth, researchers do not create new or adjust old surveys for legitimacy research. Rather, they use already existing opinion polls that are mostly designed to measure the attitudes of citizens in general. Among others, these are the World Value Surveys (Gilley, 2006a; Møller, 2016), the European Social Survey (O'Sullivan et al., 2014), or RegionalBarometers (Gilley, 2006a; Power & Cyr, 2011). As a consequence, the measurement of legitimacy can be described as eclectic to some degree since, for example, Gilley (2006a, 2009a, 2012) collects items from different surveys.

Fifth, particularly in autocratic states, attitudes may not exist or may be unreliable due to "the problem of preference falsification" (Gerscheweski, 2013, 20). To solve this,

38 Further, the first belief (beliefs about the rightful source of political authority) refers to "the rules of access to political power, the definition of the qualities appropriate to it, and the mechanisms through which consent is expressed". The second belief (beliefs about the appropriate ends or purposes that the government should serve) refers to "the kind of issue that comes within the ambit of government and the performance criteria, if any, that must satisfy" (Beetham, 1993, 489).

Gerschewski (2013, 20-21) suggests three alternative strategies to approximate legitimacy, namely (i) using behavioral data (for example, the number and intensity of public protests), (ii) using qualitative assessments (from country experts or the secondary literature), or (iii) sticking to the results of content analysis techniques (for example, to analyze the gap between perceived promises and the social reality).

Behavioral Approach. The behavioral approach coexists with the attitudinal approach. The underlying assumption is that the attitudes of the citizens lead to observable behaviors (Levi et al., 2009, 357).[39] Then, actual compliance (or non-compliance) informs about the views citizens have toward the state. Referring to Levi et al. (2009, 357), figure 6 shows this process.
First of all, the determinants of legitimacy impact value-based legitimacy, reflecting the attitudes of the citizens. According to Levi et al. (2009, 354), value-based legitimacy can be understood as "a sense of obligation or willingness to obey authorities", i.e. the state and its institutions. Finally, value-based legitimacy affects

Figure 6: From Attitudes to Behavior

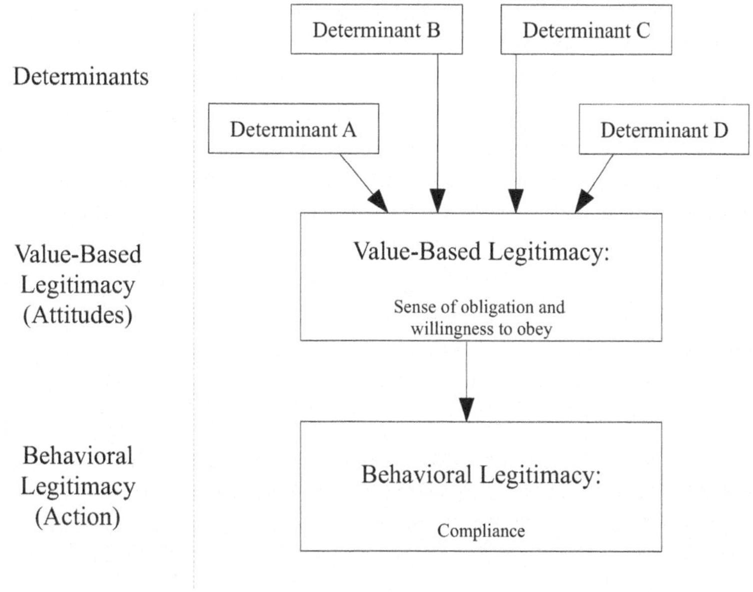

Source: Adopted from Levi et al. (2009, 357)

39 To be more precise, Levi et al. (2009, 357) argue that citizens' attitudes reflect value-based legitimacy (willingness to obey) that finally leads to behavioral legitimacy (compliance).

behavioral legitimacy. That means that the attitudes of the citizens will be "translated into actual compliance with government regulations and laws" (Levi et al., 2009, 354). Based on these considerations, various scholars argue for the behavioral approach. For example, Beetham (1991, 1993) notes that actual behavior and legitimacy are inherently connected. He (1993, 489) writes that "whatever we do is underpinned by a network of beliefs, operating at different levels, both about the way the world is and about how people should behave within it; if these beliefs were different, so too would be our behavior; sometimes there is a disjunction between what people say they believe and the way they act; and sometimes the only evidence we have about people's beliefs is from their actions; or even inactions, though the latter are notoriously difficult to interpret." In a similar fashion, Hurd (1999, 381) states that "perception affects behavior because it is internalized by the actor and helps to define how the actor sees its interests." Power and Cyr (2009, 257) also argue that "if we follow Linz's observation that legitimate political institutions are those which can demand obedience, it is certainly reasonable to ask whether such obedience actually occurs, that is, by identifying forms of compliant behavior."[40]

The main advantage of the behavioral approach is that it is objectively measurable since it is independent of subjective attitudes of the citizens and their measurement biases (Gilley, 2006a, 508). Typical indicators are voter-turnout, quasi-voluntary taxes, the use of violence in civil protest, the number and intensity of public protests, or the number of coups d'état (Dogan, 2003, 119; Gerschewski, 2013, 20-21; Gilley, 2006a, 505; 2009a, 13). However, the behavioral approach also has two essential shortcomings.

First, behavioral items are ambivalent in nature. Hurrelmann et al. (2007, 8) mention that it is "impossible to infer the motivations that underlie political action" such that the true relationship between attitudes and observed behaviors remains unclear. Gilley (2009a, 12) also notices that behavioral indicators "are based on an assumed connection between legitimacy and the indicator itself, which might not be true. Peaceful protest [...] may be more a result of the political culture, political institutions, and current political issues in a country than of legitimacy."[41] In the same fashion, Pierre et al. (2011) state that "not necessarily all actions grouped under behavioral legitimacy can be traced back to values, as instinctive behavior of fear may be as important as values to explain actual behavior. Similarly, values do not guarantee certain behaviours as different barriers or obstacles may prevent people to doing the 'right' actions. For example, citizens may vote because they support the political system, or they may support the political system, but decide not to vote since they may not believe that the current political parties and representatives rule in a way which coincides with their preferences." In the same vein, having in mind particularly autocratic states, Gerschewski (2013, 20-21) points out that the number and the intensity of public protests may be misleading as a measure of legitimacy. In

40 Repeatedly, Linz (1988, 65) defines legitimacy as "the belief that in spite of shortcomings and failures, the political institutions are better than any other that might be established, and therefore can demand obedience."

41 If citizens protest against a particular political institution (for example against institutions on immigration), this protest does not necessarily mean that the whole state is in a legitimation crisis.

particular, he (2013, 20) urges that "public protests depend on the population's ability to protest in the first place; and protest data just measure the absence of legitimation and is therefore 'one-sided'."[42] Eventually, Hurd (1999, 390) mentions that "simple compliance with a directive is not evidence of the presence of legitimacy any more than it is evidence of coercion or self-interest: to diagnose legitimacy requires a methodology for interpreting the motives for behavior rather than simply measuring behavior itself."

All these objections show that the assumption that attitudes lead to behavior may be questioned. However, if one accepts that value-based legitimacy leads to behavioral legitimacy, the second argument against behavioral items emerges: Namely that it is unclear whether they are determinants, consequences, indicators, or dimensions of legitimacy. As Easton (1975, 454) suggests, the solution of this problem depends on the theoretical judgment. For example, according to Beetham's (1991) legitimacy concept, behavioral items need to be included to account for the dimension 'acts of consent'. Gilley (2006a, 2009a, 2012) and Power and Cyr (2009) adopt this view. In contrast, if legitimacy is understood in the Weberian sense (Legitimitätsglaube), behavioral indicators are not a part of legitimacy but a consequence of it (Booth & Seligson, 2005; Easton, 1975; Levi et al., 2009; Møller, 2016).[43]

Discourse-Analytic Approach. The discourse-analytic approach refers to the legitimization process in the public sphere (Gaus, 2011, 10). It draws on the idea that discourses (primarily in quality newspapers) about the state decisively shape the attitudes of the citizens; or, as Hurrelman et al. (2013, 517) put it, that "the concept of legitimation statements is grounded in an understanding of legitimization as an act of passing judgment on the acceptability of political rule". However, one should treat the relevance of legitimation statements with care. In the first place, Hurrelmann et al. (2009, 5) point to the fact that legitimation statements "*may* shape dominant beliefs in the population and motivate political action." Thus, legitimation statements do not necessarily reflect the degree to which the state is legitimate from the view of the citizens. Further obstacles of this approach are that (i) studies may analyze only legitimation statements in selected quality newspapers (selection bias) (Hurrelmann et al., 2013), (ii) the results of discourse analyses are sensitive to legitimation attention cycles (Hurrelmann et al., 2009, 12-14), and (iii) discourse analysis requires freedom of press (otherwise, it is likely that legitimation statements are manipulated by the regime).[44]

42 Dogan (2003, 119) makes a similar statement. He writes that the "absence of revolt, however, does not imply adhesion to the regime. Revolt is possible only in certain historical circumstances, when a regime starts a process of liberalization."

43 For example, Easton (1975, 455) urges that actual behavior should be considered more "as a determinant, consequence or possible indicator of support rather than as one of its dimensions." Further, Booth and Seligson (2005) use legitimacy (or, to be precise, political support according to Norris' (1999) label) as an explanatory variable for predicting actual behavior (voting, protest participation, partisan activism). As a consequence, these views indicate that behavioral items should not be used to measure legitimacy.

44 For example, Hurrelmann et al. (2013) analyze legitimization statements in quality newspapers in the UK, Ireland, Germany, and Austria regarding EU primary law reforms in the past decade. For

To sum up, the researcher can use the attitudinal, the behavioral, or the discourse-analytic approaches for measuring state legitimacy. Each approach has advantages and shortcomings. The attitudinal approach measures legitimacy in the narrow sense (i.e. in the Weberian understanding). Shortcomings are that (i) attitudinal items may be normatively biased, (ii) attitudinal items may measure other concepts than legitimacy, (iii) some attitudinal items are not available when comparing different surveys or comparing different waves of the same survey, (iv) researchers typically use items from surveys that are not explicitly designed to measure legitimacy and, (v) attitudes themselves may be biased, in particular in autocracies. To cope with these problems, the behavioral approach can extend or replace the attitudinal approach. Based on the assumption that attitudes (value-based legitimacy) shape the actions of the citizens (behavioral legitimacy), behavioral items are appropriate to measure legitimacy. In contrast to subjective attitudinal items, one can observe behavioral items directly. However, behavioral items also have weaknesses since (i) they are ambivalent in nature and (ii) they can be treated as parts of but also as determinants or consequences of legitimacy. Finally, the discourse-analytic approach does not directly refer to the attitudes or the behaviors of citizens. Instead, the focus lies on the discourses in the newspapers. The results of the discourse analytic approach are sensitive (i) to the selection of the newspaper, (ii) to legitimation attention cycles, and (iii) to the degree of press freedom. In this thesis, the discourse-analytic approach will not be considered further.

3.2 Data Sources

This chapter offers an overview of different data sources. Since there is "no existing cross-national data set on the legitimacy of states" (Gilley, 2006a, 500), the measurement of legitimacy builds on already existing data sources that are originally not designed to measure legitimacy. Most studies use only one data source (Huang et al., 2008; Klingemann, 1999; Levi et al., 2009; Norris, 2011). In contrast, somewhat eclectically, other studies use different data sources to collect the items that are necessary since attitudinal and behavioral data are mostly not part of one data source (Gilley, 2006a, 2009a, 2012, 2012; Power & Cyr, 2009). Here, I first present data sources of attitudinal data (chapter 3.2.1) and, thereafter, focus on sources of behavioral data (chapter 3.2.2).

3.2.1 Data Sources for Attitudes

Because most countries in the world monitor the attitudes of their citizens, a variety of data sources are available for legitimacy research. For example, Gilley (2006a, 2006b, 2012), Gjefsen (2012), Møller (2016), and Norris (1999) use the World Values Survey (WVS), whereas Domański (2005) and O'Sullivan et al. (2014) draw upon the European Social Survey (ESS). Of course, scholars also use other data sources such as the Comparative Study of Electoral Systems (CSES) (Huang et al., 2008), the Afrobarometer (Levi, Sachs & Tyler, 2009; Levi & Sacks, 2009), the Eurobarometer

each country, they focus on two quality newspapers.

(Berggren et al., 2015, Gilley, 2006a), the LatinoBarómetro (Doyle, 2011; Power & Cyr, 2009), and other national surveys (Booth & Seligson, 2005; Booth & Seligson, 2009a; Seligson, 2002).[45] Due to the variety of data sources, it is not possible to survey all of them here. Rather, I focus on the World/European Values Survey (WVS/EVS) since I use this data source in the empirical part of this thesis.

World Values Survey and European Values Surveys (WVS and EVS). The World Values Survey – which builds on the European Values Survey first published in 1978 – was originally compiled by Robert Inglehart in 1981. First and foremost, Inglehart designed the WVS primarily to have an empirical data set that can be used to analyze how values change among societies in the world (Inglehart & Baker, 2000).
Besides studying values, scholars use the World Values Survey (WVS) and the European Values Survey (EVS) as an empirical basis for the measurement of legitimacy. There are two reasons for this. First, the WVS and EVS together cover more than 60 countries all over the world.[46] Thus, the WVS/EVS can be used to study cross-country differences on a global level. And second, the WVS as well as the EVS provide a variety of items that apply to the measurement of legitimacy. Table 2 offers an overview of these items. Further, table 2 also states in which waves these items are included and presents selected studies that use these items to measure legitimacy.
At the same time, table 2 sheds some light on the applicability of the WVS. There are three essential shortcomings. First, not every wave covers all items. That limits the possibility of following legitimacy scores over time since the change or the loss of items may impact on the resulting overall legitimacy values. Further, that may also explain why different scholars use different items for their measurement of legitimacy (besides different legitimacy concepts). Second, the dates of interview have a wide range in each wave. For example, the interview dates in wave 4 of the WVS vary from 1999 to 2004. This could mean that respondents of one country were interviewed in 1999 and respondents of another country were interviewed in 2004. In consequence, cross-country analyses should consider that relevant economic, social, or political changes could occur within a single wave (e.g. dot-com bubble, financial crisis, or Arab spring). And third, different waves also contain (partly) different countries, which makes it hardly possible to apply panel methods.

45 Already in 1999, Norris (1999, 14) stated that "due to an extensive international network of survey researchers we now have access to a wider range of evidence than ever before. Sources of comparative public opinion data include Almond and Verba's pathbreaking Civic Culture study, a five-nation survey in 1959/60; the Political Action Study carried out in five nations in 1974; Eurobarometers conducted twice yearly since 1973 among the expanding universe of member states of the European Union; the International Social Science Programme (ISSP) monitoring social and political attitudes every year since 1985; the World Values Study (WVS) undertaken in 1981-84, 1990-93 and 1995-7; the Central and Eastern Eurobarometer started in 1989; the New Democracies Barometer operating since 1991; and the Latinobarometro started by MORI in 1995."

46 The number of countries covered depends on the particular wave. For example, wave four of the WVS covers 41 countries and the corresponding EVS wave (1999) covers 33 countries, whereas wave six of the WVS provides data on 60 countries.

Table 2: Items of the World Values Survey Used for Legitimacy Measurement

Questions	Wave (WVS)	Study(s)
How proud are you to be a [citizen of this country]?	1-6	Klingemann (1999), Norris (2011)
Would you be willing to fight for your country?	1-6	Klingemann (1999), Norris (2011)
How much confidence do you have in the police?	1-6	Gilley(2006a, 2012), Møller (2016), Norris (2011)
How much confidence do you have in the courts (or legal system or justice system)?	1,2,3,5,6	Gilley(2012a), Møller (2016), Norris (2011)
How much confidence do you have in the civil service?	1-6	Gilley(2006a, 2012), Møller (2016), Norris (2011)
How much confidence do you have in the government?	2-6	Klingemann (1999), Møller (2016), Norris (2011)
How much confidence do you have in the parliament?	1-6	Klingemann (1999), Norris (2011)
How democratically is your country being governed today?	5,6	Gilley(2012a), Møller (2016)
On the whole are you very satisfied, rather satisfied, not very satisfied or not at all satisfied with the way democracy is developing in your country?	3,4	Gilley (2006a), Klingemann (1999), Norris (2011)
How satisfied are you with the way people now in national office are handling the country's affairs?	3-5	Klingemann (1999)
Would you say a democracy is a very good, fairly good, a fairly bad or a very bad way of governing this country?	3-6	Klingemann (1999), Norris (2011)
Do you agree that a democracy may have many problems but it's better than any other form of government?	3-5	Klingemann (1999)
How do you rate the current political system?	3,4	Gilley (2006a), Klingemann (1999)
How much respect is there for individual human rights nowadays in your country?	3-6	Gilley(2006a, 2012), Møller (2016), Norris (2011)
How much freedom of choice and control over your own life do you have?	1-6	Møller (2016)
How important is it for you to live in a country that is governed democratically?	5,6	Norris (2011)

Survey Years	Wave 1: 1981-1984	Wave 2: 1989-1994	Wave 3: 1995-1999
	Wave 4: 1999-2004	Wave 5: 2005-2009	Wave 6: 2010-2014

Source: Integrated EVS/WVS 1981-2008 Codebook (2011); WVS 6 Official Questionnaire (2012)

To sum up, the WVS/EVS can be used to measure legitimacy since the data sets provide enough items to measure the legitimacy of a particular state (or at least important aspects/dimensions of state legitimacy). However, one should notice that cross-country analyses are not exact since the dates of interviews vary across countries (which means that differences between states could just be a result of global changes). Based on this, the application of panel methods is also restricted since (i) not all waves contain all items, (ii) the number of countries varies across waves, and (iii) there is a wide range of interview dates in each wave.

Of course, other data sources may also fit for legitimacy research such as the European Social Survey (ESS), Globalbarometer Surveys, or the Eurobarometer Surveys.[47] For example, Dalton (1999, 70) partly uses the Eurobarometer Survey as an empirical basis to analyze the support for democracy in Europe. In a recent study, O'Sullivan et al. (2014) use the first five waves of the ESS to analyze how political legitimacy and its dimensions changed in Ireland during the economic crisis. Another source is the CSES which is, however, more suitable in measuring the legitimacy of democracy (democratic legitimacy) (Huang et al., 2008).[48]

Table 3: Summary of Different Selected Data Sources

Survey	Coverage: Region	Coverage: Time	Items Useful to Measure...	Data Set Useful for Legitimacy Measure of
WVS/EVS	World	6 waves (1981-2014)	legitimacy of the state	Norris (1999) Gilley (2006a)
ESS	mainly Europe	6 waves (2002-2012)	legitimacy of the state (partly)	partly Norris (1999)
GlobalBarometer	World	1 module (2003-2007)	legitimacy of the state	Norris (1999) Gilley (2006a)
CSES	World	4 modules (2001-2011)	democratic legitimacy	partly Norris (1999)

Source: Author's compilation

47 The GlobalBarometer Survey is based on regional barometer surveys (such as Afrobarometer).

48 Huang et al. (2008) use three items to measure democratic legitimacy: "On the whole, are you very satisfied, fairly satisfied, not very satisfied, or not at all satisfied with the way democracy works in [country]?", "How strongly you agree or disagree with the following statement: Democracy may have problems but it's better than any other form of government.", and "How much respect is there for individual freedom and human rights nowadays in country?" Although these items are often used in legitimacy research (Gilley, 2006a), the data set provides no information on trust in state institutions. Hence, this survey is applicable to measure the legitimacy of democracy but not of the state as a whole.

3.2.2 Data Sources for Behavior

Some authors also consider behavior when measuring legitimacy (Beetham, 1991; Gilley, 2006a, 2006b, 2009a, 2012), whereas others argue that behavior is an outcome of legitimacy (Booth & Seligson, 2005, 2009a). In any case, the question remains from where to retrieve data on actual behavior. Typically, attitude surveys include only a limited set of behavioral variables. For example, the WVS provides three items on voting:

- Voted in recent parliamentary elections? (yes/no)
- Voted in elections at the local level? (always/usually/never)
- Voted in elections at the national level? (always/usually/never)

The first item (voted in the most recent parliamentary election) is useful as a behavioral item since the answer possibilities are clearly interpretable. In contrast, the second and the third item (voted in elections at the local and national level) leave more room for interpretation since the answer possibility 'usually' remains unspecified (answer possibilities 'always' and 'never' are straight forward).

Besides voting behavior, the WVS also contains a set of items that capture political actions of the respondents. In particular, the survey respondents were asked whether they have signed a petition, joined in boycotts, attended lawful/peaceful demonstrations, joined unofficial strikes, and occupied buildings or factories. Further, two items are designed to capture whether the respondents have damaged things, have broken windows, and engaged in street and in personal violence. All these items have the answer possibilities 'have done', 'might done', or 'would never do'. Although these behavioral items could be used to proxy legitimacy, there are two shortcomings.

First, the answer possibilities do not allow one to draw conclusions on the intensity and the point in time of a specific political action. 'Have done' is ambiguous in that the respondent has, for example, joined a boycott once or several times. In addition, 'have done' could also mean that the respondent joined a boycott five years ago – or yesterday. Taking into account that state legitimacy changes over time, it is important to know when a specific political action was executed. The second shortcoming is that the WVS provides no information about the motivation of a political action. Hence, it is unclear whether the attendance of a demonstration was motivated by protests against the state or a specific actor.

An alternative to the behavioral data that is provided by attitude surveys is to use an *external source.* In this case, legitimacy is measured based on the attitudinal items of the survey and the behavioral items from the external source. Gilley (2006a, 2006b, 2009a, 2012) and Power and Cyr (2009) apply this procedure.

For example, Gilley (2006a, 2006b, 2009a, 2012) combines data from attitude surveys (WVS and Eurobarometer) with behavioral data from external sources such as

- the World Handbook of Political and Social Indicators (for data on "Use of violence in civil protest")[49],
- the International Institute for Democracy and Electoral Assistance (for data on "Voter turnout"),
- the Government Finance Yearbook of the International Monetary Fund (for data on "Quasi-voluntary taxes"), and
- the Center for Systemic Peace (for data on "Repression" and "Exclusion").

In particular, this eclectic procedure is an appropriate way to measure legitimacy at the country level (assuming a concept that includes attitudes and behaviors of the citizens). However, since attitudinal and behavioral data are nested at the country level, it is impossible to analyze legitimacy at the individual level. To analyze individual determinants of legitimacy requires that behavioral and attitudinal items are available at the individual level in the same data set. However, as noted above, surveys on attitudes do not or only in limited fashion contain useful behavioral data. That may explain why all studies that analyze individual determinants of legitimacy (such as gender, age, religion, education, wealth and income, trust, or life satisfaction) solely draw upon attitudinal items when measuring legitimacy (Booth & Seligson, 2009a; Norris, 2011).

3.3 Measurement

Since state legitimacy is a latent variable, concrete measurement approaches are manifold (for a review, see also von Haldenwang, 2016). For reasons of classification, I distinguish between (i) unidimensional and (ii) multidimensional approaches (see chapter 2). Since I stick to multidimensional ones in this thesis (chapter 3.3.2), I only provide a short overview of unidimensional approaches. After that, I divide the multidimensional approaches into those that use theory and those that are based on correlations to derive legitimacy's dimensions (chapter 3.3.2). Referring to theory-driven approaches, I focus on the contributions of Gilley (2006a, 2012). Concerning the correlation-based approaches, I particularly deal with the works of Norris (1999, 2011; see also chapter 2). Since I use both Gilley's and Norris' approach in the empirical part in this thesis, I also compare both and depict their strengths and weaknesses.

3.3.1 Unidimensional Measurement Approaches

By definition, unidimensional measurement approaches do not consider multiple dimensions. Instead, they proxy legitimacy by either (i) single items (attitudinal or behavioral) or (ii) simple indices.

49 Instead of the World Handbook of Political and Social Indicators, Power and Cyr (2009, 258) use the measure of political stability of the World Bank "because these data have not been updated and we deemed it inadvisable to use old data that are essentially episodic in nature".

Single Items. Using a single attitudinal or behavioral variable is the most 'simple' approach to measure legitimacy. It is frequently applied in the empirical literature to both legitimacy and its dimensions (table 4).

Table 4: Measurement of Legitimacy by a Single Item

Author(s)	Legitimacy Object	Measurement of Legitimacy (Item)	Source
Bornschier (1989); Weede (1996)	State (only democracies)	Mass political protest per million inhabitants (inverse)	World Handbook of Political and Social Indicators
Anderson (2005)	State (only democracies)	Winner-loser gap (regime support)	Eurobarometer
Levi & Sacks (2009)	State	Accept governments right to make people pay taxes	Afrobarometer
Levi, Sacks & Tyler (2009)	State	Tax department's right to make people pay taxes	Afrobarometer
		Police's right to make people obey the law	Afrobarometer
		Court's right to make decisions people abide	Afrobarometer
Berggren et al. (2015)	State (only democracies)	Satisfaction with democracy	EuroBarometer

Source: Author's compilation

To start with, Bornschier (1989) and Weede (1996) measure political legitimacy by the relative absence of mass political protest per million inhabitants. Since this measure includes anti-government demonstrations, riots, and political strikes, the item is clearly behavioral. However, Bornschier (1989, 220) acknowledges that a behavioral legitimacy measure also has shortcomings. He (1989, 220) refers to the typical critique that "the absence of such protest need not indicate legitimacy, but may only stand for mere toleration of the social order or may only be the consequence of government repression of mass political conflict." Similarly, Weede (1996, 218) notices that in "autocratic and repressive societies, the absence of mass protest might be due to government, (secret) police and armed forces terrorizing the people rather than to legitimacy." However, since both Bornschier (1989) and Weede (1996) restrict their analysis to Western industrial countries, they argue that this critique is of minor relevance.

Second, Anderson (2005) also measures legitimacy with a single item, namely the winner-loser gap. The winner-loser gap measures the distance between regime support of respondents who supported the winning party and regime support of respondents who supported the loser party. A small winner-loser gap indicates a legitimate political system and, vice versa, a large winner-loser gap reflects an illegitimate political system (Hechter, 2009, 281). However, due to its construction, this measure is only applicable to political systems with a functioning voting and party system (democracies).

Next, Levi and Sacks (2009) and Levi et al. (2009) use attitudinal items as a proxy for legitimacy. Levi and Sacks (2009) argue that the degree to which people accept the right of the government to make people pay taxes is a useful indicator for legitimacy (or the willingness to obey authorities). Levi et al. (2009) use the same item in their study. In addition, they (2009) further argue that the tax department's right to make people pay taxes and the court's right to make decisions people abide are powerful items to measure legitimacy.

Berggren et al. (2015) also measure legitimacy with a single variable, namely the satisfaction of respondents with the way democracy works.[50] Although they explicitly state that they measure government legitimacy, this item can also be seen as a measure of state legitimacy since they focus on 30 developed countries.

To sum up, a variety of studies use single items to measure or proxy the legitimacy of the state. Among those, some use behavioral items (Bornschier, 1989; Weede, 1996), whereas others stick to attitudinal items (Anderson, 2005; Berggren et al., 2015; Levi & Sacks, 2009; Levi et al., 2009). Explicitly or implicitly, all of those studies have the state as the object under study (some studies refer to governmental or democratic legitimacy). Further studies exist that focus on the legitimacy of specific state institutions like the police (Hough et al., 2010) or high courts (Gibson et al., 1998). Finally, one should note that an essential shortcoming of a single-item measurement approach is a lack of content validity. In particular, scholars argue that solely using a single item is not sophisticated enough to account for the latent nature of legitimacy.

Simple Indices. One strategy to increase the reliability and validity of the measurement of a latent variable is to build an *index* that consists of several items that measure the same underlying variable of interest. Here, *simple indices* label all approaches that treat legitimacy as one-dimensional at its conceptual basis. In other words, simple indices are based on several items but do not explicitly treat legitimacy as multidimensional. In the following, I offer a short review of three one-dimensional, 'simple' indices (table 5).[51]

---

50 Interestingly, Berggren et al. (2015) report that the satisfaction with the way democracy works can be approximated by the confidence in parliament and the confidence in parties (regression analysis yields an R-squared of 0.8). In detail, they use this relation to impute missing values of the actual variable of interest (satisfaction with the way democracy works).

Table 5: Measurement of Legitimacy by Simple Indices

Author(s)	Legitimacy Object	Index	Items	Source
Seligson (2002)	State (regime)	Additive (confidence in key institutions of the state)	To what extent do the courts guarantee a fair trial?	National Surveys of four Latin American Countries
			How much respect do you have for the political institutions of the country?	
			How much pride do you feel living under the political system of the country?	
			How much support do you have for the political system of the country?	
			How much trust do you have in the police?	
Domański (2005)	State	Additive	On the whole how satisfied are you with the present state of the economy in [name of the country]?	ESS
			Now thinking about the [country] government, how satisfied are you with the way it is doing its job?	
			How satisfied are you with the way democracy works?	
Doyle (2011)	State (political institutions)	Additive (trust in political institutions)	How much confidence do you have in the national parliament/congress?	Latino Barometro
			How much confidence do you have in national parties?	
			How much confidence do you have in the judiciary?	

First of all, Seligson (2002) uses an additive index that consists of five items that mainly reflect the confidence of citizens in key institutions of the state (namely the courts, the political institutions, the political system, and the police; see table 5). Interestingly, Seligson (2002, 420) writes that these items "tap into generalized support for the basic institutions of government rather than support for the incumbent government". At a closer look, it even becomes apparent that Seligon's (2002) index is a mixture of items that are part of different dimensions in the sense of Norris (1999). For example, the item 'pride of living under the political system' refers to the

51 In this context, further studies can be mentioned. For example, based on the AmericasBarometer, Seligson (2007) uses a five-variable index to measure legitimacy.

dimension political community, whereas the item 'trust in the police' refers to the dimension 'regime institutions' (see chapter 2.4.1). Since the inter-item reliability is high (Cronbach's $\alpha = 0.78$), the index seems to be appropriate for measuring state legitimacy.

Second, Domański (2005) also uses an additive index to analyze the determinants of legitimacy in Europe. Based on the ESS, he uses the items "On the whole how satisfied are you with the present state of the economy in [name of the country]?", "Now thinking about the [country] government, how satisfied are you with the way it is doing its job?", and "How satisfied are you with the way democracy works?" to assess legitimacy. Unfortunately, Domański (2005) does not state any measure that gives information on the inter-item reliability of these three items. Although Domański (2005) speaks about legitimacy, his approach mainly reflects only one dimension of legitimacy in the sense of Norris (1999), namely 'support for regime performance'.

Finally, Doyle (2011) uses three items on political trust to measure legitimacy in Latin America. Using the items "How much confidence do you have in the national parliament/congress", "How much confidence do you have in political parties", and "How much confidence do you have in the judiciary?", he constructs an additive index that is highly reliable (Cronbach's $\alpha = 0.94$) (Doyle, 2011, 1457). Similar to Domański (2005), Doyle's (2011) approach refers to only one dimension of legitimacy in the sense of Norris (1999), namely 'support for regime institutions'.

To sum up, simple indices are advantageous over single items when measuring legitimacy. The reason is that several items (as far as they are reliable) may increase (construct) validity. However, it is still problematic that these approaches treat legitimacy as uni-dimensional. When referring to Norris (1999), the approaches of Domański (2005) and Doyle (2011) refer to one dimension of political support, whereas Seligson's (2002) item battery consists of items of different dimensions.

3.3.2 Multidimensional Measurement Approaches

When dealing with multidimensional measurement approaches, one can distinguish between theory-driven and correlation-based approaches (see chapter 2). Thus, the first sub-section deals with the theory-driven approach of Gilley (2006a, 2006b, 2009a, 2012). The second sub-section focuses on correlation-based approaches, i.e. those approaches that derive the dimensions of legitimacy statistically. Since most of the empirical legitimacy literature follows the latter approach, referring to the seminal contribution by Norris (1999) (see Booth & Seligson, 2005, 2009a; Norris, 2011), I particularly focus on that approach. Finally, since both Gilley's and Norris' measurement approaches reflect the two dependent variables that will be used in the empirical part of this thesis, the last sub-section compares them and depicts their strengths and shortcomings.

Theory-Driven Measurement: Gilley's Approach

In general, theory-driven approaches derive the dimensions of legitimacy theoretically. For example, the approaches of Gilley (2006a, 2006b, 2009a, 2012) and of Møller (2016) can be classified as theory-driven. Since I stick to Gilley's approach throughout the thesis, I deal with it exclusively in the following.

Gilley's Approach. Gilley's (2006a, 2009a, 2012) seminal approach refers to the theoretical work of Beetham (1991) (see also chapter 2). Based on Beetham (1991), Gilley (2006a) defines state legitimacy as a compound of the dimensions 'views of legality', 'views of justification', and 'acts of consent' (figure 7, see also chapter 2.4.1).[52] The first two dimensions ('views of legality' and 'views of justification') are predominantly attitudinal. Following Beetham (1991), 'views of legality' refer to "the idea that the state has acquired and exercises political power in a way that accords with citizens views about laws, rules and customs" (Gilley, 2006a, 502). In contrast, 'views of justification' express the degree to which the state conforms to shared principles, ideas, and values and "refer to citizen responses to the moral reasons given by the state for the way it holds and exercises its power" (Gilley, 2006a, 502-503). The last dimension 'acts of consent' is per definition behavioral and describes "positive actions that express a citizen's recognition of the state's right to hold political authority" (Gilley, 2006a, 503). Taking all together, as Beetham (1991) already suggests, Gilley (2006a) understands legitimacy as a multidimensional concept that contains both attitudinal and behavioral aspects.

Figure 7: Legitimacy and Its Dimensions

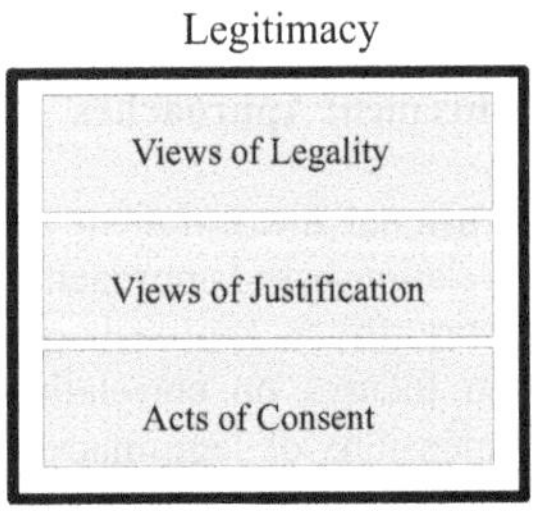

Source: Based on Beetham (1991) and Gilley (2006a)

To measure legitimacy, Gilley (2006a, 2009) offers a variety of (attitudinal and behavioral) indicators for each dimension (see Appendix C). Gilley (2006a, 2006b, 2009, 2012) uses not all of these indicators due to limited data availability. Further, one should note that Gilley (2006a, 2012) uses different items in two different papers.

52 Power and Cyr (2009, 257) raise the objection that "although Gilley refers to the state legitimacy the states in his work refer to the 72 country units. He is clearly investigating the legitimacy of political systems (regime legitimacy or system support) rather than the state as a discrete object of support in those systems."

As a consequence, I (i) review the measurement of legitimacy in his original approach (Gilley, 2006a, 2009) and (ii) dedicate some lines to the measurement of legitimacy in his subsequent article (Gilley, 2012).

Gilley's Seminal Approach. To measure state legitimacy in *circa* 2001, Gilley (2006a) selects three indicators representing 'views of legality', four indicators to depict 'views of justification', and two items to account for 'acts of consent'. The first dimension ('views of legality') solely consists of attitudinal items from the World Values Survey (WVS), namely "Provision of human rights", "Confidence in the police", and "Confidence in the civil service":

- How much respect is there for individual human rights nowadays (in our country)?
- Could you tell me how much confidence you have in the police?
- Could you tell me how much confidence you have in the civil service?

Concerning the second dimension ('views of justification'), Gilley (2006a) uses three attitudinal items and one behavioral item. He takes the attitudinal items from the WVS and several regional Barometers. These items measure "Satisfaction with the functioning of democracy", "Evaluations of the current political system", and "Satisfaction with democratic development":

- On the whole are you very satisfied, rather satisfied, not very satisfied, or not at all satisfied with the way democracy is developing in your country?
- How do you rate the current political system?[53]
- Overall, how satisfied are you with the way democracy works in your country?

He (2006a, 507) further adds a behavioral indicator that captures the "Use of violence in political protest" (the share of all citizens that are in involved in violence). This item is taken from the World Handbook of Political Science IV.

The last dimension ('acts of consent') is by definition behavioral. It is measured by "Voter turnout in parliamentary elections" and "Payment of quasi-voluntary taxes".[54] The data are taken from the Government Finance Yearbook and the International Institute for Democracy and Electoral Assistance (IDEA)).

In a next step, Gilley (2006a) normalizes all items via z-transformation into a 0 to 10 scale.[55] After that, he (2006a) calculates the sub-scores for each dimension. For the first and the third dimension ('views of legality' and 'acts of consent'), Gilley

53 The question is as follows: "People have different views about the system for governing this country. [...] Where on this scale would you put the current political system?" (WVS Codebook Wave 4).

54 Regarding quasi-voluntary taxes, Gilley (2006a, 508) assumes that more legitimate states can generate more quasi-voluntary taxes. He (2006a, 508) writes that "more legitimate governments will be able to rely more on such taxes; that their 'voluntary extractive capacity' will be higher than illegitimate governments. By contrast, states with less legitimacy will be forced to rely on alternative sources of revenue such as foreign borrowing and directly levied sales and export taxes".

computes the simple means of the items. Regarding the second dimension ('views of justification'), Gilley weights the indicator for political violence and the mean of the three attitudinal items one-half each.
Finally, Gilley aggregates the scores of the three dimensions to an overall legitimacy score. He weights 'views of justification' one-half and 'views of legality' and 'acts of consent' one-quarter each.[56] Gilley (2006a, 510) justifies this decision as follows:

> *As both Beetham (1991) and Habermas (1975) have argued, the moral justification of state power (as opposed to its legality or consent) is particularly important because that power underwrites the laws and rules that govern so much of the rest of social and economic life. It is, so to speak, the uber-power and without moral justification, its negative consequences are just too hard to bear. I thus believe that justification should be weighted more heavily for a fully theorized measure of legitimacy*

Having determined the weights of each dimension, Gilley (2006a) computes the overall legitimacy score via an additive index. In fact, I would suggest using a multiplicative index instead of an additive index. The reason is that Gilley (2006a) explicitly builds on the conceptual framework of Beetham (1991) who argues that all dimensions are necessary for legitimacy (see chapter 2.4.1; Beethamian legitimacy function). However, since the correlation between the additive and multiplicative scores is r=0.98 (using Gilley's data for ca. 2001), it has almost no practical relevance whether one uses an additive or a multiplicative aggregation strategy.[57]

Gilley's Subsequent Approach. In Gilley's subsequent article (2012), he applies the following measurement strategy. First, 'views of legality' are composed of two items, namely "Confidence in the justice system" and "Perceived respect for human rights" (WVS 2004-2008).[58]
Regarding 'views of justification', he only uses two attitudinal indicators, namely "Confidence in the civil service" and an indicator that captures the "Degree of how democratically the country is being governed" (both WVS 2004-2008), and two behavioral indicators, namely one that measures "Repression of political opposition"

55 To achieve a zero to ten scale, Gilley multiplies the z-scores with a fixed multiplier and finally adds five. Thus, the mean of each item is five and the standard deviation equals the fixed multiplier. If this procedure leads to scores higher than ten (lower than zero), Gilley simply sets these scores to ten (zero).

56 Gilley (2006a) offers two further strategies to aggregate the dimensions in this paper. The first strategy assumes that each dimension is equally important. Thus, all dimensions are weighted one-third. The second strategy is to caclulate the simple means of all attitudinal items since their inter-item correlation is high (α=0.89) (Gilley, 2006, 511). However, the latter strategy neglects that legitimacy is a multidimensional concept.

57 Thanks to Bruce Gilley for providing me his original data set.

58 Again, the original questions are "How much respect is there for individual human rights nowadays (in our country)?" and "Could you tell me how much confidence you have in the courts?"

(security legitimacy) and one that measures "Exclusion of key political actors or groups" (political legitimacy) (both from the Center for Systemic Peace).[59]
As before, the last dimension 'acts of consent' is measured by "Payment of quasi-voluntary taxes" (calculated as taxes on income, profits, and property over central government revenues less social contributions) and "Voter turnout in parliamentary elections".
As in the original paper, Gilley (2012) calculates the means of the items of the dimensions 'views of legality' and 'acts of consent'. Regarding 'views of justification', all items are weighted equally (one-fourth each) due to the fact the "'Security Legitimacy/Political Legitimacy' indicator replaces the previously used 'Incidence of Political Violence in Civic Protests' indicator" (Gilley, 2012, 694). Finally, the scores of each dimension were collapsed into the overall legitimacy score. As in the former paper, Gilley (2012) uses an additive index and weights 'views of justification' one-half and the other dimensions one-quarter.
Figure 8 presents the items of Gilley's (2006a, 2009a, 2012) original and the slightly modified measurement approach. The legitimacy scores of either approach can be found in Appendix D.

Figure 8: Gilley's Measurement of Legitimacy

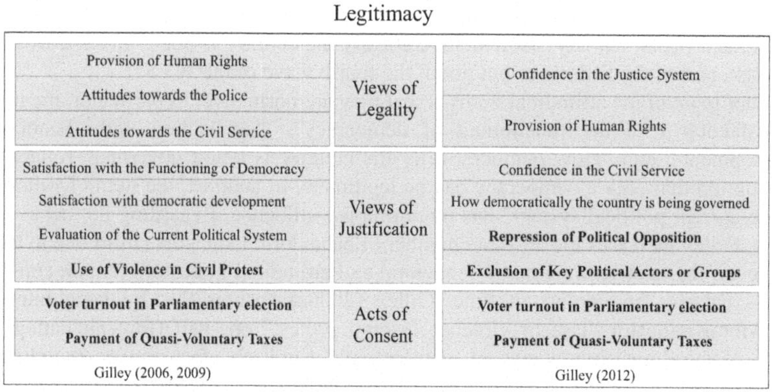

Note: Behavioral items are marked **bold**.

Source: Author's compilation based on Gilley (2006a, 2009a, 2012)

When comparing both approaches, it becomes obvious that Gilley (2006a, 2009a, 2012) makes some minor changes. First, he readdresses the item "Confidence in the civil service". Originally, this item is part of the dimension 'views of legality'. However, in the subsequent article (Gilley, 2012), "Confidence in the civil service" is part of the dimension 'views of justification'. The change impacts the overall legitimacy score since the relative weight of "Confidence in civil service" increases. In

59 The original items read as follows: "Could you tell me how much confidence you have in the civil service?" and "How democratically is this country being governed today?"

the original version (Gilley, 2006a), the item has a relative weight of one twelfth, whereas the relative weight is one eighth in the subsequent article (Gilley, 2012). Unfortunately, Gilley (2012) provides no explanation for this modification.

Second, he also modifies the dimension 'views of legality'. In contrast to the original version, Gilley (2012) drops the items "Confidence in the police" and, as shown above, "Confidence in the civil service" and adds the item "Confidence in the justice system". These modifications are somewhat puzzling since Gilley (2006a, 507) notices that "civil service and the police […] provide an effect-based way to measure views of legality [...]. Ideally, attitudes toward the judiciary would be included as well; however, this question was asked in far too few countries in the World Values Survey". Besides the civil service item, it remains unclear why Gilley drops the police item, in particular since this item is included in all waves of the WVS. Finally, as the quote shows, the item "Confidence in the justice system" is not included in the original approach due to limited data availability.[60]

Third, the dimension 'views of justification' originally consists of three attitudinal and one behavioral indicator. Gilley (2012) also updates this in his subsequent article (2012). There, 'views of justification' are represented by two attitudinal and two behavioral indicators. Regarding the attitudinal items, Gilley replaces all items mainly due to reasons of limited data availability: The items "Evaluation of the current political system" and "Satisfaction with democratic development" are available in the fourth but not in the fifth or even the sixth wave of the WVS; the new item in Gilley's subsequent paper, namely "How democratically the country is being governed", is, in contrast, part of the fifth wave but not of the fourth wave of the WVS.[61]

Another issue of the attitudinal items is that they are normative. In particular, the items "Satisfaction with the functioning of democracy", "Satisfaction with democratic development", and "How democratically the country is being governed" reflect the assumption that only a democracy can be legitimate. In contrast, the item "Evaluation of the current political system" has no normative influence. Regarding the behavioral items, Gilley increases the absolute number of behavioral indicators (from one to two). However, the relative weights of behavioral and attitudinal indicators remain constant across datasets and points in time. Gilley (2006a) ensures this by weighting the behavioral indicator "Use of violence in civil protest" one-half (for calculating the score of the dimension 'views of justification'). Similarly, focusing on the slightly modified set of indicators (Gilley, 2012), he addresses a weight of one-fourth to "repression of political opposition" as well as to "exclusion of key political actors or groups" (in sum, behavioral indicators have a weight of one-half) to obtain the sub-score for 'views of justification'.

60 The item "Confidence in the justice system" is included in all waves of the WVS except the fourth wave (which is the data basis for Gilley's (2006a) original measurement approach) (WVS Codebooks).

61 The availability of the items in the WVS/EVS is somewhat confusing. According to the integrated EVS/WVS codebook, the items "Satisfaction with the way democracy develops" (question V168 in WVS 4) and "Evaluation of current political system" (question V163a in WVS 4) are part of all waves (since the fourth wave of the WVS). However, I do not find these data in the waves published after the fourth WVS wave, neither in the integrated dataset nor in the single data sets of each wave.

All these modifications raise the question whether the item changes have a severe impact on the resulting legitimacy scores. To assess this question, a strategy would be to rebuild one of the two indices and check the correlation between both. For example, one could use the items of Gilley's original approach (2006a) and calculate the overall legitimacy scores for ca. 2008 (which correspond to Gilley's (2012) subsequent paper). If the correlation were high, the item changes would be irrelevant for the underlying concept. Unfortunately, it is not possible to apply this strategy since neither items used in the original approach are available at the time of the subsequent approach ("Evaluation of the current political system" and "Satisfaction with democratic development") nor items used in the subsequent approach are available at the time of the original approach ("How democratically the country is being governed"). As a consequence, it cannot be clarified whether the results of both approaches are consistent. Thus, they cannot be compared over time without reservations.
Although it is hardly possible to check the validity and consistency across waves, it is still possible to analyze whether the legitimacy measure is internally consistent at a point in time. Since Gilley's legitimacy measure has three theoretically derived, distinct dimensions, it is sufficient to check whether each dimension is internally consistent. Table 6 offers an overview of the internal consistency of each dimension (as measured by Cronbach's α).

Table 6: Internal Consistency of Gilley's Dimensions

	Views of Legality	Views of Justification	Acts of Consent
Cronbach's α (Gilley, 2006a)	0.75	0.51	0.32
Cronbach's α (Gilley, 2012)	0.87	0.42	0.26

Source: Author's calculation based on Gilley's (2006a, 2012) original data

According to Cronbach's α, the dimension 'views of legality' is internally consistent. In contrast, 'views of justification' and 'acts of consent' are not internally consistent since the α-values are too low (typically, α-values above 0.7 indicate that a dimension is internally consistent; some scholars also accept values larger than 0.5). However, Gilley (2009b) notices that this is not problematic since inter-item correlations are only relevant if all indicators of a dimension are substitutive (Appendix E provides more information on substitutive and constitutive indicators, see also Bollen & Lennox, 1991). In fact, 'views of justification' consists of three constitutive indicators ("Satisfaction with democratic development", "Evaluation of current political system", and "Satisfaction with operation of democracy") and one substitutive indicator ("Use of violence in civil protest") (Gilley, 2006a, 522-523); 'acts of consent' consists of two constitutive indicators ("Voter turnout" and "Quasi-voluntary taxes"). As a consequence, the low values of Cronbach's α of the dimensions 'views of justification' and 'acts of consent' do not indicate that these dimensions are internally inconsistent.

Rather, the low α-values result from addressing both constitutive and substantive indicators to each dimension.
Nonetheless, the question remains why 'views of justification' and 'acts of consent' have such low α-scores. As it turns out, the behavioral indicators are the reason for this phenomenon. Gilley (2006a, 511) already shows that the behavioral indicators are not or only weakly correlated with the attitudinal indicators. Further, the behavioral indicators themselves are not or only weakly correlated (Gilley, 2006a, 511). The same results occur when using the data of Gilley's (2012) subsequent paper.[62] Here, regarding the dimension 'views of justification', the behavioral indicator "Repression/Exclusion" is only weakly correlated with the attitudinal item "How democratically the country is being governed" and not correlated with the attitudinal item "Confidence in the civil service". Table 7 shows the correlation matrix of the items of the dimension 'views of justification'. When analyzing the dimension 'acts of consent', the correlation between the items "Voter turnout" and "Payment of quasi-voluntary taxes" also is insignificant (r=0.15).

Table 7: Inter-Item Correlations (Views of Justification)

Correlations	CCS	Demo	Rep/Ex
CCS	1	0.39***	-0.12
Demo		1	0.32**
Rep/Ex			1

Items: CCS - "Confidence in the Civil Service"; Demo - "How democratically the country is being governed"; Rep/Ex - "Repression/Exclusion" (Sum of Security Legitimacy (measure of state repression) and Political Legitimacy (measure of political factionalism and exclusion))

* - at 10%-level significant ** - at 5%-level significant *** - at 1%-level significant
Number of observations: 51

Source: Author's computation based on Gilley's (2012) (country-level) data

As a consequence, using behavioral items has a severe impact on the overall legitimacy score, in particular since behavioral and attitudinal items are only weakly or not correlated. Although this may be statistically problematic, the use of behavioral items is theoretically well-founded. In addition, Gilley (2012, 695) stresses that "it is preferable to have a behavioral indicator to balance attitudinal indicators when measuring an essentially latent concept like political legitimacy."
To conclude, Gilley (2006a, 2009a, 2012) develops a measure of state legitimacy. His measure is clearly multidimensional and based on the theoretical considerations of Beetham (1991). Thus, Gilley's dimensions are theoretically derived. That some dimensions are not internally consistent by means of Cronbach's α is not a shortcoming since the concerned dimensions are measured by both substitutive and

62 Actually, Gilley (2012) provides no information about the correlations of the items in his subsequent paper.

constitutive indicators. Further, it becomes apparent that the use of behavioral indicators counter-balances attitudinal indicators (Gilley, 2012, 695), in particular since behavioral indicators are weakly or not correlated with the attitudinal ones.

Other scholars also use Gilley's innovative contribution for further investigations. For example, Nivette and Eisner (2013) use Gilley's legitimacy scores as an independent variable to predict homicides. Further, Power and Cyr (2009, 253) adopt Gilley's measurement strategy to set up a ranking of the legitimacy of 18 Latin American countries for circa 2005. Gilley (2006a) himself also draws upon his approach to analyze the determinants of legitimacy. Finally, Nivette and Eisner (2013, 15) write that "Gilley's [...] indicator of political legitimacy [...] is beneficial over previous studies' use of singular attitudinal measures (e.g., Chamlin & Cochran, 2006; see also Weatherford, 1992) or secondary data with questionable content validity (e.g., Crespo, 2006)."

Of course, Gilley's measurement approach also has some shortcomings. First of all, one can only use Gilley's legitimacy scores to perform analyses at the country level. The reason is that Gilley collects data from different data sources to obtain the overall legitimacy scores. If he had solely used data from the WVS, it would have been possible to execute both country-level and individual-level analyses (since WVS data are available at the individual level). However, since all behavioral items are only available at the country level (for example, "Voter turnout"), a mixture of individual-level and country-level data only allows to perform analyses at the aggregated (country) level.

Second, the use of several data sources leads to the problem that all data were not collected at the same time. For example, in Gilley's (2006a) original paper, data from the WVS range from 1999 to 2004; data on the last parliamentary election range from 1995 to 2001 and data on the payment of quasi-voluntary taxes range from 1997 to 2002. In addition, the time range varies not only across countries but also within countries.[63] In fact, Gilley (2006a) averages the data and notes that his legitimacy scores represent *cicra* 2001. However, it needs to be noticed that state legitimacy may differ when comparing 1997 with 2002 due to political or economic changes (for example, the burst of the dot-com bubble in 2000 or the military conflict in Kosovo in 1998 and 1999). As a consequence, Gilley's scores do not represent legitimacy of a particular year but of a time span of four to five years. The same problem emerges in Gilley's subsequent paper (2012).

Third, Nivette and Eisner (2013, 17) point out that "Gilley's aggregate indicator did not allow the examination of different aspects of legitimacy [...]." However, this is only partly true. The reason is that Gilley (2006a, 2009a, 2012) publishes the aggregate legitimacy scores but not the sub-scores of each dimension. This limits the possibility to analyze the dimensions at a first glance. To solve this problem, one can recalculate the sub-scores of each dimension or request them from Gilley.

Fourth, Gilley uses an aggregation strategy of the dimensions that contrasts with the theoretical considerations of Beetham (1991). Since Beetham (1991) claims that all

63 Exemplary, Algerian data on the voter turnout stem from 1997, the data on the payment of quasi-voluntary taxes from 2001, and the data taken from the WVS were collected in 2002 (Gilley, 2006a, original data; WVS 4).

dimensions are necessary for legitimacy, one should abstain from aggregating the dimensions in an additive manner (since it can be derived that a multiplicative linkage of the dimensions is favorable; see chapter 2.4.2). However, the practical relevance of using an additive or multiplicative aggregation strategy is negligible (correlation between the resulting overall scores is r=0.98).

Fifth, Gilley uses behavioral indicators. Although Beetham (1991) clearly claims that 'acts of consent' are necessary to measure legitimacy, it is still difficult to find appropriate behavioral indicators that clearly indicate legitimacy. For example, Gilley uses the indicator "Voter turnout" to measure the dimension 'acts of consent'. He further assumes a monotonic positive relationship between voter turnout and legitimacy, implying that a higher voter turnout also reflects a higher degree of legitimacy. Of course, this assumption can be challenged. For example, from a rational choice perspective, an individual may find the system highly legitimate but nevertheless may abstain from voting since the expected utility from voting is lower than its costs. In this scenario, low participation in voting is basically a result of a benefit-cost assessment. Even if one assumes that legitimacy and voter turnout are positively connected, an increase in voter turnout does not necessarily mean that state legitimacy also increases since legitimacy is not the only determinant of voter turnout. To be more precise, Blais (2006) reviews various studies and finds that voter turnout is to a large degree determined by – among others – institutional factors such as compulsory voting, the electoral system, unicameralism, the voting age, and the rules designed to facilitate voting. As a consequence, cross-national differences in voting turnout could simply be the result of institutional differences. To give a concrete example, Kostadinova and Power (2007) find that voter turnout in Eastern Europe is higher than respective rates in Latin America. They further argue that these differences are the result of historical legacies and the mode of transition to democracy. As a consequence, the use of raw data on voter turnout (as done by Gilley) misses other explanatory factors. Thus, cross-country differences in voter turnout do not necessarily indicate differences in legitimacy; they could just be a consequence of different institutional settings.

Sixth, one should also notice that the overall legitimacy score of one country depends on other countries. The reason is that Gilley uses a z-transformation to standardize the items. In consequence, if one adds an observation (i.e. a country) to the data, the mean and the standard deviation of the items may change, which impacts the transformed item values. Thus, Gilley's scores have an ordinal scale level. Thus, in the narrow sense, absolute legitimacy scores as well as the distance between two legitimacy scores cannot be interpreted properly.

Despite these shortcomings, Gilley provides an innovative approach for measuring the state's legitimacy. In consequence, I update Gilley's legitimacy scores for ca. 2012, using the same items as in his (2012) subsequent paper (see Appendix D).[64] Besides Gilley's (2006a, 2009a, 2012) approach, other theory-driven approaches exist which I do not consider in this thesis (e.g. Møller, 2016).[65]

64 I have to thank Alexander Hesse who collected the items and compiled them to overall legitimacy scores.

Correlation-Based Measurement: Norris' Approach

The correlation-based measurement approaches derive the dimensions of legitimacy based on inter-item correlations and/or factor analysis (statistical methods). Since most studies following the correlation-based measurement approach build on the seminal approach of Norris (1999, 2011), I dedicate this sub-chapter to review and discuss her approach. In detail, I first review the dimensions and the indicators of Norris (1999, 2011). Thereafter, I briefly emphasize some aspects that distinguish Norris' (1999, 2011) approach from theory-driven measurement approaches.

Norris' Approach. Norris' (1999) seminal approach has its origins in the contributions of Easton (1965, 1975). Drawing on the distinction between diffuse and specific support, Norris develops a five-dimensional classification of political support. Referring to Norris' (2011) recent book *Democratic Deficit*, these five dimensions are – ordered from most diffuse to most specific – 'support for the nation-state', 'support for regime principles', 'evaluation of regime performance', 'confidence in regime institutions', and 'approval of incumbent officeholders' (Norris, 2011, 44).[66] Table 8 provides an overview of the items that belong to each dimension (all taken from the World Values Survey) and also depicts the factor loadings. In addition, I also present the factor loadings (using principal component analysis (PCA) with varimax rotation) of my replication that confirm Norris' results.[67] Since Norris (2011) uses factor analysis to extract the dimensions of political support, reliability problems (as

65 In short, Møller (2016) applies the following measurement strategy. At first, she theoretically derives three dimensions based on the works of Weber (1946), Lipset (1959), Habermas (1975), and Easton (1975) (see chapter 2.4.1), namely an input dimension (reflecting citizens' confidence in state institutions), an output dimension (referring to the performance of the state), and a dimension reflecting the degree of the rule of law. To measure these dimensions, Møller depicts all indicators from the sixth wave of the WVS. In particular, the input dimension consists of the indicators "Confidence in the courts/police/government/civil service". Further, the dimension 'rights' is measured by the respect for human rights and how much freedom of choice and control people feel. Finally, the output dimension is an index that persists of items that measure how often you or your family have gone without enough food to eat, gone without cash income, gone without medicine or medical treatment that you needed, or felt unsafe from crime in your home in the last 12 months. All items were standardized and then aggregated within dimensions in an additive manner. Applying the geometric mean, the sub-scores of each dimension were collapsed into an aggregate score. The weight of each dimension is one-third. Møller's (2016) measurement approach differs in so far from Gilley's that she (i) does not include behavioral indicators (instead, she notes that actual behavior is rather an outcome of legitimacy) and (ii) includes a performance dimension.

66 In Norris' (1999) book *Critical Citizens*, the same five-dimensional distinction can be found. However, the labels are somewhat different. Here, the dimensions – ordered from most diffuse to most specific support – are 'political community', 'regime principles', 'regime performance', 'regime institutions', and 'political actors'. (Norris, 1999, 16-21)

67 My replication differs from Norris' (2011, 45) approach in some points. First, I only use the fourth wave of the WVS, whereas Norris sticks to a pooled version of the WVS (1981-2005). Second, I partly use different items (e.g. "rating of the current political system" or "democracy may have problems but is better than other forms of government") which, however, do not alter the five-fold classification of political support. Third, I leave out items that belong to the dimension 'support for the nation state'.

measured by Cronbach's alpha) do not arise as in the case of Gilley. The reason is that factor analysis ensures that only items are part of a dimension that are highly correlated with the underlying factor and, thus, also with the other items of the same dimension.[68]

The first dimension 'support for the nation state' is the most diffuse type of political support. It consists of three items which refer to national pride, identification with the nation, and the willingness to fight for the country in a war.

The second dimension is 'regime principles'. Norris (2011) further divides this dimension into two sub-categories, namely 'approval of democratic values' and 'rejection of autocratic values'. As a result of the factor analysis, two items ("approve of having a democratic system as very/fairly good" and "the importance of living in a country being governed democratically") measure the degree to which people agree with democratic values. In contrast, an item battery consisting of the degree to which bureaucratic elites, dictators, or the military are rejected as a head of a regime measure the rejection of autocratic values.

Next, the dimension 'evaluation of regime performance' consists of two items, namely how citizens evaluate the performance of democracy and to what extent the state respects human rights.

Further, the dimension 'confidence in regime institutions' consists of items that refer to citizens' confidence in the key institutions of the state (the parliament, the parties, the government, the courts, the civil service, the police, and the armed forces).

The last dimension is 'approval of incumbent officeholders'. However, Norris (2011, 45) provides no items that belong to this dimension since it is barely possible to find items in the WVS that refer to incumbent officeholders.[69] As a consequence, factor analysis cannot extract this dimension due to limited data availability.

Eventually, three issues need to be noticed to evaluate Norris' (2011) measurement approach. First, Norris (2011) abstains from aggregating the dimensions to an overall legitimacy score. Rather, she and other colleagues analyze each dimension separately (Booth & Seligson, 2009a; Gjefsen, 2012). Second, although the measurement approach of Norris (2011) explicitly refers to political support rather than to legitimacy, various scholars adopt it and equate political support with legitimacy (see chapter 2.4.1). However, I understand political support as a wider concept than political legitimacy. In particular, this becomes obvious when comparing Norris' approach (2012) with Gilley's (2006a, 2009a, 2012), which I discuss below. Third, Norris (1999, 2011) completely sticks to attitudinal items to measure each dimension.

---

68 Based on my replication of Norris' (2011) dimensions, I also perform some reliability checks. All dimensions have an α-score above 0.5 ('regime principles: approval of democratic values' 0.601; 'regime principles: rejection of autocratic values' 0.545; 'evaluation of regime performance' 0.570; 'confidence in regime institutions' 0.825). However, reliability analyses also show that two items could be dropped. On the one hand, the omission of the item "Confidence in armed forces" increase the α-score of the dimension 'confidence in regime institutions' even further (from 0.825 to 0.828). On the other hand, the same effect results when omitting the item "Rating of current political system" of the dimension 'evaluation of regime performance' (α increases from 0.570 to 0.614).

69 The WVS contains the item 'Satisfaction with the people in the national office' that could be used as an item to operationalize the dimension 'approval of incumbent officeholders'. However, this item is only part of the third and the fourth wave of the WVS.

Table 8: Indicators of Norris' (2011) Five-Dimensional Approach

Dimension	*Items*	*Factor loadings (Norris, 2011)**	*Factor loadings (replication)***
Support for the Nation State	Strengths of feelings of national pride	0.739	-
	Strength of identification with nation	0.694	-
	Willingness to fight for country in a war	0.593	-
Regime Principles: Approval of Democratic Values	Approve of having a democratic system as 'very/fairly good'	0.803	0.796
	Importance of living in a country governed democratically	0.734	-
	Democracy may have problems but is better than other forms of government	-	0.806
Regime Principles: Rejection of Autocratic Values	Anti-bureaucratic elite rule	0.803	0.758
	Anti-dictatorship	0.765	0.742
	Anti-military rule	0.619	0.590
Evaluation of Regime Performance	Evaluation of performance of democracy	0.803	0.769
	Evaluation of respect for human rights	0.787	0.709
	Rating of current political system	-	0.788
Confidence in Regime Institutions	Confidence in the parliament	0.809	0.780
	Confidence in the parties	0.749	0.680
	Confidence in the government	0.787	0.743
	Confidence in the courts	0.760	-
	Confidence in the civil service	0.744	0.727
	Confidence in the police	0.723	0.643
	Confidence in the armed forces	0.577	0.635
Approval of Incumbent Officeholders	-	-	-

* - Factor loadings are based on the World Values Survey pooled 1981-2005.
** - Factor loadings are based on the fourth wave of the World Values Survey using principal component analysis (PCA) with varimax rotation. The mode to deal with missing values is pairwise. Items for the dimension 'support for the nation state' have not been included.

Source: Adopted from Norris (2011, 45); all items were taken from the WVS

This has the advantage that the individual data of the WVS do not need to be nested with external data. As a consequence, Norris' (2012) approach also allows for the analysis of legitimacy at the individual level.

To sum up, the correlation-driven method is an alternative way to extract the dimensions of political support and, thus, also legitimacy. A variety of other scholars also draw upon this approach. However, there are some fundamental differences between Norris' (1999, 2011) correlation-based and Gilley's (2006a, 2009, 2012) theory-driven approach. The following sub-section compares both in greater depth.

Comparing the Measurement Approaches of Gilley and Norris

In the last two sub-sections, I presented the theory-driven measurement approach by Gilley (2006a, 2009a, 2012) and the correlation-based measurement approach by Norris (1999, 2011). Although both approaches aim at measuring legitimacy, six important differences exist:

- *Method to Derive the Dimensions of Legitimacy.* To derive the dimensions of legitimacy, theory-driven and correlation-based approaches exist. In this vein, Norris (1999, 2011) clearly derives the dimensions of legitimacy in a correlation-driven fashion since she uses factor analysis to identify them. In contrast, referring to Beetham (1991), Gilley (2006a, 2009a, 2012) uses a theory-driven approach.
- *Indicator Types.* Regarding the indicator types, Norris solely uses attitudinal indicators to measure legitimacy and its dimensions. In contrast, Gilley uses both attitudinal and behavioral indicators for his measure. Whether behavioral indicators contribute to measure legitimacy is still under discussion. On the one hand, Gilley argues that behavioral indicators help to balance attitudes since both are mostly uncorrelated. On the other hand, other scholars argue that behavioral indicators are not appropriate for legitimacy research since (i) actual behavior cannot clearly be addressed to the underlying beliefs or (ii) behavior should rather be seen as an outcome of legitimacy (see chapter 3.1).
- *Data Sources.* Regarding the data sources, one should note that Norris (2011) solely sticks to one data source, namely the World Values Survey. The necessity to solely use one data source is based on the correlation-based method to derive the dimensions of legitimacy since the usage of several data sources would require interviewing the same individuals. In contrast, Gilley (2006a, 2009a, 2012) uses several data sources (aggregated) at the country level (e.g. World Values Survey, GlobalBarometer regional surveys, World Handbook of Political and Social Sciences).
- *Applicability for Further Analyses.* Due to the use of different data sources, Gilley's legitimacy scores can only be analyzed at the country level. It is not possible to analyze his data at the individual level since the behavioral data he uses are only available at the country level and, thus, cannot be disaggregated to the individual level. Thus, scholars use Gilley's legitimacy scores for descriptive statistics, correlation analyses, and regressions at the country level

(Gilley 2006b; Nivette & Eisner, 2013). In contrast, since all data are available at the individual level, Norris' approach allows both country-level and individual-level analyses. As a consequence, most analyses consist not only of descriptive statistics, correlations, and regressions at the country and individual level but also of elaborated methods that link individual and country levels such as multi-level models (Booth & Seligson, 2005, 2009a; Gjefsen, 2012; Huang et al., 2008; Norris, 1999, 2011).

- *Aggregation of the Sub-Dimenions.* Referring to the aggregation of the dimensions, Gilley (2006a, 2009a, 2012) combines the dimensions in an additive manner to obtain the overall legitimacy scores. In sharp contrast, Norris (2011) does not aggregate the dimensions at all. Rather, she and other colleagues mostly analyze each dimension separately (Booth & Seligson, 2005, 2009a; Gjefsen, 2012; Norris, 1999, 2011). For an exception, see Booth and Seligson (2009a, 247) who aggregate the dimensions 'support for regime principles', 'support for regime performance', and 'confidence in regime institutions'.
- *Legitimacy Concept.* Regarding the underlying legitimacy concept, differences between both approaches exist. Norris (1999, 2011) originally refers to political support which is a more general concept than legitimacy (legitimacy in the wider sense). In contrast, Gilley explicitly speaks about the legitimacy

Figure 9: Legitimacy Concepts of Norris and Gilley

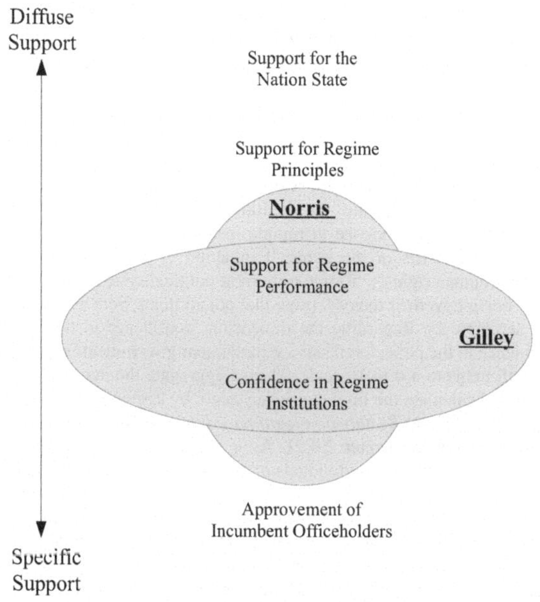

Source: Author's compilation

of the state (legitimacy in the narrow sense). The measurement approaches also reflect this conceptual difference. Gilley partly uses the same attitudinal indicators as Norris. In detail, Gilley's attitudinal indicators refer either to Norris' dimensions 'support for regime performance' (for example the indicators "Respect for human rights" or "Satisfaction/Performance of democracy") or 'confidence in regime institutions' (for example the indicator "Confidence in the civil service"); but not to Norris' dimensions 'support for the nation state', 'support for regime principles', or 'approvement of incumbent officeholders'.[70] As a consequence, Gilley's measurement approach refers to a narrow understanding of legitimacy that can be equated to two of Norris' dimensions, namely 'regime performance' and 'regime institutions' (figure 9).

The comparison shows that some important differences between Norris' and Gilley's measurement approach exist (table 9). However, both approaches are comparable under some circumstances, namely (i) when legitimacy is analyzed at the country level and (ii) when Gilley's legitimacy scores are compared to an aggregation of Norris' dimensions 'support for regime performance' and 'confidence in regime institutions'. To check this, I use the fourth, the fifth, and the sixth wave of the WVS and calculate overall legitimacy scores that consists of the dimensions 'support for regime performance' and 'confidence in regime institutions' (see Appendix F for the scores).[71] The result shows that my replicated legitimacy scores (that are based on Norris' measurement approach) are comparable to Gilley's legitimacy scores since the correlation coefficient is $r=0.71$ (fourth wave of the WVS), $r=0.72$ (fifth wave of the WVS), or $r=0.74$ (sixth wave of the WVS). Gilley (2012, 694) makes a similar comparison but only finds a correlation of $r=0.55$.[72] In both cases, the reason for the

70 Since the item 'Satisfaction/Performance of democracy' is a part of Gilley's indicators, he implicitly assumes that citizens approve of democracy (which is questionable).

71 I apply the following methodology. I almost take the same items as Norris (2012, 45). An initial factor analysis confirms the dimensions of political support as presented by Norris (2012, 45, see table 8). Then, I calculate the legitimacy scores for the dimensions 'support for regime performance' and 'confidence in regime institutions'. In fact, the dimension 'support for regime performance' consists of the items "Evaluation of performance of democracy", "Evaluation of respect for human rights", "Rating of current political system", and/or "How democratically is your country being governed today?" (note that not all items were available in the fourth, fifth, and sixth wave; see table 2). Regarding the dimension 'confidence in regime institutions', I use items on "Confidence in the police/civil service/parliament/government/parties/armed forces/courts". Then, I rescale all items to a 0 to 10 scale. Then, I aggregate the items of each dimension (simple mean). Thereafter, I calculate the final legitimacy score by aggregating the sub-scores of each dimension. I assume an underlying *Beethamian legitimacy function*. This means that I use the geometric mean of the dimensions (see chapter 2.4.2). As a result, I get a legitimacy score for each individual. Eventually, I aggregate all individuals of a country to obtain a legitimacy score at the country level.

72 The correlation of 0.55 refers to legitimacy calculations done by Seligson and Booth (2009a, 247) and the Gilley replication of Power and Cyr (2009). The calculation of Booth and Seligson's (2009a, 247) differs, however, from my methodology since they investigate how much of the citizens are triply satisfied or dissatisfied (meaning that they are simultaneously satisfied/dissatisfied with with 'regime principles', 'regime performance', and 'institutional support').

moderate correlation is the fact that the behavioral indicators are not or only weakly correlated with the attitudinal ones (see chapter 3.3.2). Nonetheless, both Norris' and Gilley's approaches allow for the measuring of legitimacy. However, whose approach a researcher should choose strongly depends on the research question (e.g. individual-level or country-level analyses; measurement of legitimacy in wider sense (political support) or in the narrow sense).

Table 9: Comparison of Norris' and Gilley's Measurement Approaches

Criterion	*Norris (1999, 2011)*	*Gilley (2006a, 2009a, 2012)*
Derivation of the Dimensions	Correlation-based	Theory-driven
Variable Types	Attitudinal items	Attitudinal and behavioral items
Data Sources	Single data source	Multiple data sources
Aggregation of the Dimensions	No aggregation	Aggregation (additive)
Applicability for Further Analyses at ...	Country and individual level	Country level
Legitimacy Concept	Legitimacy in a wider sense (Political support)	Legitimacy in a narrow sense

Source: Author's compilation

3.4 Summary

Since a precise measurement of legitimacy is a necessary precondition for the empirical investigation of the impact of economic freedom on legitimacy, this chapter offers a literature overview of various strategies to measure legitimacy. The chapter also shows that the measurement of legitimacy largely depends on the available data sources (see chapter 3.2) and the actual measurement approach (see chapter 3.3).

Regarding the data sources, the largest problem in empirical legitimacy research is that there is "no existing cross-national data set on the legitimacy of states" (Gilley, 2006a, 500). As a consequence, any approach to measure legitimacy builds on already existing data sources such as the World Values Survey, the GlobalBarometer, the European Social Survey, and others. However, those surveys are not explicitly designed to measure legitimacy. Thus, researchers have to deal with a variety of problems that are caused by the data such as:

- not every wave contains all useful items such that comparisons over time are problematic (for example, the item "Satisfaction with Democracy" in the WVS, see table 2);
- the operationalization of legitimacy is only possible with a reduction of validity due to missing items (for example, Gilley (2006a, 507) argues that the dimension 'views of legality' should ideally be measured by an item that captures the confidence in the justice system); or
- the operationalization of legitimacy is only possible when using several data sources, implying that one can only compare legitimacy scores at the country level (for example, Gilley (2006a, 2009, 2012) mainly uses attitudinal items from the WVS but also draws on other sources to collect behavioral indicators).

Besides the data sources, the way a researcher operationalizes the latent construct political legitimacy also impacts its measurement. I distinguish between unidimensional measurement approaches (single items and simple indices) and more sophisticated multidimensional ones. The latter are either theory-driven or correlation-based. In particular, I present the theory-driven approach of Gilley (2006a, 2009a, 2012) and compare his approach to the correlation-based approach of Norris (1999, 2011). Although both approaches have a variety of differences (for example regarding the variables types, the data sources, or the underlying legitimacy concept, see table 9), a comparison of the resulting legitimacy scores shows that both approaches are useful for empirical legitimacy research. The next step is to review the determinants of legitimacy.

4 The Determinants of Legitimacy: Concepts and Literature Overview

The measurement of legitimacy makes it possible to analyze the determinants of legitimacy. That also allows one to test normative theories, hypotheses, or research questions empirically. Since my research question aims at investigating the relationship between economic freedom and state legitimacy, the following chapter reviews the empirical determinants of legitimacy.[73] That is important since (i) a review of the determinants of legitimacy allows one to extract the control variables for the empirical investigation and (ii) it shows which studies already use economic freedom as an explanatory variable. To the best of my knowledge, no quantitative study explicitly links economic freedom and the state's legitimacy.[74]

This chapter is structured as follows. In the first sub-section (chapter 4.1), I present the concept of Fritz Scharpf (1970, 1999) who distinguishes between input and output legitimacy (chapter 4.1.1). Further, I extend Scharpf's classification by adding throughput legitimacy (chapter 4.1.2). Thereafter, I also offer an overview of classifications of legitimacy's determinants by other scholars and compare those with the input-throughput-output conception.

In the second sub-section (chapter 4.2), I assign variables to the input, throughput, and output distinction. To do so, I compare which variables other scholars use as determinants of legitimacy. As it turns out, it is useful to distinguish between system-level (or country-level) and individual-level variables. At the country level, the results show that one can measure (i) input legitimacy by the degree of democracy, regime tradition, and fractionalization; (ii) throughput legitimacy by the degree of corruption (or the degree of impartiality) and (iii) output legitimacy by government effectiveness, the state's absolute and relative welfare level (such as GDP per capita or the HDI), income distribution, and the unemployment rate.

Finally, the last sub-section (chapter 4.3) offers a summary of the preceding chapter and provides an outlook.

4.1 Input, Output, and Throughput Legitimacy

4.1.1 The Basic Concept: Input and Output Legitimacy

Fritz Scharpf (1970, 1999) provides a famous distinction to classify the determinants of legitimacy. Originally, Scharpf (1970, 21) applies the input-output terminology to show that theories on democracy can be distinguished into input and output theories. Output-oriented theories define the desired quality of political objectives and, thereafter, determine further requirements the political system must fulfill (Scharpf,

73 In other words, I follow a micro perspective. However, one should note that normative theories can also be used to derive the determinants of legitimacy. For example, since Rawls argues that political power is legitimate when exercised in line with constitutional essentials, the determinants of legitimacy would be the division of powers, equal basic rights and liberties, the right to vote and to participate in politics, and so forth.

74 As an exception, Gilley (2006b, 52) finds a positive correlation and notes that "economic stability of property rights and financial institutions as well as market-oriented economic governance and private economic ownership have all been seen as legitimacy-enhancing because of their role in both economic freedom and growth". See also chapter 6.

C. M. Hindermann, *The Impact of Economic Freedom on State Legitimacy*, Wirtschaft und Politik, https://doi.org/10.1007/978-3-658-23195-8_4

1970, 21).[75] In this context, Scharpf (1970, 24) acknowledges that in modern times nearly all spheres of life become more dependent on contributions offered by the state. The reason is that the modern state increasingly shapes or directs societal developments and the social system. In particular, Scharpf (1970, 24) refers to the claims of citizens that the state should provide social security, economic growth, and better opportunities in life. On the other hand, input-oriented theories focus on the will of the people and their articulated interests (rather than on the quality of the political objectives) (Scharpf, 1970, 25). Here, the question is how a political system ought to be organized to ensure that any decision is a genuine result based on equal participation of all citizens.[76]

Although Scharpf (1970) uses the input-output framework as a tool to analyze theories on democracy, various scholars borrow the input-output framework to analyze the legitimacy of political systems in general. That means that scholars apply the input-output framework not only to democracies (Scharpf, 2015) but also to other forms of government at the national (Feldmann & Mazepus, 2014) and the supranational level (such as the European Union or the European Monetary Union, Scharpf, 1999, 2015; Schmidt, 2013) and to single decisions (Lindgren & Persson, 2010; Partzsch, 2011).[77]

Scholars relabel the input-output concept, distinguishing between input and output legitimacy, to evaluate the overall legitimacy of a political system. In short, input legitimacy describes „government by the people", which refers to the participatory quality of the decision-making process (Risse, 2006, 185). Ideally, every decision that is collectively binding should be based on the preferences of the people. To ensure this, the people themselves should have the possibility to express their preferences authentically in a decision-making process (Scharpf, 2015, 1). If this principle were executed properly, the state would be legitimate since state activities and the enacted laws are self-determined by the people. Hence, people should comply with the laws and the political order, especially since laws are not imposed by an exogenous force but rather by the „will of the people" (Scharpf, 1998, 2; 1999, 6). A democratic system, or more generally a political system with open access, meets those requirements best.

75 For further details, see Scharpf (1970, 21-24). There, he names a variety of output theories (such as theories on the separation of power or liberal theories of law).

76 For further details, see Scharpf (1970, 25-28).

77 Exemplary, the input-output concept has been applied to analyze the legitimacy of the European Union. In this vein, scholars mostly argue that the European Union needs to be treated fundamentally different than nation states (since the EU has a 'democratic deficit') (Scharpf, 1999, 12; Schmidt, 2013, 5). That means that the EU can only generate legitimacy via the output dimension but not via the input dimension. The reasons for this are manifold. According to Scharpf (1999, 8), the main problem is that the European Union lacks a collective identity and still borrows its legitimacy from the nation states. Other arguments are listed by Schmidt (2013, 16): (i) EU polices cannot be approved or disapproved by the citizens since there is no government that citizens can vote in or out; (ii) EU decision-making differs from politics in the traditional sense; (iii) party differences have long been overlooked due to the search for consensus; (iv) European parties are still perceived as weak, underdeveloped, and not very cohesive; and (v) voter turnout of the European Parliament elections are rather low. As a consequence, the European Union should focus on output legitimacy. Some scholars even suggest that input legitimacy is not desired since a parliamentarization of the EU would lead to ineffective policy processes and outcomes (Follesdal & Hix, 2006, 538; see also Majone, 1998).

The reason is that people can express their preferences via voting and they can actively participate in politics themselves. Thus, democratic countries or countries with high political freedom are expected to show higher legitimacy scores than counties with an autocratic political system.

In contrast, output legitimacy expresses „government for the people". That implies that decisions that are collectively binding should serve the common interest (Scharpf, 1999, 2). Risse (2006, 185) puts this in a similar fashion: He writes that output legitimacy refers to the perceived efficiency of the rules and laws that are enacted via a decision-making process or an authority. Thus, a state is legitimate if its decisions serve the interests of the citizens.

At the same time, with output legitimacy being an interest-based concept (Scharpf, 1999, 12), it leads to a variety of problems since the decision makers need to know the interests of the citizens (or at least of the median voter). To give one example, some people may have a strong preference for an egalitarian society, preferring redistribution policies and a comprehensive social security system. In contrast, others prefer an unequal society since less redistribution may increase the benefits of individual success. Hence, the question arises which specific policies or rules should be implemented such that the political system becomes legitimate via the output channel. Scharpf (1999, 11) offers an answer: Output legitimacy can be achieved via the state's capacity "to solve problems requiring collective solutions because they could not be solved through individual action, through market exchanges, or through voluntary cooperation in civil society." Furthermore, Scharpf (1999, 11) notes it is no more required than "the perception of a range of *common interests* that is sufficiently broad and stable to justify institutional arrangements for collective action." Based on these considerations, one can derive that a general need for public goods like education, infrastructure, or national defense exists since the market may not or only insufficiently provide these goods (for example due to market failures such as externalities or the free-rider problem).

In sum, input and output legitimacy are two clearly distinguishable concepts that have been used across the literature to analyze the legitimacy of political systems. Not surprisingly, a variety of debates deal with (i) the potential trade-off between input and output legitimacy, (ii) the question whether input legitimacy is a necessary precondition for output legitimacy, (iii) how different types of democracies are related to input and output legitimacy, and (iv) the applicability of the input-output concept to autocratic regimes. Since these debates are important for the assumptions of the empirical part to follow, the subsequent enumeration provides a more detailed review:

- *Input and Output Legitimacy – A Trade-Off?* Numerous scholars raise the question whether a trade-off between input and output legitimacy exists or whether both channels are mutually reinforcing. For example, Katz and Wessels (1999, 6) write that "there is an inevitable trade-off between output legitimacy and input legitimacy, between an emphasis on government for the people and an emphasis on government by the people." A similar point is made by Höreth (2001, 13-14) who states that "greater involvement of civil society actors in decision-making and control, based on the principle of participation, could be gained probably only at the expense of efficiency in the key areas of authoritative decision-making processes, and hence of problem-solving capability." In contrast, other scholars argue that both concepts are positively related. For example, Lindgren and Persson (2010) find in an empirical study within the context of EU chemical policies that more input legitimacy also increases output legitimacy.[78] A possible explanation is that the mere opportunity to participate in a decision-making process leads to a higher probability of accepting the political outcome, even if the outcome is not ideal for the individual (Lindgren & Persson, 2010, 453).

- *Input Legitimacy as a Necessary Precondition for Output Legitimacy?* Other scholars claim that input legitimacy is a necessary precondition for output legitimacy within a democratic system. For example, Büchs (2008, 765) notes that "legitimacy can be improved only by strengthening parliamentary channels of input-legitimacy since output-legitimacy alone is inappropriate and cannot be achieved without input-legitimacy." This conclusion is based on the assumption that experts or political elites are not able to identify the preferences of the citizens appropriately since citizens' preferences are not exogenously given but shaped by the public political discussion (Büchs, 2008, 771).[79] This further implies that the preferences are not stable over time and are, thus, hard to identify by political analysts. Eriksen and Fossum (2000, 18) argue in a similar fashion and note that "deliberation transforms preferences and compels actors to give reason for why they seek a particular outcome, regardless of their resources." Following this argument, a state could not (or only randomly) achieve output legitimacy without input legitimacy. In other words, input legitimacy is necessary to identify the preferences of citizens, whereas the preferences of the citizens should be the basis for political decisions (Büchs, 2008, 771).
- *Input and Output Legitimacy and Different Types of Democracy.* According to Scharpf (1998), the type of democracy has an impact on whether input or output legitimacy predominates. In detail, he analyzes how consensual and majoritarian democracies are linked to input and output legitimacy.[80] When considering the input channel, Scharpf (1998, 3) suggests that a consensual democracy – reflecting "the widest possible agreement among the individuals and groups affected" rather than only on the preferences of the majority –

78 Lindgren and Persson (2010) measure input and output legitimacy as follows. To capture output legitimacy, they (2010, 466) ask the respondents to what degree the decision process led to the desired result (improved protection of the environment and health while also maintaining the competitiveness of European industry). In contrast, input legitimacy is measured by five survey items that measure the degree to which the decision-making process was open, representative, and inclusive (Lindgren & Person, 2010, 457, 466).

79 Büchs (2008, 771) refers, in particular, to Habermas (1998) and Eriskson and Fossum (2000) who argue that "citizens' interests do not exist independently of public political discussion and cannot be objectively identified by experts or political elites."

80 In its most extreme fashion, majoritarian systems are characterized by the rule of the majority with no veto rights for the minority. In contrast, in consensual systems, minorities have the possibility to veto. (Anderson & Guillory, 1997, 68; see also Lijphart, 1984).

should lead to more legitimacy. In contrast, majoritarian democracies are more likely to yield legitimacy through the output channel. The argument is that majoritarian democracies are more efficient in implementing an effective solution since the costs of finding a consensus are low. At the same time, Scharpf (1999, 7) stresses that the policy outcomes of a majority rule system may be "normatively indefensible" since policies could be implemented at the cost of minorities when only considering the preferences of the majority.[81] In comparison to a majoritarian democracy, divergent and conflicting preferences may hinder the implementation of effective solutions in a consensual democracy. However, once a decision process is finished, the solutions should be highly legitimated from the output-side since they are based on a consensus and, thus, should meet the preferences of the (average) citizen. Altogether, countries that focus on input legitimacy tend to implement a democracy with strong consensual elements, whereas output legitimacy oriented countries are more likely to apply majoritarian rule (Scharpf, 1998, 4).

- *Applicability of the Input-Output Conception to Autocratic Regimes.* Although originally developed to analyze theories of democracy, one can also apply the input-output conception to non-democratic regimes. By definition, non-democratic (or autocratic) regimes typically do not allow ordinary citizens to participate in the decision-making process such that input legitimacy should be low in such systems. As an example, Scharpf (1999, 26) refers to a military government and states that "choices imposed by actors that are in no way empowered by, and accountable to, the constituency in question [...] would lack input legitimacy, whatever their merits in the output dimension might be." However, autocratic systems still have the opportunity to generate very high levels of output legitimacy when implementing solutions that serve the public interest.[82] The decision-making costs are also very low (even less than in a majoritarian democracy).

To sum up, according to Scharpf's distinction, legitimacy can be achieved through the input and the output channel. The concept has been widely accepted as a conceptual scheme to analyze the legitimacy of a state. In this vein, numerous scholars also analyze the interplay between input and output legitimacy in greater detail. In particular, they investigate whether a trade-off between the two channels exists (Höreth, 2001; Katz & Wessels, 1999; Lindgren & Persson, 2010). Scholars also apply the concept to supranational organizations such as the EU (Scharpf, 1999; Schmidt, 2013). Finally, autocracies should suffer input legitimacy but should have the possibility to achieve high levels of overall legitimacy through the output channel.

81 However, this threat vanishes when a strong belief in the essential sameness of the people exists or, as Weber puts it, when a strong "*Gemeinschaftsglaube*" predominates that is based upon a common ethnic and civil identity (e.g. history, language, culture, and ethnicity) (Scharpf, 1999, 8). In this case, Scharpf (1999, 8) speaks about a nation with a "'thick' collective identity".

82 For example, Wong and Huang (2010) refer to authoritarian Singapore that still enjoys a broad public support based on the regime's ability to provide security and prosperity.

However, that requires a benevolent and competent regime that acts in line with the preferences of the citizens.[83]

4.1.2 Adding Throughput Legitimacy

Scharpf's (1970, 1999) input-output distinction is a well-founded conception to grasp the channels through which legitimacy can be achieved. However, as Schmidt (2013) suggests, the distinction is not sufficient since it misses procedural determinants. Thus, one should add a further channel, namely 'throughput' legitimacy.

Originally, Schmidt (2013) suggests extending the twofold distinction of Scharpf (1970, 1999) within the context of the legitimacy of the European Union. In this vein, Schmidt (2013, 2) notes that throughput legitimacy "is judged in terms of the efficacy, accountability and transparency of the EU's governance processes along with their inclusiveness and openness to consultation *with* the people." In greater detail, Schmidt (2013, 5) writes:

> *'Throughput' legitimacy concentrates on what goes on inside the 'black box' of EU governance, in the space between the political input and the policy output, which has typically been left blank by political systems theorists. It focuses on the quality of the governance processes of the EU as contributing to a different kind of normative legitimacy from both the performance-oriented legitimacy of output and the participation-oriented legitimacy of input. Throughput is process-oriented, and based on the interactions – institutional and constructive – of all actors engaged in EU governance.*

Schmidt (2013, 6-8) also stresses the difference between institutional and constructive throughput legitimacy. The focus of institutional throughput legitimacy lies on the efficacy, the accountability, and transparency as well as the inclusiveness and the openness of EU governance processes.[84] In contrast, constructive throughput legitimacy refers to "productive deliberative interrelationships among actors in the wide variety of throughput governance processes that make up the coordinative discourse of the policy sphere" (Schmidt, 2013, 17).[85]

Based on Schmidt's (2013) considerations, I borrow the 'throughput' conception for my research design. However, I redefine throughput legitimacy concerning two aspects. First, since my research object is not the EU, I use the state and its institutions as the object under study. And second, I follow an institutional throughput legitimacy perspective that stresses, in particular, the fairness of the procedures since "decisions and rules are more willingly accepted when they exercise their authority through

83 As an example, Gilley (2006b, 63) finds that China has a relatively high legitimacy score and ranks at the same level as Germany or Australia.

84 Schmidt (2013, 6-7) lists a variety of different examples how efficacy, accountability, transparency, inclusiveness, and openness can be achieved in the EU.

85 In fact, Schmidt (2013, 17) notes that the importance of the coordinative discourse has its origins in the works of Habermas (1996) who stresses that legitimacy mainly depends on the quality of a discourse or a deliberative process.

procedures that people experience as being fair" (Tyler, 2006, 379). Thus, I use the following definition:

> *Throughput legitimacy means the quality of governance processes of the state and itsinstitutions as judged particularly in terms of their efficacy, accountability, transparency, and fairness.*

I include the fairness criterion – in addition to the criteria efficacy, accountability, and transparency – because the *psychological* legitimacy literature provides evidence that fair procedures affect the state's legitimacy (Tyler, 2006, 382-384). For example, Tyler (2006, 382-384) emphasizes that "people are found to believe authorities are more legitimate when they view their actions as consistent with fair procedures". He further notes that "political authorities and institutions lose legitimacy when they do not adhere to procedural fairness norms".[86] In this vein, my definition of throughput legitimacy only considers what Schmidt (2013) calls institutional throughput legitimacy.

Finally, having defined throughput legitimacy, the input-throughput-output framework serves as the conceptual basis to classify the determinants of legitimacy. In other words, state legitimacy depends on determinants that operate via the input, throughput, or output channel (figure 10).

Figure 10: Input, Throughput and Output Legitimacy

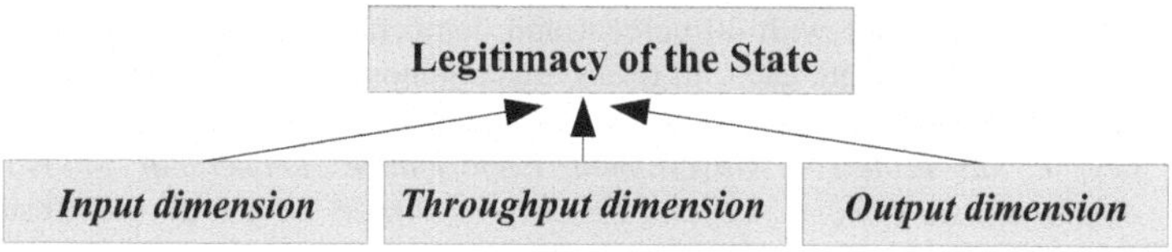

Source: Author's compilation

4.1.3 Other Classifications of Legitimacy's Determinants

Besides the Scharpfian concept, the literature provides further approaches to classifying legitimacy's determinants. Most of those can be related to the input-throughput-output distinction. The following enumeration gives a short (non-exhaustive) overview:

- *Rothstein (2009) – Electoral Democracy and Quality of Government.* Similar to Scharpf's input-output conception, Rothstein (2009) stresses the difference between electoral democracy and quality of government. Rothstein (2009) even argues that "electoral democracy is highly overrated when it comes to creating legitimacy. On the contrary, legitimacy is created, maintained, and destroyed not by the input but by the output side of the political system." Gjefsen (2012)

86 For further examples, see Tyler (2006).

investigates Rothstein's hypothesis empirically. He finds that the quality of government (measured by the Quality of Government Dataset of Teorell et al., 2015) has a significantly positive effect on legitimacy, whereas electoral democracy (measured by a combination of the Freedom House and the Polity Index) has no significant impact on legitimacy, in particular when controlling for the quality of government.

- *Gilley (2006b, 2009) – General Governance, Democratic Rights, and Welfare Gains.* Based on an empirical assessment of numerous variables at the country level, Gilley (2006b, 2009) suggests a three-part classification of legitimacy's determinants. He distinguishes between general governance, democratic rights, and welfare gains. In detail, general governance subsumes variables that account for the rule of law, control of corruption, and government effectiveness (Gilley, 2006b, 57). Within this context, Gilley (2006b, 57) also stresses that "the strength of the economic governance variable [Economic Freedom Index of the Fraser Institute; author's note] suggests that properly managed market reforms have enhanced, not diminished, the legitimacy of states". To proxy democratic rights, Gilley uses the Freedom House Index. Finally, welfare gains are measured by the percentage change in the Human Development Index. Since in his multiple regressions democratic rights and welfare gains drop out as insignificant, Gilley (2006b, 58-60) constructs a composite variable of general governance, democratic rights, and welfare gains. Based on Gilley's (2006a, 57) conclusion that "general governance [...] has a large, even overarching importance in global citizens' evaluations of the states", he weights general governance with 40 percent and democratic rights as well as welfare gains with 30 percent each. In result, this composite index explains 58 percent of legitimacy's variance.
- *Levi et al. (2009) – Government Performance, Leadership Motivations, Administrative Competence, and Procedural Justice.* Levi et al. (2009) suggest a model that explains legitimacy by government performance, leadership motivations, administrative competence, and procedural justice (government performance, leadership motivations, and administrative competence are summarized under the term trustworthiness of government). In detail, government performance refers to the provision of "public goods the population requires to ensure at least a minimal level of social welfare" (Levi et al., 2009, 358). Leadership motivations reflect the idea that legitimacy can be achieved through the ability of leaders "to persuade citizens they are trustworthy by force of character, charisma, or reference to their personal traits, histories, and identities" (Levi et al., 2009, 357). Furthermore, administrative competence refers to the government's honesty and government's capacity to implement rules and regulations (Levi et al., 2009, 358). Finally, procedural justice means that "when governments exercise their authority through procedures that people perceive as fair, they are more likely to be seen as legitimate and as deserving of deference" (Levi et al., 2009, 359). Based on these considerations, Levi et al. (2009) use a variety of different items (taken from an African Survey) to extract which of these classes explain most of legitimacy's variance in many African

countries.[87] In contrast to Gilley (2006b, 2009), Levi et al. (2009, 367) analyze these determinants at the individual level. The results show that the most important factors for individual legitimacy beliefs are administrative competence, followed by procedural justice and government performance.[88]

- *Hechter (2009) – Substantive, Procedural, and Constructivist Determinants.* Hechter (2009) also provides a useful classification of the determinants of legitimacy, which he derives from a literature overview.[89] He ends up distinguishing between substantive, procedural, and constructivist determinants. Substantive determinants reflect the performance of a regime and the provision of public goods. Based on a literature survey, Hechter (1999, 287) even concludes that state expenditures (including spending on education, public health, and security) are the most important determinant for generating legitimacy due to the improvement of citizens' quality of life.[90] In contrast, procedural determinants point to the idea that "so long as its procedures and policies do not put any category of individuals at systematically greater disadvantage or risk than others, rational people [...] will grant legitimacy to the government" (Hechter, 2009, 287). Thus, procedural determinants ensure that even people who do not benefit from particular government policies will provide compliance to the government. Evidence for this can be found in the works of Tyler (2001; 2006, 382) who concludes that "the key aspect of authorities and institutions that shapes their legitimacy and, through it, the willingness of people to defer to the decisions of authorities and to the rules created by institutions is the fairness of the procedures through which institutions and authorities exercise authority." Similarly, Sunshine and Tyler (2003) also offer evidence that people believe more in the legitimacy of authorities when their actions are in line with fair procedures. In contrast, racial profiling (Tyler & Wakslak, 2004), the application of unnecessary force (Seron et al., 2004), or other unfair procedures lead to a reduction of legitimacy. Studies that deal with fairness norms find similar results. If the authorities do

87 Since Levi et al. (2009) analyze the determinants of legitimacy at the individual level, they do not use country-level variables such as the HDI or the Polity IV Index as measures for particular classes of determinants. Rather, they stick to individual-level data that proxy administrative competence, procedural justice, and government performance. In detail, government performance is measured by an item that measures whether the citizens have never gone without food; administrative competence is measured by items like the enforcement of criminal laws, taxes, and corruption; and finally, procedural justice is measured by items that capture the degree to which citizens and their own ethnic group are treated fairly (Levi et al., 2009, 364-366).

88 Levi et al. (2009) abstain from analyzing leadership motivations in their empirical assessment due to data availability. Thus, leadership motivations are not ranked here.

89 The overview of Hechter (2009) comprises the following studies: Anderson (2005), Gilley (2006b), Jost and Major (2001), Tyler (2001, 2006), Rothstein (2009), Lake (2009), Levi et al. (2009), Hegtvedt and Johnson (2009), Horne (2009), Zhao (2009), Brady (2009), and Catlaw and Hu (2009).

90 One may question whether state expenditures or the general welfare level are most important for legitimacy since the government size typically increases when the welfare level improves (North et al., 2009).

not follow these norms, they lose legitimacy.[91] Altogether, a state that implements or already has fair decision-making procedures should be more legitimate than other states. Lastly, Hechter also names a third sub-group of determinants, namely constructivist determinants: Ideologies, symbolic scripts, and techniques of mass persuasions may be able to create legitimacy by altering the perceptions of citizens and their beliefs in the political and social order. For example, techniques of mass persuasion can be both be used to promote the ideology of the current regime and applied to persuade people that the state is performing well (Brady, 2009, 434).

A comparison of the classifications shows that they are largely congruent (but not completely uniform) with the input-throughput-output concept (table 10). This becomes apparent when noting that most scholars refer either to input legitimacy (Gilley, 2006b, 2009; Rothstein, 2009) and/or to output legitimacy (Gilley, 2006b, 2009; Hechter, 2009; Levi et al., 2009; Rothstein, 2009). The main reason why different classifications exist is the application of different derivation strategies. For example, Gilley (2006b, 2009) uses a statistical approach drawing on bivariate correlations. In contrast, Scharpf (1970, 1999) derives the input-output distinction from conceptional considerations.[92] Hechter's (2009) classification is based on an extensive literature survey (Levi et al. (2009) follow a similar strategy). A further reason is that some authors analyze legitimacy solely at the country level (Gilley, 2006b, 2009a; Rothstein, 2009), whereas other authors investigate legitimacy at the individual level (Levi et al., 2009). Since procedural determinants are typically measured by items at the individual level (such as the question whether one's own ethnic group is treated fairly, see Levi et al., 2009, 366), scholars that analyze country-level variables do not explicitly refer to procedural determinants.

Table 10: Classifications of Legitimacy's Determinants

Scharpf (1970, 1999)	*Input Legitimacy*	*Output Legitimacy*		*Throughput Legitimacy*
Rothstein (2009)	Electoral Democracy	Quality of Government		
Gilley (2006b, 2009a)	Democratic Rights	General Governance; Welfare Gains		(General Governance)
Levi et al. (2009)		Government Performance	Leadership Motivations	Procedural Justice; Administrative Competence
Hechter (2009)		Substantive Determinants	Constructivist Determinants	Procedural Determinants

Source: Author's compilation

91 Tyler (2006, 382) provides a more extensive overview.
92 Rothstein (2009) also uses the input-output distinction.

Unfortunately, I need to disavow leadership motivations and constructivist determinants (see Hechter, 2009; Levi et al., 2009) in the following since they do not fit into the standard input, throughput, and output concept. Regarding leadership motivations, I assume that they refer to what Norris calls 'support for incumbents in office'. Thus, they do not fit in the more narrow legitimacy conception I employ here. Second, concerning constructivist determinants (such as propaganda), I drop those because they are difficult to measure empirically. I am aware that the government (and other state institutions as well) may use propaganda as a tool to maintain political stability since it allows to shape the citizens' underlying values (for example toward regime principles or the nation state as whole) and to alter the citizens' interests (in a way that citizens are more in favor with the outcome of the political system).

The literature overview (table 10) also helps to assess which channel is most important for generating legitimacy (Hechter, 2009). Referring to scholars that stress the predominance of the output channel, Rothstein (2009, 313) argues – having in mind Scharpf's input-output methodology – that "electoral democracy is highly overrated when it comes to creating legitimacy. On the contrary, legitimacy is created, maintained, and destroyed not by the input but by the output side of the political system. In brief, political legitimacy depends on the quality of government, not the quality of elections or political representations." To underline this, he not only provides a variety of examples (democracy in Iraq, Krajina Serbs) that show that the mere procedures of representative democracy are not able to provide policies and public goods that are in line with the interests of people; he also points to well established electoral democracies and the decline of people's trust in major political institutions although they are close to a normative ideal. Gjefsen (2012) analyzes Rothstein's (2009) suggestion empirically and finds evidence that output determinants have a greater impact on state legitimacy (as measured in terms of 'regime principles', 'regime performance', and 'regime institutions') than input determinants. Similar to Rothstein (2009), Gilley (2006a, 57) also concludes that the output channel is most important for the state's legitimacy. As also cited above, he (2006a, 57) states that "general governance [...] has a large, even overarching importance in global citizens' evaluations of the states".

In contrast, applying regression analyses and using the African Social Survey as data basis, Levi et al. (2009) find partly opposing results. In their work, the output channel in terms of government performance (measured by the ability of the government to make sure that citizens do not go without food) has only little impact on legitimacy (measured in terms of tax department's right to make people pay taxes, police's right to make people obey the law, and court's right to make decisions by which people abide). Rather, throughput legitimacy in terms of administrative competence (measured in terms of the enforcement of taxes and the corruption among the tax administration) and in terms of procedural justice (measured in terms of the treatment of one's own ethnic group and treatment of citizens in general) has the strongest influence on legitimacy. Similarly, Tyler (2001; 2006) argues that the key determinant of state legitimacy is the perceived fairness of the decision-making process. He even concludes that perceived fairness (and thus throughput legitimacy) is more important than the provision of resources, output, or opportunities. An explanation for this may be that fair procedures foster the creation of social values that make people feel morally obliged in accepting decisions and their outcomes as long as the procedures are fair (Tyler, 2006, 382).

Input legitimacy seems to play a subordinate role when analyzing the determinants of legitimacy. For example, Gilley (2006b) acknowledges that democratic rights (which is a proxy for the participation in the decision-making process) are an important determinant of legitimacy but stresses that the influence of output legitimacy is overarching. Similarly, Gjefsen (2012) finds that input legitimacy in terms of electoral democracy has no or even a negative impact on different dimensions of political support ('regime principles', 'regime performance', and 'regime institutions'), in particular in regression equations that control for determinants that refer to output legitimacy.[93] Finally, Booth and Seligson (2009a, 139) note that the history of democracy (reflecting input legitimacy) explains the 'support for regime principles'. However, other dimensions of political support can be better explained by output variables ('regime institutions' by government effectiveness and 'regime performance' by GDP growth).[94]

4.2 Variables to Address Legitimacy

The input-throughput-output concept provides a basis to classify the channels through which legitimacy can be generated. However, it remains unclear which concrete variables or indices can be used to explain legitimacy. Since legitimacy is a variable that captures individual attitudes and behaviors, the determinants of legitimacy should ideally be objectively measurable.

One can distinguish between variables at the system level and at the individual level. The input-throughput-output concept serves to classify the determinants at the system level (chapter 4.2.1). Since a variety of studies show that individual variables (such as age, income level, or educational level) have explanatory power (Booth & Seligson, 2009a; Gjefsen, 2012; Norris, 2011), I also present those (chapter 4.2.2). The last sub-chapter summarizes the results (chapter 4.2.3).

93 For example, the impact of electoral democracy on 'support for regime institutions' is negative. That means that more democracy leads to less support for regime institutions. A possible explanation is that citizens are tendentiously more critical in democratic societies since they have better access to information (Gjefsen, 2012, 71).

94 Besides the determinants that refer to input, output, and throughput legitimacy, other scholars argue that constructivist determinants may have the strongest impact on political legitimacy. For example, in the case of China, Zhao (2009) argues that during Mao's reign China's sole base of legitimacy was founded on the communist ideology and Mao's charisma. In contrast, China's state legitimacy was primarily founded on performance (or substantive determinants) before and after the reign of Mao. According to Zhao (2009), confucianism was the main driver in supporting performance legitimacy during imperial China. At that time, the emperor had no 'right' to rule but rather a 'Heavenly Mandate' to fulfill his duties (Zhao, 2009, 421). After the communist era, the basis of China's state legitimacy shifted gradually back from ideology to performance. Hence, Zhao (2009) concludes that government performance is the sole base of legitimacy today. However, Brady (2009) partly challenges this view, instead arguing that China's legitimacy depended on both economic growth and mass persuasion during the years from 1989 to 2007.

4.2.1 System-Level Variables

To find appropriate variables that measure input, throughput, and output legitimacy is a difficult task. This has several reasons. First, Scharpf (1999, 12) explicitly notes that output legitimacy is by definition interest-based. As a consequence, to address the correct variables would ideally require knowing what decisions are in line with the interests of the citizens. As a consequence, to some extent, it is inevitable that a researcher has to assume what leads to output legitimacy. This problem emerges at the system and also at the individual level. Second, it is sometimes problematic to disentangle output and throughput legitimacy, in particular since some indicators are a conglomerate of items that reflect aspects of both output and throughput legitimacy. Third, both input, throughput, and output legitimacy can be measured by a variety of different indicators which have the same underlying concept but vary in their actual measurement. As a consequence, I focus on each dimension separately and investigate which indicators are most suitable for the later statistical analyses.

Indicators to Address Input Legitimacy

According to Scharpf (1970, 1999), input legitimacy hinges on two important aspects. First, input legitimacy refers to the participatory quality of the decision-making process. As a consequence, indicators are also required that proxy the participatory quality of the decision-making process. Since a democratic government comes closest to meeting this requirement, the degree of democracy is expected to have an impact on state legitimacy (Dahl, 2006; see also Rothstein, 2009, 314-316). Second, Scharpf (1999, 7-10) further states that input legitimacy is an identity-based concept. As a consequence, I expect a state to be more legitimate that has (i) a long regime tradition (since a long regime tradition may ensure that the citizens identify with a current political regime and its political values) and that has (ii) a homogeneous ethnic composition (since a homogeneous ethnic composition increases the probability that citizens identify not only with the political system but also with all other spheres of the state and its institutions). Table 11 shows that all three aspects (degree of democracy, democratic tradition, and ethnic fractionalization) are part of empirical legitimacy studies.

Degree of Democracy. The most frequently applied indicators to measure the degree of democracy are the Polity IV Index and the Freedom House Index (Gilley, 2006b; Gjefsen, 2012; Levi & Sacks, 2009; Norris, 2011; Power & Cyr, 2009). The Voice and Accountability Index (which belongs to the World Bank's Governance Indicators) has also been applied (Power & Cyr, 2009).[95] Thus, the question remains which indicator to choose. I exclude the Voice and Accountability Index since using this indicator leads to endogeneity problems.[96] The reason is that the Voice and Accountability Index –

95 Other measures of democracy are listed and discussed by Munck (2009; see also Hadenius & Teorell, 2005).

96 The Voice and Accountability Index captures the "perceptions of the extent to which a country's citizens are able to participate in selecting their government, as well as freedom of expression,

Table 11: Variables to Address Input Legitimacy

	Source	Studies	Data Type	Remarks
Degree of Democracy				
Voice and Accountability Index	World Bank	Power & Cyr (2009)	Ordinal - admixture of survey data and expert assessment	endogeneiety problems
Civil and Political Liberties	Freedom House	Booth & Seligson (2009); Gilley (2006b); Gjefsen (2012); Levi & Sacks (2009); Power & Cyr (2009)	Ordinal - based on assessment by external analysts	too wide, maximalist definition of democracy
Democracy Index	Polity IV Index	Gjefsen (2012); Norris (2011)	Ordinal - based on assessment by experts	minimalist definition of democracy
Regime Tradition				
Democratic Tradition	MBP Index	Power & Cyr (2009)	Quasi-metric - mean democracy score	
History of Democracy	Vanhanen Democracy Index	Booth & Seligson (2009)	Quasi-metric - mean democracy score	
Fractionalization				
Ethnic Fractionalization	Fearon's (2003) Cultural Diversity Index; Alesina et al. (2003)	Gilley (2006b); Gjefsen (2012); Power & Cyr (2009)	Metric - probability that two randomly selected people of a country belong to different groups	limited time-series data

Source: Author's compilation

similar to the other Governance Indicators of the World Bank – is not only based on expert assessments but also on survey data that include questions that refer to citizens' trust in the police, the parliament, or the courts (data stem from the Afrobarometer, the Gallup World Poll, the Latinobarometro, the Americas' barometer, see Kaufmann et al., 2009, 42, 55, 61, 70). However, since legitimacy is to a large extent measured by trust or confidence items (see Gilley, 2006a; Norris, 1999, 2011), it is problematic from an econometric point of view to use the Voice and Accountability Index as an independent variable due to endogeneity (even though the share of survey data to expert assessments is rather low). As a consequence, I stick to the Polity IV and the Freedom House Index. I follow the suggestion of Hadenius and Teorell (2005) who recommend using a combined Polity IV/FH Index to capture political democracy. Following Dahl (1971, 4-6), political democracy is constituted by contestation and

freedom of association, and a free media." (Kaufmann et al., 2009, 6)

participation. Hadenius and Teorell (2005, 8) also adopt this conception and define political democracy by "fundamental procedural rights— i.e., the rules and institutions that make popular influence over political life possible". Those are basically expressed in "the combination of fair and honest elections with the existence of essentially unlimited political freedoms" such as freedom of assembly and association and of the press (Hadenius & Teorell, 2005, 8). Hadenius and Teorell's (2005) suggestion results from the fact that both indices miss the definition of political democracy to some extent. On the one hand, the Freedom House Index applies a too wide, maximalist definition (Munck, 2009, 36).[97] That means that political democracy is measured along the dimensions political rights and civil liberties, whereas both dimensions cover not only "the entire range of basic democratic criteria" but also "some other things that seem dubious or directly irrelevant" (Hadenius & Teorell, 2005, 16).[98] In detail, Hadenius and Teorell (2005, 16) note that the dimension political rights also includes the possibility that elections can be substituted by the possibility of consultation with the people. Further, they (2005, 16) also question whether "self-determination for minority groups, or neutrality in relation to different ethnic groups" should be part of political rights. Similarly, civil rights do not only reflect basic democratic criteria but also socioeconomic aspects such as "free enterprise, property rights, a lack of corruption, and equality and independence in work and family life" (Hadenius & Teorell, 2005, 16, see also Munck, 2009, 17). Thus, since these socio-economic aspects partly reflect a market-based economic system, the Freedom House Index understands democracy also in terms of economic features. On the other hand, in contrast to the Freedom House Index, the Polity IV Index applies a minimalist definition. That means that the Polity IV Index omits what Dahl (1971) calls participation (Munck, 2009, 17, 36). In particular, Hadenius and Teorell (2005, 20-21) point out that in the Polity IV Index (i) "questions touching on the breadth of the suffrage and the correctness of elections are lacking", (ii) there is no "heed paid to the actual power attached to elective offices", and (iii) "with the possible exception of freedom of organisation", there is no heed paid "to the incidence of political freedoms". As a consequence, both indices show weaknesses at the conceptional level.[99] To cope with these, as Hadenius and Teorell (2005) suggest, I use a combined FH/Polity IV Index (the mean of both indices). Since the Freedom House's over-conceptualization and Polity IV's under-conceptualization may annul each other, a

97 The problem of a maximalist definition is that it typically includes also attributes that correspond to other concepts. Thus, the concept under consideration is not properly delimited. (Munck, 2009, 16)

98 Referring to the basic democratic criteria, political rights comprise a variety of electoral aspects such as "the right of opposition parties to take part, the fairness of the electoral process, the real power attached to elective organs" and others (Hadenius & Teorell, 2005, 15). In contrast, civil liberties subsume aspects such as "freedom for media and organizations, including political parties; the right of assembly; the absence of political prisoners and of political control over the judiciary" (Hadenius & Teorell, 2005, 15-16). (Freedom House, 2015)

99 Beyond this, Munck (2009, 36) as well as Hadenius and Teorell (2005) list a variety of other shortcomings regarding the aggregation strategy and measurement issues (not discussed in greater detail here).

combined index seems to fit best when measuring Dahl's (1971) concept of democracy.

Regime Tradition. Regarding the regime tradition, the argument runs that a long democratic tradition improves the legitimacy of the state (Booth & Seligson, 2009a, 139; Power & Cyr, 2009, 261-262). In this vein, scholars measure democratic tradition by calculating the mean of a country's democratic history. For example, Booth and Seligson (2009a, 139) use the democracy scores of the Vanhanen Democracy Index and average these scores for the time period from 1900 to 1989. Their results show that a country's democratic history has a positive impact on dimensions of political support (in particular, on the dimensions 'political community' and 'regime principles'). Similarly, Power and Cyr (2009, 261-262) use the regime classification of Mainwaring et al. (2007) and calculate the mean democracy score of three 20-year periods beginning in 1945. Interestingly, Power and Cyr (2009, 262) find that in Latin America "a democratic tradition from 1945 to 1964 is a better predictor of present-day legitimacy than is the regime experience of a given country in the period from 1964 to 1985. What is interesting is that the totality of democratic experience in the postwar period (represented by the mean of the full 60 years of the MBP time series) is a better predictor than any one of the three 20-year stretches, which correspond roughly to the Second Wave of democracy, the military-authoritarian era and the Third Wave of democracy, respectively." Thus, one can derive that legitimacy increases if a country has a longer democratic history. A possible explanation is that the surveillance of and the experience with democratic institutions have an impact on how a political culture develops within a country (Booth & Seligson, 2009a, 123). However, as an alternative to Booth and Seligson (2009a) and Power and Cyr (2009), one could also argue that non-democratic institutions shape the political culture. That means, in other words, that countries with a long non-democratic tradition may also show, holding all other factors constant, higher legitimacy scores since the citizens of that country may be used to the existing regime and its political culture. To account for this possibility, I use an interaction term (mean centered) between a country's democracy score and a country's democratic history score.[100] If the coefficient of the interaction term is significantly positive, autocracies will also be legitimate if the country has an autocratic history.

Fractionalization. A further measure to capture the identity part of input legitimacy is fractionalization. Most scholars use Fearon's (2003) Cultural Diversity Index that expresses the probability that two randomly selected people of a country belong to different ethnic groups (ethnic fractionalization).[101] Others use the measure of Alesina

100 As an alternative, one could also use regime durability (as measured by the Polity IV Index in terms of the "number of years since the last substantive change in authority characteristics" has taken place; Marshall & Jaggers, 2007, 13) of the regime type to measure the impact of the experience with a given political system in general. However, I abstain from using this measure since the regime durability is rather a consequence of legitimacy (since legitimacy leads to system stability).

101 The index is based on 822 ethnic and "ethno-religious" groups that reflect at least 1% of the population of a country. 160 countries were considered. The index ranges from 0 to 10. A 0

et al. (2003) (e.g. Power & Cyr, 2009, 267); this index also calculates the probability that two randomly selected people of a country belong to different groups, but it distinguishes between ethnic, religious, and linguistic groups (see also Quality of Government Dataset, Dahlberg et al., 2015). The basic idea is that the citizens of more homogeneous countries are also more likely to share the same values and norms (Gjefsen, 2012, 49). If that is the case, the state can more easily consider the 'will of the people'. Gilley (2006b, 51) also notes that "*ethnic homogeneity* will enhance legitimacy by making it easier for a state to embody particular ethnic values. If the state was seeking 'congruence' with underlying cultural values, then this would be easier if those values were largely homogeneous, such as where they derive from shared ethnic identity." Several studies use ethnic fractionalization as an explanatory variable for the state's legitimacy with partly opposing results. For example, Gilley (2006b, 53) finds no correlation between ethnic homogeneity (measured by Fearon's Cultural Diversity Index) and legitimacy in his world-wide cross-country study. In contrast, replicating Gilley's legitimacy score for 18 Latin American countries, Power and Cyr (2009, 267) find that ethnic fractionalization (measured by the index of Alesina et al., 2003) highly correlates with legitimacy and remains even significantly negative when controlling for socio-economic modernization and democratic tradition.[102] In opposition to that finding, Gjefsen (2012) concludes that ethnic fractionalization has a positive effect on legitimacy, in particular on political support's dimensions 'regime principles', 'regime performance', and 'regime institutions'.

As this short overview shows, scholars typically refer to ethnic fractionalization but ignore religious and linguistic fractionalization. According to the results of Alesina et al. (2003), at least ethnic and religious fractionalization should be treated as two independent types of fractionalization. The reason is that ethnic and linguistic fractionalization are strongly correlated ($r=0.697$), whereas religious fractionalization is almost not related to linguistic or ethnic fractionalization (correlations are $r=0.269$ and $r=0.142$ respectively). Hence, one could argue that ethnic and linguistic fractionalization reflect the same type of fractionalization, whereas religious fractionalization has other sources. To give some evidence, ethnic fractionalization negatively correlates with GDP per capita and the democracy index. Further, it is also negatively related to economic growth and the quality of government (Alesina et al., 2003, 157; see also Easterly & Levine, 1997). A possible reason for the negative relationship between the democracy index and ethnic fractionalization is given by Aghion et al. (2004). They (2004) argue that it is more likely in more fragmented societies that a group imposes limitations on political liberties to control other groups, whereas in more homogeneous societies a democratic rule is more likely due to a lesser intensity of conflicts (see also Alesina et al., 2003, 173). In contrast, religious fractionalization seems to be positively correlated with measures of good governance

symbols totally homogeneous societies and a 10 reflects highly fractionalized societies (Teorell et al., 2015, 52).

102 A reason for the negative impact of ethnic fractionalization may also be that Latin American countries are composed of ethnically diverse populations with culturally and historically distinct heritages which may, in particular, shape citizens' 'views of legality'. For example, since some Latin American countries have large indigenous populations, there are not only formal judicial systems which operate in the state but also indigenous legal institutions. (Power & Cyr, 2009, 265)

and in some specification also with a democracy index. In this vein, Alesina et al. (2003, 158) note that "measured religious fractionalization tends to be higher in tolerant and free societies, like the United States, which in fact displays one of the highest levels of religious fractionalization." Hence, religious fractionalization may be a proxy for how tolerant and free a society is and measures whether an identity of a tolerant and free society leads, ceteris paribus, to higher legitimacy scores. However, since I do not aim to investigate whether religious fractionalization impacts legitimacy and since, to the best of my knowledge, no study has explicitly addressed this question, I do not furter explore religious fractionalization in the further thesis.[103] In sum, I solely use ethnic fractionalization in my empirical analysis. Again, ethnic fractionalization captures the conflict potential of different underlying cultural values. Thus, it should have an adverse impact on state legitimacy.

Indicators to Address Throughput Legitimacy

As defined above, throughput legitimacy refers to "the quality of governance processes of the state and its institutions as judged particularly in terms of their efficacy, accountability, transparency, and fairness." As a consequence, indicators need to measure to which degree the state and its institutions are efficient, accountable, transparent, and/or fair. Referring to the literature, scholars apply three measures to address throughput legitimacy, namely (i) the degree of corruption, (ii) the rule of law, and (iii) the degree of impartiality (Gilley, 2006b; Gjefsen, 2012; Power & Cyr, 2009; Rothstein & Teorell, 2012; Seligson, 2002; see also table 12).

Degree of Corruption. Various studies show that corruption undermines the legitimacy of the state (Gilley, 2006b; Seligson, 2002; Power & Cyr, 2009). For example, using individual-level data from national samples of four Latin American countries (El Salvador, Nicaragua, Paraguay, and Bolivia), Seligson (2002) provides evidence that more corruption leads to less legitimacy. Similar evidence is provided by authors who follow a country-level strategy. For example, Power and Cyr (2009, 262) find that the absence of corruption (measured by the TI Corruption Perceptions Index) is highly correlated with legitimacy (r=0.726). Using the Control of Corruption Index of the World Bank, Gilley (2006b, 57) also concludes that the absence of corruption, as a part of general governance, has a positive impact on legitimacy.

On the system level, scholars use two corruption measures as determinants of legitimacy, namely the TI Corruption Perception Index and the Control of Corruption Index of the World Bank. The TI Corruption Perception Index defines corruption as "the abuse of entrusted power for private gain" (Transparency International, 2016). Further, it "can be classified as grand, petty and political, depending on the amounts of

103 Religious fractionalization is uncorrelated with legitimacy except in the ca. 2012 wave (which may be a statistical artifact) (r_{2001}= 0.13, r_{2008}= 0.16, r_{2012}=0.31**). However, since all correlations are positive, this may indicate that societies that have a liberal identity show higher legitimacy scores than less liberal societies.

Table 12: Variables to Address Throughput Legitimacy

	Source	Studies	Data Type	Remarks
Degree of Corruption				
Control of Corruption Index	World Bank	Gilley (2006b)	Ordinal/quasi-metric - experts assessments & survey data	no year-to-year comparisons possible
TI Corruption Perceptions Index	Transparency International	Power & Cyr (2009); Seligson (2002)	Ordinal/quasi-metric - experts assessments & survey data of experts	no year-to-year comparisons possible until 2012
Rule of Law				
Rule of Law Index	World Bank	Gilley (2006b); Power & Cyr (2009)	Ordinal/quasi-metric - experts assessments & survey data	endogeneiety problems / refer strongly to economic freedom
Degree of Impartiality				
Impartiality Index	Quality of Government Dataset	Rothstein and Teorell (2012); Gjefsen (2012)	Ordinal/quasi-metric - experts assessments	limited time-series data

Source: Author's compilation

money lost and the sector where it occurs" (Transparency International, 2016).[104] The index is based on a variety of different data sources from different institutions that were standardized and aggregated to an overall score which varies from 0 (highest level of corruption) to 100 (lowest level of corruption).[105] As an alternative, the Control of Corruption Index of the World Bank captures the "perceptions of the extent to which public power is exercised for private gain, including both petty and grand forms of corruption, as well as 'capture' of the state by elites and private interests" (Kaufmann et al., 2009, 6). Regarding the data sources, the Control of Corruption Index uses data sources from the Corruption Perception Index in addition to further sources (Rohwer, 2009, 48). Similar to other World Governance Indicators, the Control of Corruption Index is a standardized index that has a mean of zero and a standard

104 In greater detail, grand, petty, and political corruption are described as follows: "Grand corruption consists of acts committed at a high level of government that distort policies or the central functioning of the state, enabling leaders to benefit at the expense of the public good. Petty corruption refers to everyday abuse of entrusted power by low- and mid-level public officials in their interactions with ordinary citizens, who often are trying to access basic goods or services in places like hospitals, schools, police departments and other agencies. Political corruption is a manipulation of policies, institutions and rules of procedure in the allocation of resources and financing by political decision makers, who abuse their position to sustain their power, status and wealth." (Transparency International, 2016)

105 The amount of data sources varies over time. For example, in 1995, seven different data sources were used, whereas in 2004 eighteen different data sources made up the index (Rohwer, 2009, 45). More recently, the index of 2014 is based on 12 different data sources from eleven different institutions (Transparency International, 2015).

deviation of one (nearly all scores fit into the range from -2.5 to 2.5) (Teorell et al., 2013, 136; Rohwer, 2009, 49). Although both indices are based on expert assessments and survey data, the problem of endogeneity (as in the case when measuring the degree of democracy with the help of the World Bank's Voice and Accountability Index) does not emerge. The reason is that the survey questions are strongly related to corruption and do not refer to citizens' confidence in major state institutions (or other items that constitute legitimacy). However, another problem of both indices is that year-to-year comparisons are only possible to a limited extent (Rohwer, 2009, 50). Regarding the World Bank's Control of Corruption Index, it is not recommended to use this index for short-run year-to-year comparisons but for trends over long periods (World Bank, 2016).[106] Regarding TI's Corruption Perceptions Index, comparisons over time were not possible until 2012 (Rohwer, 2009, 50; Transparency International, 2015).[107] After that, the aggregation strategy was simplified such that a comparison of the corruption scores over time became possible without methodological problems (Transparency International, 2015). In fact, both corruption measures are highly correlated (r_{2001}=0.979; r_{2008}=0.987) such that it has no practical relevance which one is chosen.

Rule of Law. Another important variable to grasp throughput legitimacy is the rule of law. For example, Gilley (2006b) concludes that the presence of the rule of law (as part of general governance) improves the legitimacy of the state. Power and Cyr (2009) also find that the rule of law positively correlates with the legitimacy of several Latin American states. Both scholars use the Rule of Law Index from the World Bank. The Rule of Law Index is designed to capture the "perceptions of the extent to which agents have confidence in and abide by the rules of society, and in particular the quality of contract enforcement, property rights, the police, and the courts, as well as the likelihood of crime and violence" (Kaufmann et al., 2009, 6). Although scholars use the rule of law as an explanatory variable, I abstain from using the rule of law to set up the basic model in the next chapter. This has several reasons. First, the Rule of Law Index of the World Bank is to a large extent economical (for example, it includes property rights and contract enforcement). Since property rights are connected with economic freedom (see also the Economic Freedom of the World Index by the Fraser Institute), I deal with them in the upcoming chapter (chapter 6). Second, as in the case of the Voice and Accountability Index of the World Bank, the Rule of Law Index contains a variety of questions that refer to trust in the police or the courts (see Kaufmann et al., 2009, 42, 55, 61, 70). Thus, if I were to use this index, endogeneity problems would emerge since similar questions constitute the legitimacy measure and the Rule of Law Index.

106 The reason is that the Control of Corruption scores may not only change due to actual changes in corruption but also due to (i) changes in the underlying data sources, (ii) the addition of new data sources, and (iii) changes in weighting. For further details, see World Bank (2016).

107 Similar to the World Bank's Control of Corruption Index, the reasons for this lies in the standardization and aggregation procedures. The score of a country can, ceteris paribus, change if (i) the perception of corruption in another country changes or (ii) new countries were added or already existing countries drop out (Rohwer, 2009, 50; Transparency International, 2015).

Degree of Impartiality. A further possibility to measure throughput legitimacy is the degree of impartiality as suggested by Rothstein and Teorell (2012). Based on an extensive literature review, they (2012, 16) argue that "neither the absence of corruption, nor representative democracy, nor the size of government, nor the rule of law, nor administrative effectiveness capture what should be counted as quality of government." Rather, they suggest using impartiality as a criterion to measure quality of government since it is (i) based on a normative theory and (ii) can be applied universally. Impartiality reflects a basic norm in executing public power. It is defined as follows: "When implementing laws and policies, government officials shall not take anything about the citizen or case into consideration that is not beforehand stipulated in the policy or the law" (Rothstein & Teorell, 2012, 18 qt. in Rothstein & Teorell, 2008, 170). Although Rothstein and Teorell (2012, 17) argue that impartiality belongs to the output side of the political system, I address the Impartiality Index to the throughput channel. The reason is that the impartiality criterion strictly refers to procedures rather than to the content of policies: "Since QoG [Quality of Government, author's note] as impartiality is a procedural norm confined to the exercise of public power, one important field that is not affected by this conception is the substance of the content of policies" (Rothstein & Teorell, 2012, 19). For empirical applications, they (2012) design the Impartiality Index that consists of five different questions that were aggregated to an overall index (all questions were answered by experts). Gjefsen (2012) uses the Impartiality Index to explain different dimensions of political support ('support for regime principles', 'support for regime performance', and 'support for regime institutions'). Independent of the dimensions, the coefficient of the Impartiality Index indicates a significantly positive effect (Gjefsen, 2012, 53-75). Although the Impartiality Index fits well as a measure of throughput legitimacy, it also has some shortcomings. Most notably, only one wave of the Impartiality Index has been published to date. The underlying data were generated during 2008 and 2011. As a consequence, the Impartiality Index only fits as an explanatory variable when dealing with legitimacy scores that refer to the same time period. When considering the World Values Survey, this is problematic since the 2008 to 2011 time period overlaps with the fifth (2005 to 2009) and the sixth (2010-2014) wave (chapter 3.2.1). Thus, when using the fifth wave of the WVS, it could be the case that a country's legitimacy score stems from 2005, whereas the score from the Impartiality Index stems from 2011.[108] Another problem is that the world wide economic crises occurred during the time period (2008 to 2011). This may have had an impact on how experts evaluated a country's impartiality. Since only one wave has been published to date, the Impartiality Index has no time series character. Thus, the usability of the Impartiality Index is limited for my research since my analyses extend beyond the fifth and the sixth waves of the WVS. In sum, I abstain from using the Impartiality Index due to its restricted availability over time.[109]

108 Despite these facts, Gjefsen (2012) use the Impartiality Index to explain the regime's legitimacy based on the fifth wave of the WVS.

109 When using the Impartiality Index for the fifth and the sixth waves of the WVS, one needs to assume that the degree of impartiality does not alter significantly over a ten-year horizon.

Indicators to Address Output Legitimacy

Finally, it is necessary to find indicators that address output legitimacy. That is a difficult task due to two reasons. First, since output legitimacy refers to the content or the outcome of the political system, all outcomes of the political system should be relevant, i.e. economic outcomes but also social, ecological, military, and other policies. For example, Feldmann and Mazepus (2014, 5-6) note that "output of government is not only understood in terms of economic growth but also in terms of general quality of government. Hence, outcome favourability [...] is linked to the quality of government and can involve many aspects of state-society relations" such as "impartiality, protection of human rights, improvement of social welfare, equality, education, supraethnicity or secularism of the state, accountability of government and many others [...]."[110] In other words, ideally, all policy outcomes should be considered when dealing with output legitimacy. Second, since output legitimacy is an interest-based concept (Scharpf, 1999, 12), the evaluation of the outcomes of the political system strongly depends on the interests of the citizens. This could mean that a specific policy is favored by one group of the society but not by another group.[111] This could also mean that a specific policy increases legitimacy in one country but leads to a reduction in another country due to different preferences or interest structures. Finally, it could also be the case that some policies that were favored in the past may not be favored in the presence or the future due to changing underlying values. As a consequence, scholars typically do not analyze specific policies when analyzing legitimacy at the country level but use measures that are widely acknowledged as legitimacy-increasing. These measures reflect the wealth of a nation in terms of GDP per capita (Domański, 2005; Levi & Sacks, 2009; Power & Cyr, 2009), the GDP growth rate (Gjefsen, 2012; Power & Cyr, 2009), or the Human Development Index (HDI) (Gilley, 2006b; Power & Cyr, 2009). Alternatively, scholars use indices that reflect the effectiveness of the government (in terms of the Government Effectiveness Index of the World Bank) (Booth & Seligson, 2009a; Gilley, 2006b), the unemployment rate (Domański, 2005), or the degree of income inequality (Gjefsen, 2012). Table 13 provides an overview.

Welfare Level Indicators (GDP per Capita and HDI). The general welfare level may have an influence on legitimacy. To capture this, scholars typically use GDP per capita or the Human Development Index (HDI) as measures of the welfare standard. Since it makes no sense to use both GDP per capita and HDI as independent variables simultaneously (since GDP per capita is a sub-dimension of the HDI), one has to decide for one indicator:

110 The enumeration of Feldman and Mazepus (2014) contains elements that refer to output and throughput legitimacy. For example, I address impartiality as an indicator to measure throughput legitimacy.

111 On the individual level, one could overcome this problem when controlling for the policy position and individual characteristics of the respondents (Lindgren & Persson, 2010, 458).

Table 13: Variables to Address Output Legitimacy

	Source	Studies	Data Type	Remarks
Welfare Level				
GDP per Capita	World Bank	Domański (2005); Gilley (2006b); Levi & Sacks (2009); Power & Cyr (2009)	Metric	may explain too much (Gilley, 2006a)
Human Development Index (HDI)	United Nations	Power & Cyr (2009)	Ordinal/quasi-metric - composite index	applied in absolute values and as change over time
Welfare Change				
GDP per Capita Growth Rate	World Bank; World Development Indicators	Gjefsen (2012); Power & Cyr (2009)	Metric	may be sensitive to the interval defined (e.g. 10 or 20 years)
HDI (Relative Change)	United Nations	Booth & Seligson (2009a); Gilley (2006b)	Ordinal/quasi-metric - composite index	applied in absolute values and as change over time
Other Output Indicators				
Government Effectiveness	World Bank	Booth & Seligson (2009a); Gilley (2006b)	Ordinal - based on expert assessments & survey data	minor endogeneiety problems
Income Distribution (Gini Index)	World Bank	Gjefsen (2012)	Metric	-
Unemployment Rate	World Bank	Domański (2005)	Metric	-

Source: Author's compilation

- *GDP per Capita.* Several scholars find a positive relationship between legitimacy and GDP per capita. For example, Domański (2005, 82) concludes that a higher GNP per capita leads to higher legitimacy scores in 21 European countries. In detail, on a legitimacy scale from 0 to 30, Domański (2005, 82) notes that "[w]hen GNP increases by one thousand Euro per capita, legitimacy increases by .11 point other things equal. It suggests that although much depends on reliability of politicians it seems generally better to rule in wealthy than in poor nations." Gilley (2009b, 33) also finds that legitimacy and GDP per capita are highly correlated (r=0.69 using the ca. 2001 data and r=0.55 using the ca. 2008 data). Similarly, Power and Cyr (2009, 262) find that GDP per capita of 18 Latin American countries is highly correlated with legitimacy (r=0.678). Despite this strong evidence, one should treat the relationship between GDP per capita and legitimacy with caution. The reason is that the relationship between

Figure 11: Legitimacy and GDP per Capita

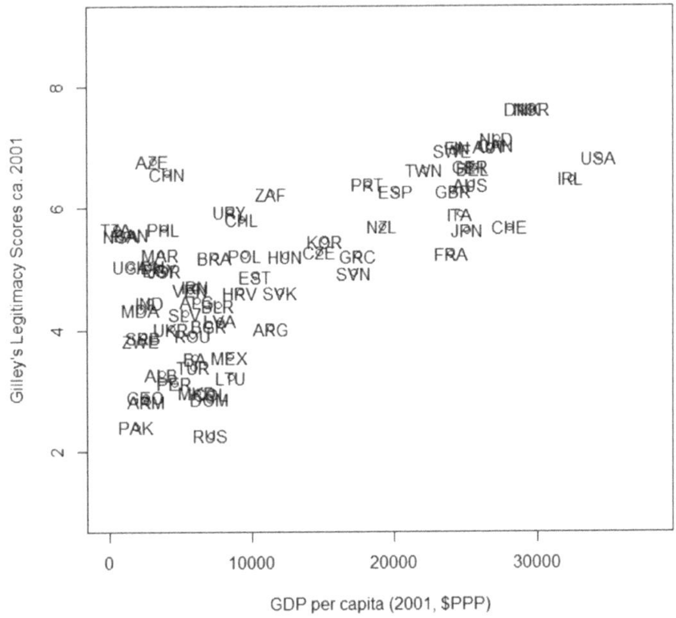

Source: Own representation based on Gilley's (2006a) legitimacy scores

GDP per capita and legitimacy shows a high level of heteroscedasticity as figure 11 shows (see also Gilley, 2009b, 33).[112] In particular, figure 11 depicts no relationship between GDP per capita and legitimacy when considering low-income countries but a strong positive correlation when observing high-income countries in ca. 2001. The same pattern emerges (i) when using Gilley's (2012) legitimacy scores for ca. 2008 and ca. 2012 and (ii) when using the legitimacy scores of my Norris replication (that consists of 'support for regime performance' and 'regime institutions') for the fourth, fifth, and sixth wave of the WVS (see Appendix G for graphs). Since the pattern between GDP per capita and legitimacy is constant over several periods of time, I suggest the following stylized pattern between GDP per capita and legitimacy (figure 12). The pattern shows that legitimacy and GDP per capita are uncorrelated in the low GDP per capita area but positively correlated in the high GDP per capita area. The "breakthrough level" divides the low GDP per capita area from the high GDP per capita area. As suggested by Gilley (2009b, 33), the "breakthrough level" roughly corresponds to a GDP per capita of 14000$ (PPP). Based on this value, table 14 shows the correlations between GDP per capita

112 To cope with heteroskedasticity, one could use the log instead of the raw values.

Figure 12: Legitimacy and GDP per Capita: A Stylized Pattern?

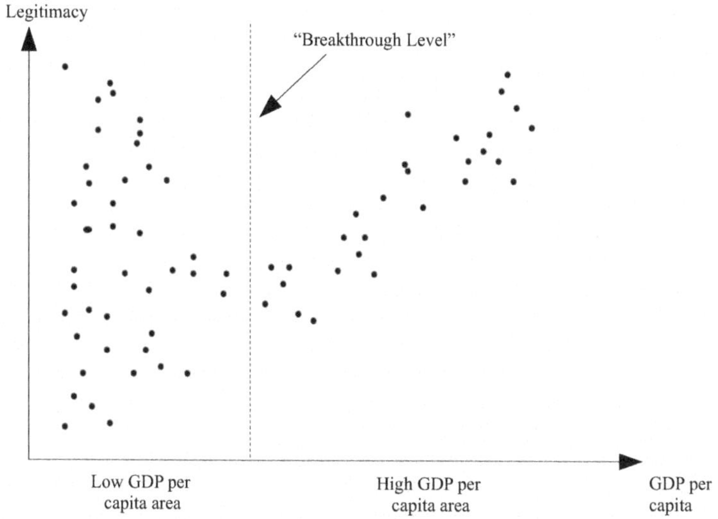

Source: Own representation

Table 14: Legitimacy and GDP per Capita: Correlation Analysis

Legitimacy Measure	*Year*	*Correlations*		
		Full sample	*Restricted Sample (GDP per Capita Smaller than 14000$)*	*Restricted Sample (GDP per Capita Larger than 14000$)*
Gilley (2006a)	ca. 2001[a]	0.69^{***}	0.03	0.66^{***}
Gilley (2012)	ca. 2008[b]	0.55^{***}	-0.09	0.80^{***}
	ca. 2012[c]	0.59^{***}	0.15	0.66^{***}
Norris Replication	ca. 2001[c]	0.28^{**}	-0.24	0.56^{***}
	ca. 2008[c]	0.21	-0.28	0.42^{**}
	ca. 2012[c]	0.47^{***}	-0.14	0.73^{***}

* - at 10%-level significant ** - at 5%-level significant *** - at 1%-level significant
[a] - GDP per capita values refer Gilley's (2006a) original data (2001, $PPP).
[b] - GDP per capita values refer Gilley's (2012) original data (GNI , $PPP, 2008, WDI).
[c] - GDP per capita values were taken from the World Bank ($PPP, 2012).

Source: Author's compilation

and legitimacy for several legitimacy measures and several points in time. Furtermore, I also distinguish between the correlations of the full sample and the correlations of two restricted samples (one refers to countries with a GDP per capita lower than 14000$ and the other refers to countries with a GDP per capita equal or larger than 14000$). When considering the full sample, the results show that the correlations between GDP per capita and legitimacy vary between r=0.21 and r=0.69 depending on the measure and the point in time. When analyzing the countries with a GDP per capita larger than 14000$, strong positive correlations between GDP per capita and legitimacy arise. In contrast, when analyzing the countries with a GDP per capita less than 14000$, the correlation coefficients become insignificant, varying between r= -0.28 and r=0.15. The results of the low-income countries also are largely congruent with the findings of Levi et al. (2009, 363) who find that logged GDP per capita has no significant impact on their measures of legitimacy using survey data of low-income African countries. Since the correlation between GDP per capita and legitimacy is highly sensitive to income levels (heteroskedasticity, see figure 11 and Appendix G), it remains questionable whether one can use GDP per capita as an explanatory variable. Besides the statistical argument to ignore GDP per capita as a determinant of legitimacy, Gilley (2006b, 56) also suggests to "put aside income levels (GDP per capita), not because it tells us too little about causal factors, but too much." He (2006b, 56) further notes that "any state's income levels are a syndrome of choices over a whole range of variables for which income levels are only a proxy, from better governance to reduced poverty to enhanced education."[113] However, despite Gilley's objections, GDP per capita can be used as an explanatory variable as also done by others. However, one should use logged GDP per capita values (to cope with heteroskedasticity) and control for other variables (e.g. governance) to extract the true effect of the welfare level.

- *Human Development Index (HDI).* Another measure to address the welfare standard is the Human Development Index (HDI), which reflects the socioeconomic modernization of a country (Power & Cyr, 2009, 262). In detail, the HDI is a composite index that consists of three basic dimensions of human development. Those are life expectancy (measured by life expectancy at birth), education (measured by the mean of schooling and expected years of schooling), and living standard (measured by the GDP per capita) (Jahan, 2015, 3). Studies suggest that the HDI is a strong predictor of legitimacy (Booth & Seligson, 2009a, 43; Gilley, 2006b, 65; Power & Cyr, 2009, 262). For example, Gilley (2006b, 54) finds a positive correlation between legitimacy and the absolute level of the HDI. Similarly, Power and Cyr (2009, 262) observe a strong correlation between legitimacy and the HDI in Latin America (r=0.521). When plotting the HDI and legitimacy, heteroskedasticity again arises (see Appendix H). In addition, correlation analyses suggest a "breakthrough level" that corresponds to an HDI value of roughly 0.7.[114] As a consequence, when

113 The same argument could be made to exclude the HDI as a measure of the welfare standard.

114 Using HDI values smaller than 0.7, the correlations between the HDI and legitimacy are zero or close to zero (r_{2001}= -0.19; r_{2008}=0.11; r_{2012}= 0.07). Otherwise, using only those countries with a HDI value larger than 0.7, the correlations between the HDI and legitimacy are strongly positive

using the HDI as an explanatory variable, the same shortcomings emerge as in the case of GDP per capita.

In sum, a researcher has to decide whether he or she uses GDP per capita or the HDI. Both absolute welfare measures have the same shortcomings. Since GDP per capita is a part of the HDI, one should only use one of the two measures in regressions. In this thesis, I stick to the HDI.

Welfare Change Indicators. Besides the absolute level of welfare, scholars also suggest analyzing the relative change of the welfare standard in terms of the GDP growth rate or the relative change of the HDI. Since GDP per capita is part of the HDI, one should use either the GDP growth rate or the relative change of the HDI as a control variable in regression equations.

- *GDP per Capita Growth Rate.* Several studies use the GDP growth rate to proxy the recent economic development of a particular country. The basic idea is that sustained economic growth – which enables the state to provide public goods and to distribute material welfare to the citizens – leads to higher legitimacy (Easton, 1965; see also Gjefsen, 2012, 52).[115] Concerning the measurement, scholars typically use the average growth rate of GDP per capita of the last decade. For example, Gilley (2006b, 64) uses the annual real growth rate of GDP per capita between 1990 and 2001 to explain legitimacy in ca. 2001.[116] Similarly, Booth and Seligson (2009a, 129-131) use the national GDP growth from 1990 to 2003 to analyze legitimacy (in particular, 'regime performance') in 2003. Finally, Gjefsen (2012, 41) also uses the average GDP growth rate of the last five and ten years prior to measuring legitimacy. Despite the theoretical reasoning that economic growth should create legitimacy, the empirical evidence is limited. To begin with, Booth and Seligson (2009a, 131) find that economic performance has a significantly positive effect (at 10% level) on 'support for regime performance' in Latin America. In contrast, Gjefsen (2012, 62) finds no significant relationship between economic growth and 'support for regime performance' when considering countries all over the world. Coming to opposite conclusions, Gjefsen (2012, 69) reports that economic growth has a significantly positive effect on 'support for regime institutions'; and Booth and Seligson (2009a, 126) find no significant relationship between economic growth and 'support for regime institutions' in their sample. Power and Cyr (2009, 262) (who replicate Gilley's legitimacy scores for a variety of Latin American countries) also report that economic growth is not significantly correlated with legitimacy. Gilley (2006b, 54) finds only a moderate correlation between economic growth and legitimacy ($r=0.41$).

($r_{2001}=0.81$; $r_{2008}=0.77$; $r_{2012}=0.90$).

115 In addition to the growth rate, one may also consider the volatility of the growth rate as an explanatory variable. Gilley (2006b, 50; see also Clarke et al., 1993; Finkel et al., 1989) notes that a "large literature in political economy has explored how short- or medium-term fluctuations in economic growth can have a profound effect on regime support".

116 Gilley (2006b, 64) uses discounted growth rates because poorer countries in general have a greater growth potential than richer countries.

To sum up, economic growth seems to have no or only a small effect on legitimacy, in particular when controlling for other factors. However, one should notice that the results may be sensitive to the interval defined (last ten years or last five years).[117] Nonetheless, economic growth (the average annual GDP change of the last ten years prior to the legitimacy measurement legitimacy) is one option to capture the welfare change.

- *Relative Change of the HDI.* As an alternative, one could also use the relative change of the HDI (for example, the relative change of the HDI during the last ten years) (Booth & Seligson, 2009a, 110; Gilley, 2006b, 65). In detail, Booth and Seligson (2009a, 110) use the percentage change of the HDI between 1975 and 2003 to meausre the long-term change of the welfare standard. Alternatively, Gilley (2006b, 54, 65) compiles the "percentage change between 1990 and 2002 in the logit value of the Human Development Index" and finds a moderate correlation between welfare change and legitimacy (r=0.59).[118]
  Similar to the absolute welfare level, one should decide whether one uses the relative change of the HDI or the GDP growth rate. Since I use the absolute level of the HDI, I also use the relative change of the HDI.

Government Effectiveness. When referring to government effectiveness, it needs to be clarified when a government or the state is effective. According to Lipset (1959, 86), a political system's effectiveness depends on the "extent to which the system satisfies the basic functions of the government as defined by the expectations of most members of a society, and the expectations of powerful groups within it which might threaten the system, such as the armed forces."[119] Since Lipset's (1959) definition states that the political system needs to satisfy the expectations of the members of a society, one has to make assumptions about those expectations. The Government Effectiveness Index of the World Bank makes such assumptions since it refers to the "perceptions of the

---

117 To check whether the interval has an influence, I compile both five-year and ten-year time intervals. Then, I calculate the correlations between growth rates and legitimacy (Gilley's scores). The results show that no method is superior. The correlations of the five-year time intervals (r_{2001}= -0.01; r_{2008}= -0.43; r_{2012}= 0.12) are not significantly higher or lower than the correlations of the ten-year time intervals (r_{2001}=0.09; r_{2008}= -0.39; r_{2012}= 0.02).

118 Gilley (2006b, 54) only states the R^2 when regressing legitimacy against the relative change of the HDI, which is 0.35.

119 A seminal contribution that stresses the importance of the state's effectiveness goes back to Lipset (1959) who coined the expression performance legitimacy. Originally, Lipset (1959) stresses that the stability of a political regime depends on the relationship between legitimacy and effectiveness of a political system. His argument is that both concepts are intertwined and that the presence or absence of one can influence the development of the other in the long run. According to theory, if legitimacy is high, a short-run crisis of effectiveness does not threaten the stability of the system. The high level of legitimacy "creates a reservoir of goodwill on which the authorities can draw in difficult times and increases considerably the willingness of people to tolerate shortcomings of effectiveness" (Dogan, 2003, 123). The idea is that legitimacy and effectiveness are two independent factors in the short-run that influence the stability of the regime. However, the situation changes in the long-run perspective. Here, the argument runs that both concepts are interdependent such that long-term effectiveness has a positive effect on legitimacy. In the same vein, Rothschild (1977, 488) mentions that "effectiveness and legitimacy are linked to each other and in practice they interact organically".

quality of public services, the quality of the civil service and the degree of its independence from political pressures, the quality of policy formulation and implementation, and the credibility of the government's commitment to such policies" (Kaufmann et al., 2009, 6). Thus, government effectiveness is understood in terms of the quality of the provision of public goods.[120] Regarding the empirical application, scholars find that government effectiveness (as measured by the World Bank) is a strong predictor of legitimacy (table 13). For example, Booth and Seligson (2009a, 125-126) use the Government Effectiveness Index to explain 'support in regime institutions' and find a strong positive relation, i.e. more effective governance increases citizens' legitimacy beliefs in major regime institutions. Further, Gilley (2006b, 64) also concludes that the Government Effectiveness Index (as a part of a composite index that contains the Government Effectiveness Index, Control of Corruption Index, and the Rule of Law Index of the World Bank) is a strong predictor of state legitimacy. Although scholars apply the Government Effectiveness Index widely, the index also has one minor shortcoming. Similar to the other Governance Indicators of the World Bank, endogeneity may be a problem since the Government Effectiveness Index includes a survey item that captures the trust in government (see Kaufmann et al., 2009, 61). However, since only a single item may cause endogeneity problems, I assume that no severe statistical problems arise. Thus, I use the Government Effectiveness Index as a measure of the quality of public goods and bureaucracy.

Income Distribution. Some scholars suggest that the income distribution may be an explanatory factor for legitimacy (Easton, 1965). The argument is that legitimacy is likely to be lower in an unequal society than in an equal society due to, for example, relative deprivation.[121] However, this argument cannot be supported by empirical evidence since studies typically find no correlation between income inequality (as measured by the Gini Index) and legitimacy (Gilley, 2006b, 53; Gjefsen, 2012, 77). The psychological literature also investigates this phenomenon (Costa-Lopes et al., 2013; Tyler, 2006). There, the legitimization of inequality is explained by 'system-justifying ideologies or beliefs'. Those are a set of beliefs that "can explain or make sense of a social system in ways that provide a rationale for the appropriateness or reasonableness of differences in authority, power, status, or wealth" (Tyler, 2006, 376). For example, system-justifying beliefs subsume the set of beliefs that refer to meritocratic ideology, fair market ideology, economic system justification, belief in a just world, and others (Jost & Hunyday, 2005, 261; see also Costa-Lopes et al., 2013, 233).[122] As the psychological research shows, "system-justifying ideologies are

120 This also becomes apparent when investigating the underlying survey items of the Government Effectiveness Index since they explicitly refer to the public sector, in particular to public goods (see Kaufmann et al., 2009, 42, 44, 46, 53, 58, 60) and to the administrative quality of the state (see Kaufmann et al., 2009, 40, 43, 45, 50, 62, 65, 67, 71, 72).

121 One should note that income distribution is not the only equality measure. Besides, one could also check for the wealth distribution or social mobility (see also Great Gatsby Curve; Krueger, 2012).

122 In greater detail, the meritocratic ideology assumes that "[t]he system rewards individual ability and motivation, so success is an indicator of personal deservingness"; the fair market ideology reflects the belief that "[m]arket-based procedures and outcomes are not only efficient but are

potentially powerful tools for legitimating inequality, perpetuating social disparities, and maintaining support for the status quo" (Costa-Lopes et al., 2013, 233). Thus, the empirical results of Gilley (2006b) and Gjefsen (2012) are in line with the psychological literature. Nonetheless, I use the Gini Index to set up the basic model in the next chapter since it is a standard explanatory variable. However, I expect the Gini Index to be insignificant.

Unemployment Rate. To the best of my knowledge, there is only one study that explicitly uses the unemployment rate as an explanatory variable. In detail, Domański (2005, 83) concludes that there "is a clear decrease (by .09 points) of legitimacy [on a 0-30 scale; author's note] with every one percent of unemployment increase which shows that the latter weakens credibility of the political system and ruling class." Thus, I also use the unemployment rate as an explanatory variable.

As the review shows, scholars use a variety of variables to address legitimacy at the system level. In accordance with an extended Scharpfian perspective, I assign the variables to the input, throughput, and output channel. Thus, I use the following variables in chapter 5 to set up the basic model:

- **Input Legitimacy:** Degree of democracy, democratic history, ethnic fractionalization, and an interaction term (democracy* democratic history);
- **Throughput Legitimacy:** Degree of corruption;
- **Output Legitimacy:** Government effectiveness, income distribution, unemployment rate, Human Development Index (HDI), and relative change of the HDI.

4.2.2 Individual-Level Variables

Besides system-level variables, scholars also find that numerous individual-level variables explain legitimacy (Booth & Seligson, 2009a; Domański, 2005; Gjefsen, 2012; Levi & Sacks, 2009; Levi et al., 2009). The following enumeration offers a short overview and derives hypotheses how the individual-level variables are potentially related to legitimacy (as measured by my Norris replication; see chapter 3):

- *Age.* Age is one of the most standard individual-level variables. The empirical literature shows diverging results regarding the relationship between age and legitimacy: Most studies find no significant relationship at all (Gjefsen, 2012, 65; Levi & Sacks, 2009, 28; Levi et al., 2009, 364-366), whereas others find a weak positive relationship (Gjefsen, 2012, 69; Levi et al., 2009, 365). Since a deeper look at the study of Booth and Seligson (2009a, 126) reveals a u-shaped

inherently fair, legitimate, and just"; the economic justification ideology refers to the idea that "[e]conomic inequality is natural, inevitable, and legitimate; economic outcomes are fair and deserved"; and the belief in a just world ideology refers to the idea that "[p]eople typically get what they deserve and deserve what they get; with regard to outcomes, what 'is' is what 'ought' to be" (Jost & Hunyday, 2005, 261).

pattern with lowest legitimacy values (here, support for regime institutions) in the age range from 31 to 50, one may question whether the results of the other studies are appropriate. The reason is that none of those studies implemented a quadratic age term or several age dummies to control for the possibility that age could be u-shaped or even inverted u-shaped. In contrast to the empirical findings, Booth and Seligson (2009a, 114) even argue that younger citizens should show lower legitimacy beliefs since "they may engage less with the political system since they have less at stake in terms of family, property, and the like" and they may "experience higher rates of unemployment and have lower incomes than do older citizens"; similarly, elder citizens should also show lower legitimacy beliefs since they are "often confronted with difficult economic circumstances". In sum, there is no unambiguous relationship between legitimacy and age; thus, the relationship could be linear, u-shaped, or even inverted u-shaped.

- *Gender.* Another important individual-level variable is gender. However, the effect of gender on legitimacy is hardly derivable from other studies, since (i) some studies do not include gender at all (Domański, 2005; Gjefsen, 2012) and (ii) other studies find results that partly diverge. For example, Levi et al. (2009, 364-366) point to the tendency that females show lower legitimacy beliefs. In the same vein, Booth and Seligson (2009a, 126, 131) also find that to be female decreases the 'support for regime performance'. However, referring to the results of Booth and Seligson (2009a), it is not possible to argue that women find the state less legitimate since to be female increases 'support for regime institutions' (and Norris' legitimacy scores are a composite index that comprises 'regime institutions' and 'regime performance'). To sum up, I suppose that to be female has either no significant or only a small negative effect on legitimacy.
- *Education.* Next, a person's educational level may be an explanatory variable. Since educated persons are expected to have more capacity to critically analyze the regime, they should show lower legitimacy beliefs (Booth & Seligson, 2009a, 115). However, this variable seems to have no significant impact on legitimacy. For example, Domański (2005, 82) finds no relationship between years of schooling and legitimacy. Similarly, the educational level (as measured by highest educational degree) has – except for a positive effect due to college education – no impact on 'regime performance' (Gjefsen, 2012, 62, Booth & Seligson, 2009a, 131). In contrast, more educated persons seem to have less trust in state institutions (Gjefsen, 2012, 69; Booth & Seligson, 2009, 126). Thus, I suspect that the educational level has no or only a minor negative effect on legitimacy.
- *Economic Situation.* To capture the economic situation, scholars focus on wealth or income levels. Although the assumption predominates that more economic resources increase a person's legitimacy perceptions, the literature provides mixed evidence. On the one hand, Domański (2005, 82) finds a negative impact of log family income on legitimacy, but he notes at the same time that satisfaction with income is a positive predictor of legitimacy. On the other hand, measures of wealth (approximated by household artifacts such as

cars, television, bikes, radio, or computers) are insignificant or positively related to legitimacy (Booth & Seligson, 2009a, 126, 131; Levi & Sacks, 2009, 28; Levi et al., 2009, 364-366). Despite this mixed evidence, I strongly suppose that a better economic situation is positively related to a person's legitimacy perceptions.

- *Employment Status.* Citizen's employment status may also shape his or her legitimacy beliefs. However, only limited evidence exists since to be employed has in most regressions no significant influence and in some regressions a positive or a negative effect (Levi & Sacks, 2009, 28; Levi et al., 2009, 364-366). The occupational category (as divided into professionals and managers, lower professionals and managers, owners, skilled workers, unskilled workers, and farmers and agricultural laborers) has no influence on a person's legitimacy beliefs (Domański, 2005, 82). Thus, I assume that the employment status has no influence on legitimacy. Regarding occupational category, I suppose that the division of occupations chosen by Domański (2005, 82) is misleading. Rather, assuming an in-group-out-group perspective (following Social Identity Theory (SIT); Tajfel & Turner, 1986), I suppose that people who are employed by the state show higher legitimacy beliefs than persons who work in the private sector.
- *Religion.* Whether a person belongs to a particular religion may shape legitimacy beliefs. For example, Booth and Seligson (2009a, 126, 131) find that Christians (in particular Catholics) show higher 'support for regime institutions' in Latin America (however, there is no relationship to 'regime performance'). I suppose that the religion of a person matters in particular in states where religion (or the church) is closely associated with the state (e.g. Israel or Islamic Republics). In that case, to be part of a particular church should increase legitimacy beliefs. In contrast, in states where religion (or the churches) and the state are strongly separated, religion should have no influence on legitimacy (e.g. Germany).
- *Place of Residence.* The place of residence may also be a factor shaping legitimacy beliefs. The empirical results show the tendency that citizens living in larger cities show lower legitimacy scores than citizens living in rural areas (Booth & Seligson, 2009a, 126, 131).

Besides standard socio-demographic variables, legitimacy research also focuses on variables that capture personal experiences and attitudes. The empirical results show that

- media contact increases 'support for regime institutions' (Booth & Seligson, 2009a, 126),
- politically informed people evaluate the state as less legitimate (Booth & Seligson, 2009a, 126, 131),
- more right-wing persons evaluate the state as more legitimate (Domański, 2005, 82),

- voting for the presidential winner increases a person's legitimacy perceptions tremendously (Booth & Seligson, 2009a, 126, 131),
- interpersonal trust (social capital) has a clear positive effect on legitimacy (Booth & Seligson, 2009a, 126, 131; Domański, 2005, 82; Gjefsen, 2012, 62, 69),
- life satisfaction is clearly positively related to legitimacy (Booth & Seligson, 2009a, 126, 131; Domański, 2005, 82),
- if a person has been a victim of crime, feels unsafe, or has been solicited by a public official to bribe, lower legitimacy beliefs ensue (Booth & Seligson, 2009a, 126, 131).

As far as data are available, I use the individual-level variables to set up the basic model in the next chapter when using Norris' legitimacy scores. For further details regarding the theoretical relationship between individual-level variables and legitimacy see Booth and Seligson (2009a, 113-118) who provide a more comprehensive overview.

4.3 Summary and Outlook

This chapter reviews the determinants of legitimacy. I follow an extended Scharpfian (1979, 1990) perspective, which means that I use Scharpf's original input and output framework and extend it by a further dimension, namely throughput legitimacy. Based on this conceptual framework, I screen the empirical literature to find appropriate system-level variables for each of the three legitimacy channels. The results show that (i) input legitimacy can be measured by the degree of democracy, the regime tradition, and ethnic fractionalization; (ii) throughput legitimacy can be addressed via the degree of corruption (or the degree of impartiality); and (iii) output legitimacy can be addressed by government effectiveness, income distribution (Gini Index), the unemployment rate, and the absolute level of welfare and its relative change (HDI). In addition to system-level variables, scholars also incorporate individual-level variables in regressions as far as individual-level data are available. Here, the results show that not only standard socio-demographic variables (such as age, gender, education, economic situation, or place of residence) help to explain legitimacy but also personal experiences and attitudes (such as media contact, political alignment, interpersonal trust, and others).

The chapter also provides valuable information about the fact that, to the best of my knowledge, economic freedom (at the system level) or attitudes toward economic freedom (at the individual level) have not explicitly been addressed as determinants of legitimacy. Only Gilley (2006b, 52) provides an exception, noting that the "economic stability of property rights and financial institutions as well as market-oriented economic governance and private economic ownership have all been seen as legitimacy-enhancing because of their role in both economic freedom and growth". Finding a positive correlation between economic freedom and legitimacy, Gilley (2006b, 54, 56) concludes that "properly managed market reforms have enhanced, not diminished, the legitimacy of states". However, before analyzing the role of economic freedom and legitimacy, the next chapter sets up a basic model based on the variables of input, output, and throughput legitimacy. This basic model serves as a reference model when analyzing the impact of economic freedom on legitimacy.

5 The Determinants of Legitimacy: A Basic Model

This chapter sets up a basic model based on the determinants presented in chapter 4. The basic model serves as the reference model when analyzing the impact of economic freedom on legitimacy (chapter 6). To date, there is no standard model in the literature due to the following reasons:

(i) *Legitimacy Measure.* Scholars use different legitimacy measures (see Booth & Seligson, 2009a, 2009b; Domański, 2005; Gilley, 2006b; Power & Cyr, 2009). As a consequence, the extracted determinants, their levels of statistical significance, and their signs may be sensitive to the legitimacy measure.

(ii) *Spatial Differences.* The levels of significance and the signs of the determinants may also depend on the regional scope of legitimacy studies. For example, Gilley (2006b) analyzes the determinants of legitimacy in a global set. In contrast, Power and Cyr (2009) and Booth and Seligson (2009a) focus on Latin American countries. Domański's (2005) results refer to European countries.

(iii) *Control Variables.* The chosen control variables also may impact on the signs and the levels of significance of the determinants. That becomes apparent when noticing that some studies only control for system-level variables (Gilley, 2006b; Power & Cyr, 2009), whereas other studies also include individual-level variables (Booth & Seligson, 2009a; Domański, 2005; Gjefsen, 2012). Further, the set of system-level and individual-level variables also differs from study to study.

(iv) *Methodological Differences.* The relevance of different variables may also depend on the methodology. Some studies mainly focus on simple correlations (Gilley, 2006b; Power & Cyr, 2009), whereas other studies use multiple regression models such as OLS (Domański, 2005) or multi-level analysis (Booth & Seligson, 2009a; Gjefsen, 2012).

In addition to these (statistical or econometric) reasons, there is, to the best of my knowledge, no empirical study that explicitly uses Scharpf's classification to address system-level determinants. In this vein, it remains open whether statistical analyses support the theoretical idea to differentiate between an input, a throughput, and an output channel.

In this chapter, I apply extrapolative methods to determine the basic model since I do not want to test theoretical hypotheses here. To find a statistically robust model, I apply two different legitimacy measures throughout this chapter (namely Gilley's original scores and the legitimacy scores I replicated based on Norris' approach; see chapter 3). This chapter also servers to answer the following questions:

- Are the determinants of my basic model congruent with the determinants proposed by Gilley (2006b)?
- Are the results sensitive to the point in time (2001, 2008, 2012)?

C. M. Hindermann, *The Impact of Economic Freedom on State Legitimacy*,
Wirtschaft und Politik, https://doi.org/10.1007/978-3-658-23195-8_5

- Are the results sensitive to the applied method (OLS, ordered logit models, multi-level analysis)?
- Are the results sensitive to the applied legitimacy measure?

The upcoming chapter is structured as follows. In chapter 5.1, I stick to Gilley's legitimacy scores as dependent variables. Since Gilley's scores are available at the country level, I solely use system-level variables as independent variables (see chapter 4). Since Gilley's (2006a, 2012) legitimacy scores are available for three points in time (ca. 2001, 2008, and 2012), I initially investigate each point in time separately. Based on these results, I derive a general basic model. In short, the results suggest that it is sufficient to differentiate between an input and an output channel at the country level (due to the statistical closeness of output and throughput measures). In particular, it turns out that (i) better general governance (in terms of government effectiveness and control of corruption) leads to more legitimacy, (ii) states with a higher welfare standard (as measured by the Human Development Index) show, ceteris paribus, lower legitimacy scores (particularly in low-income countries), and (iii) democracies are not necessarily more legitimate than autocracies (since the impact of democracy on legitimacy seems to depend on a country's democratic history and also varies over time). The findings support the statement of Rothstein (2009) that "legitimacy is created, maintained, and destroyed not by the input but by the output side of the political system". At the same time, the findings also challenge the results of Gilley (2006b) who uses the same legitimacy scores (those that refer to ca. 2001) but finds partly different results, in particular regarding the role of democracy and the role of welfare.

In chapter 5.2, I replace Gilley's (2006b, 2012) with Norris' legitimacy scores and perform robustness checks. Since Norris' legitimacy scores are available at the individual level, it is possible to analyze both system-level and individual-level variables. Based on the legitimacy scores of three points in time (fourth, fifth, and sixth wave of the WVS), I apply two different estimations strategies. First, I compute OLS regressions (using the determinants of the basic model of chapter 5.1 as independent variables). The results show the same patterns as when using Gilley's (2006a, 2012) legitimacy scores. Second, I also perform multilevel analyses since Norris' legitimacy scores are available at the individual level, allowing to control for both system-level and individual-level variables. These results provide the same insights regarding the country-level variables as before, namely that better general governance leads to more legitimacy and states with a higher welfare standard show lower legitimacy scores. As in the previous investigations, the role of democracy remains a puzzle. Finally, chapter 5.3 serves to summarize the basic model.

5.1 A Basic Model at the System Level Based on Gilley's Legitimacy Scores

This sub-chapter uses the legitimacy scores provided by Gilley (2006a, 2012) for ca. 2001 and ca. 2008 as dependent variables. In addition, I also compile legitimacy scores for ca. 2012 following the Gilley methodology (see Appendix D). Thus, there are three points in time to analyze.

To derive the basic model, I first discuss a variety of methodological issues (chapter 5.1.1). In particular, this refers to (i) the data preparation of the independent variables, (ii) the choice of an appropriate estimation strategy (which depends on the assumption about legitimacy's scale type), and (iii) a short discussion about critical model assumptions. Thereafter, chapter 5.1.2 presents the results of an initial correlation analysis and the OLS regressions. To determine the basic model, I make use of two extrapolative model selection strategies (backward regression and Bayesian model averaging). Finally, I apply ordered logit models as a robustness check. In short, the results show that the basic model should consist of the following variables: Democracy, democratic history, an interaction between democracy and democratic history, general governance, the absolute welfare level, and the unemployment rate. General governance and the absolute welfare level are the most important variables across waves.

5.1.1 Methodological Issues

Data Preparation of the Independent Variables

Before analyzing the determinants of legitimacy, it is necessary to prepare the independent variables. Regarding input legitimacy, four variables are relevant, namely the degree of democracy, democratic history, the interaction between democracy and democratic history (mean centered), and ethnic fractionalization.

Degree of Democracy. To measure the degree of democracy, I use a combined index that consists of the Freedom House Index and the Polity IV Index. I proceed as follows. First, concerning the Freedom House Index, I simply add the two sub-indices (Political Rights and Civil Liberties; each range from 1 to 7; lower scores highlight more democratic values) to obtain an overall FH Index (which varies between 2 and 14, whereas 2 means politically free and 14 politically not free). Then, I standardize the FH overall Index to a 0 to 10 scale (such that 10 means absolutely democratic and 0 means absolutely autocratic).[123] Applying a similar strategy, I also recode the Polity IV Index which originally ranges from -10 (absolutely autocratic) to 10 (absolutely democratic).[124] In the last step, I calculate the mean of both standardized indices (the correlation between both indices is r=0.886 in the 2001 sample). Data on Bosnia and Herzegovina is missing in the Polity IV Index in the ca. 2001 wave. In this case, I just take the data of the standardized FH Index.

Democratic History. To measure a country's democratic history, I calculate the mean standardized Polity IV score from 1945 to one year prior to the legitimacy score.[125]

123 In greater detail, I transform the FH overall index in such a manner that a 2 becomes a 10 of the standardized FH overallindex and that a 14 becomes a 0 of the standardized FH overall index. All other values are evenly addressed with a distance of 0.833.

124 Again, I transform the Polity IV Index in such a manner that an original -10 becomes a 0 and an original 10 becomes a 10 of the standardized Polity IV Index. All other values in between are evenly addressed with a distance of 0.5.

125 That means that the democratic history score for 2001 (2008; 2012) is based on the mean standardized Polity IV score from 1945 to 2000 (1945 to 2007; 1945 to 2011).

However, this procedure leads to various problems since some countries became independent (former colonies or states that were former parts of larger states such as the USSR) or united during this period (e.g. Germany). To cope with these problems, I apply the following strategies:

- *Former Colonial States:* A variety of states were under colonial domination, mostly until the 1950s or 1960s. In these cases, I calculate the mean standardized Polity IV scores beginning in the year of the state's independence. To give an example, Morocco was a French protectorate until 1956. Thus, the Moroccan democratic history score is the mean of the standardized Polity IV Index of the years 1956 to 2000 (in the case of the legitimacy score for ca. 2001). The footnote below provides an overview of the states that are affected by this procedure.[126]
- *Former Soviet States (Parts of USSR):* Concerning former Soviet states, I calculate the democratic history score based on the standardized Polity IV score of the USSR from 1945 to 1990 and the standardized Polity IV score of the particular country from 1991 to 2000 (2007 or 2011 respectively). The states affected by this procedure are listed below.[127]
- *Former Yugoslav States:* Similar to former Soviet states, I deal with former Yugoslav states. Thus, I calculate the democratic history scores based on the standardized Polity IV score of Yugoslavia from 1945 to 1990 and the standardized Polity IV scores of the particular country from 1991 to 2000 (2007 or 2011 respectively). That procedure applies to Croatia, Macedonia, and Slovenia. However, there are three exceptions. First, for Serbia and Montenegro (in the 2001 sample), I take the values of Yugoslavia from 1945 to 1991 and the values of the Federal Republic of Yugoslavia from 1992 to 2000. Second, for Serbia (in the 2008 sample), the democratic history score is based on the values of Yugoslavia from 1945 to 1991, the Federal Republic of Yugoslavia from 1992 to 2002, Serbia and Montenegro from 2003 to 2006,

126 In each of the three samples (2001, 2008, 2012), the following states have a colonial background (year ofindependence in parenthesis): Algeria (1962; before under French colonial rule), Bahrain (1971; before under British colonial rule), Burkina Faso (1960; before under French colonial rule), Cyprus (1960; before under British colonial rule), Ghana (1960; before under British colonial rule), India (1950; before under British colonial rule), Kuwait (1963; before under British colonial rule), Qatar (1971; before under British colonial rule), Lybia (1951, before under allied occupation), Malaysia (1963; before under British colonial rule), Morocco (1956; before under French colonial rule), Mali (1960; before under French colonial rule), Nigeria (1960; before under British colonial rule), Pakistan (1947; before under British colonial rule), Rwanda (1961; before under Belgian colonial rule), Singapore (1959; before under British colonial rule), Tanzania (1961; before under British colonial rule), Trinidad & Tobago (1962; before under British colonial rule), Tunisia (1959; before under French protectorate), Uganda (1962; before under British colonial rule), Zambia (1964; before under British colonial rule), and Zimbabwe (1970, before under British colonial rule (Southern Rhodesia)).

127 In the 2001 sample, the procedure is applied to Armenia, Belarus, Estonia, Georgia, Latvia, Lithuania, Moldova, Russia and Ukraine. In the 2008 sample, Georgia, Moldova, Russia and Ukraine are considered. In the ca. 2011 sample, this is applied to Armenia, Azerbaijan, Belarus, Estonia, Georgia, Kazakhstan, Kyrgyzstan, Russia, and Ukraine.

and Serbia in 2007. And third, for Bosnia and Herzegovina (in the 2001 sample), I take the data of Yugoslavia from 1945 to 1990 and the data of Bosnia from 1991 to 1994 (after 1994, no data are available).

- *Other Divisions of States:* Other states also separated since 1945. First, the Czech Republic and Slovakia formed Czechoslovakia from 1945 to 1992. Thus, to calculate the democratic history of the Czech Republic (Slovakia), I take the values of former Czechoslovakia from 1945 to 1992 and the Czech Republic (Slovakia) from 1993 to 2000. Second, since Bangladesh was a part of Pakistan until 1972, the democratic history score of Bangladesh is the result of the Pakistani values (from 1947 to 1972) and the values of Bangladesh (from 1973 to 2000). Third, since South Korea became independent from Japan in 1948, I take the values of South Korea from 1948 to 2000 (2007 and 2011 respectively). No values for Japan from 1945 to 1947 are available. Fourth, because Taiwan has been independent from China since 1949, I calculate the democratic history score of Taiwan based on the Chinese values from 1945 to 1948 and the Taiwanese values from 1949 to 2000 (2007 and 2011 respectively).
- *Unification of States:* Some states reunited during the period from 1945 to date. This applies to Germany, Vietnam, and Yemen. Concerning Germany, I apply a weighted strategy in three steps. First, I calculate the mean democratic history score of East and West Germany from 1949 to 1990 separately. Then, I compute the mean score for the 1949 to 1990 period by weighting the West Germany score with 4 and the East Germany score with 1 (which approximately reflects the population size of both countries). Second, I compute the mean democratic history score of united Germany from 1991 to 2000 (2007 and 2011 respectively). Third, I calculate the final democratic history score of Germany. Here, I weight the democratic history score of separated Germany with 41 and the democratic history score of united Germany with 10 (17 and 22 respectively) (weights correspond to the number of years before and after unification). Concerning Vietnam, I calculate in a first step the mean of North Vietnam (from 1954 to 1976) and the mean of South Vietnam (from 1955 to 1976). Then, I calculate the mean value of both. Next, I calculate the mean democracy score of reunited Vietnam (from 1976 to 2000 or 2007 respectively). In the last step, I compute the mean of separated and united Vietnam, weighting the score of separated Vietnam with 21 and the score of reunited Vietnam with 24 (31 respectively). Finally, regarding Yemen, I calculate the mean of Northern and Southern Yemen (from 1967 to 1989) separately and collapse both values into an index. Then, I calculate the mean democracy score of reunited Yemen from 1990 to 2011. Thereafter, I weight the first value (separated Yemen from 1967 to 1989) with 22 and the second value (reunited Yemen from 1990 to 2011) with 21 to obtain the overall democratic history score.

*Interaction Term (Democracy*Democratic History).* To calculate the interaction term, I first center both variables by the mean mainly to avoid multicollinearity problems (mean centering). That means that I subtract the mean democracy score (mean democratic history score) from a country's democracy score (democratic history score). Thereafter, I multiply the centered democracy score by the centered democratic history score.

Fractionalization. To measure ethnic fractionalization, I use the data of Alesina et al. (2003) as provided by the Quality of Government Dataset (Teorell et al., 2015). Since the data stem from the early to mid-1990s, one could argue that the data are obsolete. However, when assuming that fractionalization changes only very slowly over time, this objection vanishes. Alesina et al. (2003, 160) also note that this is "a reasonable assumption at the 30 year horizon" since group "changes are sufficiently stable that changes only have a minor impact on fractionalization measures". In the 2012 sample, data on Palestine, Hong Kong, and Yemen are missing.
Regarding throughput and output variables, the degree of corruption, government effectiveness, economic distribution, the unemployment rate, and the Human Development Index (HDI) in absolute and relative terms need to be prepared.[128]

Degree of Corruption. To measure the degree of corruption, I use the Control of Corruption Index by the World Bank for the years 2000 (2001 not available), 2008, and 2012. No values are missing (except Palestine in 2012). Since there are a variety of missing values in 2001, I abstain from using the TI Corruption Index.[129]

Government Effectiveness. Regarding government effectiveness, I rely on the Government Effectiveness Index by the World Bank. Here, I take the data from 2000 (2001 data not available), 2008, and 2012. There are no missing values (except Palestine in 2012).

Income Distribution. To measure income distribution, I use the Gini coefficient and take the data from the World Bank. However, in most cases, there are no data available for the years of interest (2001, 2008, 2012). In these cases, I take the Gini coefficient of the year that is closest to the corresponding year.[130] For example, I take the Algerian Gini coefficient of 1995 since there is no value for the year of interest (here, 2001) available. The footnote below gives a more extended enumeration of the cases to which this procedure applies.[131] Another problem is that the World Bank does not

128 As measures of welfare, I stick to the HDI (in absolute and relative terms). Of course, it is also possible to use GDP per capita and the GDP per capita growth rate.

129 The TI Corruption Perceptions Index does not cover the following countries in the 2001 sample: Albania, Algeria, Armenia, Belarus, Bosnia and Herzegovina, Georgia, Iran, Macedonia, Morocco, and Serbia/Yugoslavia.

130 In the case of OECD countries, data availability for the Gini coefficient is better when taking the OECD data. However, I stick to the data of the World Bank to have a consistent procedure.

131 Regarding the 2001 wave, the following countries are affected (year of the Gini coefficient in parenthesis): Algeria (1995), Albania (2002), Austria (2000), Bangladesh (2000), Belgium (2000), Great Britain (1999), Canada (2000), Chile (2000), China (2002), Czech Republic (1996), Denmark (2000), Egypt (2000), Finland (2000), France (2000), Germany (2000), Greece (2000), India (2005), Indonesia (2002), Iran (1998), Ireland (2000), Italy (2000), Japan (2008), Jordan (2003), Latvia (2002), Macedonia (2002), Mexico (2002), Netherlands (1999), Nigeria (2004),

provide a Gini coefficient for some countries at all. In these cases, I use the data of the World Factbook (cases are listed below).[132] Data on Bahrain, Kuwait, Lebanon, Libya, Palestine, and Qatar are missing.

Unemployment Rate. Again, the World Bank data are the basis for the unemployment rate. There is only one missing value in each wave (2001, 2008, 2012), namely Taiwan. Thus, I take the unemployment data from the World Factbook in this case. In addition, data on Palestine are missing for 2012.

Welfare Measures. I use the Human Development Index (HDI) to approximate the welfare level and the welfare change of a country.

- *HDI (Absolute):* For the 2001 wave, I take of HDI data of 2000 (2001 not available). Three countries are missing, namely Macedonia, Nigeria, and Taiwan. For 2008, I stick to the HDI data of 2010 (2008 not available). For 2012, I simply take the HDI data of 2012. There are no data for Taiwan.
- *HDI (Relative Change):* For the 2001 wave, I use the HDI's growth rate from 1990 to 2000 to measure the change of the welfare level. Unfortunately, there are missing values for Azerbaijan, Belarus, Bosnia and Herzegovina, Georgia, Macedonia, Nigeria, and Taiwan. For the 2008 wave, I stick to the HDI's growth rate from 2000 to 2010. Here, data on Burkina Faso and Taiwan are missing. For the ca. 2012 wave, I calculate the growth rate of the HDI from 2000 to 2012.[133] As before, data on Taiwan are missing.

Norway (2000), Pakistan (2002), Philippines (2002), Portugal (2004), Serbia (2002), Slovakia (2004), Slovenia (2002), South Africa (2000), Spain (2000), Sweden (2000), Switzerland (2000), Tanzania (2000), Turkey (2000), Uganda (2002), Ukraine (2002), and USA (2000).

With respect to the 2008 wave, there are the following exceptions: Australia (2003), Burkina Faso (2009), Canada (2007), Chile (2009), Ethiopia (2005), Finland (2007), France (2005), Germany (2007), Ghana (2006), India (2010), Iran (2005), Malaysia (2007), Mali (2010), Morocco (2007), Netherlands (2007), Norway (2007), Rwanda (2006), South Africa (2009), Spain (2007), Sweden (2005), Switzerland (2004), UK (2007), United States (2007), Zambia (2006), and Trinidad & Tobago (1992).

Finally, regarding the 2012 wave, the following exceptions are being made: Algeria (1995), Azerbaijan (2008), Argentina (2011), Australia (2003), Belarus (2011), Chile (2011), China (2011), Estonia (2011), Egypt (2008), Germany (2010), Ghana (2006), Japan (2008), Jordan (2010), Kazakhstan (2010), Kyrgyzstan (2011), Malaysia (2009), Morocco (2007), Netherlands (2010), Nigeria (2010), Pakistan (2011), Poland (2011), Russia (2009), Rwanda (2011), Slovenia (2011), South Africa (2011), Spain (2010), Sweden (2005), Thailand (2010), Trinidad and Tobago (1992), Tunisia (2010), Turkey (2011), Ukraine (2010), USA (2010), Yemen (2005), and Zimbabwe (2006).

132 I use the data of the World Factbook for the 2001 wave in the following cases: New Zealand (1997), South Korea (2013), Taiwan (2012), Zimbabwe (2006). For the 2008 wave, the following countries are affected: Cyprus (2005), South Korea (2013), New Zealand (1997), Taiwan (2012). Regarding the 2012 wave, this affects Cyprus (2014), New Zealand (1997), Singapore (2014), South Korea (2014), and Taiwan (2014).

133 When data for 2000 are not available, I calculate the average growth rate from 2010 to 2012 and multiply it by six. This applies to Lebanon, Palestine, and Nigeria.

Estimation Strategies

The estimation strategy to extract the basic model strongly depends on the scale type of the dependent variable. Here, it is possible to assume that legitimacy is either (i) an ordinal or (ii) a (quasi-)metric variable.

First, in the narrow sense, legitimacy should be treated as an ordinal variable since a state with a legitimacy score of ten is not double as legitimate as a state with a legitimacy score of five. Thus, under this assumption, it is only possible to note which state is more legitimate than another but not to what degree. In this vein, (ordered) logit or (ordered) probit models are appropriate methods to analyze the determinants of legitimacy.[134] The advantage of these models is that they treat legitimacy according to its true scale type. In contrast, (ordered) logit or (ordered) probit models require a categorical dependent variable. Since Gilley's legitimacy scores are continuous, one needs to define discrete categories. Since the values can vary between 0 and 10, one could define 11 discrete categories or even less, for example four. In both cases, that procedure leads to a reduction of the original variance which is, however, necessary to extract the impact of the determinants properly. In other words, one neglects more within group variance when using fewer categories.

Second, to overcome both problems, one could make the (critical) assumption that legitimacy scores are (quasi-)metric. Then, the basic model can be estimated via standard OLS. In this case, the advantage is that one loses no variance. That is of particular importance when one makes the assumption that measured differences in legitimacy reflect true differences. In addition, the coefficients are estimated efficiently due to the properties of OLS (requiring that the OLS model assumptions hold).

To sum up, both estimation strategies have advantages and disadvantages. The most important advantage of (ordered) logit or (ordered) probit models is that they account for legitimacy's true scale level (which is ordinal). In contrast, the OLS estimation strategy has better estimation properties, in particular since the number of observations are rather low. As a consequence, I use both estimation strategies to analyze legitimacy's determinants. Thus, I initially investigate the determinants of legitimacy using OLS (implying the assumption that legitimacy is metric). Thereafter, mainly to check the robustness of the OLS results, I also apply (ordered) logit models.

Model Structure

It is also necessary to make some assumptions about the model structure. Those refer to (i) the direction of causality between legitimacy and the independent variables and (ii) the relationship between the three legitimacy channels (input, output, and throughput).

Direction of Causality. Regarding the direction of causality, I assume that all determinants clearly precede legitimacy. However, this assumption may be critical

134 The basic difference between logit and probit models lies in the assumption about the distribution of errors. Logit models assume that the error terms are standard logistically distributed, whereas probit models assume that error terms are normally distributed. (Train, 2009)

since legitimacy may be a predictor of its assumed antecedents. For example, Rothschild (1977, 489, see also Feldman & Mazepus, 2014, 5) notes that the relationship between state effectiveness and legitimacy is circular: State effectiveness increases legitimacy and legitimacy increases state effectiveness in return. Similarly, Weede (1996) also finds that legitimacy increases the GDP growth rate of a country.[135] Further, Berggren et al. (2015) find some evidence that (governmental) legitimacy positively affects the growth rates, but only if the government size is small.[136] If the government size is high, high values of (governmental) legitimacy are associated with lower growth rates. Despite these objections, I assume that state effectiveness (or growth rates) are strict determinants of legitimacy and, thereby, avoid dealing with endogeneity issues. I am aware that this assumption may be controversal.[137]

Interactions between the Three Channels. Concerning the legitimacy channels (input, throughput, and output legitimacy), one could assume that they are independent or interrelated. If one assumes an interrelation, it is necessary to model interaction effects. Those reflect the possibility (i) that a trade-off between the channels may exist or (ii) that input legitimacy is a precondition for output legitimacy (see chapter 4.1.1). In the following, I assume that all three channels are independent and leave it to another study to relax this assumption.[138]

5.1.2 Results

Correlation Analysis

Before applying multiple regression models, an initial correlation analysis is useful to get an understanding of the data. Thus, I initially present bivariate correlations (i) between legitimacy and each independent variable and (ii) between the independent variables.

(i) Bivariate Correlations between Legitimacy and the Independent Variables. To receive an impression about the direction and the strength of causality, table 15

135 From a theoretical perspective, Weede (1996) notes that legitimacy's impact on growth is not clearly identifiable in advance since the impact may be positive or negative. On the other hand, legitimacy should have a positive impact on growth since social control costs and transaction costs should be lower (Weede, 1996, 218). On the other hand, legitimacy can reduce the growth rates since those in command "can buy it by making promises to special interest groups". Thus, the size of the state may increase and an efficient allocation of resources may be hampered (Weede, 1996, 218; see also Olsen, 1982).

136 According to Berggren et al. (2015), there are five different channels through which legitimacy impacts the growth rate. For more details, see Appendix I.

137 One could apply a Hausman-Test to check for endogeneity. For example, the fraction of tropical areas could be used as instrumental variable for the GDP growth rate per capita (Sala-i-Martin et al., 2004). I abstain from performing this test since the GDP growth rate per capita (and the relative change of the HDI) will be no part of the basic model (see below, chapter 5.1.2).

138 A strategy to analyze whether the channels interact could be to calculate a score for each channel (for example, based on regression coefficients). Then, one could check correlations between the input and the output score.

Table 15: Correlations between Legitimacy and the Independent Variables

Independent Variables	Gilley ca. 2001	Gilley ca. 2008	Gilley ca. 2012
	(1)	(2)	(3)
Input Variables			
Democracy	0.34^{***}	0.34^{**}	0.43^{***}
Democratic History	0.55^{***}	0.54^{***}	0.51^{***}
Interaction Term	0.44^{***}	0.16	0.20
Ethnic Fractionalization	-0.34^{***}	-0.39^{***}	-0.24^{*}
Throughput Variables			
Degree of Corruption	0.73^{***}	0.66^{***}	0.71^{***}
Output Variables			
Government Effectiveness	0.74^{***}	0.66^{***}	0.70^{***}
Income Distribution	-0.27^{**}	-0.13	0.03
Unemployment Rate	-0.47^{***}	-0.31^{**}	-0.39^{***}
Welfare Level (HDI)	0.50^{***}	0.36^{***}	0.45^{***}
Welfare Change (HDI)	0.16	-0.31^{**}	-0.11

* - at 10%-level significant ** - at 5%-level significant *** - at 1%-level significant

presents the results of bivariate correlations between legitimacy and its potential determinants for each wave (ca. 2001, ca. 2008, and ca. 2012).

As the results show, the correlations of all input variables are stable across different waves regarding the sign and the strength. In the first place, democracy is positively related to legitimacy in each wave, which is in line with theoretical considerations ($r_{2001}=0.34^{***}$, $r_{2008}=0.34^{**}$, $r_{2012}=0.43^{***}$). Similarly, the democratic history of country is also positively correlated with legitimacy ($r_{2001}=0.55^{***}$, $r_{2008}=0.54^{**}$, $r_{2012}=0.51^{***}$). However, this result needs to be treated with caution since a high democratic history score typically goes along with a high democracy score. To account for this, one can focus on the interaction term (mean centered) between democracy and democratic history. Here, the correlations are positive but vary in magnitude and level of significance across waves ($r_{2001}=0.44^{***}$, $r_{2008}=0.16$, $r_{2012}=0.20$). Concerning ethnic fractionalization, the correlations are in line with theoretical considerations ($r_{2001}= -0.34^{***}$, $r_{2008}= -0.39^{**}$, $r_{2012}= -0.24^{*}$). More ethnically fractionalized societies are less likely to share the same identity such that legitimacy is lower in these countries.

When focusing on the throughput variable, the correlations show the expected signs throughout all waves. The degree of corruption (higher values mean less corruption) is clearly positively correlated with legitimacy ($r_{2001}= 0.73^{***}$, $r_{2008}= 0.66^{***}$, $r_{2012}=0.71^{***}$). States have higher legitimacy values if they fight corruption more effectively.

In slight contrast to the input and throughput dimension, not all variables of the output dimension have the same sign and/or level of significance across waves, in particular in the case of welfare change. In detail, government effectiveness is clearly positively correlated with legitimacy as theoretically expected (r_{2001}=0.74***, r_{2008}=0.66**, r_{2012}=0.70***). This means that legitimacy increases if the state improves the quality of public and civil services. Regarding the income distribution, correlations are likely to be negative, but they are only significant in one wave (r_{2001}= -0.27**, r_{2008}= -0.13, r_{2012}= 0.03). This may indicate that income inequality reduces the legitimacy perceptions of citizens. However, this effect may largely be mitigated by system-justifying beliefs (that foster the perception that economic inequality is a legitimate outcome of the system; see chapter 4.2.1). Thus, income inequality seems to have no or only limited explanatory power. Next, the unemployment rate is clearly negatively correlated with legitimacy, confirming the finding of Domański (2005) (r_{2001}= -0.47***, r_{2008}= -0.31**, r_{2012}= -0.39***). Further, the absolute welfare level (as measured by the HDI) also shows a significantly positive correlation with legitimacy (r_{2001}=0.50***, r_{2008}=0.36***, r_{2012}=0.45***). At a first glance, this means that more developed countries show higher legitimacy scores than less developed countries. In contrast to the other output variables, the coefficients of welfare change are not stable across waves since correlations are insignificant in the 2001 and 2012 waves but significantly negative in the 2008 wave (r_{2001}=0.16, r_{2008}= -0.31**, r_{2012}= -0.11).[139] This change may be a result of the outbreak of the worldwide financial crises (assuming that high legitimacy countries, which are on average also high developed countries, were more heavily hit by the financial crises; thus, countries with a high level of legitimacy also show lower rates of welfare change). Another potential reason may be that the three waves consist of partly different countries (and also a different amount of observations in total).

(ii) Bivariate Correlations between the Independent Variables. To indicate and to cope with potential multicollinearity problems, it is reasonable to check the bivariate correlations between the independent variables.[140] Thus, I plot the correlation matrices for legitimacy and its independent variables for all three waves (figures 13-15; correlations within the frame). As the correlation matrices show, most correlations between the independent variables show the expected signs. For example, it is not surprising that democracy positively correlates with HDI (absolute) since democracies are typically developed countries (r_{2001}=0.73***; r_{2008}=0.6***; r_{2012}=0.48***). Similarly, the absolute level of welfare (HDI) is also highly correlated with corruption (r_{2001}=0.80***; r_{2008}=0.70***; r_{2012}=0.70***) and government effectiveness (r_{2001}=0.80***; r_{2008}=0.77***; r_{2012}=0.74***). Interestingly, the correlations between the relative change of HDI and the other independent variables change significantly over time. In the 2001 sample, the relative change of HDI is uncorrelated with all other variables. In contrast, in the 2008 sample, the relative change of HDI is partly strongly correlated with variables such as

139 The same pattern emerges when investigating the correlations between legitimacy and the average GDP per capita growth rate (r_{2001}=0.09, r_{2008}= -0.38**, r_{2012}=0.01). This is not surprising since the HDI consists of the GDP per capita. Thus, when calculating the relative change of the HDI, it contains the average GDP growth rate per capita such that, ceteris paribus, both variables change in the same direction (in other words, if the GDP per capita growth rate increases, the relative change of the HDI also increases, all other indicators of the HDI held constant).

140 Of course, bivariate correlations between the independent variables are not sufficient to indicate multicollinearity since linear dependency may also occur in multiple regressions due to the interplay of several independent variables.

Figure 13: Bivariate Correlations (Gilley ca. 2001)

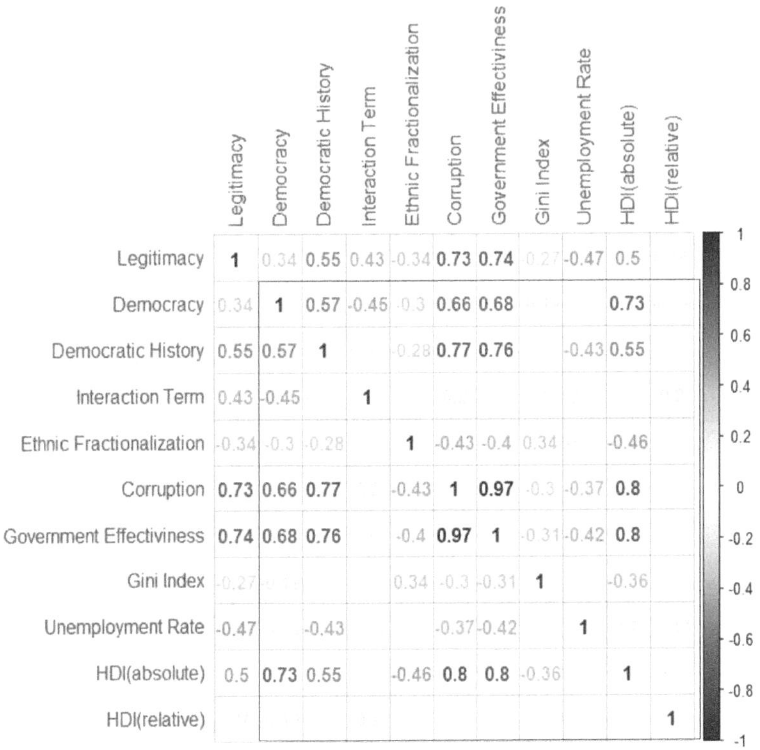

Source: Author's compilation; based on R package 'corrplot'

democracy, democratic history, control of corruption, government effectiveness, or the absolute level of HDI. In fact, this observation supports the idea that the financial crises mostly impacted developed countries. Thus, in developed countries, the growth rate dropped more dramatically than in developing or non-developed countries.[141] In other words, highly developed countries (those with a high HDI score) lost more in terms of HDI change than non-developed countries. In addition to this, more developed countries generally have lower growth rates than developing countries and, thus, the relative change of HDI is by definition tendentiously lower in comparison to

141 At least, it turns out that (i) developed countries have lower growth rates than developing countries in general and (ii) the growth rate of developed countries show greater negative numbers than the growth rates of emerging countries in the year of the financial crisis (Blanchard et al., 2010, 264). Thus, the change of the HDI (over a ten-year horizon) should be lower in developed countries than in developing countries.

Figure 14: Bivariate Correlations (Gilley ca. 2008)

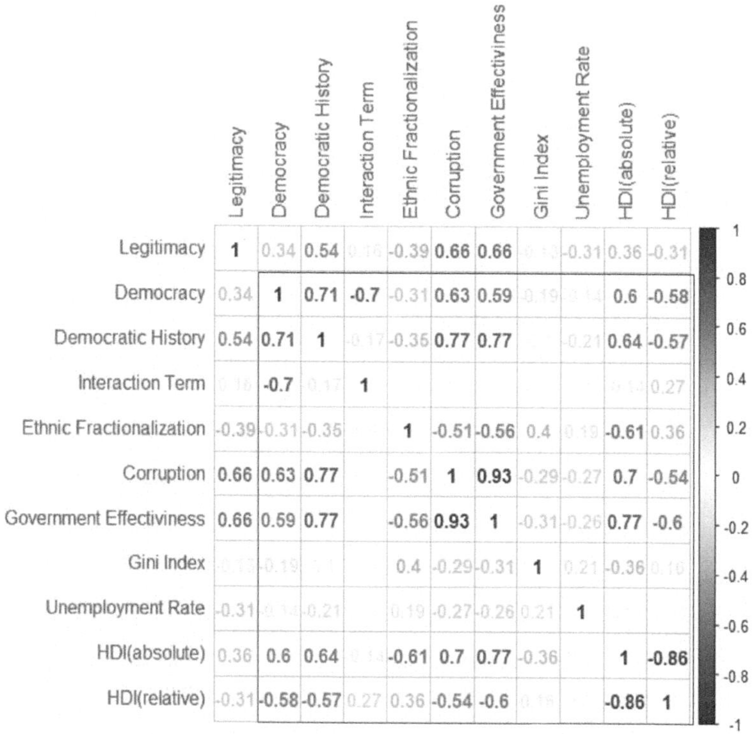

Source: Author's compilation; based on R package 'corrplot'

non-developed countries.[142] However, I want to stress that these explanations (in particular the financial crisis hypothesis) need to be investigated in greater detail (which is not done here). Thus, it remains a puzzle why the correlations between the relative change of HDI and legitimacy are not stable across waves. Similarly, it is also unclear why the correlations between the relative change of HDI and the other independent variables change significantly over time.

To avoid multicollinearity in regression analyses, it is important to check whether some independent variables are highly correlated (i.e. the correlation coefficient is

142 Sticking to the average GDP growth rate, Gilley (2006b, 64) suggests discounting the growth rates of the countries with respect to their status of development. The reason is that – assuming absolute beta-convergence – developing countries have a higher growth potential (assuming conditional beta-convergence challenges this assumption). One could also apply a similar strategy when using the relative change of the HDI. However, I abstain from this modification and leave this to another study.

Figure 15: Bivariate Correlations (Gilley ca. 2012)

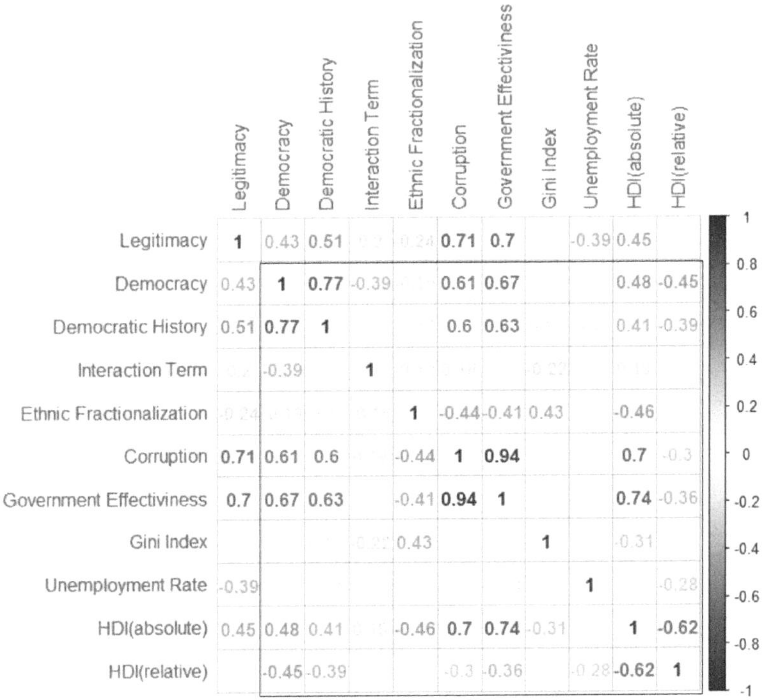

Source: Author's compilation; based on R package 'corrplot'

above 0.90). In fact, the Control of Corruption Index and the Government Effectiveness Index are highly correlated ($r_{2001}=0.97^{***}$; $r_{2008}=0.93^{***}$; $r_{2012}=0.94^{***}$). As a consequence, severe multicollinearity problems arise if one uses both variables as independent variables in regression analyses. To account for this problem, I follow the strategy of Gilley (2006b) and build an index ('general governance') that consists of the Control of Corruption Index and the Government Effectiveness Index, weighting each index equally. Although one can easily apply this procedure from a statistical point of view, it causes severe theoretical problems since I mix up items that belong to different channels of legitimacy, namely throughout and output legitimacy. Thus, the findings strongly challenge the assumption that throughput and output legitimacy are two distinct channels at the country level. Rather, they suggest that throughput legitimacy can be subsumed under the output channel. As a consequence, I only distinguish between input and throughput/output legitimacy. This signals that three

channels exist theoretically, but it shows at the same time that there are statistical reasons to treat throughput and output legitimacy as one channel.
To sum up, the correlation analyses offer a variety of insights. First, bivariate correlations between legitimacy and the independent variables largely have the expected signs (except welfare change). In some cases, I partly find insignificant correlation coefficients (ethnic fractionalization, income distribution, and welfare change). Second, since the Government Effectiveness Index and the Control of Corruption Index are highly correlated, I collapse both into one index called 'general governance' to avoid multicollinearity problems. I am aware that this challenges the theoretical considerations that three distinct legitimacy channels exist. Third, the relationship between the relative change of HDI and legitimacy remains unclear since the size and the significance of the correlation coefficient is highly sensitive to the point in time. Nonetheless, I do not drop this variable at this stage. Thus, the upcoming multiple regression analyses (OLS and ordered logit models) stick to the following variables:

- **Input variables:** Degree of democracy, democratic history, ethnic fractionalization, interaction term (democracy * democratic history);
- **Throughput/Output variables:** General governance, income distribution (Gini Index), unemployment rate, Human Development Index (absolute and relative).

OLS Estimates

There are a variety of strategies to find an appropriate model. An initial suggestion is to use a *kitchen-sink approach*, which means using all independent variables as regressors. However, this procedure mostly leads to insignificant coefficients (table 16).
In greater detail, concerning the output variables, only the variables general governance and HDI (absolute) are significant in two of the waves. The positive sign of general governance indicates that states can generate legitimacy via the output channel if they provide better governance (in terms of higher state effectiveness and less corruption). In contrast, the negative sign of HDI (absolute) indicates that more developed states are, ceteris paribus, less legitimate than less developed states. Thus, more developed states have to perform better in other output variables (for example in terms of general governance) and/or in the input channel to achieve high legitimacy. However, this interpretation should be treated with caution since the sign of the HDI (absolute) variable is negative in the regression but positive in the bivariate case. This phenomenon may be caused by multicollinearity or a suppression effect. Regarding the other three output variables (Gini Index, HDI (relative), and the unemployment rate), the kitchen-sink approach provides no clear evidence since, for the most part, the coefficients are not significant at all. That already raises the question whether one should exclude these variables from the model.
With respect to the input variables, there is some evidence in the ca. 2001 wave that the degree of democracy, a country's democratic history, and the interaction between

Table 16: OLS Estimates Based on Gilley's Legitimacy Scores – Kitchen-Sink Approach

Dependent: Legitimacy	Gilley ca. 2001			Gilley ca. 2008			Gilley ca. 2012		
	(1)			(2)			(3)		
	Coeff.	t-value	p-value	Coeff.	t-value	p-value	Coeff.	t-value	p-value
Intercept	6.43***	5.73	0.000	11.43***	2.72	0.010	5.09	1.65	0.11
Input Variables									
Democracy	0.21**	2.54	0.014	0.17	0.78	0.442	0.08	0.59	0.557
Democratic History	-0.08*	-1.70	0.095	0.03	0.28	0.784	-0.01	-0.06	0.955
Democracy*DemocraticHistory[1]	0.08***	3.95	0.000	0.07	1.45	0.156	0.06	1.60	0.117
Ethnic Fractionalization	-0.42	-0.95	0.349	-1.26	-1.27	0.211	0.60	0.68	0.503
Throughput/Output Variables									
General Governance	1.05***	4.80	0.000	1.19***	2.77	0.008	1.03***	3.20	0.003
Gini Index	-0.00	-0.11	0.910	0.01	0.24	0.811	0.01	0.53	0.601
HDI (absolute)	-4.20***	-2.82	0.007	-9.85**	-2.60	0.013	-1.53	-0.53	0.597
HDI (relative)	0.14	0.95	0.345	-1.01*	-1.91	0.064	-2.52	-0.05	0.958
Unemployment Rate	-0.02	-1.30	0.200	-0.03	-1.03	0.308	-0.08**	-2.27	0.029
R^2		0.767			0.589			0.597	
Adjust. R^2		0.729			0.497			0.506	
Observations		65			50			50	

[1] - Interaction term is mean centered.
* - at 10%-level significant ** - at 5%-level significant *** - at 1%-level significant

Note: Normality assumption of the error term is not violated.

democracy and democratic history are able to explain legitimacy. Again, this result should be treated with caution since the results are only significant in the first wave but not in the second and third wave (although one should notice that the signs of the second wave are similar to the first wave; a potential reason could be that each wave contains partly different countries). Since the interaction term is mean centered, the coefficient of democracy equals the marginal effect at the mean of democracy. Since the coefficient of the interaction term is positive, input legitimacy is high in countries in which both the values of democracy and democratic history are larger (or smaller) than their mean values. In contrast, it is possible that legitimacy declines if the democracy score is larger (smaller) than the mean democracy score and the democratic history scores is smaller (larger) than the mean democratic history score (see Appendix J for a mathematical and graphical illustration). This implies that more democracy can reduce legitimacy if the country has no democratic history. In other words, the importance of democracy is higher in countries which have a long democratic history. In contrast, if a country has no democratic history, it is legitimacy-enhancing to put an autocratic regime into place. These findings support the idea that democracies cannot easily be 'exported' to countries with no democratic history since the state would run into a legitimacy crisis. Instead of shock therapy, a gradual transformation from an autocratic system to a democratic system seems to be the better alternative to maintain legitimacy during the transformation process. However, although the sign of the interaction term is positive in all three waves, one should note that the coefficients are not significant in the second and the third wave. In this vein, the interaction term should be interpreted with caution. Similar to the throughput/output channel, the question remains whether one should exclude some variables from the model (in particular, ethnic fractionalization since it is insignificant in all waves).

Although the kitchen-sink approach already provides some fruitful insights, it remains the question why most of the coefficients are insignificant. There are two reasons. First, insignificant coefficients could be caused by multicollinearity since multicollinearity leads to higher standard errors. To check for this, I calculate the variance inflation factors (VIFs) for all three waves (table 17). A variance inflation factor (VIF) larger than 10 signals severe multicollinearity.[143] As table 17 shows, democracy is affected by multicollinearity in the 2008 wave (VIF=11.16). This may also explain why democracy is insignificant in the 2008 wave since the t-value of democracy would be 3.34 (which is the square root of 11.16) times larger if democracy were uncorrelated with all other independent variables.[144] Besides democracy, other independent variables also show relatively high VIFs such as general governance (VIF_{2001}=7.21; VIF_{2008}=5.74; VIF_{2012}=4.24) and HDI (absolute) (VIF_{2001}=5.28; VIF_{2008}=9.09; VIF_{2012}=5.06). This is not surprising since both variables are highly correlated ($r_{2001}=0.81^{***}$; $r_{2008}=0.74^{***}$, $r_{2012}=0.73^{***}$). However, although the VIFs of democracy, general governance, and HDI (absolute) are high, multicollinearity seems to have only a minor impact on the results, in particular since the variables affected are significant in most cases (or the variables not affected by multicollinearity are insignificant) with the exception of the variable democracy.

143 The variance inflation factor (VIF) is the R^2 of an auxiliary regression in which all independent variables except one try to explain the omitted variable. A VIF above 10 means that the independent variables can explain more than 90% of the variance of the omitted variable, thereby indicating linear dependency.

144 The square root of the variance inflation factor of democracy indicates how much larger the standard error (or much smaller the t-values) is in comparison to the situation where democracy is uncorrelated with all other independent variables (Montgomery et al., 2012, 297).

Table 17: Kitchen-Sink Approach – Variance Inflation Factors

VIFs	Gilley ca. 2001	Gilley ca. 2008	Gilley ca. 2012
	(1)	(2)	(3)
Input Variables			
Democracy	5.62	**11.16**	6.72
Democratic History	3.12	4.37	5.20
Democracy*DemocraticHistory	2.64	5.99	2.73
Ethnic Fractionalization	1.38	1.93	1.71
Throughput/Output Variables			
General Governance	7.21	5.74	4.24
Gini Index	1.36	1.49	1.61
HDI (absolute)	5.28	9.09	5.06
HDI (relative)	1.13	5.60	3.14
Unemployment Rate	1.42	1.21	1.41

Source: Own computation, based on R package 'HH'

Second, an insignificant coefficient could simply indicate that the particular independent variable has no explanatory power. In this case, the models stated in table 16 are over-specified. Thus, following the principle of parsimony, one should exclude all regressors that have no explanatory power. There are several procedures to exclude regressors from the model (such as selecting the model with the lowest AIC or BIC). Here, to find an appropriate basic model for all three waves, I apply the backward regression technique and the Bayesian model averaging (BMA) procedure (the latter to confirm the results of the backward regression).

(i) Backward Regression. The backward regression technique starts with all variables and excludes – step-by-step – those variables that cause the smallest decrease in R^2 when removed from the whole model (Kvanli et al., 2005, 502). This process continues as long as the decrease in R^2 is insignificant (or stops when the decrease in R^2 is significant). Table 18 provides the results for the three waves under investigation. The backward regressions provide some insights. First, one may call the relevance of the input variables into question since (i) both democratic history and ethnic fractionalization are not part of the model in all waves and (ii) both democracy and the interaction term (democracy * democratic history) are only part of the model in the first wave. Second, when investigating the output variables, general governance is the most important variable for explaining legitimacy since it is part of the model in all three waves. In addition, in two of the three waves, the absolute welfare level is also part of the model. Similar to table 16, the signs of the welfare level are negative. Further, the unemployment rate is only part of the model in the ca. 2012 wave. The other two variables (Gini Index and the relative change of the welfare level) should be excluded. In sum, the backward regressions already support the suggestion of

Table 18: OLS Estimates Based on Gilley's Legitimacy Scores – Backward Regression

Dependent: Legitimacy	Gilley ca. 2001			Gilley ca. 2008			Gilley ca. 2012		
	(1)			(2)			(3)		
	Coeff.	t-value	p-value	Coeff.	t-value	p-value	Coeff.	t-value	p-value
Intercept	5.81***	6.79	0.000	7.35***	5.25	0.000	5.48***	19.87	0.000
Input Variables									
Democracy	0.16**	2.02	0.048						
Democratic History									
Democracy*DemocraticHistory[1]	0.07***	3.72	0.000						
Ethnic Fractionalization									
Throughput/Output Variables									
General Governance	0.98***	5.55	0.000	1.63***	5.89	0.000	1.05***	6.82	0.000
Gini Index									
HDI (absolute)	-3.78***	-2.84	0.006	-4.10**	-2.11	0.040			
HDI (relative)									
Unemployment Rate							-0.08**	-2.78	0.008
R^2		0.738			0.501			0.542	
Adjust. R^2		0.721			0.480			0.523	
Observations		64			50			50	

[1] - Interaction term is mean centered.
* - at 10%-level significant ** - at 5%-level significant *** - at 1%-level significant

Rothstein (2009) that the throughput/output channel has the strongest impact on legitimacy.

The backward regression procedure shows that democratic history, ethnic fractionalization, the Gini Index, and the relative change of the welfare level (HDI (relative)) should not be part of the basic model. However, since the interaction term consists of democratic history, it is common statistical practice to keep this variable. Thus, I follow this convention. Further, the *core variables* are general government and the absolute welfare level (HDI (absolute)). Democracy, the interaction term, and the unemployment rate are *important variables* since they seem to have explanatory power but not, for whatever reason, in every wave. Finally, ethnic fractionalization, the Gini Index, a country's democratic history, and the relative welfare change are *less important variables* since they may have explanatory power which is, however, to a wide extent mitigated when controlling for other variables (i.e. they become statistically insignificant).

Bayesian Model Averaging (BMA). As an alternative to the backward regression technique, it is also possible to apply Bayesian model averaging (BMA) as a model selection strategy. Here, I use BMA to confirm the results above. In short, BMA estimates all possible models (which equals 2^K models, where K is the amount of independent variables) and gives back the probability that a particular independent variable is part of the model (for further details, see Zeugner, 2011).

Table 19: Bayesian Model Averaging - R Output

Dependent: Legitimacy ca. 2001

	PIP	Post Mean	Post SD	Cond.Pos.Sign
General Governance	**0.99966**	**1.0003716**	**0.2223673**	**1.000000**
Democracy*DemocraticHistory	**0.96704**	**0.0559008**	**0.0232020**	**1.000000**
HDI (absolute)	**0.62498**	**-2.0500454**	**1.9857633**	**0.000000**
Democracy	0.39363	0.0601637	0.0953863	0.980577
Unemployment Rate	0.25009	-0.0053414	0.0120945	0.000000
Democratic History	0.20466	-0.0114056	0.0318724	0.000220
HDI (relative)	0.20175	0.0366807	0.1008855	1.000000
Ethnic Fractionalization	0.15239	-0.0557144	0.2222308	0.000000
Gini Index	0.12903	-0.0007989	0.0045470	0.004341

Dependent: Legitimacy ca. 2008

	PIP	Post Mean	Post SD	Cond.Pos.Sign
General Governance	**0.97654**	**1.3364841**	**0.4098366**	**1.000000**
HDI (absolute)	**0.53986**	**-2.8150815**	**3.5010437**	**0.000625**
Democracy*DemocraticHistory	0.31970	0.0151593	0.0327922	1.000000
HDI (relative)	0.23700	-0.1052736	0.3558760	0.294904
Democracy	0.19254	0.0137543	0.1087416	0.410282
Unemployment Rate	0.19165	-0.0062033	0.0190828	0.000000
Ethnic Fractionalization	0.18718	-0.1631576	0.5624745	0.021171
Democratic History	0.15604	0.0111114	0.0497320	1.000000
Gini Index	0.14830	0.0018051	0.0095525	0.925744

Dependent: Legitimacy ca. 2012

	PIP	Post Mean	Post SD	Cond.Pos.Sign
General Governance	**0.99876**	**1.0366329**	**0.2181715**	**1.000000**
Unemployment Rate	**0.79603**	**-0.0609933**	**0.0404231**	**0.000000**
Democracy*DemocraticHistory	0.34398	0.0129472	0.0227815	1.000000
Democratic History	0.20556	0.0167029	0.0487943	0.999077
HDI (absolute)	0.18782	-0.3625570	1.1739132	0.004468
Ethnic Fractionalization	0.17624	0.1196938	0.4203177	0.999475
Gini Index	0.16868	0.0024561	0.0093398	0.994928
HDI (relative)	0.15375	2.7747772	16.314086	0.865498
Democracy	0.15239	-0.0005130	0.0412641	0.366670

One has to make some assumptions to run BMA. First, although having a theoretical background (which is the input-output framework), I assume that the true model is unknown. This implies that I abstain from including some fixed regressors which should be part of the model according to theory. Second, I assume that each model has an equal probability to be selected (in terms of BMA, I apply a uniform model prior). Having nine different independent variables (K=9), the expected model size is K/2=4.5 (Sala-i-Martin et al., 2004, 818).[145] In turn, this also means that the prior inclusion probability is 4.5/9=0.5 (Sala-i-Martin et al., 2004, 823).[146] Based on these assumptions, table 19 presents the results for the three waves (using the R package BMS with default settings). To show which variables have inclusion probabilities larger than 0.5, I mark them bold. As table 19 shows, the inclusion probabilities (PIP) differ across waves. However, this is not surprising since the coefficients of the kitchen-sink approach (table 16) and the backward regression technique (table 18) already suggest that not all variables are equally important in every wave. When focusing on the variables with a posterior inclusion probability larger than 0.5, these are nearly the same variables as in the case of the backward regression (except democracy in the ca. 2001 wave). Thus, the results of BMA correspond to the results of the backward regressions. Interestingly, BMA also confirms that the sign of HDI (absolute) is negative in multiple regression analyses (cond. pos. sign is close to zero), although the bivariate correlation between HDI (absolute) and legitimacy is positive.
Both strategies (backward regression and BMA) lead to comparable results. Thus, I argue that the basic model consists of both *core variables* and *important variables* plus democratic history (since it is part of the interaction term):

- **Input variables:** Degree of democracy, democratic history, interaction term (democracy * democratic history);
- **Throughput/Output variables:** General governance, unemployment rate, HDI (absolute).

Based on these variables, I again perform OLS regressions (table 20). The resulting coefficients are largely comparable to those of the kitchen-sink approach (table 16). Regarding the input variables, the coefficients have the same signs and similar levels of significance in all waves. This supports the hypothesis that the importance of democracy for legitimacy depends on the democratic history of a country. When focusing on the throughput/output variables, the levels of significance and the signs of the coefficients largely equal those of the kitchen-sink approach (exceptions are the coefficient of the unemployment rate which becomes significant at the 1%-level in the ca. 2012 wave and the coefficient of general governance which becomes significant at the 5%-level in the ca. 2008 wave). Referring to HDI (absolute), I suggest to interpret the coefficient as follows: An increase of the welfare level of a country, ceteris paribus,

145 Theoretically, the expected model size $\bar{k}$ is K/2 for a uniform model prior (K = amount of independent variables). Of course, a researcher can assume a model size that is larger or smaller. (Sala-i-Martin et al., 2004, 818)

146 The prior inclusion probability can be calculated by dividing the expected model size $\bar{k}$ over the amount of independent variables K ($\bar{k}$/K). (Sala-i-Martin et al., 2004, 818)

Table 20: OLS Estimates Based on Gilley's Legitimacy Scores – The Basic Model

Dependent: Legitimacy	Gilley ca. 2001			Gilley ca. 2008			Gilley ca. 2012		
	(1)			(2)			(3)		
	Coeff.	t-value	p-value	Coeff.	t-value	p-value	Coeff.	t-value	p-value
Intercept	5.92***	6.32	0.000	4.92**	2.57	0.014	6.38***	4.69	0.000
Input Variables									
Democracy	0.20**	2.29	0.026	0.18	0.86	0.397	0.06	0.52	0.606
Democratic History	-0.08*	-1.69	0.097	0.05	0.497	0.622	0.02	0.16	0.873
Democracy*De mocraticHistory[1]	0.09***	4.41	0.000	0.07	1.444	0.156	0.05	1.58	0.121
Throughput/Output Variables									
General Governance	0.99***	4.53	0.000	1.06**	2.49	0.012	1.08***	4.17	0.000
HDI (absolute)	-3.45**	-2.42	0.018	-3.21**	-1.72	0.093	-2.23	-1.26	0.214
Unemployment Rate	-0.02	-1.49	0.145	-0.02	-0.70	0.498	-0.09***	-3.19	0.003
R^2		0.726			0.539			0.637	
Adjust. R^2		0.700			0.476			0.591	
Observations		70			51			54	

[1] - Interaction term is mean centered.
* - at 10%-level significant ** - at 5%-level significant *** - at 1%-level significant

Note: Normality assumption of the error term is not violated. Democracy is close to multicollinearity in the ca. 2008 wave (VIF=10.59).

reduces legitimacy. A first explanation for this finding is that a higher welfare level increases the demands of the citizens toward the state due to raising aspirations.

All in all, the basic model fits well to explain legitimacy across states since only six variables explain a huge part of legitimacy's variance.[147] However, the determinants of the basic model are only partly congruent with the determinants proposed by Gilley (2006b), in particular regarding (i) the role of democracy and (ii) the role of welfare (gains):

- *The Role of Democracy.* Gilley (2006b) argues that democratic rights (measured in terms of Freedom Houses' civil liberties scores) enhance state legitimacy. In

147 Plots of the predicted legitimacy values against the original legitimacy values can be found in Appendix K.

slight contrast to this, I find that the impact of the degree of democracy on legitimacy depends on a country's democratic history. This relationship becomes even more apparent when analyzing only low GDP per capita countries (< 14000 $) (see Appendix K). In the case of high GDP per capita countries (> 14000 $), the effect vanishes due to statistical reasons.[148] Hence, one cannot simply argue that more democracy leads to more legitimacy. Rather, it is necessary to control for the democratic history of a country, which shapes citizens' attitudes toward democracy. As a logical consequence, a rapid increase of the degree of democracy may lead to a temporary legitimacy crisis. This idea is not new. For example, Lipset (1959, 87) argues that "crises of legitimacy occur during a transition to a new social structure". Similarly, Habermas (1975, 48) also notes that "legitimation crises result from a need for legitimation that arises from changes in the political system (even when normative structures remain unchanged) and that cannot be met by the existing supply of legitimation."

- *The Role of Welfare.* Gilley (2006b, 57) also argues, based on bivariate correlations, that welfare gains (measured as the relative change of the HDI) increase legitimacy. In contrast, I find that the welfare change (i.e. welfare gains) has no explanatory power as both backward regressions and BMA indicate. Instead, strongly challenging previous legitimacy research (see chapter 4.2.1), I argue that a higher welfare *level*, ceteris paribus, lowers legitimacy.[149] An explanation for this may be that a higher welfare level raises citizens' demands toward the state due to higher aspirations, thereby causing a decline in legitimacy. The economics of happiness provide similar results (Easterlin, 2001; Frey & Stutzer, 2002; Graham, 2005). According to Easterlin (2001), a raising level of welfare (in terms of GDP per capita) does only increase national happiness up to a certain level; beyond this point, even more welfare has no positive effect on happiness. A potential explanation is that higher income levels lead to higher aspirations, mitigating the positive effect of income over time (Easterlin, 2001, 473). Another reason for the negative relationship between the welfare level and legitimacy may be that a higher welfare level is a proxy for i) value pluralism or ii) changing values (e.g. Gjefsen (2012) finds that post-material values negatively impact legitimacy). In both cases, it is harder for the state to enact policies that are in accordance with (heterogeneous) interests (and values) of the citizens such that legitimacy declines.[150]

148 However, it is not surprising that the effect in high-income countries vanishes since i) there is very little variance in the degree of democracy, ii) the models consist only of a few observations, and iii) the models are over-specified since multicollinearity problems arise. See Appendix L for the results.

149 As above, when splitting the sample into low and high-income countries (GDP per capita larger or lower than 14000 $), it turns out that the negative sign of the HDI is mainly driven by the low-income countries. See Appendix L for further details.

150 Alesina and Spolaore (2005) come to a similar conclusion. However, they argue that a larger state size increases preference heterogeneity, which makes it harder to govern the state.

Multiple regression analyses also show that both input and throughput/output variables matter for explaining legitimacy, although the results strongly suggest that legitimacy mainly depends on the output side. Nonetheless, there is evidence that legitimacy hinges on at least two distinct channels as proposed by Scharpf (1970, 1999). Furthermore, the basic model roughly explains between 50% and 70% of legitimacy's variance, depending on the particular wave.[151] Thus, the basic model captures not all factors that impact legitimacy. Finally, despite all evidence, I treat legitimacy as a metric variable in this chapter. Since legitimacy is an ordinal variable in the narrow sense, it thus remains the question whether the results are robust when applying models for ordinal variables.

Robustness of the Basic Model: Ordered Logit Estimates

Although I already found a sound basic model, it may be problematic to treat legitimacy as a (quasi-)metric variable. In order to cope with methodological shortcomings, this chapter assumes that legitimacy is an ordinal variable and investigates whether applying discrete choice models leads to similar results. To approach this research question, one needs (i) to define legitimacy as a discrete variable and (ii) to choose a discrete choice model. Regarding the first point, I define two different discrete legitimacy variables, namely one that has four and one that has ten categories:[152]

- *Legitimacy (Four Discrete Categories).* The first discrete legitimacy variable consists of four categories (1 to 4). Table 21 displays how I address Gilley's continuous legitimacy scores to the four discrete categories.

Table 21: Legitimacy as Four-Categorical Variable

Gilley's Legitimacy Scores	[0,2.5)	[2.5,5)	[5,7.5)	[7.5,10]
Discrete Category	1	2	3	4

- *Legitimacy (Ten Discrete Categories).* As an alternative, I also define a discrete legitimacy variable that consists of ten categories (1 to 10). Again, I use Gilley's continuous legitimacy scores (2006a, 2012). Table 22 indicates this procedure.

Table 22: Legitimacy as Ten-Categorical Variable

Gilley's Legitimacy Scores	[0,1.5)	[1.5,2.5)	[2.5,3.5)	[3.5,4.5)	[4.5,5.5)
Discrete Category	1	2	3	4	5
Gilley's Legitimacy Scores	[5.5,6.5)	[6.5,7.5)	[7.5,8.5)	[8.5,9.5)	[9.5,10]
Discrete Category	6	7	8	9	10

151 Although the basic model explains legitimacy within the entire set of countries, one should note that the results are mainly driven by low-income countries. When focusing solely on high-income countries, the model seems to be overspecified (mainly due to multicollinearity problems and the limited amount of observations) (see Appendix L).

152 I define two legitimacy variables to check whether the results are dependent on the amount of categories defined.

Second, I need to choose a discrete choice model (ordered logit or ordered probit). Here, I use ordered logit models. The reason is that ordered logit models are easier to interpret (in terms of the odds ratio; in fact, I am solely interested in the signs and the levels of significance of the coefficients). Based on these considerations, I estimate ordered logit models with legitimacy as a four-categorical variable and a ten-categorical variable. Tables 23 and 24 provide the results.
The results show that, in most cases, the signs and levels of significance are congruent with the OLS models (table 20). In greater detail, I find the following similarities or differences:

- *Democracy.* Concerning democracy, the ordered logit results are similar to those of OLS, irrespective of applying a four-categorical or a ten-categorical variable. In the 2001 wave, democracy is significantly positive, but it is not in the 2008 and 2012 waves.
- *Democratic History*. Regarding democratic history, all coefficients are insignificant when applying ordered logit models. This is in slight contrast to

Table 23: Ordered Logit Estimates Based on Gilley's Legitimacy Scores – The Basic Model

Dependent: Legitimacy (four categorical)	Gilley ca. 2001			Gilley ca. 2008			Gilley ca. 2012		
	(1)			(2)			(3)		
	Coeff.	Wald-statistics	p-value	Coeff.	Wald-statistics	p-value	Coeff.	Wald-statistics	p-value
Input Variables									
Democracy	0.96**	6.033	0.014	0.31	0.650	0.420	0.03	0.008	0.927
Democratic History	-0.03	0.019	0.891	0.20	0.982	0.322	0.36	2.243	0.134
Democracy*DemocraticHistory[1]	0.38***	9.529	0.002	0.13	2.116	0.146	0.15*	3.015	0.083
Throughput/Output Variables									
General Governance	3.09***	8.351	0.004	2.35**	6.213	0.013	2.33***	7.654	0.006
HDI (absolute)	-13.12**	4.881	0.027	-4.87	3.278	0.138	-4.67	1.091	0.296
Unemployment Rate	-0.07	1.107	0.293	-0.01	0.009	0.923	-0.14**	4.901	0.027
Pseudo R^2 (Cox and Snell)	0.605			0.479			0.583		
Observations	69			51			54		

[1] - Interaction term is mean centered.
* - at 10%-level significant ** - at 5%-level significant *** - at 1%-level significant

Table 24: Ordered Logit Estimates Based on Gilley's Legitimacy Scores – The Basic Model

Dependent: Legitimacy (ten categorical)	Gilley ca. 2001 (1)			Gilley ca. 2008 (2)			Gilley ca. 2012 (3)		
	Coeff.	Wald-statistics	p-value	Coeff.	Wald-statistics	p-value	Coeff.	Wald-statistics	p-value
Input Variables									
Democracy	0.60^{**}	6.619	0.010	0.35	1.158	0.282	0.09	0.173	0.677
Democratic History	-0.22	2.683	0.101	0.08	0.236	0.627	0.06	0.126	0.723
Democracy*DemocraticHistory[1]	0.25^{***}	16.646	0.000	0.13^{*}	2.871	0.090	0.08	1.976	0.160
Throughput/Output Variables									
General Governance	2.59^{***}	15.673	0.000	1.59^{**}	5.561	0.018	2.03^{***}	13.727	0.000
HDI (absolute)	-9.56^{**}	6.093	0.014	-5.02^{*}	3.042	0.081	-3.22	0.964	0.326
Unemployment Rate	-0.05	1.448	0.229	-0.03	0.356	0.551	-0.13^{**}	6.242	0.012
Pseudo R^2 (Cox and Snell)	0.688			0.538			0.601		
Observations	69			50			54		

[1] - Interaction term is mean centered.
* - at 10%-level significant ** - at 5%-level significant *** - at 1%-level significant

the OLS results, according to which democratic history is significantly negative in the 2001 wave. In sum, one may suspect that the true effect of democratic history on legitimacy is zero.

- *Interaction Term (Democracy * Democratic History).* The results of the interaction term (democracy * democratic history) are similar to the OLS results. However, there are two exceptions. First, in the 2008 wave, the coefficient is significant at the 10%-level when applying a ten-category legitimacy measure. Second, the coefficient is also significant at the 10%-level in the 2012 wave when applying a four-category legitimacy measure. The results indicate that the impact of democracy on legitimacy depends on a country's democratic history.
- *General Governance.* Regarding general governance, the results of the ordered logit models confirm the OLS results. Improving the level of general governance has a strong positive effect on legitimacy.

- *HDI (absolute).* When analyzing the absolute welfare level with ordered logit models, the results are similar to those when applying OLS (in the case of the ordered logit models, the coefficients are likely to be less significant). Again, this shows that, ceteris paribus, more developed countries are less legitimate. Thus, developed states have to perform better (for example in terms of general governance) to maintain legitimacy.
- *Unemployment Rate.* The coefficients of the unemployment rate show the same pattern, irrespective of applying ordered logit models or OLS. They are insignificant in the ca. 2001 and ca. 2008 waves but highly significant in the ca. 2012 wave. As a consequence, one could raise the question whether the unemployment rate should be a part of the basic model.

5.2 Norris' Legitimacy Scores – An Alternative Legitimacy Measure

As an alternative to Gilley (2006a, 2012), I use Norris' legitimacy values as dependent variables in this chapter.[153] These are a composite index that consists of the dimensions 'support for regime performance' and 'confidence in regime institutions' (Norris, 1999, 2011; see also chapter 3.3.2). One of the main differences between both legitimacy measures is that Gilley's (2006b, 2012) measure is based on attitudinal and behavioral items, whereas Norris' measure solely relies on attitudinal items. Since Norris' legitimacy scores are solely based on items from the World Values Surveys (table 9), they are available at the individual level. This implies two advantages. First, using Norris' legitimacy scores allows one to analyze the determinants of legitimacy not only at the system but also at the individual level.[154] Second, Norris' legitimacy values refer to an exact year. This makes the analyses more accurate with respect to time (in Gilley's case in contrast, it is only possible to refer to a 'circa' date (ca. 2001, ca. 2008, and ca. 2012) since he uses data from different sources that differ in time).

The following chapter has two tasks. First, I investigate whether the determinants of the basic model show the same signs and levels of significance when replacing Gilley's (2006b, 2012) with Norris' legitimacy values at the system level (chapter 5.2.1). This serves as a further robustness check of the basic model (table 21). In short, when using Norris' legitimacy scores, the results show largely the same patterns as in Gilley's case (chapter 5.1): General governance has a positive impact and the absolute welfare level has a negative impact on legitimacy; however, the role of democracy seems puzzling. Second, I use both individual-level and system-level variables in one model to analyze what shapes an individual's legitimacy belief. Again, the focus lies on the question to what extent system-level variables are relevant (chapter 5.2.2). To deal with variables at different contextual levels, I use multilevel analysis as also conducted by other scholars (Booth & Seligson, 2009a, 2009b; Domański, 2005;

153 There is a strong correlation between Norris' and Gilley's legitimacy scores ($r_{2001}=0.71^{***}$; $r_{2008}=0.72^{***}$; $r_{2012}=0.73^{***}$). Thus, both measures reflect the same underlying concept (see chapter 3.3.2).

154 To obtain a score for each state, I aggregate the individual-level legitimacy scores (simple mean of the legitimacy values of all respondents of a country). Appendix F provides the legitimacy values for each country.

Gjefsen, 2012; Levi et al., 2009). Again, the results indicate that general governance and the absolute welfare level are the most robust variables. The role of democracy remains unclear.

5.2.1 Robustness of the Basic Model: OLS Estimates

Before analyzing the determinants of legitimacy based on Norris' legitimacy scores, two aspects should be considered. First, in every wave, some states are no part of Gilley's (2006b, 2012) but part of the Norris' legitimacy data and vice versa.[155] Thus, the observations (i.e. the countries) are not completely congruent. Second, since Norris' legitimacy values refer to a concrete year, I modify the independent variables with respect to the date of survey of the dependent variable.[156] This approach differs from the approach when using Gilley's scores as dependent variables (since I simply use the data that correspond to 2001, 2008, and 2012 according to Gilley's suggestion). Regarding the data preparation, I follow the same strategy as above (see chapter 5.1.1). Based on these modifications, I run a regression for each wave with the determinants of the basic model as independent variables. Table 25 shows the results.
As the results indicate, the variables of the basic model have different explanatory power in the three waves since R^2 varies between 0.453 and 0.585 (adjusted R^2 varies between 0.383 and 0.539 respectively). Further, the significance of the coefficients varies across waves. On the one hand, the impact of general governance and the absolute welfare level (HDI) is stable across waves (always significant at the 5% level at minimum). In addition, the unemployment rate is also significant in two out of the three waves. On the other hand, the role of input variables is unclear since they are mostly insignificant (except in the ca. 2001 wave). A short analysis of each wave is provided in the following:

- *Ca. 2001 Wave.* When analyzing the ca. 2001 wave, the determinants of the basic model explain Norris' legitimacy scores very well (R^2=0.581 and adjusted R^2=0.539). The coefficients of the input and output variables are mostly significant (except democracy) and show the expected signs. When plotting the predicted legitimacy scores of the model against the actual legitimacy scores (see Appendix K), one can identify two potential outliers (Vietnam and

155 In greater detail, regarding the 2001 wave, I add Iceland, Iraq, Kyrgyzstan, Luxembourg, Saudi Arabia, and Vietnam to the data. And further, I drop Armenia, Austria, Azerbaijan, Brazil, Colombia, Dominican Republic, El Salvador, Georgia, New Zealand, Norway, Switzerland, Taiwan, and Uruguay due to no data. With respect to the 2008 wave, Andorra, Guatemala, Hungary, and Iraq are added.

156 Exceptions are the absolute HDI values. Here, I take the 2000 HDI values for all countries of the ca. 2001 wave and the mean of the 2000 and 2010 HDI value for all countries of the ca. 2006 wave (when not possible, I take the 2010 values).
Another problem is the computation of the democratic history values of some countries. That affects Iceland (I assume the value ten since no democratic history value is available), Malta (I approximate Malta's democratic history with value 6.5 since the Freedom House index suggests some partly free periods during the 70s and 80s) in the 2001 wave, and Andorra (I assume the value five since it is democratic in modern times but was not in the 70s according to the Freedom House index) in the ca. 2006 wave.

Table 25: Robustness of the Basic Model: Alternative Legitimacy Measure – OLS Estimates

Dependent: Legitimacy (Norris)	Norris ca. 2001			Norris ca. 2006			Norris ca. 2012		
	(1)			(2)			(3)		
	Coeff.	t-value	p-value	Coeff.	t-value	p-value	Coeff.	t-value	p-value
Intercept	8.57***	8.261	0.000	8.31***	7.074	0.000	8.63***	8.584	0.000
Input Variables									
Democracy	0.11	1.27	0.211	-0.18	-1.481	0.145	-0.14	-1.628	0.110
Democratic History	-0.10*	-1.89	0.063	0.03	0.363	0.718	-0.00	-0.028	0.978
Democracy*DemocraticHistory[1]	0.08***	3.80	0.000	0.02	0.591	0.557	0.02	1.072	0.289
Throughput/Output Variables									
General Governance	0.73***	3.37	0.001	1.06***	3.913	0.000	0.87***	4.583	0.000
HDI (absolute)	-6.20***	-4.13	0.000	-3.46**	-2.540	0.014	-3.23**	-2.425	0.019
Unemployment Rate	-0.04**	-2.46	0.017	-0.01	-0.202	0.841	-0.06***	-2.982	0.004
R^2		0.581			0.453			0.585	
Adjust. R^2		0.539			0.383			0.533	
Observations		66			54			55	

[1] - Interaction term is mean centered.
* - at 10%-level significant ** - at 5%-level significant *** - at 1%-level significant

Note: Normality assumption of the error term is violated in regression (1).

Morocco). When excluding these countries from the data, the model fit even increases (R^2=0.649 and adjusted R^2=0.612).[157]

- *Ca. 2006 Wave.* When using the ca. 2006 legitimacy scores, the basic model seems to be over-specified since a variety of coefficients are insignificant. When plotting the predicted legitimacy scores against the actual legitimacy scores (see Appendix K again), I again find two potential outliers (Vietnam and Ethiopia). When excluding these countries from the data, the model fit increases

157 In this case, the coefficients are basically the same. The coefficient of democracy even turns significant at the 1% level and the coefficient of the unemployment rate becomes significant at the 10% level.

visibly (R^2=0.582 and adjusted R^2=0.525).[158] Since the model seems to be over-specified, a stepwise exclusion of the insignificant independent variables leads to the result that, using the adjusted R^2 as the selection criterion, only democracy, general governance, and the absolute welfare level remain as explanatory variables (adjusted R^2=0.412). When excluding the potential outliers (Vietnam and Ethiopia) from the data, the model fit increases as well (adjusted R^2=0.550). Thus, a minimalist model seems better to explain Norris' legitimacy scores in ca. 2006 (table 26). Interestingly, democracy has a significantly negative effect on legitimacy in this case.

Table 26: Minimalist Model (Norris ca. 2006) – OLS Estimates

Dependent: Legitimacy (Norris)	Norris ca. 2006			Norris ca. 2006		
	(1)			(2)		
	Full Sample			Without Vietnam and Ethiopia		
	Coeff.	t-value	p-value	Coeff.	t-value	p-value
Intercept	8.81***	9.581	0.000	9.83***	11.592	0.000
Input Variables						
Democracy	-0.23***	-3.743	0.000	-0.19***	-3.538	0.000
Throughput/Output Variables						
General Governance	1.21***	6.044	0.000	1.35***	8.014	0.000
HDI (absolute)	-3.45**	-2.627	0.011	-5.37***	-4.649	0.000
R^2	0.445			0.576		
Adjust. R^2	0.412			0.550		
Observations	54			52		

* - at 10%-level significant ** - at 5%-level significant *** - at 1%-level significant

- *Ca. 2012 Wave.* In the ca. 2012 wave, the basic model seems to be over-specified since none of the input variables turn significant.[159] A stepwise exclusion of the most insignificant variables leads to the result that the adjusted R^2 (adjusted R^2=0.542) becomes maximal when dropping democratic history.[160]

158 Here, all levels of significance and all signs of the coefficients stay the same (except the absolute welfare level which becomes significant at the 1% level).

159 When plotting predicted against actual legitimacy scores, a potential outlier may be Qatar (plot is provided in Appendix M). However, since a drop of Qatar leads to a reduced R^2 and adjusted R^2, I leave it in the sample.

160 I am aware of the convention that one should not have an interaction term (democracy * democratic history) in the regression without the main effects (democracy). Nonetheless, although

The remaining variables are democracy (coeff.= -0.14**, p-value=0.01), the interaction term (coeff.=0.02, p-value=0.228), general governance (coeff.=0.87***, p-value=0.000), the unemployment rate (coeff.=-0.064***, p-value=0.003), and the absolute level of welfare (coeff.=-3.22**, p-value=0.015). Interestingly, similar to the ca. 2006 wave, the degree of democracy has a significantly negative impact on legitimacy.

To sum up, using Norris' legitimacy scores as dependent variables basically leads to the same patterns as when using Gilley's (2006a, 2012) legitimacy scores.[161] On the one hand, two variables show a stable impact on legitimacy across waves, namely general governance (always shows a strong positive effect on legitimacy) and the absolute welfare level (HDI) (always has a strong negative effect on legitimacy). In particular, the negative impact of the absolute welfare level on legitimacy again indicates that citizens of more developed states may have higher aspirations and, thus, also higher expectations of the state. If the state is not able to meet these expectations, citizens' legitimacy beliefs will decline such that a legitimacy crisis might occur.

On the other hand, the impact of the other variables (democracy, democratic history, interaction term, and unemployment rate) is not stable across waves. Regarding the unemployment rate, empirical evidence suggests a negative effect of the unemployment rate on legitimacy since all coefficients point in this direction (always negative, also in Gilley's (2006a, 2012) case, table 21). However, since I only find significant coefficients in two of the three waves (and only one significant coefficient in Gilley's case, table 21), one should be careful in concluding that a higher unemployment rate leads, ceteris paribus, to less legitimacy. When focusing on the input variables, the role of democracy is puzzling. In the basic model setting (table 26), democracy is insignificant in two of the three waves and only significant at the 5% level in interaction with democratic history in the ca. 2001 wave. When excluding insignificant independent variables in the ca. 2006 and the ca. 2012 wave, I find a significant but negative impact of democracy on legitimacy, which contrasts with the underlying theory (Scharpf, 1970).

To conclude, the determinants of legitimacy are largely the same, irrespective of using Gilley's (2006a, 2012) or Norris' legitimacy scores. The basic model seems to be appropriate, although one should mention that the results are dependent on the particular wave.

5.2.2 Robustness of the Basic Model: Multi-Level Analysis

Since Norris' legitimacy values are available at the individual level, it is possible to perform multi-level analyses (MLA). Multi-level analysis is one of the most widely applied statistical method in legitimacy research since it is possible to control for

the interaction effect is still part of the model, the exclusion of the main effect improves the model fit.

161 In the case of Norris' legitimacy scores, dividing into a low-income and high-income country sub-sample (GDP per capita less or more than 14000$) largely leads to similar results as when using the whole sample. See Appendix N for further details.

individual-level and system-level determinants (Booth & Seligson, 2009a; Domański, 2005; Gjefsen, 2012; Levi et al., 2009).
To account for the two levels (individual and country level), I apply a random intercept model (Bickel, 2007). Thus, I assume that individual-level determinants have the same impact on individual legitimacy beliefs *L* in all countries. In a formalized fashion, the coefficient ($\beta_1,...,\beta_n$) of each individual-level variable ($X_1,...,X_n$) is the same for all individuals in all countries. The intercept $\beta_{0,j}$ captures country differences (equation [19]).

$$L=\beta_{0,j}+\beta_1 X_1+...+\beta_n X_n+r \qquad [19]$$

Each country's intercept β_{0j} is explained by the determinants at the country level ($W_1,...,W_n$) (equation [20]).

$$\beta_{0,j}=\gamma_0+\gamma_1 W_1+...+\gamma_n W_n+u_{0,j} \qquad [20]$$

In sum, one can plug equation [19] into equation [20] to obtain the combined model that consists of individual-level and country-level variables (equation [21]).

$$L=\gamma_0+\gamma_1 W_1+...+\gamma_n W_n+u_{0,j}+\beta_1 X_1+...+\beta_n X_n+r \qquad [21]$$

I perform multi-level analyses (restricted maximum likelihood model (REML)) for the fourth, fifth, and sixth wave of the World Value Surveys using the MIXED procedure of SPSS (Baltes-Götz, 2013).[162] To do so, I merge the original WVS files (that contain the legitimacy beliefs and the individual-level variables) with a file that contains the country-level variables. The country-level variables equal the variables of the basic model, namely democracy, democratic history, an interaction term (democracy * democratic history), general governance, the unemployment rate, and the absolute level of welfare (HDI) (see chapter 5.1.2). Regarding the individual-level variables, I rely on the variables suggested by the existing literature (see chapter 4.2.2):

- *Age.* To measure the impact of a person's age, I apply a continuous age variable. Since the relationship between age and legitimacy could be linear, u-shaped, or inverted u-shaped, I also add age squared.[163]
- *Gender.* To account for the gender of a person, I include a dummy variable (1=male, 0=female).
- *Education.* A further variable is education. Here, I use five dummy variables (no education completed, completed primary education, completed secondary education, completed college education, and completed university education). In the regression, I incorporate the dummies for completed primary education,

162 Concerning the fourth wave of the WVS, I only have 33 countries in my sample. Since Gilley (2006a) merges the WVS and the EVS, he has more observations (>60).

163 Age and age squared are highly correlated, which may cause multicollinearity. However, since it is common practice to incorporate both variables into the regression (in particular in other research fields such as labor market econometrics), I follow this convention.

completed secondary education, completed college education, and completed university education. No education completed is the reference category.

- *Income Level.* Originally, the WVS provides ten ordinal income categories (from lowest to highest income group in a country).[164] Although the most precise strategy would be to code these variables as dummy variables, I treat the income variable as continuous ranging from 1 to 10 mainly due to reasons of space. Using income dummies leads to largely similar results (see below).
- *Religion.* Regarding religion, I code three dummies (religious person, no religious person, convinced atheist). In the regressions, I incorporate the religious person and atheist person dummies. No religious person is the reference category.
- *Media Contact.* Concerning media contact, it is necessary to differentiate between the different waves. In the fourth wave of the WVS, it is not possible to operationalize media contact since no appropriate items are available.[165] In the fifth wave of the WVS, I build the media contact variable based on three questions, namely whether the respondent has used newspaper, TV/Radio, and Internet/E-Mail in the last week. Finally, in the sixth wave, I build an index (mean of the items; assuming a quasi-metric scale level) of how often a person consumes daily news, TV news, radio news, and the internet (1 – never, 2 – less than monthly, 3 – monthly, 4 – weekly, 5 – daily).
- *Political Interest.* Next, regarding the political interest of the respondent, I use a dummy variable (1 – very/somewhat interested in politics, 0 – not very/not interested in politics).
- *Interpersonal Trust.* For interpersonal trust as well, I apply a dummy variable (1 – most people can be trusted, 0 – one needs to be very careful). Note that this item is only available in the fifth and the sixth wave of the WVS.
- *Life Satisfaction.* For measuring life satisfaction, I use the variable given by the WVS that varies from 1 (absolutely dissatisfied) to 10 (absolutely satisfied) (assuming that this variable is quasi-metric).
- *Victim of Crime.* To operationalize whether the respondent was a victim of crime, I apply a dummy variable (1 – respondent was a victim of a criminal act in the past year, 0 – respondent was not a victim of a criminal act in the past year). This item is only available in the sixth wave of the WVS.
- *Feeling of Safety.* Finally, the feeling of safety is measured by the question "In the last 12 months, how often have you or your family: Felt unsafe from crime in your own home?" (WVS Codebook, 2012, 14). Since the answer possibilities range from 1 (never) to 4 (often), I assume that it is a continuous variable. Similar to the item "Victim of crime", this item is only available in the sixth wave of the WVS.

---

164 Precisely, the question is: "On this card is an income scale on which 1 indicates the lowest income group and 10 the highest income group in your country. We would like to know in what group your household is. Please, specify the appropriate number, counting all wages, salaries, pensions and other incomes that come in." (WVS Codebook, 2012, 18)

165 I only find one item that could be used to measure media contact, namely how often a person watches TV. However, since this item has a lot of missing values, I abstain from using it in the regressions.

I do not include all individual-level variables that the literature suggests. This has different reasons and concerns the following variables:

- *Place of Residence and Political Positioning.* All three waves of the WVS contain items to capture both the place of residence of the respondent and its political positioning. Regarding the place of residence, it is possible to calculate five dummies that represent rural area (size of town under 2000 inhabitants), a small city/town (between 2000 and 20000 inhabitants), a medium city (between 20000 and 200000 inhabitants), a large city (between 100000 and 500000 inhabitants), and a metropolis (more than 500000 inhabitants). In a similar fashion, the political positioning of the respondent (originally measured on a continuous scale from 1 – left and 10 – right) can also be considered. I simply recommend calculating a dummy for left, center, and right political positioning.[166] However, although these items are available in every wave, I do not incorporate both items in the multi-level analyses due to missing values (both items have more than 20000 missing values in every wave). For example, in the fourth wave of the WVS, there are 33 observations at the country level when excluding the residence dummies and the political positioning dummies. When including both, the number of observations at the country level drops to 21.[167] Thus, I exclude both variables from the multi-level analyses. However, if I were to include both variables, the results would be in line with the findings of the existing literature: Respondents that are politically left-of-center (right-of-center) show significantly lower (higher) legitimacy beliefs than those in the center. Regarding the place of residence, I find a strong tendency that people living in larger cities show lower legitimacy values.[168]
- *Employment Status.* Concerning the employment status, it is possible to code eight dummies (full-time employed, part-time employed, self-employed, retired, housewife, students, unemployed, and other). Since the inclusion of the employment dummies leads in most cases to insignificant results (which is in line with previous findings), I drop the employment status dummies mainly for reasons of space. Appendix O shows the regression coefficients.
- *Sector of Employment.* An interesting question is whether people that are employed by the state show higher legitimacy values than people who work in private business. However, since the inclusion of such an item excludes all respondents that do not work, I omit this item.[169]

166 In detail, the dummy left political positioning is based on the values 1, 2, and 3 of the original scale. Center political positioning is based on 4,5,6, and 7. Right political positioning is based on 8,9, and 10.

167 Similarly, in the fifth wave of the WVS, the number of observations at the country level is 31 when including both variables and increases to 42 when excluding them. In the sixth wave, 40 observations are available when including the residence dummies and the political positioning dummies and 51 observations when excluding these variables.

168 See Appendix O. There, results are provided that contain the residence and the political positioning dummies.

169 See Appendix O, where a multi-level analysis is performed with employment sector dummies included.

- *Voting for Presidential Winner.* The literature suggests including a variable that shows whether the respondent has voted for the presidential winner. Unfortunately, to the best of my knowledge, the WVS does not provide an appropriate item.

Before performing multi-level analyses, I initially check the intra-class correlation coefficients (ICCs).[170] Since the ICCs are above 0.05 (ICC_{2001}=0.289, ICC_{2008}=0.351, ICC_{2012}=0.264), multi-level analyses should be preferred to (fixed effect) OLS estimations (Hayes, 2006, 394).[171]
Next, I need to decide whether the independent variables should be centered or not. There are three possibilities: Using the raw data, centering the variables at their grand mean, or centering the variables at their group means.[172] Here, I use raw data due to two reasons. First, the intercept and the coefficients can easily be interpreted. The intercept shows the average legitimacy value if all individual-level variables are zero.[173] Second, since I use no cross-level interaction terms (i.e. no random slopes), multicollinearity problems do not arise (which would make grand mean centering necessary). The coefficients of the independent variables do not change when using raw or grand mean centered data (Hox, 2002, 54-58).
Based on these considerations, I run several regressions for every wave. Tables 27-29 state the results. For each wave, I state several models: The basic model (all system-level variables included) and models that result when excluding step-by-step the most insignificant country-level variables. This procedure ends when the information criteria (AIC/BIC) stop decreasing. I also state the pseudo-R^2.[174] Note that the coefficients and the p-values of the individual-level variables do not change when excluding country-level variables (since I use a random intercept model such that the country-level variables only explain the intercept).

Results of Fourth Wave of the WVS (Norris ca. 2001). Table 27 provides the results of the multi-level analyses of the fourth wave. Concerning the individual-level variables, most coefficients show the expected signs (see chapter 4.2.2). First of all, there is a highly significant u-shaped relationship between age and legitimacy. According to the coefficients, people at an age of ca. 30 have the lowest legitimacy beliefs. Second, gender does not matter for legitimacy since it is insignificant, which is in line with previous findings (see chapter 4.2.2). Concerning education, the results indicate that

170 The intra-class correlation coefficient (ICC) shows how much of legitimacy's total variance is explained by country differences. Scholars mostly argue that an ICC above 0.05 (which means that at least 5% of legitimacy's variance is explained by country differences) indicates that a multi-level analysis should be executed. (Hayes, 2006, 394)

171 Note that the numerical values of the ICCs above may slightly change in regression analyses if one adds control variables with missing observations.

172 For further details on grand mean and group mean centering see Bickel (2007) or Heck and Thomas (2015).

173 Scholars argue that variables such as age cannot reasonably be interpreted when being zero. Thus, they prefer grand mean centering to avoid this problem.

174 I calculate the pseudo-R^2 according to Bickel (2007, 133). This is one minus the sum of the residuals and the intercept variance of the model over the residuals and the intercept variance of the null model.

higher educated people have lower legitimacy beliefs. A potential reason is that higher educated people are more critical of the state and its institutions. Fourth, a higher income lowers people's legitimacy beliefs (using dummies instead of the continuous variable leads to similar results). Fifth, religious persons show higher legitimacy beliefs than non-religious persons, whereas non-religious persons still have higher legitimacy beliefs than convinced atheists. Booth and Seligson (2009a, 114) provide a potential explanation for this phenomenon noting that "membership in particular denominations may expose one to certain political cues that might shape one's evaluations of the polity." Sixth, legitimacy beliefs are higher among those that are more politically interested. Finally, people with higher life satisfaction are also likely to have higher legitimacy beliefs. Having discussed the individual-level variables, I now turn to the analysis of the country-level variables. Model (1) includes all variables of the basic model. However, this model seems to be inappropriate since some variables are insignificant. As a consequence, I first exclude democracy and democratic history to obtain model (2). Since the information criteria (AIC/BIC) decrease, this step is reasonable. In model (2), both the unemployment rate and general governance are insignificant. Since general governance has the highest p-value in model (3), I suggest excluding general governance. However, since the exclusion of general governance leads to an increase of the information criteria, I do not follow this plan. Instead, I exclude the unemployment rate since this leads to a further reduction of the information criteria (however, pseudo-R^2 decreases). According to the information criteria, model (3) is the best model. Thus, multi-level analyses suggest that legitimacy beliefs can be explained at the country level by the interaction term, general governance, and the absolute welfare level. In greater detail, the effect of democracy on legitimacy seems to depend on a country's democratic history. This is the same result as in previous investigations (see chapters 5.1.2 and 5.2.1). Next, I find a positive effect of general governance on legitimacy (although only significant at the 10% level). This is also in line with the previous results. Moreover, the absolute welfare level has a negative impact on legitimacy. Again, this supports the interpretation that respondents of more developed countries have higher aspirations toward the state and, thus, also higher expectations of the services that the state has to provide.

Table 27: Multi-Level Analyses (Norris ca. 2001)

Model	(1)		(2)		(3)	
	Coeff.	p-value	Coeff.	p-value	Coeff.	p-value
Individual-Level Variables						
Intercept	7.777***	0.000	6.964***	0.000	7.506***	0.000
Age	-0.012***	0.000	-0.012***	0.000	-0.012***	0.000
Age^2	0.0002***	0.000	0.0002***	0.000	0.0002***	0.000
Male	0.011	0.543	0.011	0.543	0.011	0.543
Compl. primary school[a]	-0.221***	0.000	-0.221***	0.000	-0.221***	0.000
Compl. secondary school[a]	-0.318***	0.000	-0.318***	0.000	-0.318***	0.000
Compl. college[a]	-0.406***	0.000	-0.406***	0.000	-0.406***	0.000
Compl. university[a]	-0.447***	0.000	-0.447***	0.000	-0.447***	0.000
Income (continuous)	-0.022***	0.000	-0.022***	0.000	-0.022***	0.000
Religious Person[b]	0.256***	0.000	0.256***	0.000	0.256***	0.000
Atheist Person[b]	-0.252***	0.000	-0.252***	0.000	-0.252***	0.000
Media Contact	-	-	-	-	-	-
Political Interest	0.507***	0.000	0.507***	0.000	0.507***	0.000
Interpersonal Trust	-	-	-	-	-	-
Life Satisfaction	0.079***	0.000	0.079***	0.000	0.079***	0.000
Victim of Crime	-	-	-	-	-	-
Feels Unsafe	-	-	-	-	-	-
Country-Level Variables						
Democracy	0.072	0.553	-	-	-	-
Democratic History	-0.111	0.228	-	-	-	-
Democracy*DemocraticHistory[1]	0.097***	0.008	0.093***	0.000	0.091***	0.000
General Governance	0.543	0.182	0.335	0.279	0.532*	0.071
HDI (absolute)	-4.984**	0.035	-3.867*	0.054	-5.237***	0.006
Unemployment Rate	-0.040	0.108	-0.037	0.127	-	-
-2LL	165083		165079		165076	
AIC/BIC	165087/165104		165083/165100		165080/165097	
Pseudo-R^2	0.2334		0.2359		0.2281	
Observations (individual level)	41260		41260		41260	
Observations (country level)	33		33		33	

[1] - Interaction term is mean centered.
* - at 10%-level significant ** - at 5%-level significant *** - at 1%-level significant
[a] - reference category: no primary school completed [b] - reference category: no religious person
Note. I exclude both Democracy and Democratic History in two steps, but I state only the final result in model (2) due to reasons of space.
Note: When using dummies for Income instead of a continuous variable, legitimacy decreases – on average – in rising income quintiles. All other variables do not change significantly.

Results of the Fifth Wave of the WVS (Norris ca. 2008). Concerning the individual-level variables of the fifth wave of the WVS, some results are different compared to the fourth wave. First, the u-shaped age pattern can hardly be replicated since the coefficient of age is insignificant (the p-value is only slightly above 0.10). Since the quadratic term is significant, this suggests that legitimacy beliefs increase in age in a quadratic fashion. Second, the income variable is significantly positive (there is also a clear positive effect of income on legitimacy when using income dummies). Third, two new variables are part of the regressions, namely media contact and interpersonal trust. Here, the results show that more media contact seems to increase legitimacy beliefs.An explanation may be that "the more one sees, hears, or reads the news [...], the more likely this exposure would be to affect support for institutions" or the regime as a whole (Booth & Seligson, 2009a, 116). Similarly, interpersonal trust has a positive impact on legitimacy beliefs. This reflects the idea that "persons disposed by experience or by their personalities to place trust in others would be more likely to believe that government attends to or promotes their interests" (Booth & Seligson, 2009a, 116). Besides these differences, all other individual-level variables show the same impact as in the fourth wave (no significant effect of gender; more educated people show lower legitimacy beliefs; religious people show higher legitimacy beliefs than non-religious people, and non-religious people show still higher values that convinced atheists; and a positive impact of political interest and life satisfaction).

Concerning the country-level variables, a stepwise exclusion of the most insignificant explanatory variables leads to the result that democracy, general governance, and the absolute level of welfare are the most important variables (model (3)). These results are largely similar to those of the fourth wave. However, one should note that the measure of welfare is insignificant. A further exception is the role of democracy. In the fourth wave, the results suggest that the impact of democracy on legitimacy depends on a country's democratic history. In contrast, in the fifth wave, democracy seems to be independent of a country's democratic history and has, ceteris paribus, a negative effect on legitimacy beliefs. These findings mostly conform to those in chapter 5.2.1.

Table 28: Multi-Level Analyses (Norris ca. 2008)

Model	(1)		(2)		(3)	
	Coeff.	p-value	Coeff.	p-value	Coeff.	p-value
Individual-Level Variables						
Intercept	5.941***	0.000	5.959***	0.000	6.208***	0.000
Age	-0.004	0.118	-0.004	0.118	-0.004	0.118
Age^2	0.0001***	0.002	0.0001***	0.002	0.0001***	0.002
Male	-0.004	0.815	-0.004	0.815	-0.004	0.815
Compl. primary school[a]	-0.249***	0.000	-0.249***	0.000	-0.249***	0.000
Compl. secondary school[a]	-0.295***	0.000	-0.295***	0.000	-0.295***	0.000
Compl. college[a]	-0.322***	0.000	-0.322***	0.000	-0.322***	0.000
Compl. university[a]	-0.421***	0.000	-0.421***	0.000	-0.421***	0.000
Income (continuous)	0.038***	0.000	0.038***	0.000	0.038***	0.000
Religious Person[b]	0.290***	0.000	0.290***	0.000	0.290***	0.000
Atheist Person[b]	-0.240***	0.000	-0.240***	0.000	-0.240***	0.000
Media Contact	0.074***	0.000	0.074***	0.000	0.074***	0.000
Political Interest	0.375***	0.000	0.375***	0.000	0.375***	0.000
Interpersonal Trust	0.480***	0.000	0.480***	0.000	0.480***	0.000
Life Satisfaction	0.114***	0.000	0.114***	0.000	0.114***	0.000
Victim of Crime	-	-	-	-	-	-
Feels Unsafe	-	-	-	-	-	-
Country-Level Variables						
Democracy	-0.205	0.129	-0.206	0.114	-0.199***	0.004
Democratic History	0.053	0.486	0.053	0.468	-	-
Democracy*DemocraticHistory[1]	0.003	0.922	0.003	0.922	-	-
General Governance	0.732**	0.028	0.736**	0.021	0.868***	0.000
HDI (absolute)	-1.622	0.290	-1.647	0.266	-1.705	0.240
Unemployment Rate	-0.001	0.982	-	-	-	-
-2LL	203638		203633		203625	
AIC/BIC	203642/203660		203637/203655		203629/203647	
Pseudo-R^2	0.166		0.171		0.178	
Observations (individual level)	52496		52496		52496	
Observations (country level)	43		43		43	

[1] - Interaction term is mean centered.
* - at 10%-level significant ** - at 5%-level significant *** - at 1%-level significant
[a] - reference category: no primary school completed [b] - reference category: no religious person
Note: I exclude both Democratic History and the Interaction Term in two steps, but I state only the final result in model (3) due to reasons of space.
Note: When using dummies for Income instead of a continuous variable, legitimacy increases – on average – in rising income quintiles. All other variables do not change significantly.

Results of the Sixth Wave of the WVS (Norris ca. 2012). Concerning the individual-level variables, I obtain the following results. Similar to the fourth wave, a u-shaped relationship between age and legitimacy emerges. Regarding gender, male respondents show significantly lower legitimacy scores than female respondents. As in the previous waves, better-educated people show lower legitimacy beliefs. Regarding income, similar to the fifth wave, I find a significantly positive effect. This is in sharp contrast to the fourth wave (where income and legitimacy are negatively related).[175] Similar to the other waves, religious people show higher legitimacy beliefs than non-religious people; and non-religious people show still higher values than convinced atheists. In the same vein, legitimacy beliefs significantly increase when respondents have more media contact, higher political interest, more interpersonal trust, and higher life satisfaction. Finally, when a respondent was a victim of crime or feels unsafe, its legitimacy beliefs are significantly lowered. Here, a potential explanation is that "citizens victimized by crime might conclude that their victimization could have been prevented by more vigilant or effective public security efforts" such that they make the state responsible for the criminal act or the unsafe environment (Booth & Seligson, 2009a, 117). Regarding the country-level variables, the stepwise exclusion of the most insignificant independent variables leads to model (3) that contains democracy, general governance, the absolute welfare level, and the unemployment rate. Similar to the fifth wave, democracy has a negative impact on legitimacy beliefs. This challenges previous findings where (i) the effect of democracy depends on a country's democratic history or (ii) democracy has a positive impact on legitimacy. As in the previous empirical analyses, general governance has a significantly positive effect on legitimacy and the absolute welfare level has a negative effect. Finally, in this wave, I find that the coefficient of the unemployment rate is highly significant. Thus, the results suggest that a higher general unemployment rate leads to a reduction of state legitimacy.

In sum, multi-level analysis provides the same insights regarding the country-level variables since the positive effect of general governance and the negative effect of the absolute welfare level are robust across all three waves (signs always point in the same direction; however, in some waves, coefficients are insignificant). As in the previous investigations, the role of democracy is puzzling. In the fourth wave, the results suggest the inclusion of an interaction between democracy and democratic history. In contrast to this, in the fifth and sixth wave, democracy has a negative impact on state legitimacy. Regarding democratic history and the unemployment rate, there is no clear conclusion since their level of significance varies across waves. Thus, one could argue that, for example, the significant coefficient of the unemployment rate in the sixth wave either shows the impact of the financial crisis (considering that the unemployment rate lags behind the business cycle) or is just a statistical artifact. Thus,

175 Evidently, the impact of the income variable on legitimacy depends on the sample/wave. Since this result seems to be odd at the first glance, it might be possible that it is caused by different control variables that have been used in the different waves. Thus, I again check the income coefficient when solely using the variables that have been used in wave four in all three waves (this means that I exclude media contact and interpersonal trust in wave five; and I exclude media contact, interpersonal trust, victim of crime, and feels unsafe in wave six). However, the results remain largely stable. The income coefficients remain significantly positive in the fifth (0.03^{***}, $p=0.000$) and the sixth wave (0.070^{***}, $p=0.000$).

Table 29: Multi-Level Analyses (Norris ca. 2012)

Model	(1)		(2)		(3)	
	Coeff.	p-value	Coeff.	p-value	Coeff.	p-value
Individual-Level Variables						
Intercept	7.693***	0.000	7.661***	0.000	7.883***	0.000
Age	-0.012***	0.000	-0.012***	0.000	-0.012***	0.000
Age^2	0.0002***	0.000	0.0002***	0.000	0.0002***	0.000
Male	-0.053***	0.000	-0.053***	0.000	-0.053***	0.000
Compl. primary school[a]	-0.070**	0.017	-0.070**	0.017	-0.070**	0.017
Compl. secondary school[a]	-0.167***	0.000	-0.167***	0.000	-0.167***	0.000
Compl. college[a]	-0.175***	0.000	-0.175***	0.000	-0.175***	0.000
Compl. university[a]	-0.334***	0.000	-0.334***	0.000	-0.334***	0.000
Income (continuous)	0.057***	0.000	0.057***	0.000	0.057***	0.000
Religious Person[b]	0.253***	0.000	0.253***	0.000	0.253***	0.000
Atheist Person[b]	-0.198***	0.000	-0.198***	0.000	-0.198***	0.000
Media Contact	0.124***	0.000	0.124***	0.000	0.124***	0.000
Political Interest	0.405***	0.000	0.405***	0.000	0.405***	0.000
Interpersonal Trust	0.423***	0.000	0.423***	0.000	0.423***	0.000
Life Satisfaction	0.110***	0.000	0.110***	0.000	0.110***	0.000
Victim of Crime	-0.184***	0.000	-0.184***	0.000	-0.184***	0.000
Feels Unsafe	-0.079***	0.000	-0.079***	0.000	-0.079***	0.000
Country-Level Variables						
Democracy	-0.149*	0.063	-0.165***	0.001	-0.208***	0.000
Democratic History	-0.016	0.793	-	-	-	-
Democracy*DemocraticHistory[1]	0.024	0.196	0.022	0.177	-	-
General Governance	0.831***	0.000	0.829***	0.000	0.928***	0.000
HDI (absolute)	-3.735***	0.003	-3.647***	0.002	-3.386***	0.004
Unemployment Rate	-0.060***	0.006	-0.059***	0.006	-0.057***	0.007
-2LL	262941		262937		262933	
AIC/BIC	262945/262963		262941/262960		262937/262955	
Pseudo-R^2	0.2127		0.2145		0.2128	
Observations (individual level)	65416		65416		65416	
Observations (country level)	52		52		52	

[1] - Interaction term is mean centered.
* - at 10%-level significant ** - at 5%-level significant *** - at 1%-level significant
[a] - reference category: no primary school completed [b] - reference category: no religious person

Note: When using dummies for income instead of a continuous variable, legitimacy increases – on average – in rising income quintiles. All other variables do not change significantly.

more empirical research needs to be performed to extract the true impact of the unemployment rate and a country's democratic history on legitimacy.
Concerning the individual-level variables, most results are in line with those of the existing empirical literature. Despite some insignificant results in some waves, the relationship between age and legitimacy seems to be u-shaped, gender has no influence on legitimacy beliefs, more education reduces a person's legitimacy beliefs, and religion has a positive impact. Further, more media contact, more political interest, more interpersonal trust, and more life satisfaction increase one's legitimacy beliefs. If a person's feeling of safety is threatened, legitimacy beliefs decline. The only exception is the role of income. Here, one cannot conclude that richer or poorer people have higher or lower legitimacy beliefs since the results vary too much across waves.

5.3 Summary of the Basic Model

This chapter extracts a basic model that explains Gilley's (and Norris') legitimacy scores. In this vein, my aim is to analyze the following four research questions:

- Are the determinants of my basic model congruent with the determinants proposed by Gilley (2006b)?
- Are the results sensitive to the point in time (2001, 2008, 2012)?
- Are the results sensitive to the applied method?
- Are the results sensitive to the applied legitimacy measure?

Regarding the first question, I find that the determinants of the basic model are partly congruent with Gilley's (2006b, 48) proposed determinants (good governance, democratic rights, and welfare gains). However, in contrast to Gilley (2006b), I derive the conclusion that the determinants impact legitimacy differently. Since Gilley (2006b) constructs a composite index of the three determinants, he assumes that more good governance, more democratic rights, and more welfare gains increase legitimacy. In contrast to this, I find that the degree of democracy does not per se increase legitimacy. Rather, the role of democracy is puzzling. This has two reasons:

1. When using Gilley's legitimacy scores as dependent variables, there is no stable impact of democracy and/or the interaction term on legitimacy since the coefficients are not significant in all waves (table 20). Nonetheless, the interaction term is statistically more relevant, in particular in low-income countries (see Appendix L). These results are independent of applying OLS (table 20) or ordered logit models (tables 23 and 24).
2. When using Norris' legitimacy scores, the results are similar to those of Gilley's legitimacy scores when applying the basic model (table 25). There, democracy and the interaction term have positive effects on legitimacy in one wave. However, in the other two waves, no statistically significant effects can be found. These results change when applying a minimalist model (just based on democracy, general governance, and the absolute welfare level). Then, the sign changes and democracy has a negative impact on legitimacy (table 26). Similar

results occur when applying multi-level analysis (tables 27-29). There, I find a positive effect of the interaction term in one wave and a negative effect of democracy on legitimacy in the other two waves.

In sum, the impact of democracy on legitimacy depends on the wave, the legitimacy measure, and the applied method. Thus, there is no statistical support for the argument that democracy is necessary for or leads to legitimacy as proposed by Scharpf (1970, 1999). Rather, the results indicate that the relevance of democracy depends on a country's democratic history. Further, model selection strategies indicate that welfare gains have no effect on legitimacy. Instead, it turns out that the welfare level has a negative effect, in particular when controlling for other factors. The negative impact of the absolute welfare level on legitimacy is consistent, independent of the point in time, the legitimacy measure, and the method. This implies that more developed countries need to provide better governance to sustain legitimacy. Potential explanations for this finding are that (i) citizen's expectations of the state are higher in highly developed countries or (ii) highly developed countries show higher value pluralism, which makes it more difficult for the state to implement policies that meet the citizens' preferences.
In sum, my results challenge Gilley's (2006b) findings since I argue (i) that the role of democracy remains a puzzle and that (ii) the absolute level of welfare negatively influences legitimacy. Regarding the role of general governance, my results are in line with Gilley's (2006b) since I find a strong and robust positive relationship between general governance and legitimacy.
Concerning the second question whether the results are sensitive to the point in time, one can conclude that this depends on the particular variable. The impact of general governance and the absolute welfare level on legitimacy is robust, whereas the other output (the unemployment rate) and input variables may have alternating signs and different levels of significance in different waves. For example, the unemployment rate is highly significant when using multi-level analyses in ca. 2012 (table 29) but not significant in the other two waves (tables 27 and 28). Similar findings apply to the input variables (tables 20, 23-25).
Next, regarding the third question, one can conclude that the results are to a large extent independent of the applied method. When using Gilley's (2006a, 2012) legitimacy scores, OLS and ordered logit models come to similar results with only minor differences, in particular regarding the significance of the coefficients (tables 20, 24, and 25). When using Norris' legitimacy scores, one can also conclude that OLS estimates largely produce the same results as the multi-level analyses (when comparing the country-level variables) (tables 25, 27-29).
Further, the results indicate that both legitimacy measures reflect the same underlying concept. When applying OLS (tables 20 and 25), the main determinants (general governance, absolute level of welfare, and input variables) show similar signs and levels of significance. Differences mainly occur when focusing on further output variables (e.g. the unemployment rate).
Finally, one should notice that the analyses have some shortcomings which may influence the results:

- *Theoretical Framework.* Initially, I assume that state legitimacy theoretically depends on the input, the throughput, and the output channel. However, since the measure of throughput legitimacy (Control of Corruption Index of the World Bank) and one measure of output legitimacy (Government Effectiveness Index of the World Bank) are highly correlated, I merge both items into a general governance index. However, this procedure challenges the assumption that throughput and output legitimacy are different channels.
- *Model Assumptions.* I assume that all legitimacy channels (input and throughput/output) are independent. If one relaxes this assumption, one should account for the possibility that both channels may interact. However, I leave this to another study.
- *Data Preparation.* One needs to notice that the data preparation of some independent variables lacks consistency. For example, it is not possible to calculate the democratic history of post-colonial states with 1945 as the starting point. Thus, it remains open to what degree my calculated democratic history values of post-colonial states are exact. Second, I use both the Polity IV and the Freedom House Index to calculate the democracy score. However, this is in slight contrast to the calculation of the democratic history score, which is solely based on the Polity IV Index. The reason for this procedure is that only the Polity IV Index provides data that begin even before 1945. Eventually, for the 2008 wave, I use the 2010 data of the HDI to measure welfare gains because no data for 2008 are available.
- *Legitimacy Values.* Another shortcoming of the study may be the fact that Gilley (2006a, 2012) changes the items of his legitimacy measures. As shown in chapter 3.3.2, Gilley (2006a, 2012) modifies the items of the dimensions 'views of legality' and 'views of justification'. Hence, it remains open to what extent these changes impact the validity of the legitimacy measure. A further problem is that Gilley (2006a, 2012) compiles legitimacy values from items that were elicited in different years. For example, concerning the legitimacy values of ca. 2001, the underlying items of the WVS stem from the years 1999 to 2004 (see table 2). Furthermore, the OLS analyses assume that Gilley's legitimacy scores are (quasi-)metric. Although ordered logit models lead to similar results, the assumption that legitimacy is metric is not correct in a narrow sense.

6 Economic Freedom and Legitimacy

In the previous chapter, I analyzed the determinants of legitimacy but ignored economic institutions. The results show that the most important variables refer to political freedom (the degree of democracy and democratic history) and the output of the political but also the economic system (the general development level, general governance, and the unemployment rate). Although these variables explain a large part of legitimacy's variance, scholars largely neglect one important variable, namely the institutional setting of the economic system – in other words, the degree of economic freedom. Concerning empirical legitimacy studies, only Gilley (2006b, 52) explicitly mentions that market-friendly institutions (i.e. more economic freedom) have a positive effect on legitimacy. In line with liberal scholars (Friedman, 1969; Hayek, 1944, 1960), Gilley (2006b, 52) notes that "*economic stability* of property rights and financial institutions as well as *market-oriented economic governance* and *private economic ownership* have all been seen as legitimacy- enhancing because of their role in both economic freedom and growth".

In this chapter, I investigate whether a more market-friendly institutional setting (i.e. more economic freedom) leads to more legitimacy. Although Gilley's (2006b, 54, 57) investigations already suggest that "properly managed market [pro-market, author's note] reforms have enhanced, not diminished, the legitimacy of states", there is still a need to validate Gilley's finding and to prove the hypothesis that economic freedom increases legitimacy. This has several reasons. First, as mentioned above, only Gilley (2006b) investigates the empirical relationship between economic freedom and legitimacy. Thus, empirical evidence is limited. Second, Gilley's (2006b) conclusion is based on a bivariate correlation between legitimacy and economic freedom (as measured by the Economic Freedom of the World (EFW) Index of the Fraser-Institute). Since bivariate correlations do not control for other variables, the positive correlation between legitimacy and economic freedom may be spurious. Third, Gilley (2006b) only analyzes the overall EFW Index. Since the EFW Index consists of different areas, it is interesting to investigate which of those areas enhance legitimacy.

Before approaching the research question, one should note that – following Wegner (2009; 2012) – two different theoretical approaches seek to justify why liberalism is legitimacy-enhancing: A substantive and a procedural version. *Substantive economic liberalism* concentrates on the empirical and theoretical proof that the wealth of the citizens can be promoted best if the functions of the state are limited (in a way to be further specified by economic theory; model of limited state activity). It "gives economic freedom first priority but has to find an answer whether economic freedom expresses the will of citizens rather than representing one idiosyncratic political ideal" (Wegner, 2009, 543). This perspective claims that the state should leave economic issues to the market sphere except when there is a need to interfere due to market failures (Wegner, 2012, 34). Market failures are understood in a restrictive manner, implying that "any plea for governmental activity carries the burden of proof that private coordination cannot lead to sufficient outcomes" (Wegner, 2009, 540). State interventions are only justified in the case of systematic failures of market allocation (in contrast to temporary market imperfections) (Wegner, 2012, 35). In this sense,

C. M. Hindermann, *The Impact of Economic Freedom on State Legitimacy*,
Wirtschaft und Politik, https://doi.org/10.1007/978-3-658-23195-8_6

substantive economic liberalism refers to the thought of classical economic liberalism (Wegner, 2009, 541). Among others, Friedrich August von Hayek and Milton Friedman are the main representatives of this perspective.

On the other hand, *procedural economic liberalism* "demands that policies be grounded on agreement by citizens whatever the preferences about policies may be" (Wegner, 2009, 541). To achieve agreement, this perspective demands universal consent (unanimity), where all members of a society have an equal voting weight (i.e. no discrimination). In other words, consent can only be achieved if no member of a society issues a veto, which is not feasible in practice. In consequence, it suffices that "only general principles or rules be based on consent" and that "in-period politics within the rules follows the majority rule" (Wegner, 2009, 542). Thus, it remains unclear in advance whether the procedural version "constrain[s] politics to the extent that SEL [substantive economic liberalism, author's note] requires" (Wegner, 2009, 543). For example, following Buchanan, citizens (who act as "impartial spectators") would not agree on "rules that permit in-period policies on behalf of groups or individuals; since these policies deny equal participation in markets and accept that outsiders are to be discriminated against, everyone must consider the chance of becoming an outsider himself" (Wegner, 2009, 544).[176] Important representatives of this perspective are social contract theorists such as James Buchanan.

This chapter follows the substantive version of economic freedom. Thus, in the next sub-chapter (chapter 6.1), I present the concept of economic freedom mainly referring to Hayek (1944, 1960). Since economic freedom is a latent construct, chapter 6.2 deals with the areas of economic freedom, discusses the theoretical relationships of those areas to legitimacy, and presents their measurement. In this vein, I use the Economic Freedom of the World Index (EFW) since it is constructed in accordance with substantive economic liberalism (Wegner, 2012, 74). Thereafter, in chapter 6.3, I add the EFW Index and its areas to the basic model (chapter 5). In short, the results suggest that the area 'legal system and property rights' (reflecting the rule of law) is the main driver of legitimacy. Regarding the other areas of economic freedom ('government size', 'sound money', 'freedom to trade internationally', and 'regulation'), no robust positive or negative effects emerge at the country level. Finally, chapter 6.4 performs analyses at the individual level. According to Scharpf's (1970, 1999) theory, an individual's legitimacy belief becomes maximized if the economic situation is in line with his or her interests. Based on market-attitude items, the results provide evidence in favor of that hypothesis.[177] Legitimacy declines (i) if the degree of economic

176 To give another example, citizens should resolve a social contract with the agreement that they abstain from using costly organizations for generating a majority of votes to avoid irrational distribution (or rent-seeking) battles. In return, citizens gain a variety of advantages such as (i) reliable expectations that losing or winning an election (i.e. to be part of the majority or the minority) has no impact on the distribution, (ii) resources that have previously been used to generate the majority of votes, (iii) the advantage that rent-seeking of particular interest groups will be pushed back in the long-run, and (iv) a stable economic policy. (Wegner, 2012, 45)

177 Precisely, I use four different items. The first item reflects the degree to which an individual has a pro-market attitude (approximated by the degree to which an individual favors competition). The other three items refer to which degree an individual is satisfied with the given economic situation (as measured by items that capture the degree to which an individual wants more or less income

freedom is higher or lower than an individual's pro-market attitude or (ii) if an individual wants a change of the current economic situation (in terms of perceived inequality, government responsibility, or private ownership of businesses).

6.1 The Concept of Economic Freedom

This chapter defines economic freedom and shows at the conceptual level why and how economic freedom affects legitimacy. Following Hayek (1944, 1960), economic freedom means the absence of coercion (chapter 6.1.1).[178] Based on this definition, I present Hayek's (1944) argument that an economically free society is superior to a planned economy and, thus, legitimacy-enhancing. The reason is that an economically free society allows the individuals to follow their own preferences (chapter 6.1.2). At the same time, a high degree of economic freedom also goes along with a high degree of individual responsibility. Since too much responsibility may lead to dissatisfaction, it may be the case that too much economic freedom causes a reduction of legitimacy (chapter 6.1.3). Thus, the net effect of more economic freedom on legitimacy is unclear at the very conceptual level.

6.1.1 Definition of Economic Freedom

In *The Constitution of Liberty*, Hayek (1960) defines freedom in a negative manner as the absence of coercion.[179] By coercion, Hayek means (1960, 19) "such control of the environment or circumstances of a person by another that, in order to avoid greater evil, he is forced to act not according to a coherent plan of his own but to serve the ends of another" (Hayek, 1960, 19). Thus, Hayek (1960, 19) sees coercion as an evil: It "eliminates an individual as a thinking and valuing person and makes him a bare tool in the achievement of the ends of another." In turn, free action means that an individual can pursue his own aims without being forced by others (Hayek, 1960, 19). Thus, "freedom [...] presupposes that the individual has some assured private sphere, that there is some set of circumstances in his environment with which others cannot interfere" (Hayek, 1960, 13).

However, Hayek (1960, 19) also notes that coercion "cannot be altogether avoided because the only way to prevent it is by the threat of coercion." As a consequence, to prevent coercion of private persons, the state typically has the monopoly of coercion. Hayek (1960, 20) notes:

> *Free society has met this problem by conferring the monopoly of coercion on the state and by attempting to limit this power of the state to instances where it is required to prevent coercion by private persons. This is possible only by the*

inequality, government responsibility, or private ownership of businesses).

178 Following Spector (2010), four basic categories of freedom exist. Those are derived from the distinctions between negative and positive liberty and liberal and republican liberty.

179 In fact, Hayek (1960, 11-21) notes that liberty or freedom (defined as the absence of coercion) should not be confused with political liberties or "inner" freedom (the freedom to do what an individual wants by his own will).

> *state's protecting known private spheres of the individuals against the interference by others and delimiting these private spheres, not by specific assignation, but by creating conditions under which the individual can determine his own sphere by relying on rules which tell him what the government will do in different types of situations.*

Hayek (1960, 20) further mentions that the degree of coercion executed by the state should be "reduced to a minimum and made as innocuous as possible by restraining it through known general rules, so that in most instances the individual need never be coerced unless he has placed himself in a position where he knows he will be coerced." The important point is that impersonal, general, and abstract rules exist. These ensure that coercion is "confined to limited and foreseeable duties, or at least made independent of the arbitrary will of another person" (Hayek, 1960, 20). Altogether, a person can only be coerced if he does not follow the known general rules that are given beforehand. Thus, within the framework of known rules, an individual can pursue his own ends, is free do decide whatever he wants, and cannot "be used for the ends of others" (Hayek, 1960, 20).

To sum up, economic freedom means the absence (or at least the minimization) of coercion in the economic field. Within a given framework of general and abstract rules, nobody can be coerced to spend his time for the ends of others. The only exception is that the state has the power to coerce an individual if he or she trespasses the boundaries of the rules. Based on these considerations, one can derive several constituting areas of a free society (see chapter 6.2).

6.1.2 Economic Planning Versus Economic Freedom

In the book *The Road to Serfdom,* Hayek (1944) gives a first intuition why economic freedom should lead to legitimacy. There, Hayek (1944) shows that central planning inevitably leads to the danger of tyranny and a reduction of individual freedom.

To understand this, one should consider which requirements are necessary for a legitimate single economic plan. According to Hayek (1944, 60), the most important requirement is the existence of a *complete ethical code* since "a single plan presupposes that every one of our needs is given its rank in an order of values which must be complete enough to make it possible to decide between all the different courses which the planner has to choose." Otherwise, if a complete ethical code does not exist, it will not be possible for the planner "to decide between all the different courses" (Hayek, 1944, 60). However, Hayek (1944, 61) concludes that "no such complete ethical code exists". The reason is that "the attempt to direct all economic activity according to a single plan would raise innumerable questions to which the answer could be provided only by a moral rule, but to which existing morals have no answer and where there exists no agreed view on what ought to be done" (Hayek, 1944, 61). Hayek (1944, 62-63) derives this conclusion based on an individualist position, according to which (i) each individual has an own scale of values and preferences in his or her mind and (ii) these scales of values and preferences differ among individuals.[180]

As a consequence, Hayek (1944, 62-63) concludes that every individual should be allowed to follow his own values and preferences since dictations of the government or other authorities inevitably conflict with the individual's preferences at some time. Thus, although an economic plan may satisfy some needs of an individual, other preferences cannot be met, irrespective of whether the economic plan is set up by a dictator or is a result of a democratic process. In this vein, Hayek (1944, 67-68) also notes that: "An economic plan, to deserve the name, must have a unitary conception. Even if the parliament could, proceeding step by step, agree on some scheme, it would certainly in the end satisfy nobody. A complex whole where all the parts must be carefully adjusted to each other, cannot be achieved through a compromise between conflicting views."

Thus, an economic plan cannot guarantee that all individuals of a country can follow their values and preferences. The simple reason is that no complete ethical code exists since values and preferences differ among individuals. As a consequence, any economic plan, which can only be the result of "a compromise between conflicting views" (Hayek, 1944, 68), hinders the individuals to follow their own values and preferences, which should also lead to declining legitimacy beliefs.

6.1.3 Economic Freedom as Individual Responsibility

Although economic freedom increases individuals' possibilities to pursue their own ends, one should note that economic freedom also means individual responsibility. Hayek (1960, 63) notes:

> *Liberty not only means that the individual has both the opportunity and the burden of choice; it also means that he must bear the consequences of his actions and will perceive praise or blame for them. Liberty and responsibility are inseparable. A free society will not function or maintain itself unless its members regard it as right that each individual occupy the position that results from his action and accept it as due to his own action.*

Thus, economic freedom and individual responsibility are strongly connected. Hayek (1960, 70) already acknowledges that it is one of the most difficult tasks for men to use their individual responsibility in an appropriate manner such that the freedom of

180 In detail, Hayek (1944, 62-63) writes that: "It [individualism, author's note] merely starts from the indisputable fact that the limits of our powers of imagination make it impossible to include on our scale of values more than a sector of the needs of the whole society, and that, since, strictly speaking, scales of value can exist only in individual minds, nothing but partial scales of values exist, scales which are inevitably different and often inconsistent with each other. From this the individualist concludes that the individuals should be allowed, within defined limits, to follow their own values and preferences rather than somebody else's, that within these spheres the individual's system of ends should be supreme and not subject to any dictation by others. It is this recognition of the individual as the ultimate judge of his ends, the belief that as far as possible his own views ought to govern his actions, that forms the essence of the individualist position."

choice has been a major source of dissatisfaction. In detail, he (1960, 70) writes that: "The burden of choice that freedom imposes, the responsibility for one's own fate that a free society places on the individual, has under the conditions of the modern world become a main source of dissatisfaction." The reason for this observation is that in modern times "the success of a man will depend not on what special abilities he possesses in the abstract but on these abilities being put to the right use" (Hayek, 1960, 70). In other words, the mere fact that an individual has some special abilities does not guarantee that he or she will be successful. Again, Hayek (1960, 71) comments:

> *It is of the essence of a free society that a man's value and remuneration depend not on capacity in the abstract but on success in turning it into concrete service which is useful to others who can reciprocate. [...] What makes the individual unique in this respect is not his generic but his concrete knowledge, his knowledge of particular circumstances and conditions.*

As a consequence, an individual has not only the responsibility to decide for an occupation that fits with his or her abilities but also to ensure that his or her profession is useful to fulfill the needs of others. In this vein, individual responsibility goes along with a high degree of uncertainty since it is often not sure in advance whether the individual can use his or her abilities in a useful manner. That may even trigger resentments against a free society. Hayek (1960, 72) observes:

> *All that a free society has to offer is an opportunity of searching for a suitable position, with all the attendant risk and uncertainty which such a search for a market for one's gifts must involve. There is no denying that in this respect a free society puts most individuals under a pressure which is often resented. But it is an illusion to think that one would be rid of such pressure in some other type of society; for the alternative to the pressure that responsibility for one's own fate brings is the far more invidious pressure of personal orders that one must obey.*

Thus, if the perceived pressure of market freedom (for instance due to uncertainty or feelings of permanent burden caused by the speed of market-driven societal change) is larger than the perceived benefits of free choice, too much economic freedom, which may be accompanied by too much individual responsibility, may reduce legitimacy. In the same vein, too little economic freedom also may lower legitimacy if the cost of illiberalism outweigh the benefits of less individual responsibility. In sum, the relationship between economic freedom and legitimacy could be inverted u-shaped. According to this hypothesis (which is not explicitly tested in the empirical part), legitimacy declines if economic freedom (and, thus, individual responsibility) exceeds or falls below the optimal level.

6.2 Areas of Economic Freedom: Theory and Measurement

Economic freedom is a latent concept. Thus, to analyze the impact of economic freedom on legitimacy, one should understand (i) which areas constitute economic freedom, (ii) the theoretical relationship between each area of economic freedom and legitimacy, and (iii) the measurement of those areas. The most widely applied measures are the Economic Freedom of the World Index by the Fraser Institute (EFW) and the Index of Economic Freedom by the Heritage Foundation (IEF). In the further thesis, I stick to the EFW Index.

Ranging from 0 (minimum freedom) to 10 (maximum freedom), the EFW Index consists of five areas, namely (i) 'legal system and property rights', (ii) 'size of

Table 30: General Structure of the EFW Index (2015 Edition)

Legal System and Property Rights [0.2]	Judicial independence (0.11)
	Impartial courts (0.11)
	Protection of property rights (0.11)
	Military interference in rule of law and politics (0.11)
	Integrity of the legal system (0.11)
	Legal enforcement of contract (0.11)
	Regulatory costs of the sale of real property (0.11)
	Reliability of police (0.11)
	Business costs of crime (0.11)
Size of Government [0.2]	Government consumption (0.25)
	Transfers and subsidies (0.25)
	Government enterprises and investment (0.25)
	Top marginal tax rate[a] (0.25)
Sound Money [0.2]	Money growth (0.25)
	Standard deviation of inflation (0.25)
	Inflation: most recent year (0.25)
	Freedom to own foreign currency bank accounts (0.25)
Freedom to Trade Internationally [0.2]	Tariffs[a] (0.25)
	Regulatory trade barriers[a] (0.25)
	Black-market exchange rates (0.25)
	Controls of the movement of capital and people[a] (0.25)
Regulation [0.2]	Credit market regulations[a] (0.33)
	Labor market regulations[a] (0.33)
	Business regulations[a] (0.33)

[a] - Component consists of further sub-components.

Sources: Gwartney et al. (2015, 4)

government', (iii) 'sound money', (iv) 'freedom to trade internationally', and (v) 'regulation'. Each of these areas contains further components. Table 30 gives an overview of a recent index (2015 edition) (weighting scheme in parentheses) (Gwartney et al., 2015, 4).

As table 30 shows, the five areas of economic freedom are equally weighted (20 percent each). Similarly, the components of each area are equally weighted as well. However, Berggren (2003, 194-195) already notes that the areas and components of the EFW Index as well as the weighting schemes changed over time. Thus, one should be careful when taking the EFW Index from different editions. As a consequence, to see whether these changes are relevant, table 31 provides a short overview of the amount of areas, the amount of components, and the weighting scheme of the EFW indices from 2001 to 2015.[181]

Table 31: Comparing Different Editions of the EFW Index

Edition(s)	Correspond to Year(s)	Amount of Areas	Amount of Sub-Components	Weighting Scheme
2012-2015	2010-2013	5	24	Simple Means
2007-2011	2005-2009	5	23	Simple Means
2002-2006	2000-2004	5	21	Simple Means
2001	1999	7	19	Different Weights

Sources: Various Economic Freedom of the World Annual Reports (Gwartney et al., 2001-2015)

As table 31 shows, the EFW Index is based on the same aggregation principle across the editions from 2002 to 2015 (which corresponds to the years 2000 to 2013). Before the 2002 edition, there were more than five areas of economic freedom that were collapsed into the overall index, using different weights.[182] Thus, the editions before 2002 are not comparable to the editions from 2002 to 2015. Fortunately, since I use legitimacy data that start in 1999, it is possible to use the EFW Index that consists of five areas in nearly all cases. For reasons of consistency, I use the EFW data that correspond to the year 2000 when legitimacy data stem from 1999. As a consequence, it is sufficient to deal with those five areas that constitute the EFW Index since 2000. I refer to the EFW's annual report of 2015 to present the areas and its components (Gwartney et al., 2015).

In the following, I deal with each area of economic freedom separately (chapters 6.2.1-6.2.5). In particular, I discuss why each area is important for economic freedom, show how each area should be related to legitimacy from a theoretical point of view, and present the measurement of each area. The latter helps to understand how changes at the disaggregated (or area) level impact the overall index and, thus, also legitimacy.[183] Finally, I summarize the findings and derive a variety of hypotheses (chapter 6.2.6).

181 I start with the Annual Report of 2001 (i.e. the EFW index for 1999) since the legitimacy data I use in my later analyses start in 1999.

182 See also Heckelman and Stroup (2005).

183 If not specified otherwise in the following five sub-chapters, Gwartney et al. (2015, 203-215) provide more details on the exact measurement procedure of the EFW's components/items.

For reasons of completeness, I also sketch alternative hypotheses (chapter 6.2.7) before summarizing (chapter 6.2.8).

6.2.1 The First Area: Legal System and Property Rights

The first area of the EFW Index measures the quality of the legal system and property rights. Gwartney et al. (2015, 5) label this area as "the most important function of government". This is in line with Hayek (1944, 1960) who stresses the importance of the rule of law, property rights, and the freedom of contract.

Rule of Law. One of the most important elements of economic freedom is the rule of law, ensuring that coercion can only be used under the law (Friedman, 1969; Hayek, 1944, 1960). In greater detail, the rule of law means "that government in all its actions is bound by rules fixed and announced beforehand – rules which make it possible to foresee with fair certainty how the authority will use its coercive powers in given circumstances, and to plan one's individual affairs on the basis of this knowledge" (Hayek, 1944, 75-76). Thus, the rule of law not only provides security that the government will not interfere in the private sphere (unless the individual has broken the law), it also allows the individuals to anticipate what the government or any other authority will do under particular circumstances.
However, ideally, the rules (that are fixed and announced beforehand) restrict any government action. Since the ideal case can never be fully realized in practice, Hayek (1944, 76) claims that the rules given should leave the least amount of coercive power to the authorities:

> *[...] the essential point, that the discretion left to the executive organs wielding coercive power should be reduced as much as possible, is clear enough. While every law restricts individual freedom to some extent by altering the means which people may use in the pursuit of their aims, under the Rule of Law the government is prevented from stultifying individual efforts by ad hoc action. Within the known rules of the game the individual is free to pursue his personal ends and desires, certain that the powers of government will not be used deliberately to frustrate his efforts.*

Thus, the rule of law means that the given (abstract and general) rules apply to the government and the authorities in such ways that they cannot interfere in the private sphere by ad hoc action. Of course, this also applies to economic resources such as labor or capital. In detail, Hayek (1944, 76) stresses that "under the first [rule of law, author's note] the government confines itself to fixing rules determining the conditions under which the available resources may be used, leaving to the individuals the decisions for what ends they are to be used." The important point is that the government solely sets up the conditions – which are a specific set of rules that every individual and every authority has to follow – of how individuals can use the resources but abstains from deciding for what ends the individuals should use them. In contrast, if the government were to decide for what ends the resources should be used, not the law but an arbitrary government would rule. In detail, Hayek (1944, 76) writes that "under the second [an arbitrary government, author's note] the government directs the use of the means of production to particular ends."

A further requirement of the rule of law concerns the formulation and the content of the rules. According to Hayek (1944, 78), general abstract rules that are formulated in advance constitute the rule of law. In greater detail, general abstract rules apply to "certain types of situation, defined in general terms, without reference to time and place or particular people" (Hayek, 1944, 78). Thus, a rule should not be limited to a specific period, a specific region, and a specific group of people. This implies that an abstract rule is "useful to yet unknown people, for purposes for which these people will decide to use them, and in circumstances which cannot be foreseen in detail" such that "they do not involve a choice between particular ends or particular people" (Hayek, 1944, 78).

Altogether, according to Hayek (1944, 1960), the rule of law should have the following properties:

1. The rule of law requires that government actions are bound by rules that are fixed and announced beforehand (no ad hoc actions). (Hayek, 1944, 75-76)
2. The government's possibility to use coercive power should be reduced as much as possible. (Hayek, 1944, 76)
3. The formal rules themselves should be general abstract rules. (Hayek, 1944, 78).

Under these conditions, the rule of law makes it possible that the individuals can effectively follow their individual plans since they can predict the actions of the state. In this vein, Hayek (1944, 79) claims that "the state should confine itself to establishing rules applying to general types of situations, and should allow the individuals freedom in everything, which depends on the circumstances of time and place because only the individuals concerned in each instance can fully know these circumstances and adapt their actions to them. If the individuals are to be able to use their knowledge effectively in making plans, they must be able to predict actions of the state which may affect these plans". Further, he (1944, 84) notes that "the important question is whether the individual can foresee the action of the state and make use of this knowledge as a datum in forming his own plans, with the result that the state cannot control the use made of its machinery, and that the individual knows precisely how far he will be protected against the interference from others, or whether the state is in a position to frustrate individual efforts."

Hayek (1944, 84) stresses that the state can, of course, set up regulations, for example setting pollution allowances or determining safety laws. The important point is that the fixed rules have a general abstract character and are permanent such that an individual can predict the actions of the state and is protected against the interference from others. Altogether, Hayek (1944, 87) finally notes:

> *The Rule of Law thus implies limits to the scope of legislation: it restricts it to the kind of general rules known as formal law, and excludes legislation either*

> *directly aimed at particular people, or at enabling anybody to use the coercive power of the state for the purpose of such discrimination. It means, not that everything is regulated by laws, but, on the contrary, that the coercive power of the state can be used only in cases defined in advance by the law and in such a way that it can be foreseen how it will be used. (Hayek, 1944, 87)*

In sum, besides the fact that any individual can follow their own ends, the predictability of the state's action is the main gain of the rule of law. Thus, countries are expected to have high legitimacy scores if the rule of law is strong. As mentioned before, the reason is that the rule of law ensures that state actions are predictable and that individuals can pursue their ends without having the fear that the state uses coercive power to frustrate individual efforts.

Property Rights and Enforceability of Contracts. Property rights and the rule of law are necessarily intertwined. The reason is that the rule of law requires that an individual has some private sphere that is protected against interference from other individuals as well as the state. Hayek (1960, 122) also writes that "since coercion is the control of essential data of individual's action by another, it can be prevented only by enabling the individual to secure for himself some private sphere where he is protected against such interference."

To ensure a private sphere, it requires that men accept general rules that govern "the conditions under which objects or circumstances become part of the protected sphere of a person or persons" (Hayek, 1960, 123). All those objects and circumstances that are part of the protected sphere, one can call property rights. Thus, Hayek (1960, 123) concludes that property rights are an "essential condition for the prevention of coercion [...]". In this vein, property rights are also an essential condition for the rule of law since "the recognition of property is clearly the first step in the delimitation of the private sphere" (Hayek, 1960, 123).

However, although property rights are a necessary condition to protect an individual against coercion, they are not a sufficient condition. In addition to the mere existence of property rights, Hayek (1960, 123) further stresses that not all material means should be in the exclusive control of one agent but sufficiently dispersed. To be precise, Hayek (1960, 123) writes that "the essential requisite for the protection of the individual against coercion is not that he possess property but that the material means which enable him to pursue any plan of action should not be all in the exclusive control of one other agent." Further, he (1960, 124) stresses that "property should be sufficiently dispersed so that the individual is not dependent on particular persons who alone can provide him with what he needs or who alone can employ him."

Typically, property is dispersed among the individuals that live in a country. Thus, men may trade or exchange property to follow their individual ends. As a consequence, the existence of property rights also requires the enforceability of contracts. Hayek (1960, 124) notes:

> *That other people's property can be serviceable in the achievement of our aims is due mainly to the enforcibility of contracts. The whole network of rights*

> *created by contracts is as important a part of our own protected sphere, as much the basis of our plans, as any property of our own. The decisive condition for mutually advantageous collaboration between people, based on voluntary consent rather then coercion, is that there be many people who can serve one's needs, so that nobody has to be dependent on specific persons for the essential conditions of life or the possibility of development on some direction. It is competition made possible by the dispersion of property that deprives the individual owners of particular things of all coercive power.*

Finally, Hayek (1960, 124) also stresses that public goods and the right to share them are an important part of the private sphere:

> *The rules of property and contract are required to delimit the individual's sphere where the resources or services needed for the pursuit of his aims are scare and must, in consequence, be under the control of some man or another. But if this is true of most of the benefits we derive from men's effort, it is not true of all. There are some kinds of services, such as sanitation or roads, which, once they are provided, are normally sufficient for all who want to use them. The provision of such services has long been a recognized field of public effort, and the right to share in them is an important part of the protected sphere of the individual.*

To sum up, property rights are an essential part of a free society since they ensure that any individual has a private sphere which is protected by general abstract rules against interference. Since property is dispersed among the members of society, it requires that contracts between individuals can be enforced to ensure exchange and trade. As a consequence, assuming the enforceability of contracts and the existence of property rights, the rule of law prevails since the private sphere is protected against coercion. Thus, similar to the rule of law, countries with better enforcement of property rights should also show higher legitimacy scores. The simple reason is that under the existence of property rights, men can follow their individual ends without having the fear that they will be coerced to use their property for other ends than their own.

Based on the theoretical considerations, several items constitute the area 'legal system and property rights', namely (i) judicial independence, (ii) impartial courts, (iii) protection of property rights, (iv) military interference in rule of law and politics, (v) integrity of legal system, (vi) legal enforcement of contracts, (vii) regulatory costs of the sale of real property, (viii) reliability of the police, and (ix) business costs of crime (Gwartney et al., 2015, 205-207). The following enumeration presents each component in greater detail:

- *Judicial Independence.* The measurement of the judicial independence bases on a survey item from of the Global Competitiveness Report, namely "Is the judiciary in your country independent from political influences of members of government, citizens, or firms?" (Gwartney et al., 2015, 205).[184] An independent judiciary is necessary for a free society since it ensures that special interests groups (such as firms or political actors) are also bound to the rule of law (i.e. to the rules that are fixed and announced beforehand, Hayek, 1944, 75-76, see above). If the state were to influence the judiciary, it would use its coercive power to deviate from the rules that were fixed and announced beforehand and to violate the private sphere of the individuals. An example is a state which neglects the property rights of an individual (for example, in terms of expropriation). Thus, judicial independence is a necessary condition for the rule of law. Judicial independence also implies that the predictability of individuals' actions increase, which leads to more economic growth (Feld & Voigt, 2003). In contrast, economic freedom declines if interest groups influence the judiciary and, thus, circumvent the rule of law.

- *Impartial Courts.* As above, the measurement of the courts' impartiality stems from the Global Competitiveness Report: "The legal framework in your country for private businesses to settle disputes and challenge the legality of government actions and/or regulations is inefficient and subject to manipulation (= 1) or is efficient and follows a clear, neutral process (= 7)" (Gwartney et al., 2015, 205). Impartial courts are important since they guarantee that no discrimination takes place between individuals or interest groups. If the courts were non-impartial, the decisions of the courts would become uncertain. That could mean either that the individual would be favored by the courts if he or she belonged to the favored group or that the individual would be disadvantaged by the courts if he or she belonged to the disfavored group. In addition, it also remains unclear which groups are favored since the favored groups may change over time. Thus, only neutral or impartial courts guarantee a fair process that allows an individual to act freely due to lower uncertainty.
- *Protection of Property Rights.* The component 'protection of property rights' also stems from the Global Competitiveness Report: "Property rights, including over financial assets, are poorly defined and not protected by law (= 1) or are clearly defined and well protected by law (= 7)" (Gwartney et al., 2015, 205). The protection of property rights is an essential feature of economic freedom. As Hayek (1960, 139) notes, property rights are necessary to define the private sphere which protects individuals against arbitrary interference from the state (see above). In this vein, "the conditions under which objects or circumstances become part of the protected sphere of a person or persons" define property rights (Hayek, 1960, 140). Thus, well-defined property rights are essential for a free society and also lead to economic progress.[185]

---

184 The answer possibilities range from "No – heavily influenced (=1)" to "Yes – entirely independent (=7)". The raw data were rescaled to a 0-to-10 scale. (Gwartney et al., 2015, 205).

185 Property rights are essential for economic growth and progress. The reason is that they provide certainty since every individual can own private property that is protected. As a consequence, private property increases the incentive to act since one is protected against 'theft'. Further reasons why property rights lead to economic growth are given by Gwartney and Stroup (1995) (see also Mehlkop, 2002, 79-81).

- *Military Interference.* A further component is 'military interference'. This item is taken from the International Country Risk Guide (Political Component G. Military in Politics) and measures the degree to which the military is involved in politics (Gwartney et al., 2015, 205). To understand why this component is important for economic freedom, one should note that "the military is not elected" and "diminishes democratic accountability" (Gwartney et al., 2015, 205). In consequence, a government that has been taken over by the military will not only show diminishing effectiveness but also "become corrupt, and create an uneasy environment for foreign businesses" (Gwartney et al., 2015, 205). Then, economic freedom declines since it remains unclear whether the military governs under the principles of the rule of law. This lowers the predictability of the future and increases the uncertainty of investments and property rights.
- *Integrity of the Legal System.* To measure the component 'integrity of the legal system', Gwartney et al. (2015, 206) take an item from the International Risk Guide (Political Risk Component I for Law and Order). On the one hand, this item measures the impartiality of the legal system ('law') (see also the component impartial courts). On the other hand, the item also measures the popular observance of the law ('order'). In particular, the latter item is important since the popular observance of the law reflects the de facto rule of law which may deviate from the de jure rule of law.
- *Legal Enforcement of Contracts.* The enforcement of contracts is a necessary condition to ensure property rights and, thus, the rule of law (Hayek, 1960, 141). To measure this component, Gwartney et al. (2015, 206) use Doing Business Data to calculate the time and the money required for a plaintiff to collect a debt. In detail, countries receive higher ratings if the time costs (fewer calendar days from the filing of the lawsuit until the payment) and the monetary costs (as costs in percentage of the debt) are lower (Gwartney et al., 2015, 206).
- *Regulatory Costs of the Sale of Real Property.* This item stems from the Doing Business Data and measures the time and the costs "to transfer ownership of property that includes land and a warehouse" (Gwartney et al., 2015, 206). The importance of this item becomes apparent when considering that high regulatory costs (for example bureaucratic costs) may alter the decisions of the individuals to sell real property (since total costs may be too high such that a sale of real property may not occur). Countries receive a higher rating if transfers take less time (measured in days to transfer ownership) and if the monetary costs of the transfers are lower (in percentage of the property value) (Gwartney et al., 2015, 206).
- *Reliability of Police.* The rule of law not only needs to be formally enacted (de jure rule of law) but also appropriately enforced (de facto rule of law). The latter is the typical task of the police. Thus, this component (taken from the Global Competitiveness Report) captures the degree to which the police is reliable: "To what extent can police services be relied upon to enforce law and order in your country? (1 = Cannot be relied upon at all; 7 = Can be completely relied upon)." (Gwartney et al., 2015, 206)

- *Business Costs of Crime.* This component captures the business costs of crime (taken from the Global Competitiveness Report): "To what extent does the incidence of crime and violence impose costs on businesses in your country? (1 = To a great extent; 7 = Not at all)" (Gwartney et al., 2015, 207). If the rule of law prevails, the business costs of crime should be low since the law and the institutions protect businesses against criminal activities. In contrast, if crime imposes high costs on businesses, the rule of law does not correctly function since parts of the police or the courts may be corrupt and circumvent the de jure rule of law.

In sum, all nine components serve well to measure the area 'legal system and property rights'. In all cases, Gwartney et al. (2015) assume a linear relationship between the components and the legal system, which is an appropriate procedure. In this vein, the measurement of the rule of law also fits with the theoretical considerations of Hayek (1944, 1960).

6.2.2 The Second Area: Size of Government

The next area of economic freedom is 'government size'. In a free society, the activities of the state are restricted. First of all, according to Hayek (1960, 195-196), the state should have the monopoly of coercion which should be the only monopoly of the state. In detail, Hayek (1960, 195-196) writes that "a free society demands not only that the government have the monopoly of coercion but that it have the monopoly only of coercion and that in all other respects it operate on the same terms as everybody else."

Second, besides the monopoly of coercion, the state should provide public goods that the market cannot provide. Hayek (1960, 195) distinguishes between two types of public goods. On the one hand, he (1960, 195) stresses the importance of public goods that "provide a favorable framework for individual decisions" and, thus, "supply means which individuals can use for their own purposes". Those government activities are, for example, the provision of a monetary system, statistics, and the support of some kind of education (Hayek, 1960, 196). On the other hand, Hayek (1960, 196) notes that the state should also provide "all those services which are clearly desirable but which will not be provided by competitive enterprise because it would either be impossible or difficult to charge the individual beneficiary for them." As examples, Hayek (1960, 196) mentions sanitary and health services or the construction and maintenance of roads. However, he (1960, 196) further notes that, although government activities may be useful in some fields at a particular time, it is more efficient when independent agencies (instead of the state) provide the services needed. In particular, he (1960, 196) writes that "in most instances, moreover, it is by no means necessary that government engage in the actual management of such activities; the services in question can generally be provided, and more effectively provided, by the government's assuming some or all of the financial responsibility but leaving the conduct of the affairs to independent and in some measure competitive agencies."

Furthermore, Hayek (1960, 196) also notes that any state enterprise is a risk to economic freedom. The reason is that the state could always use its coercive power to turn the position of any state enterprise into a monopoly. To solve this problem, he (1960, 196) suggests that

> *[...] it would be necessary that any special advantages, including subsidies, which government gives to its own enterprises in any field, should also be made available to competing private agencies. There is no need to emphasize that it would be exceedingly difficult for government to satisfy these conditions and that the general presumption against state enterprise is thereby considerably strengthened. But this does not mean that all state enterprise must be excluded from a free system. Certainly it ought to be kept within narrow limits; it may become a real danger to liberty if too large a section of economic activity comes to be subject to the direct control of the state. But what is objectionable here is not state enterprise as such but state monopoly.*

Hayek (1960, 196) acknowledges that state enterprises (that operate under the same conditions as private ones) are not necessarily a threat to a free society. Rather, the state monopoly is the most dangerous threat to economic freedom and liberty.

In sum, following Hayek (1960), the state has two main tasks, namely to hold the monopoly of coercion and to provide public goods that the market cannot provide. However, Hayek (1960) claims that public goods should only be provided to a necessary minimum. As a consequence, only a small (or limited) government size is compatible with a free society. In this vein, Gwartney et al. (2014, 3) note that "when government spending increases relative to spending by individuals, households, and businesses, government decision-making is substituted for personal choice and economic freedom is reduced."

However, a lower government size does not necessarily lead to more state legitimacy. The reason is that, as Hayek (1960) proposes, the state should undertake at least a minimum of activities, in particular providing public goods. Thus, the relationship between government size and legitimacy may be inverted u-shaped. If the government size is too low (i.e. the state provides no or only an inadequate degree of public goods such as roads, schooling, or other), legitimacy should decline since the state is not able to fulfill at least its very basic tasks. Similarly, if government size is too large (i.e. the state does not only provide public goods that are necessary but also goods that the market could offer), legitimacy should decline as well since the state's decisions reduce individual choice. Legitimacy beliefs should be highest if the state fulfills its main tasks (i.e. a limited government size) and leaves as much economic activity as possible to the individuals.

Although limited government size should be legitimacy-enhancing according to a (substantive) liberal perspective, there is also reasoning for the opposite. For example, according to Buchanan (1992, 42), a welfare state (which is typically characterized by a large government size) can be seen as (quasi)-legitimate. However, this requires that the citizens have a preference for a welfare state (e.g. it is seen to provide security against poverty due to redistribution policies) and, thus, agree on a large government

(procedural liberalism) (see also Mehlkop, 2002, 60-67). In fact, Ochsner (2016) finds that the legitimacy of western states increases with welfare spending.
To measure this area, Gwartney et al. (2015) use four components, namely (i) 'government consumption', (ii) 'transfers and subsidies', (iii) 'government enterprises and investment', and (iv) 'top marginal tax rate'. In line with liberal principles, fewer government consumption, less transfers and subsidies, fewer government enterprises and investments, and lower marginal tax rates lead to more economic freedom. In turn, this means that fewer government consumption leads to higher values in this area and, thus, overall economic freedom (which may be a problem since too little government consumption may imply that the state cannot even undertake its core tasks). Gwartney et al. (2015, 203-204) measure the four components of this area as follows:

- *Government Consumption.* 'Government consumption' is calculated by dividing the general government consumption by total consumption.[186] Thus, a monotonic negative relationship between government consumption and the sub-score exists (i.e. more government consumption leads to a lower score and vice versa). However, this assumption should be treated with caution, particularly when noting that liberal scholars such as Hayek (1960) argue that the state should undertake at least a minimum of core tasks (such as the provision of public goods that cannot be provided by the market). According to a calculation of Gwartney et al. (1998), the state can provide its core tasks with government consumption as a share of GDP of 10 to 15 percent. According to this calculation, the score for government consumption of the EFW Index is slightly biased: The score for government consumption should be maximal if the state's actual government consumption lies between 10 and 15 percent; however, countries receive the maximum score with a government consumption of 6 percent (see Gwartney et al., 2015, 203). Further, this also means that the score for government consumption should decline if a state's actual government consumption (as a share of the GDP) were lower or higher than 10 to 15 percent. Thus, the measurement procedure should be modified such that any deviation from the ideal value should lower economic freedom. Based on these considerations, some scholars, such as De Haan and Sturm (2000), even question whether government consumption (as calculated in the EFW Index, Gwartney et al., 2015) is an appropriate indicator to measure a country's economic freedom since even a free state needs to undertake a limited degree of government consumption.
- *Transfers and Subsidies.* The component 'transfers and subsidies' is measured by the share of general governance transfers and subsidies in GDP. Similar to 'government consumption', Gwartney et al. (2015, 203) assume a negative

186 According to the World Bank (2015), general government consumption (recently labeled general government final consumption expenditures) includes "all government current expenditures for purchases of goods and services (including compensation of employees)" and "expenditures on national defense and security, but excludes government military expenditures that are part of government capital formation." And further, total consumption (recently labeled as final consumption expenditures) is the sum of private consumption and general government consumption.

linear relationship between the share of transfers and subsidies and the sub-score (i.e. countries with a higher share of transfers and subsidies receive lower scores and vice versa). Again, one may question whether the construction of this component is in line with Hayek's thoughts. On the one hand, Hayek (1993, 96) clearly argues that the state should abstain from redistribution policies. He (1993, 96) further notes that social justice has no meaning since "in a society of free men whose members are allowed to use their own knowledge for their own purposes the term 'social justice' is wholly devoid of meaning or content". However, on the other hand, Hayek (1993, 71) also acknowledges that the results of the market sphere (i.e. the outcomes of "the game of catallaxy") lead to winners and losers. As a consequence, Hayek (1993, 87) does not want to reduce transfers to zero but argues for a guaranteed minimum income that makes survival of those people possible that cannot help themselves. In particular, he (1993, 87) writes that "there is no reason why in a free society government should not assure to all protection against severe deprivation in the form of an assured minimum income, or a floor below which nobody need to descend." Therefore, following Hayek (1960, 262), the state should provide "a uniform minimum for all who are unable to maintain themselves". Under these considerations, there should be an ideal value of transfers and any deviation from this value should reduce the score of this component. In this vein, the construction of the transfers and subsidies score in the EFW Index may be somewhat biased since Gwartney et al. (2015) assume a linear relationship between the share of transfers and subsidies in GDP and the sub-score.

- *Government Enterprises and Investment.* To measure the component 'government enterprises and investment', Gwartney et al. (2015, 203-204) calculate the share of government investment in total investment. Countries with a lower (higher) share receive higher (lower) values.[187] When comparing this component with Hayek's thoughts, the indicator seems to be appropriate since some degree of government investment needs to exist to ensure the provision of public goods such as sanitary and health services or the construction and maintenance of roads (Hayek, 1960, 223, see above). However, Hayek (1960, 196) also points out that government activities may be useful in some fields at a particular time, but he also notes that it is in most parts more efficient when independent agencies provide the services needed rather than the state. In particular, Hayek (1960, 196) sees the problem that any state enterprise could always use the coercive power of the state to turn its position into a monopoly (for example, the state could use its tax revenues to subsidize state enterprises). Thus, he (1960, 196) concludes that: "Certainly it [the state enterprise, author's note] ought to be kept within narrow limits; it may become a real danger to liberty if too large a section of economic activity comes to be subject to the direct control of the state." Similar objections to state

187 In detail, Gwartney et al. (2015, 203-204) assign the following scores to the shares: If the share of government investment lies below 15%, the country receives 10 points. If the share lies between 15% and 20% (20% and 25%, 25% and 30%, 30% and 40%, 40% and 50%), countries get the value 8 (7, 6, 4, 2). If the share lies above 50%, the country receives value 0.

enterprises are also put forward by other scholars (Gwartney et al., 1996; see also Mehlkop, 2002, 67-69).

- *Top Marginal Tax Rate.* The last component of the first area is 'top marginal tax rate'. This component assigns lower ratings to countries with (i) a high top marginal income tax rate and (ii) a high top marginal income and payroll tax rate that take effect at lower income thresholds (Gwartney et al., 2015, 204). This component is relevant since marginal tax rates "deny individuals the fruits of their labor" (Gwartnet et al., 2015, 3). To see why taxation is an obstacle to economic freedom, Mehlkop (2002, 71) lists a variety of reasons. First, higher marginal tax rates reduce the incentives to work and, thus, the aggregate labor supply. That means that people may prefer to enjoy more vacation or retire earlier since the high tax rates may not pay off for additional work. Second, high marginal tax rates may impact investment decisions. Assuming that domestic tax rates are higher than foreign tax rates, domestic investors are more likely to invest abroad or, vice versa, foreign investors may invest less in the domestic market. Third, high marginal tax rates may alter the decisions of the individuals. For example, this means that people (in particular company owners) may more likely buy depreciable goods instead of non-depreciable goods (since depreciation lowers profits and, thus, the tax burden). All these examples show that high tax rates may alter the individuals' decisions and may lead to results that differ from those without taxation. A weakness of this component is that it solely derives the score based on the top marginal tax level but does not account for the tax system design. For example, Hayek (1960, 272) finds that a progressive tax system is not compatible with a free society: "[U]nlike proportionality, progression provides no principle which tells us what the relative burden of different persons ought to be. It is no more than a rejection of proportionality in favor of a discrimination against the wealthy without any criterion for limiting the extent of this discrimination." In the same vein, Spicer (1995), who analyzes Hayek's works with respect to taxation, concludes that (i) horizontal equity and neutrality and (ii) stable tax policies constitute a liberal tax system since it is non-discriminatory and predictable. Thus, one should ideally add a further sub-component that captures the degree of progression and the relative stability of a particular tax system.[188]

To sum up, the area 'government size' measures the degree to which the state interferes with the market sphere. In this vein, states with fewer government activities

188 One should note that Hayek (1960, 307) does not want to abandon all progressive taxes. Instead, he allows that some single taxes have a progression if this leads to the result that all taxes together are not progressive. He (1960, 307) writes that "it should be said at once that the only progression with which we shall be concerned and which we believe cannot in the long run be reconciled with free institutions is the progression of taxation as a whole, that is, the more than proportionally heavy taxation of the larger incomes when all taxes are considered together. Individual taxes, and especially the income tax, may be graduated for a good reason – that is, so as to compensate for the tendency of many indirect taxes to place a proportionally heavier burden on the smaller incomes. This is the only valid argument in favor of progression. It applies, however, only to particular taxes as part of a given tax structure and cannot be extended to the tax system as a whole."

(in terms of consumption, transfers, investments, and taxation level) receive a higher score. Although these assumptions are plausible and fit with a liberal view, one should note that some components may be wrongly specified, in particular when following a Hayekian perspective:

- The EFW Index assumes a linear relationship between government consumption and economic freedom. However, when following Hayek, an inverted u-shaped relationship seems to be more appropriate since the state has to provide some core tasks.
- Similarly, the EFW Index assumes a linear relationship between transfers and economic freedom. Again, when considering Hayek's claims that the state should provide at least a minimum of transfers for those that cannot maintain themselves, an inverted u-shaped relationship seems to fit better.
- Finally, the top marginal tax rate concept may be incomplete. In addition to the level of the tax rate, one should also evaluate the progression of the tax system.

Thus, one may expect that the relationship between 'government size' and legitimacy may be linear or even inverted u-shaped (since a smaller government size leads, according to the construction of this area, to more economic freedom; however, this violates the idea that the state has to undertake at least a minimum of state activities).

6.2.3 The Third Area: Sound Money

Next, liberal economists stress the importance of 'sound money' for economic freedom. According to Hayek (1944, 92-93), money is "one of the greatest instruments of freedom ever invented by man". In detail, he (1944, 92-93) writes:

> *The ultimate ends of the activities of reasonable beings are never economic. Strictly speaking there is no "economic motive" but only economic factors conditioning our striving for other ends. What in ordinary language is misleadingly called the "economic motive" means merely the desire for general opportunity, the desire for power to achieve unspecified ends. If we strive for money it is because it offers us the widest choice in enjoying the fruits of our efforts. Because in modern society it is through the limitation of our money incomes that we are made to feel the restrictions which our relative poverty still imposes upon us, many have come to hate money as the symbol of these restrictions. But this is to mistake for the cause the medium through which a force makes itself felt. It would be much truer to say that money is one of the greatest instruments of freedom ever invented by man. It is money which in existing society opens an astounding range of choice to the poor man, a range greater than that which not many generations ago was open to the wealthy. We shall better understand the significance of this service of money if we consider what it would really mean if, as so many socialists characteristically propose, the "pecuniary motive" were largely displaced by "non-economic incentives". If all rewards, instead of being offered in money, were offered in the form of*

> *public distinctions or privileges, positions of power over other men, or better housing or better food, opportunities for travel or education, this would merely mean that the recipient would no longer be allowed to choose, and that, whoever fixed the reward, determined not only its size but also the particular form in which it should be enjoyed.*

As the quote shows, money allows us to choose freely among opportunities and to follow our own ends. As a consequence, the state or the monetary authorities should not only provide money but also ensure that the individuals can rely on money and its value. In a later work, Hayek (1976) even argues for *free money*, allowing also private actors to put money into circulation.

Friedman (1969, 38) also notes that "it is desirable that we use government to provide a stable monetary framework for a free economy".[189] This becomes apparent when considering the three functions of money, namely as a medium of exchange, as a unit of account, and as a store of value. As long as the monetary framework is stable, the functions of money enable individuals to save money without fearing devaluation, to make wise investments on predictable prices, and to use money as a medium of exchange. However, if the monetary framework becomes unstable, one can observe a variety of reactions. A high inflation rate typically reduces the demand for money (due to higher opportunity costs). Thus, individuals start to buy tangible assets, leading to transaction costs (e.g. shoe-leather costs or menu costs). In the case of very high inflation rates, individuals may even substitute money by foreign currencies or other substitutes (for instance, the use of a cigarette currency). Especially in the latter case, money loses all its functions and men their freedom to spend money according to their own ends (Hayek, 1944, 92-93).

Besides the functions of money, a stable monetary framework (in terms of low and stable inflation rates) also has an impact on economic growth (Barro, 1995, 1996; Bruno & Easterly, 1998; Fischer, 1993), leads to higher life satisfaction (Di Tella et al., 2001), and avoids real fiscal drag (or bracket creep) (Heinemann, 2001; Immervoll, 2005). As a consequence, countries with a better monetary framework should show higher legitimacy scores. Thus, I assume a positive relationship between 'sound money' (i.e. less inflation, the freedom to use foreign currencies, and a sound control of the monetary supply) and the legitimacy of the state.[190]

Gwartney et al. (2015) use four components to measure this area, namely (i) money growth, (ii) standard deviation of inflation, (iii) inflation of the most recent year, and (iv) freedom to own foreign currency bank accounts:

- *Money Growth.* Money growth is an important component since too high rates of money growth typically lead to high inflation rates or an increased risk of bubbles. Gwartney et al. (2015, 207) calculate "the average annual growth of

189 To ensure a stable monetary framework, Friedman (1969, 51-54) suggests that the money supply should be controlled by rules instead of (discretionary) authorities.

190 Some people may favor an unstable monetary framework since it could be beneficial (for example, according to the creditor-debtor hypothesis or the development of real wages). However, I do not consider this opportunity here.

the money supply in the last five years minus average annual growth of real GDP in the last ten years." That procedure directly refers to Fisher's equation of exchange (or quantity equation) [22],

$$M_1 * v = P * Y \qquad [22]$$

where M_1 stands for the M1 money supply, v for the velocity of money, P for the price level and Y for the real GDP. When taking the first derivative with respect to the time (of the log values), one obtains equation [23].

$$\frac{\Delta M_1}{M_1} + \frac{\Delta v}{v} = \frac{\Delta P}{P} + \frac{\Delta Y}{Y} \qquad [23]$$

Assuming that the velocity of money v is constant over time ($\Delta v = 0$), one can rearrange equation [23] such that the inflation rate equals the growth rate of the money supply (M_1) minus the growth rate of the real GDP (Y) (equation [24]).

$$\frac{\Delta M_1}{M_1} - \frac{\Delta Y}{Y} = \frac{\Delta P}{P} \qquad [24]$$

That shows that the price level increases if the money supply rises faster than real GDP. In this vein, if the money supply increases too fast, the risk of high inflation rates (or emerging bubbles, see Schnabl & Hoffmann, 2008) increases as well and the monetary framework may become unstable. As a consequence, countries receive lower ratings if the expansion of the money supply exceeds the real GDP growth rate.

- *Standard Deviation of Inflation.* The component standard deviation of inflation reflects the volatility of the inflation rate, which is a measure of monetary uncertainty. If the volatility of the inflation rate is high, it is hardly possible to predict future prices, limiting economic actions of the individual and leading to unpredictable costs or redistribution. To demonstrate this, one can refer to the development of real wages or the debtor-creditor hypothesis. In both cases, because the actual inflation rate and the anticipated inflation rate may diverge, one party wins and the other party loses. Regarding the development of real wages, workers win if the actual inflation rate is lower than the expected inflation rate (which is the basis for wage agreements) since nominal wages rise faster than the price level. When referring to the debtor-creditor hypothesis, the debtor wins if the expected inflation rate is higher than the actual inflation rate since the real interest rate (defined as the nominal interest rate minus the expected inflation, Fisher equation) becomes lower. To measure this component, Gwartney et al. (2015, 207) use the GDP deflator (or, if not available, the Consumer Price Index) to calculate "the standard deviation of the inflation rate over the last five years." Countries with a higher standard deviation of inflation receive lower scores, whereas countries with zero standard deviation receive 10 points.

- *Inflation of the Most Recent Year.* Since inflation (in particular high rates) negatively impacts the functions of money and increases uncertainty (see above), very high inflation rates reduce economic freedom. In this vein, countries with a high (low) inflation rate should have a lower (higher) degree of economic freedom. To measure this component, Gwartney et al. (2015, 207-208) use the CPI (or, if not available, the GDP deflator) of the most recent year.
- *Freedom to Own Foreign Currency Bank Accounts.* The area's last component is freedom to own foreign currency bank accounts. In particular if domestic inflation rates are high, this freedom is important since individuals can easily substitute the domestic currency by foreign (more stable or credible) currencies to preserve the value of the money (Gwartney et al., 2015, 5). Otherwise, if the conversion of currencies is not possible, individuals lose the possibility to preserve the original value of the domestic currency. In this vein, Friedman (1969, 57) also notes that direct controls on foreign exchange are a threat to economic freedom. He (1969, 57) writes that "there is much experience to suggest that the most effective way to convert a market economy into an authoritarian economic society is to start by imposing direct controls on foreign exchange. This one step leads inevitably to the rationing of imports, to control over domestic production that uses imported products or that produces substitutes for imports, and so in a never-ending spiral." Regarding the measurement, Gwartney et al. (2015, 208) rate a country 10 "when foreign currency bank accounts were permissible without any restrictions both domestically and abroad", 5 when "foreign currency bank accounts were permissible domestically but not abroad (or vice versa)", and zero when foreign accounts are restricted at all.

In sum, the area 'sound money' contains components that measure the stability of the monetary framework. Since all components show a strict monotonic relationship with economic freedom, the measurement of the components is reasonable and fits with underlying theoretical considerations. Thus, I expect a positive relationship between 'sound money' and legitimacy.

6.2.4 The Fourth Area: Freedom to Trade Internationally

Economists widely believe that international trade is a positive sum game and increases the wealth of nations (due to the Ricardian principle of comparative advantage).[191] Thus, since people may want to engage in economic activities with foreign partners, the area 'freedom to trade internationally' is an essential part of economic freedom. If the state restricts these activities (by tariffs, quotas, regulations, or controls of the movement of capital and people), the freedom to trade with foreign

191 There is mixed evidence in the empirical literature that trade freedom necessarily leads to more growth. For example, Cebula (2013) and Berggren and Jordahl (2005) provide evidence that trade freedom has a positive impact on growth. In contrast, Carlsson and Lundström (2002) provide partly opposing results. For a more comprehensive overview of studies that deal with growth and trade freedom, see Carlsson and Lundström (2002, 337).

partners becomes limited. In most cases, those trade restrictions are enacted "at the urging of protectionist critics and special-interest groups" (Gwartney et al., 2015, 6). In particular, special-interest groups may favor trade restrictions to protect themselves against foreign competition. In consequence, domestic producers can either sell their products at a too high price (a price that lies above the competitive (world market) price) or lower the quality of their products. This situation has advantages and disadvantages. On the one hand, the domestic producers gain from restrictions to trade since they can generate a higher rent (rent-seeking). In this vein, the domestic workforce is also protected against unemployment (in particular if the migration of labor is restricted). On the other hand, consumers lose their freedom to choose between domestic and foreign (imported) products and they have to accept the (higher than global market) price of the domestic producers. Furthermore, restrictions that increase the shipping time hinder free trade. These delays may be a "result of administrative inefficiency while in other instances they reflect the actions of corrupt officials seeking to extract bribes" (Gwartney et al., 2015, 6).

Liberal economists typically argue for trade freedom. For example, Friedman (1969, 57) notes that imposing economic controls "in order to 'solve' balance of payment problems" is a threat to economic freedom. In this vein, freedom to trade means that exchange rates are freely floating and there are no other restrictions on trade (such as tariff and non-tariff restrictions) (Friedman, 1969, 67-74). Studies even suggest that trade liberalization has a positive effect on economic growth (Wacziarg & Welch, 2008), unless the economy's labor market and business sector are excessively regulated (Bolaky & Freund, 2004).

Although scholars of substantive economic liberalism favor free trade, it does not necessarily increase the legitimacy of the state. As argued above, the reason is that trade freedom has effects on the production and the consumption sphere. On the one hand, trade freedom has a positive effect on the consumption sphere (due to lower prices, higher quality of products, and a larger range of products). On the other hand, trade freedom may have negative effects on the production sphere. In detail, this means that people may be negatively affected by trade freedom due to a higher risk of unemployment and/or lower wages due to labor migration or the insolvency of ineffective domestic firms (which would survive in a less competitive environment). As a consequence, the relationship between trade freedom and legitimacy is not determinable in advance. According to the liberal perspective, one should expect that any restriction on trade (in terms of tariffs, regulatory barriers, or control of capital, and/or people movement; Gwartney et al., 2014, 4) should lead to less legitimacy. The rationale is that individuals' freedom of choice declines if they do not have access to the international markets. However, as mentioned earlier, people may evaluate more trade freedom as an 'evil', in particular if they lose their jobs due to foreign competition or if trade freedom threatens the standards of products (e.g. TTIP where the German public fears the 'chlorine chicken'; Klodt, 2015, 1). This could mean that too much trade freedom reduces legitimacy. Thus, it is hardly possible to say whether state legitimacy is higher in more closed or more open economies. In consequence, I expect either a positive or an inverted u-shaped relationship between the area 'freedom to trade internationally' and legitimacy.

This area of economic freedom consists of four components, namely (i) tariffs, (ii) regulatory trade barriers, (iii) black-market exchange rates, and (iv) controls of the movement of capital and people. The following enumeration gives a more comprehensive review:

- *Tariffs.* Tariffs typically lead to an increase in the price of foreign products in the domestic market. In consequence, people's freedom to choose declines. That not only means that foreign products may become more expensive (or even unaffordable), but also may force foreign producers to retreat from the domestic market. Unsurprisingly, the tariff level is a determinant of the trade volume and its growth rates (Baier & Bergstrand, 2001). To measure this component, Gwartney et al. (2015, 208-209) use three distinct sub-components, namely (i) the revenues from trade taxes in percent of the trade sector (a higher share of revenues means a lower rating), (ii) the (unweighted) mean tariff rate (a higher tariff rate leads to a lower rating), and (iii) the standard deviation of tariff rates (a higher variation of tariff rates leads to lower ratings since "wide variations in tariff rates indicate greater efforts towards central planning of the economy's production and consumption patterns") (Gwartney et al., 2015, 208-209).
- *Regulatory Trade Barriers.* Regulatory trade barriers are another factor that restricts international trade (Disdier et al., 2008). Gwartney et al. (2015, 6) note that "the volume of trade is also reduced if the passage of goods through customs is onerous and time consuming." Other studies come to similar conclusions (Chen et al., 2006; Djankov et al., 2010; Maskus et al., 2005; Nordås et al., 2006). For example, Nordås et al. (2006) find that time reduces the trade volume and stress that lengthy export and import procedures lower "the probability that firms will enter export markets for time sensitive products at all." Chen et al. (2006, 2) also note that "testing procedures and lengthy inspection procedures by importers reduce exports by 9% and 3%, respectively." To measure this component, Gwartney et al. (2015, 209) use two distinct sub-components, namely (i) non-tariff trade barriers (countries with higher tariff and non-tariff barriers receive lower ratings) and (ii) compliance cost of importing and exporting (a higher final rating corresponds to lower time costs for export and import procedures) (Gwartney et al., 2015, 209).
- *Black-Market Exchange Rates.* A premium on black-market exchange rates signals a limited convertibility of the domestic currency. Since free trade requires a freely convertible currency, a high black market premium is a signal of restricted trading opportunities. To measure this component, Gwartney et al. (2015, 210) calculate "the percentage difference between the official and the parallel (black) market exchange rate." A higher black market premium lowers the rating of a country. In the case of a fully convertible currency without any restrictions, a country receives the score 10.
- *Controls of the Movement of Capital and People.* On the one hand, controls of the movement of capital and people are an impediment to free trade. For example, Tamirisa (1999, 84) finds that "capital controls [...] reduce bilateral trade for developing and transition economies, but not for industrial countries."

> On the other hand, the scientific literature shows that capital controls can also have advantages. For example, Ostry et al. (2010) note that capital controls can have a positive effect on a country's liability structure and its resilience to economic crisis. To measure this component, Gwartney et al. (2015, 210) use three sub-components, namely (i) foreign ownership of companies and investment restrictions (a higher degree of foreign ownership and a lower degree of investment restrictions lead to a higher score), (ii) capital controls (a country receives lower ratings when employing more capital controls), and (iii) the freedom of foreigners to visit (a country receives lower ratings when "the percentage of countries for which a country requires a visa from foreign visitors" is higher) (Gwartney et al., 2015, 210).

In sum, this area of economic freedom measures the degree of trade freedom. When referring to the components, countries receive a high rating when tariffs are low, the administration of customs is efficient, the domestic currency is freely convertible, and only a few controls on the movement of labor and capital exist (Gwartney et al., 2015, 6). Unfortunately, no item directly captures quotas, which is a shortcoming in this area. Although the components are in line with liberal thinking, it is not clearly derivable whether more trade freedom also leads to more legitimacy. The reason is that more trade freedom also implies more competition from foreign firms. If domestic firms have a low competitiveness, individuals (who profit from trade freedom as customers) are likely to lose their jobs or get lower wages. Thus, if the people perceive more trade freedom as a threat, their legitimacy beliefs will decline. To have a working hypothesis, I expect that the relationship between the area 'freedom to trade internationally' and legitimacy is either positive or inverted u-shaped.

6.2.5 The Fifth Area: Regulation

The degree of regulation also determines economic freedom. Gwartney et al. (2015, 6) note that "when regulations restrict entry into markets and interfere with the freedom to engage in voluntary exchange, they reduce economic freedom." However, one needs to acknowledge that economic freedom does not necessarily mean that the state is not in the business of not regulating at all. Rather, as Hayek (1960, 193) notes, "freedom of economic activity had meant freedom under the law, not the absence of all government action." In particular, Hayek (1960, 197) stresses that regulatory activities are compatible with a free society under some assumptions.

First, any regulation has to satisfy the principles of the rule of law. That means that a regulation should be a general and abstract rule; or, as Hayek (1960, 197) puts it, "[…] a free system does not exclude on principle all those general regulations of economic activity which can be laid down in the form of general rules specifying conditions which everybody who engages in a certain activity must satisfy." Further, regulations should be published in advance and should leave as little discretionary power as possible to the authorities. Again, Hayek (1960, 198) notes that: "Regulations drawn up by the administrative authority itself but duly published in advance and strictly adhered to will be more in conformity with the rule of law than will vague discretionary powers conferred on the administrative organs by legislative action." Second, regulations should not discriminate arbitrarily between persons (which is a consequence of the first point). In particular, Hayek (1960, 199) stresses that it should make no difference "who is to be allowed to provide different services or commodities, at what prices or in what quantities—in other words, measures designed to control the access to different trades and occupations, the terms of sale, and the amounts to be produced or sold." Although restrictions on the freedom of occupation and the freedom to set prices and quantities threatens economic freedom, Hayek (1960, 199) underlines that some occupations require a minimum level of qualification. That does not necessarily violate the liberal principle as long as every individual that possesses "the necessary qualification has the right to practice the occupation in question and, if necessary, can have his claim examined and enforced by an independent court".[192] In contrast, Hayek (1960, 199-200) argues that any control of prices or quantities violates the liberal principle because any kind of control "must in their very nature be discretionary and arbitrary" and, thus, gives "it [the authorities, author's note] power [...] to determine what is to be produced, by whom, and for whom." Hayek (1960, 199-200) names a variety of arguments to underline that:

> *In the first place, it is impossible to fix prices according to long-term rules which will effectively guide production. Appropriate prices depend on circumstances which are constantly changing and must be continually adjusted to them. On the other hand, prices which are not fixed outright but determined by some rule (such as that they must be in a certain relation to cost) will not be the same for all sellers and, for this reason, will prevent the market from functioning. A still more important consideration is that, with prices different from those that would form on a free market, demand and supply will not be equal, and if the price control is to be effective, some method must be found for deciding who is to be allowed to buy or sell. This would necessarily be discretionary and must consist of ad hoc decisions that discriminate between persons on essentially arbitrary grounds.*

Third, regulations fit with the liberal principle when the additional costs of regulations help to achieve a given end or help to avoid external costs. In detail, Hayek (1960, 197) writes that: "They [regulations, author's note] will normally raise the cost of production or, what amounts to the same thing, reduce over-all productivity. But if this effect on cost is fully taken into account and it is still thought worthwhile to incur the cost to achieve a given end, there is little more to be said about it."[193]

---

192 In this vein, Hayek (1960, 199) also notes that licensing authorities should be abandoned according to the liberal principle: "The restriction of coercion to the enforcement of general rules require, however, that any one possessing these qualifications have an enforcible claim to such permission and that the grant of the permission depend only on his satisfying the conditions laid down as a general rule and not on any particular circumstances (such as "local need") which would have to be determined by the discretion of the licensing authority."

193 As an example, Hayek (1960, 225) refers to phosphorus matches. He (1960, 225) notes that: "But if, for instance, the production and sale of phosphorus matches is generally prohibited for reasons

Based on these considerations, countries with fewer regulations (regarding prices, quantities, and labor) show a higher degree of economic freedom since people are less restricted in following their own ends (Gwartney et al., 2014, 6). Thus, at first glance, fewer regulatory restrictions should also lead to a higher degree of legitimacy. However, there are some arguments against a linear relationship between 'regulation' and legitimacy. First, as argued above, since some regulations are compatible with a free society (such as regulations to avoid external effects in the production sphere or labor market regulations to ensure that only qualified individuals can work in a particular job), too little regulation may also be harmful and, thus, leads to less legitimacy. Second, not all people may prefer fewer regulations since some people may benefit from existing (or planned) regulations. For example, the abandonment of licenses would increase competition and lower the rents of existing firms in a particular sector (e.g. taxi driver licenses). In consequence, the relationship between the degree of regulation and legitimacy is by no means unidirectional: It depends on whether an individual wins or loses from a regulation. To have a working hypothesis, I expect a linear or an inverted u-shaped relationship between 'regulation' and legitimacy.

The EFW Index assumes that more regulation reduces economic freedom. In greater detail, the area 'regulation' consists of three sub-dimensions, namely (i) credit market regulations, (ii) labor market regulations, and (iii) business regulations (all of those consist of several components):

- *Credit Market Regulations.* This sub-dimension consists of three components that reflect "the conditions in the domestic credit market"; countries receive a better rating when using "a private banking system to allocate credit to private parties" and refraining "from controlling interest rates" (Gwartney et al., 2015, 6). The sub-components are (i) ownership of banks (as measured by "the percentage of bank deposits held in privately owned banks"; countries with a higher share of deposits held in private hand receive a higher score), (ii) private-sector credit (as measured by "the extent of government borrowing relative to private-sector borrowing"; a higher degree in government borrowing leads to lower ratings), and (iii) interest rate controls/negative real interest rates (countries receive a higher rating when the market determines the interest rates, the monetary policy is stable, and the spread between the real-deposit and the lending rate is reasonable) (Gwartney et al., 2015, 211-212).
- *Labor Market Regulations.* As mentioned above, some degree of labor market regulation is reasonable, particularly when ensuring that only people with a minimum level of qualification can enter a specific occupation (Hayek, 1960, 199). On the other hand, too much regulation of the labor market leads to harmful effects. For example, Loayza et al.(2005, 1) note that "a heavier regulatory burden --particularly in product and labor markets-- reduces growth and induces informality", which may diminish the legitimacy of the state. In

of health or permitted only if certain precautions are taken, or if night work is generally prohibited, the appropriateness of such measures must be judged by comparing the over-all costs with the gain; it cannot be conclusively determined by appeal to a general principle."

this vein, a small degree of labor market regulations should maximize the state's legitimacy. Gwartney et al. (2015, 6) use six components to reflect the degree to which "minimum wages, dismissal regulations, centralized wage setting, extension of union contracts to nonparticipating parties, and conscription" restrict the freedom of employees and employers. In particular, these are (i) hiring market regulations (countries receive higher ratings when it is less difficult to hire people), (ii) hiring and firing regulations (countries with a lower degree of hiring and firing regulations receive higher ratings), (iii) centralized collective bargaining (countries receive higher ratings when collective bargaining is less centralized), (iv) hours regulation (countries receive higher ratings when hours – in terms of restrictions on night work, weekly holiday work, the length of the workweek, overtime, and vacation – are less regulated), (v) mandated cost of worker dismissal (countries receive higher ratings when the cost "of the advance notice requirements, severance payments and penalties due when dismissing a redundant worker with 10 years tenure" are lower), and (vi) conscription (countries with longer conscription periods receive lower ratings since affected people cannot enter the labor market) (Gwartney et al., 2015, 212-214).

- *Business Regulations.* The third sub-dimension of this area is business regulations. According to Gwartney et al. (2015, 7), this component is "designed to identify the extent to which regulations and bureaucratic procedures restrain entry and reduce competition." That means that economic freedom increases if countries allow the market to determine prices and if regulations do not increase the costs of productions and hinder the entry to markets (Gwartney et al., 2015, 7). As known from standard textbook economics, entry barriers may diminish the positive effects of competition due to an emerging dead-weight loss. As an empirical example, Schivardi and Viviano (2011) find that – in the Italian retail trade sector – "entry barriers are associated with substantially larger profit margins and lower productivity of incumbent firms." Thus, a liberalization of business regulations lowers the rent of the producers but increases the rent of consumers such that total welfare increases. Regarding the measurement, this sub-area is an index consisting of six components. Those are (i) administrative requirements (countries with burdensome administrative requirements receive lower ratings), (ii) bureaucracy costs (countries with lax or non-existent bureaucracy costs receive higher ratings), (iii) starting a business (countries receive higher ratings when "the amount of time and money it takes to start a new limited liability business" is lower), (iv) extra payment/bribes/favouritism (countries receive higher ratings when the degree to which extra payments or bribes are necessary for running a business is lower), (v) licensing restrictions (countries receive higher ratings when "the time in days and monetary costs required to obtain a license to construct a standard warehouse" are lower), and (vi) cost of tax compliance (countries receive higher ratings when the "time required per year for a business to prepare, file, and pay taxes on corporate income, value added or sales taxes, and taxes on labor" are lower) (Gwartney et al., 2015, 214-215).

To sum up, regulations are a severe obstacle to economic freedom. To give some examples, too much regulation may foster monopolies (when entry barriers are too high), may decrease the willingness of potential entrepreneurs to set up a new business (due to high entry costs in terms of time and money), or may lead to unpleasant allocations of labor (due to too restrictive hiring and firing regulations). On the other hand, regulations are sometimes necessary, particularly to diminish negative external effects, to lower the degree of asymmetric information, or to prevent the emergence of (natural) monopolies or cartels. In this vein, it is difficult to predict an optimal level (or a legitimacy-enhancing level) of regulation in advance. In addition, since regulatory affairs subsume credit market regulations, labor market regulations, and business regulations, it would be interesting to analyze which of these fields are important for legitimacy and which are not. In the following, I hypothesize that no regulation at all (which leads to the maximum degree of economic freedom) should undermine the legitimacy of the state since the costs of external effects may exceed the benefits of freedom. Furthermore, when regulations are too high (economic freedom becomes low), people may feel unfree or imprisoned such that legitimacy should decrease. Thus, a small degree of regulations should be legitimacy-enhancing (e.g. such regulations that avoid external effects in the production sphere or labor market regulations to ensure that only qualified individuals can work in a particular job). As a consequence, as also mentioned above, I expect either a linear or an inverted u-shaped relationship between 'regulation' and legitimacy.

6.2.6 Summarizing the Hypotheses

The analyses above show that the relationship between the areas of economic freedom and legitimacy is by no means unidirectional or simply linear. For example, I expect that the relationship between 'government size' and legitimacy is inverted u-shaped. Then, a reduction of the government size increases economic freedom but the impact on legitimacy remains unclear since it could be positive or negative. Assuming a reduction of the government size below the minimal level that is proposed by Hayek (i.e. the state does not provide any public goods), economic freedom increases (according to the construction of the EFW Index) but legitimacy decreases. Thus, in this example, I expect that an increase of economic freedom leads to a reduction of legitimacy. The same considerations also apply to the areas 'regulation' and 'freedom to trade internationally' (since I also expect an inverted u-shaped relationship between these areas and legitimacy). Table 32 summarizes the hypotheses.

Based on these hypotheses, one can derive that the relationship between economic freedom and legitimacy is not determinable in advance. To show this mathematically, legitimacy *L* depends on economic freedom *EF* as expressed in equation [25] (all other factors impacting legitimacy are suppressed).

$$L = L(EF) \qquad [25]$$

Since economic freedom *EF* consists of five areas, one can substitute these into the equation, which leads to equation [26] (where *RoL* stands for the rule of law (i.e. 'legal

Table 32: Areas of Economic Freedom and Expected Relationships to Legitimacy

Area of Economic Freedom (EFW index)	Expected Relationship to Legitimacy
Legal System and Property Rights	Positive (linear)
Size of Government	Positive (linear) or inverted u-shaped
Sound Money	Positive (linear)
Freedom to Trade Internationally	Positive (linear) or inverted u-shaped
Regulation	Positive (linear) or inverted u-shaped

system and property rights'), *GS* is the abbreviation of the 'government size', *SM* expresses 'sound money', *FT* symbolizes 'freedom to trade internationally', and *R* means 'regulation').

$$L = L(RoL, GS, SM, FT, R) \quad [26]$$

For analyzing the impact on legitimacy, one can take the total derivative, receiving equation [27].

$$dL = L_{RoL}\, d\,RoL + L_{GS}\, d\,GS + L_{SM}\, d\,SM + L_{FT}\, d\,FT + L_R\, d\,R \quad [27]$$

Now, one can assume that each area of economic freedom increases by one (i.e. also overall economic freedom increases) as expressed in equation [28].

$$d\,RoL = d\,GS = d\,SM = d\,FT = d\,R = 1 \quad [28]$$

In this case, the overall impact on legitimacy ΔL is the sum of the partial derivatives (equation [29]).

$$dL = L_{RoL} + L_{GS} + L_{SM} + L_{FT} + L_R \quad [29]$$

Based on the expected relationships to legitimacy (table 32), the signs of the partial derivatives can be either positive (in the cases of the 'rule of law' and 'sound money') or not clearly identifiable (which means that the signs can be positive, negative, or zero in the cases of 'government size', 'regulation', and 'freedom to trade internationally'). Thus, in mathematical terms, one finds that $L_{RoL} > 0$, $L_{GS} \lesseqgtr 0$, $L_{SM} > 0$, $L_{FT} \lesseqgtr 0$, $L_R \lesseqgtr 0$. When plugging the partial derivatives into equation [29], equation [30] shows that the overall impact on legitimacy is not clearly identifiable.

$$dL \lesseqgtr (>0) + (\lesseqgtr 0) + (>0) + (\lesseqgtr 0) + (\lesseqgtr 0) \quad [30]$$

Thus, referring to the areas of economic freedom, one cannot simply argue that more economic freedom leads to more legitimacy. However, since two areas of economic freedom should have a clear positive effect on legitimacy and the other three may be positive as well, there is a high probability that more economic freedom also leads to more legitimacy. The result strongly depends on the starting position of the country. If a country has a very large government size with a maximum degree of regulation, an increase of economic freedom should also lead to more legitimacy. In contrast, if a country is already on the ideal level of economic freedom regarding 'government size' and 'regulation', any increase or decrease of these areas (and, thus, ceteris paribus, also economic freedom) should lead to a reduction of legitimacy.

6.2.7 Alternative Arguments

Besides the relationships between economic freedom's areas and legitimacy, further arguments exist for and against economic freedom for which I do not account in the later empirical part. Nonetheless, for reasons of completeness, I present these arguments in the following.

At first, as Hayek (1944, 1960) stresses, economic freedom also means individual responsibility, which may place too much pressure on the individuals. As argued in chapter 6.1.3, if the perceived pressure of market freedom is larger than the perceived benefits of free choice, too much economic freedom may reduce legitimacy; and if the costs of illiberalism outweigh the benefits of less individual responsibility, too little economic freedom also may lower legitimacy. As a consequence, the relationship between economic freedom and legitimacy may not be simply linear.

Second, according to psychological findings, evaluations of the market and economic freedom may be based on systematic cognitive failures, in particular the anti-market and the anti-foreign bias (Caplan, 2007, 23-49). Following Caplan (2007, 30), the anti-market bias is defined as "a tendency to underestimate the economic benefits of the market mechanism." If the individuals underestimate the economic benefits of the market mechanism (in particular competition), they may conclude that more competition (and so economic freedom) is harmful. If that were true, more economic freedom would lead to less legitimacy. The same considerations also apply to the anti-foreign bias which is defined as "a tendency to underestimate the economic benefits of interaction with foreigners" (Caplan, 2007, 36). Here, the individuals may not consider that trade with foreigners typically leads to trade gains (which increase wealth due to absolute and/or comparative advantages). In the same fashion, that also applies to the immigration of labor. Here, citizens not only often ignore the benefits of labor migration but also see migration as a threat to the domestic labor market. Thus, individuals may come to the conclusion that more trade freedom (and thus more economic freedom) damages the society.

Third, economic freedom may be morally undesirable. Based on a discourse-analytic approach, Nullmeier (2013) investigates the legitimacy of the market economy based on quality newspapers. Although his results suggest that the market economy has no legitimacy deficit, he (2013, 39) extracts three moral arguments that are typically put forward against the market: (i) The market economy destroys the moral foundation of the society since it makes social cohesion and solidarity impossible; (ii) the market economy is based on old-boy networks and insufficient virtues of leadership; and (iii) in the market economy, pure greed governs the society.

Fourth, the impact of economic freedom on legitimacy may depend on the underlying beliefs (in terms of economic history). If that were the case, the net effect of increasing economic freedom on legitimacy would depend on the history of economic freedom (which is similar to the idea that the impact of democracy on legitimacy depends on a country's democratic history). In a study that deals with the legitimization of capitalism in the post-communist transition, Kluegel et al. (1999, 252) note that "if the postcommunist states are to successfully navigate the transition from state socialism to capitalism, their populations will also have to develop a sense of 'market justice' and to abandon, in part at least, their former beliefs in 'socialist justice'." If that is true, one can derive that the impact of economic freedom on legitimacy depends on the underlying beliefs toward the market, which can be approximated by the history of economic freedom. Then, an increase of economic freedom also leads to more legitimacy if the citizens have (historically shaped) pro-market attitudes. In contrast, if the underlying beliefs favor a socialist system, an increase in economic freedom should result in decreasing legitimacy. To check this, one could implement a further variable (economic history). However, since the EFW Index was first published in 1996, the data basis is not appropriate to calculate an economic history score. Thus, I leave this task to another study.

6.2.8 Summary

As this chapter shows, economic freedom may be an important determinant of the state's legitimacy, which can be derived in particular from the works of Hayek (1944, 1960) and partly also Friedman (1969). On the conceptual level, the argument is that more economic freedom gives the individuals the possibility to follow their own ends without interference from others. In this sense, freedom is the absence of coercion (Hayek, 1944). For measuring economic freedom, several indices exist such as the EFW or the IEF. In this thesis, I stick to the EFW Index. A deeper analysis of the EFW Index shows that economic freedom is a multidimensional concept that consists of several areas, namely (i) 'legal system and property rights' (reflecting the rule of law), (ii) 'government size', (iii) 'sound money', (iv) 'freedom to trade internationally', and (v) 'regulation'. I also pointed out that not all areas of economic freedom theoretically have a linear positive relationship to legitimacy. For example, the areas 'government size', 'freedom to trade internationally', and 'regulation' may have an inverted u-shaped relationship to legitimacy. Thus, the net effect of an increase of the EFW Index on legitimacy is indeterminable in advance (which is also the result when considering alternative hypotheses, see above). Based on these considerations, one should use not only the overall EFW Index as an independent variable but also the areas of economic freedom. This allows the analysis which areas drive the relationship between the EFW Index and legitimacy at the aggregated level.

6.3 Empirical Investigations at the Country Level

In the previous sub-chapters, I discussed the relationships between the areas of economic freedom and legitimacy. This chapter analyzes these relationships statistically at the country level. To approach this task, I apply the basic model and its control variables (see chapter 5). As dependent variables, I use both Gilley's and Norris' legitimacy scores, which are available at three points in time (ca. 2001, 2008, and 2012). The idea is to add the EFW Index and its areas to the basic model and to investigate which areas of economic freedom are statistically significant.
In short, the results suggest that the most important area for enhancing legitimacy is 'legal system and property rights', reflecting the rule of law. The other areas have no robust impact on legitimacy. The areas 'government size', 'sound money', and 'freedom to trade internationally' show only statistically significant coefficients in a few regressions. In fact, there is even some evidence that a large government size enhances legitimacy, which contrasts with the liberal perspective. When focusing on trade freedom, the results are ambivalent, meaning that one can find significantly positive and significantly negative coefficients. Regarding 'sound money', there is weak evidence that a stable monetary framework increases the state's legitimacy. No significant coefficients emerge when referring to the area 'regulation'.
The remainder of this section is structured as follows. In chapter 6.3.1, I first deal with some methodological issues: A presentation of the econometric strategy, a discussion of the model specification, and some information about the data preparation. In the next sub-section (chapter 6.3.2), I present the results. In particular, I first state correlations between legitimacy and economic freedom's areas. After that, I add each area to the basic model and discuss the results. At first, I do this with Gilley's legitimacy scores as the dependent variable. To check the robustness of the results, I perform the same procedure with Norris' legitimacy scores as the dependent variable. Chapter 6.3.3 summarizes the results and offers a conclusion.

6.3.1 Methodological Issues
Econometric Strategy and Discussion of the Specification

To analyze whether economic freedom impacts legitimacy, I add the EFW Index or its areas to the basic model (see chapter 5). In a formalized fashion, the regression equations read as follows,

$$Legitimacy = \beta_0 + \boldsymbol{\beta} \boldsymbol{X} + \alpha_1 \, EFW + \epsilon \qquad [31]$$

$$Legitimacy = \beta_0 + \boldsymbol{\beta} \boldsymbol{X} + \boldsymbol{\alpha} \, \boldsymbol{AREAS}_{EFW} + \epsilon \qquad [32]$$

where $\boldsymbol{X}$ reflect the (control) variables, *EFW* stands for the Index of Economic Freedom, $\mathbf{AREAS}_{\mathbf{EFW}}$ refer to the vector (or the combination) of areas of economic freedom under investigation, and ε reflects the error term. Since the areas of economic freedom may have different impacts on legitimacy, the results of equation [31] serve as a starting point. It is more interesting to extract which areas of economic freedom actually impact legitimacy.

However, my econometric strategy also has some theoretical shortcomings. These emerge (i) from the interdependence of economic and political freedom and (ii) from classifying economic freedom as belonging to the output channel.

- *Dependence between Political and Economic Freedom.* Since the econometric strategy is to add the EFW Index (and its areas) to the basic model, both political freedom (democracy) and economic freedom (EFW Index) are part of the right-hand side of the equation. However, one should be careful in assuming that both types of freedom are independent. For example, Friedman (1969, 7) notes that "it is widely believed that politics and economics are separate and largely unconnected; that individual freedom is a political problem and material welfare an economic problem; and that any kind of political arrangements can be combined with any kind of economic arrangements". However, according to Friedman (1969, 8), "such a view is a delusion" since "there is an intimate connection between economics and politics, that only certain combinations of political and economic arrangements are possible [...]." Thus, Friedman (1969, 10) stresses that "the relation between political and economic freedom is complex and by no means unilateral." In the same vein, Scharpf (1999, 29) also notes that "the democratic state and the capitalist economy coexist in symbiotic interdependence." Different theoretical explanations exist why economic and political freedom are interrelated (North et al., 2009; Hayek, 1960; Friedman, 1969).

  According to the Friedman-Hayek hypothesis, economic freedom is a necessary condition for political freedom; or with the words of Lawson and Clark (2010, 230), "societies with high levels of political freedom must also have high levels of economic freedom." In contrast, the hypothesis allows for the possibility that political freedom is low while economic freedom is high (famous examples are countries like Singapore or Hong Kong). In other words, Lawson and Clark (2010, 231) note that the hypothesis "does not say that economically free societies must be politically free." Hayek (1944, 74) writes:

  > *Our point, however, is not that dictatorship must inevitably extirpate freedom, but rather that planning leads to dictatorship because dictatorship is the most effective instrument of coercion and the enforcement of ideals, and as such essential if central planning on a large scale is to be possible. The clash between planning and democracy arises simply from the fact that the latter is an obstacle to the suppression of freedom which the direction of economic activity requires.*

  The hypothesis bases on Hayek's argument that voters will not accept decisions made by economic planners. The reason is that "the making of an economic plan involves the choice between conflicting or competing ends" among which the planner has to decide (Hayek, 1944, 68). Thus, central planning contains the risk that the economic plan does not serve the ends of individuals. In this sense, a democratic society cannot coexist with central planning. Instead, voters in a democracy would vote for parties that enhance economic liberty. That ensures that the individuals can follow their own ends (Lawson & Clark, 2010). According to Lawson and Clark (2010), empirical evidence supports the Friedman-Hayek hypothesis.[194]

The Friedman-Hayek hypothesis suggests that economic freedom is a necessary precondition for political freedom. Thus, since both political and economic freedom are determinants of legitimacy, the question emerges how to deal with both freedoms in statistical analyses.[195] In different research contexts, various scholars treat economic and political freedom as two separate independent variables (Barro,1996; Farr et al., 1998; Goel & Nelson, 2005; De Soysa & Vadlammanati, 2013).[196] In contrast, others not only use both variables separately but also add interactions (Stroup, 2007; 2008). For example, Stroup (2007; 2008) also includes interaction terms that consist of (i) economic freedom and a dummy that reflects high political freedom and (ii) political freedom and a dummy that reflects high economic freedom. In the following empirical analyses, I follow the first strategy, namely to include both variables (economic and political freedom) without any interaction term. The reason is that I use not only the EFW Index but also its areas in the upcoming regressions.

- *Economic Freedom in an Input-Output Framework.* Regarding the input-output framework of legitimacy, economic freedom and its areas clearly belong to output legitimacy. This means that the economic institutional setting is the result of a decision-making process (which could be democratic or autocratic) that is collectively binding.[197] Then, if economic institutions – that are in accordance with substantive liberalism – serve the common interest („government for the people", see Scharpf, 1999, 2), they are legitimacy-enhancing. In this vein, unless one knows the interests of the people, one cannot say in advance that liberal economic institutions (for example, only few regulations) are legitimacy-enhancing. Or in other words, one can only say in advance whether liberal economic institutions enhance legitimacy if the interests of the people are known. If that were the case, one could simply check

194 In greater detail, Lawson and Clark (2010) find that (a) only a few cases exist where political freedom is high but economic freedom is low and (b) the amount of cases violating the Hayek-Friedman hypothesis diminish over time.

195 A variety of studies find a strong positive correlation between economic freedom and political freedom (see Lawson & Clark, 2010 for a literature overview). In addition, I also find a positive relationship between economic freedom (EFW index) and political freedom (democracy index) in my data (r_{2001}=0.64; r_{2008}=0.60; r_{2012}=0.25).

196 Barro (1997) uses a rule-of-law index (which can be interpreted as one area of economic freedom) and a democracy index.

197 Following Wegner (2009, 540), it does not matter for substantive economic liberalism (SEL) „whether the nature of the state is autocratic or democratic; rather, SEL reminds us that politics in democracy, as in any other state, makes use of coercive power and thus potentially restricts private coordination in various ways".

whether the economic institutional setting is in line with the interests and, if not, one could change the economic institutional setting in a decision-making process. However, since I assume that the interests of the people are unknown, statistical investigations help to extract whether economic freedom is in line with the common interest of the people or not.

Although I treat economic freedom as an output variable in the following statistical analyses, economic freedom (as a part of the output dimension) is also linked to both the input dimension and other variables of the output dimension. Regarding economic freedom's relationship to input legitimacy, it is important to notice that the input channel (mainly the degree of democracy) and economic freedom are theoretically interdependent (see above). To be more precise, according to the Friedman-Hayek hypothesis, economic freedom is a necessary condition for political freedom (see above). In a similar vein, North et al. (2009) speak about a "double balance" between economic and political freedom. When referring to the relationships between economic freedom and other economic output variables, one should note that economic freedom (or at least some areas of economic freedom, see Heckelman & Stroup, 2005) is a predictor of the GDP growth rate (Berggren, 2003; Heckelman & Stroup, 2005) and, thus, also an antecedent of the welfare level in the long run (Goldsmith, 1997).[198]

In this sense, economic freedom predicts other determinants of legitimacy. To model this correctly, one should ideally use lagged variables for economic freedom in the regressions, use multi-stage models, or, if data were available, apply time series models. However, I leave these tasks to other studies and follow the strategy to add economic freedom and its areas to the basic model. The reason is that the interest of this thesis lies in investigating the relevance of the institutions themselves for legitimacy.

Data Preparation

This chapter uses the same data as chapter 5 (extraction of the basic model). To this data, I add the EFW Index and its areas. Overall, I do this six times, namely three times when using Gilley's and three times when using Norris' legitimacy scores (ca. 2001, 2008, and 2012 each).

In the cases of Gilley's legitimacy scores, I simply add the scores of the EFW Index or its areas from 2001, 2008, and 2012 to the data. In the ca. 2001 wave, EFW scores for Armenia, Azerbaijan, Belarus, Bosnia & Herzegowina, Georgia, Macedonia, Moldova, and Serbia are missing. In addition, for Albania, Algeria, Iran, Parkistan, Tanzania, and Uganda, no values for labor and business regulations exist. Referring to the ca. 2008 and ca. 2012 waves, there are no missing values. In the cases of missing items, I drop the observations.

In the cases of Norris' legitimacy scores, I add the scores of the EFW Index or its areas from the year that corresponds to the survey date of the legitimacy scores. That means

198 Note again that not all areas of economic freedom have a positive impact on the growth rate (Carlsson & Lundström, 2002).

that I take the EFW scores from 2000 when the legitimacy scores stem from 2000. When the date of interview was 1999, I take the EFW scores from 2000. The reason is that the EFW Index has seven areas before 2000 (table 33). Similarly, when the date of interview was 2014, I take EFW data from 2013 since data from 2014 were not available at the time of investigation. In the case of the ca. 2001 wave, scores for Belarus, Bosnia and Herzegovina, Macedonia, Serbia, Vietnam, Moldova, Saudi-Arabia, Kyrgyzstan, and Iraq are missing. In addition, for Albania, Algeria, Croatia, Iran, Luxembourg, and Malta, no values for labor and business regulations are available. When referring to the ca. 2008 wave, no EFW values are available for Andorra and Iraq. Similarly, in the ca. 2012 wave, scores are missing in the cases of Belarus and Iraq. As above, I drop the observations in the case of missing items.

6.3.2 Results

Gilley's Legitimacy Scores as Dependent Variable

To get a first impression, I calculate the correlations between legitimacy and the EFW Indices for the three waves under investigation.[199] Table 33 presents the results.

Table 33: Correlations between Legitimacy (Gilley) and Economic Freedom

Correlations	Gilley ca. 2001	Gilley ca. 2008	Gilley ca. 2012
	(1)	(2)	(3)
Economic Freedom (EFW)	0.61***	0.48***	0.48***
Size of Government	-0.42***	-0.18	-0.18
Legal System and Property Rights	0.75***	0.60***	0.72***
Sound Money	0.57***	0.40***	0.31**
Freedom to Trade Internationally	0.54***	0.29**	0.37***
Regulation	0.49***	0.32**	0.42***
Credit Market Regulation	0.48***	0.40***	0.34**
Labor Market Regulation	0.02	0.09	0.24*
Business Regulation	0.60***	0.27*	0.39***

* - at 10%-level significant ** - at 5%-level significant *** - at 1%-level significant

The correlations between the EFW Index and legitimacy are significantly positive in all waves ($r_{2001}=0.61^{***}$, $r_{2008}=0.48^{***}$, $r_{2012}=0.48^{***}$). Although this indicates that economic freedom is positively related to legitimacy, one should abstain from concluding that more economic freedom leads, ceteris paribus, to more legitimacy. The reason is that economic freedom is typically high in countries which also have good general governance and a high level of welfare.

199 In this chapter, I assume that both the legitimacy scores as well as the EFW index (and its areas) are metric variables. This allows me to calculate simple correlations and to use the OLS method.

Focusing on economic freedom's areas reveals that the area 'legal system and property rights' shows the highest correlations in all three waves (r_{2001}= 0.75***, r_{2008}= 0.60***, r_{2012}= 0.72***). That indicates that this area drives the correlations between the EFW Index and legitimacy, in particular since the sizes of the correlations of the other areas are lower. To begin with, the area 'government size' shows negative correlations, indicating that a larger government size increases legitimacy. In fact, this finding contradicts the liberal perspective. However, since the correlations are insignificant in two of the three waves, there is only limited evidence that the area 'government size' matters (r_{2001}= -0.42***, r_{2008}= -0.18, r_{2012}= -0.18). Next, the positive correlation of the area 'sound money' indicates that low inflation rates and a stable price level may enhance legitimacy, which fits with the theoretical considerations (r_{2001}= 0.57***, r_{2008}= 0.40***, r_{2012}= 0.31**). Similarly, the correlations between the area 'freedom to trade internationally' and legitimacy are significantly positive, showing that more open countries also have higher legitimacy scores (r_{2001}= 0.54***, r_{2008}= 0.29**, r_{2012}= 0.37***). Finally, the area 'regulation' also correlates positively with legitimacy (r_{2001}= 0.49***, r_{2008}= 0.32**, r_{2012}= 0.34**). Again, this indicates that countries with fewer regulatory activities show higher legitimacy beliefs (in particular less credit market regulation and less business regulation; labor market regulation seems to be irrelevant).

To check whether the relationship between the areas 'government size', 'freedom to trade internationally', and 'regulation' are inverted u-shaped, I regress each area and its squared term (here, mean centered to avoid multicollinearity) on legitimacy (that means three regressions per wave). Table 34 shows the results.

Table 34: Testing for Non-Linearity

Dependent: Legitimacy	Gilley ca. 2001	Gilley ca. 2008	Gilley ca. 2012
	(1)	(2)	(3)
Regression 1: Only Government Size			
Size of Government	-0.37***	-0.14	-0.24
Size of Government²	0.01	0.18	-0.03
Regression 2: Only Trade Freedom			
Freedom to Trade Internationally	0.64***	0.36	0.88***
Freedom to Trade Internationally²	0.10**	-0.32	0.27**
Regression 3: Only Regulation			
Regulation	0.70***	0.63**	0.79***
Regulation²	0.07	0.27	0.10

* - at 10%-level significant ** - at 5%-level significant *** - at 1%-level significant
Note: All independent variables are mean centered.

Interestingly, only the squared terms of the area 'freedom to trade internationally' are significant in the ca. 2001 and ca. 2012 waves. However, since the linear and the squared term is positive, the regressions provide no evidence for an inverted u-shaped relation. Thus, I just use the linear terms in the following.

Next, although the correlations show for the most part that the areas of economic freedom are related to legitimacy, one should be careful to conclude that an increase in a particular area *leads* to more or less legitimacy. The reason is that the areas of economic freedom are not independent. In consequence, to see which areas remain significant when controlling for the other areas, I run regressions with legitimacy as the dependent variable and the areas of economic freedom as independent variables. Table 35 presents the results.

Table 35: Regressing Legitimacy (Gilley) on Economic Freedom's Areas

Dependent: Legitimacy	Gilley ca. 2001		Gilley ca. 2008		Gilley ca. 2012	
	(1)		(2)		(3)	
	Coeff.	p-value	Coeff.	p-value	Coeff.	p-value
Intercept	3.02***	0.002	0.11	0.964	0.66	0.669
Size of Government	-0.15*	0.097	-0.01	0.944	0.09	0.529
Legal System and Property Rights	0.37***	0.000	0.70***	0.001	0.97***	0.000
Sound Money	0.17*	0.081	0.12	0.594	-0.11	0.526
Freedom to Trade Internationally	-0.06	0.650	-0.11	0.731	-0.17	0.531
Regulation	-0.02	0.924	0.05	0.850	0.04	0.887
R^2	0.60		0.37		0.53	
Adjust. R^2	0.57		0.30		0.48	
Observations	64		51		52	

* - at 10%-level significant ** - at 5%-level significant *** - at 1%-level significant

The results show that the area 'legal system and property rights' (reflecting the rule of law) is the most important area of economic freedom since it is the only area that has a significant coefficient in all three waves (β_{2001}= 0.37***, β_{2008}= 0.70***, β_{2012}= 0.97***). All other areas become insignificant or only significant at the 10%-level. The same pattern emerges when performing a stepwise exclusion of the most insignificant independent variables or when using the sub-areas of 'regulation' ('credit market regulation', 'labor market regulation', and 'business regulation').[200]

Based on these findings, it may be questionable whether one should use the overall EFW Index as an independent variable of the basic model. As table 36 shows, adding the EFW Index to the basic model produces insignificant coefficients (β_{2001}= -0.11, β_{2008}= -0.17, β_{2012}= -0.04). Considering the investigations above (tables 34 and 35), this

200 Regarding the ca. 2001 wave, 'legal system and property rights' is highly significant when using all variables. The areas 'government size' and 'sound money' are only significant at the 10%-level. A stepwise exclusion of the areas 'regulation' and 'freedom to trade internationally' leads to the same result. Similar results occur when using the sub-areas of 'regulation', instead of 'regulation' itself. Regarding the ca. 2008 and the ca. 2012 wave, only the area 'legal system and property rights' is highly significant. The stepwise exclusion of the other insignificant areas leads to the result that solely the area 'legal system and property rights' remains significant. One obtains a similar result when using the sub-areas of 'regulation'. See Appendix P for further details.

Table 36: The Basic Model Plus EFW – OLS Estimates

Dependent: Legitimacy (Gilley)	Gilley ca. 2001			Gilley ca. 2008			Gilley ca. 2012		
	(1)			(2)			(3)		
	Coeff.	t-value	p-value	Coeff.	t-value	p-value	Coeff.	t-value	p-value
Intercept	7.03***	5.335	0.000	5.91*	1.838	0.073	6.50**	2.465	0.012
Input Variables									
Democracy	0.22**	2.498	0.016	0.19	0.881	0.383	0.08	0.599	0.552
Democratic History	-0.09*	-1.834	0.072	0.05	0.440	0.662	0.01	0.143	0.887
Democracy*DemocraticHistory[1]	0.08***	4.056	0.000	0.07	1.437	0.158	0.04	1.418	0.163
Throughput/Output Variables									
General Governance	1.20***	4.952	0.000	1.14**	2.370	0.022	1.11***	3.237	0.002
HDI (absolute)	-4.46***	-3.028	0.004	-3.01	-1.547	0.129	-2.49	-1.304	0.199
Unemployment Rate	-0.01	-0.615	0.541	-0.02	-0.674	0.504	-0.08***	-2.847	0.007
EFW	*-0.11*	*-0.706*	*0.483*	*-0.17*	*-0.385*	*0.702*	*-0.01*	*-0.025*	*0.980*
R^2		0.753			0.541			0.612	
Adjust. R^2		0.721			0.466			0.549	
Observations		62			51			51	

[1] - Interaction term is mean centered.
* - at 10%-level significant ** - at 5%-level significant *** - at 1%-level significant
Note: Democracy is close to multicollinearity in the ca. 2008 wave (VIF=10.70).

is not surprising since the EFW Index is composed of different areas that are partly differently related to legitimacy.

In consequence, it is more reasonable to use the areas of economic freedom as independent variables. Since the area 'legal system and property rights' (i.e. the rule of law) explains legitimacy best (table 35), I initially add it to the basic model (table 37). Interestingly, the results show that the area 'legal system and property rights' is either not significant at all or highly significant (β_{2001}= -0.01, β_{2008}= -0.15, β_{2012}= 0.66**). At the same time, when the area 'legal system and property rights' becomes significant in the ca. 2012 wave, the coefficient of general governance turns insignificant. These changes in size and significance of the coefficients of general governance point toward multicollinearity problems. To check for this, I investigate the variance inflation factors (VIFs) of each wave and also check correlations between general governance

Table 37: The Basic Model Plus Legal System and Property Rights – OLS Estimates

Dependent: Legitimacy (Gilley)	Gilley ca. 2001			Gilley ca. 2008			Gilley ca. 2012		
	(1)			(2)			(3)		
	Coeff.	t-value	p-value	Coeff.	t-value	p-value	Coeff.	t-value	p-value
Intercept	6.45***	5.582	0.000	5.67**	2.207	0.033	2.35	1.091	0.281
Input Variables									
Democracy	0.20**	2.292	0.026	0.18	0.836	0.408	0.10	0.799	0.429
Democratic History	-0.08*	-1.674	0.099	0.05	0.450	0.655	0.09	0.949	0.348
Democracy*DemocraticHistory[1]	0.08***	3.668	0.000	0.08	1.497	0.142	0.02	0.615	0.542
Throughput/Output Variables									
General Governance	1.16***	3.765	0.000	1.24**	2.087	0.043	0.20	0.430	0.670
HDI (absolute)	-4.37***	-2.910	0.005	-3.06	-1.601	0.117	-2.52	-1.412	0.165
Unemployment Rate	-0.01	-0.558	0.580	-0.02	-0.690	0.494	-0.07**	-2.689	0.010
Legal System	*-0.01*	*0.118*	*0.912*	*-0.15*	*-0.443*	*0.660*	*0.66***	*2.458*	*0.018*
R^2		0.751			0.541			0.660	
Adjust. R^2		0.718			0.467			0.605	
Observations		62			51			51	

[1] - Interaction term is mean centered.
* - at 10%-level significant ** - at 5%-level significant *** - at 1%-level significant
Note: Besides the general governance variables, democracy also is close to multicollinearity in the ca. 2008 wave (VIF=10.60).

and 'legal system and property rights'. When including the area 'legal system and property rights' to the regression, severe multicollinearity problems arise since the VIFs are above 10 ($VIF_{2001}^{GeneralGov}$= 13.08, $VIF_{2008}^{GeneralGov}$= 10.65, $VIF_{2012}^{GeneralGov}$= 10.26). A similar result emerges when focusing on the bivariate correlations between general governance and 'legal system and property rights'. All of these indicate that the area 'legal system and property rights' highly correlates with general governance (r_{2001}=0.91***, r_{2008}=0.88***, r_{2012}=0.86***).[201]

201 Correlations between 'legal system and property rights' and government effectiveness also are very high (r_{2001}=0.90; r_{2008}=0.85; r_{2012}=0.84). Similarly, 'legal system and property rights' and control of corruption also are highly correlated (r_{2001}=0.90; r_{2008}=0.87; r_{2012}=0.86).

In consequence, to avoid multicollinearity problems, I add the area 'legal system and property rights' to the general governance index.[202] Thus, the 'new' general governance index consists of the variables government effectiveness, control of corruption, and 'legal system and property rights'; it, thus, equals Gilley's (2006b) general governance index that consists of the variables government effectiveness, control of corruption, and rule of law (all taken from the World Bank). The advantage of this procedure also becomes apparent when analyzing the VIFs of the 'new' general governance variable of the 'new' basic models (i.e when using the 'new' general governance index as an independent variable instead of the 'old' general governance index) since these are significantly below 10 ($VIF_{2001}^{NewGeneralGov}$= 6.37, $VIF_{2008}^{NewGeneralGov}$= 5.17, $VIF_{2012}^{NewGeneralGov}$= 3.10).

This procedure also implies that one should abstain from using the overall EFW Index in the regression (since one of its areas is already part of the 'new' general governance variable). As a consequence, it remains to analyze whether the other four areas ('government size', 'sound money', 'freedom to trade internationally', and 'regulation') have an impact on legitimacy. To do so, I perform several regression runs for each wave (tables 38-40). Each table states the 'new' basic model (1), the 'new' basic model plus one of the areas or sub-areas of economic freedom (model (2)-(8)), and the 'new' basic model plus all four remaining areas of economic freedom (model (9)).

The statistical results indicate that the other four areas of economic freedom have no or only little relevance for explaining legitimacy. Regarding the area 'government size', the regressions show that the true effect of this area remains unclear since the results partly differ across waves. In the ca. 2001 wave, I find a significantly negative coefficient (β_{2001}= -0.15**), which indicates that a smaller (larger) government size reduces (increases) legitimacy. This finding contrasts with the liberal perspective. However, this result could also be a statistical artifact since no significant effect of 'government size' on legitimacy emerges in the ca. 2008 and ca. 2012 waves (β_{2008}= 0.08, β_{2012}= -0.01). That is not surprising since a look at the scatter plots show high-legitimacy states with a low government size (Hong Kong, Singapore, Australia, China, Canada) but also high-legitimacy states with a large government size (Sweden, Finland, Norway, Netherlands, Germany) (see Appendix R). In sum, the effect of the area 'government size' on legitimacy remains a puzzle since the results are not stable across waves. When analyzing the area 'sound money', the regressions provide no evidence for a relationship between 'sound money' and legitimacy since all coefficients do not differ significantly from zero (β_{2001}= 0.08, β_{2008}= 0.03, β_{2012}= -0.14). Thus, the results do not indicate that sound money (in terms of lower inflation rates and price stability) increases state legitimacy as proposed by a liberal view. Similarly, there is no evidence that the area 'freedom to trade internationally' impacts legitimacy. In all waves, the particular coefficients do not differ significantly from zero (β_{2001}= 0.08, β_{2008}= -0.26, β_{2012}= 0.01). Again, the results do not explicitly support the liberal perspective. Finally, the degree of 'regulation' also has no impact on legitimacy since

202 Note that I use the z-transformed values of the area 'legal system and property rights' (since the World Bank's Government Effectiveness Index and the Control of Corruption Index also provide z-scores).

Table 38: The 'New' Basic Model Plus Areas of Economic Freedom (Gilley ca. 2001)

	(1)	(2)	(3)	(4)	(5)	(6)	(7)	(8)	(9)
Intercept	6.01***	6.97***	5.48***	5.69***	7.62***	5.99***	7.50***	8.77***	7.41***
Input Variables									
Democracy	0.17*	0.20**	0.15*	0.15	0.17*	0.17*	0.11	0.04	0.17*
Democratic History	-0.05	-0.03	-0.04	-0.04	-0.04	-0.05	-0.03	-0.03	-0.02
Interaction Term	0.07***	0.07***	0.07***	0.07***	0.07***	0.07***	0.05*	0.04	0.06***
Throughput/Output Variables									
New General Governance	1.05***	0.93***	0.99***	1.04***	1.27***	1.06***	1.21***	1.60***	1.00***
HDI (absolute)	-3.45**	-3.56**	-3.42**	-3.76**	-3.83***	-3.45**	-4.24**	-4.04**	-4.15***
Unemployment Rate	-0.01	-0.01	-0.01	-0.01	-0.01	-0.01	-0.01	-0.01	-0.01
+ Government Size		-0.15**							-0.13*
+ Sound Money			0.08						0.14
+ Freedom to Trade				0.08					-0.01
+ Regulation					-0.24				-0.22
+ Credit Market						0.00			
+ Labor Market							-0.09		
+ Business								-0.29*	
R^2	0.738	0.758	0.744	0.740	0.750	0.737	0.733	0.745	0.778
adjusted R^2	0.709	0.727	0.711	0.707	0.717	0.704	0.694	0.708	0.734
Observations	62	62	62	62	62	62	56	56	62

[1] - Interaction term is mean centered.
* - at 10%-level significant ** - at 5%-level significant *** - at 1%-level significant
Note: New general governance is close to multicollinearity in model (8) (VIF=11.95) and model (9)(VIF=10.30).
Note: The inclusion of a squared term (in the cases of 'government size', 'freedom to trade internationally', and 'regulation') leads to insignificant results (results are shown in Appendix Q).

all coefficients are insignificant (β_{2001}= -0.24, β_{2008}= -0.20, β_{2012}= -0.03). The same results emerge when including the sub-areas of 'regulation' in the regressions (except 'business regulation' in the ca. 2001 wave).

As the investigations show, one cannot simply argue that enhancing or limiting economic freedom affects legitimacy positively or negatively. The most important area of economic freedom is 'legal system and property rights' (as a part of the 'new' general governance variable) since it has a clear positive effect on legitimacy. This not only shows that the rule of law is important to maintain a legitimate state but also underlines the importance of the works of Hayek (1944, 1960) who stresses that (general and abstract) rules are the key element to economic freedom and also to legitimacy. Furthermore, the area 'government size' *may* explain legitimacy, but the

Table 39: The 'New' Basic Model Plus Areas of Economic Freedom (Gilley ca. 2008)

	(1)	(2)	(3)	(4)	(5)	(6)	(7)	(8)	(9)
Intercept	4.66**	4.13*	4.53**	5.91**	6.39**	3.26**	5.53**	8.86***	6.26*
Input Variables									
Democracy	0.23	0.22	0.22	0.28	0.19	0.25	0.22	0.12	0.22
Democratic History	0.07	0.07	0.07	0.05	0.08	0.07	0.09	0.07	0.07
InteractionT erm	0.07	0.07	0.07	0.07	0.06	0.08	0.07	0.05	0.06
Throughput/Output Variables									
New General Governance	0.91**	0.94**	0.90**	0.99**	1.06**	0.77*	0.94**	1.42***	1.09**
HDI (absolute)	-3.15	-3.17	-3.28	-2.70	-3.39*	-3.37*	-3.45*	-4.14**	-3.40
Unemployment Rate	-0.02	-0.02	-0.03	-0.03	-0.03	-0.02	-0.03	-0.02	-0.03
+ Government Size		0.08							0.10
+ Sound Money			0.03						0.13
+ Freedom to Trade				-0.26					-0.25
+ Regulation					-0.20				-0.17
+ Credit Market						0.15			
+ Labor Market							-0.11		
+ Business								-0.43	
R^2	0.526	0.528	0.526	0.534	0.532	0.532	0.534	0.552	0.542
adjusted R^2	0.461	0.451	0.449	0.458	0.456	0.456	0.458	0.479	0.428
Observations	51	51	51	51	51	51	51	51	51

[1] - Interaction term is mean centered.
* - at 10%-level significant ** - at 5%-level significant *** - at 1%-level significant

Note: The inclusion of a squared term (in the cases of 'government size' and 'regulation') leads to insignificant results. When including a squared term for 'freedom to trade internationally', the coefficient of the squared term turns negative (significant at the 1%-level). This indicates that more trade freedom reduces legitimacy (results are shown in Appendix Q).

evidence is mixed. Finally, the areas 'sound money', 'freedom to trade internationally', and 'regulation' seem to be irrelevant for legitimacy. These results are the same irrespective of adding each area separately (models (2)–(5)) or of adding all areas simultaneously (model (9)). Before starting the final discussion, I check the robustness of the results by replacing Gilley's with Norris' legitimacy scores.

Table 40: The 'New' Basic Model Plus Areas of Economic Freedom (Gilley ca. 2012)

	(1)	(2)	(3)	(4)	(5)	(6)	(7)	(8)	(9)
Intercept	6.68***	6.76***	7.57***	9.23***	6.62***	6.26***	7.35***	6.26***	8.30***
Input Variables									
Democracy	0.07	0.07	0.08	0.07	0.07	0.07	0.06	0.08	0.10
Democratic History	0.05	0.05	0.04	0.05	0.05	0.05	0.05	0.05	0.03
Interaction Term	0.03	0.03	0.03	0.02	0.03	0.03	0.03	0.03	0.03
Throughput/Output Variables									
New General Governance	1.17***	1.17***	1.26***	1.45***	1.17***	1.14***	1.22***	1.12***	1.43***
HDI (absolute)	-2.84	-2.86	-2.59	-3.14*	-2.84	-2.98	-2.98**	-2.82	-2.93
Unemployment Rate	-0.08***	-0.08***	-0.07**	-0.07**	-0.08***	-0.08***	-0.09***	-0.08***	-0.06**
+ Government Size		-0.01							0.06
+ Sound Money			-0.14						-0.10
+ Freedom to Trade				-0.32					-0.38
+ Regulation					0.01				0.18
+ Credit Market						0.06			
+ Labor Market							-0.08		
+ Business								0.05	
R^2	0.645	0.645	0.653	0.664	0.645	0.647	0.649	0.645	0.673
adjusted R^2	0.596	0.587	0.597	0.610	0.587	0.590	0.591	0.587	0.592
Observations	51	51	51	51	51	51	51	51	51

[1] - Interaction term is mean centered.
* - at 10%-level significant ** - at 5%-level significant *** - at 1%-level significant

Note: The inclusion of a squared term (in the cases of 'government size', 'freedom to trade internationally', and 'regulation') leads to insignificant results (results are shown in Appendix Q).

Robustness Check: Norris' Legitimacy Scores as Dependent Variable

To check the robustness of the previous results, I replace Gilley's with Norris' scores and modify the independent variables slightly according to the year of interview (see chapter 6.3.1). Then, I perform the same analyses as before. To start with, I calculate the correlations between Norris' legitimacy scores and the EFW Index and its areas.

As table 41 shows, the correlations between Norris' legitimacy scores and the EFW Index are smaller in size than the correlations between Gilley's legitimacy scores and the EFW Index (table 35) (r_{2001}= 0.37***, r_{2008}= 0.25*, r_{2012}= 0.37***). This already indicates that the correlations depend on the applied legitimacy measure. The same observations emerge when analyzing the areas of economic freedom. Here, correlations are more likely to be insignificant (in table 34, all but two correlations of the EFW Indices and legitimacy are significantly different from zero). Only the area

Table 41: Correlations Between Legitimacy (Norris) and Economic Freedom

Independent Variables	Norris ca. 2001	Norris ca. 2008	Norris ca. 2012
	(1)	(2)	(3)
Economic Freedom (EFW)	0.37^{***}	0.25^{*}	0.37^{***}
Size of Government	-0.11	-0.15	-0.07
Legal System and Property Rights	0.32^{**}	0.49^{***}	0.57^{***}
Sound Money	0.48^{***}	0.12	0.12
Freedom to Trade Internationally	0.17	0.02	0.20
Regulation	0.19	0.22	0.46^{***}
Credit Market Regulation	0.19	0.17	0.25^{**}
Labor Market Regulation	0.13	0.08	0.34^{**}
Business Regulation	0.16	0.25^{*}	0.54^{***}

*- at 10%-level significant **- at 5%-level significant ***- at 1%-level significant

'legal system and property rights' shows significant correlations in all three waves ($r_{2001}= 0.32^{**}$, $r_{2008}= 0.49^{**}$, $r_{2012}= 0.57^{***}$). Except for the area 'sound money' in the ca. 2001 wave and the area 'regulation' in the ca. 2012 wave, all other areas are not significantly correlated with legitimacy. These findings again underline that the area 'legal system and property rights' (i) drives the correlation between the overall EFW Index and legitimacy and, thus, (ii) is most relevant for the state's legitimacy. Since the areas 'sound money' and 'regulation' show only significant correlations in one of the three waves, one should abstain from arguing that these areas have a robust impact on legitimacy.

To prove this intuition, I again run regressions with legitimacy as the dependent variable and the areas of economic freedom as independent variables. This helps me to see which areas remain significant when controlling for all areas of economic freedom. As table 42 shows, the area 'legal system and property rights' has a strong impact on legitimacy in two of the three waves ($r_{2001}= 0.13$, $r_{2008}= 0.52^{***}$, $r_{2012}= 0.64^{***}$). This again indicates that the rule of law is a strong predictor of legitimacy. That the area 'sound money' is highly significant in the ca. 2001 wave should not be overemphasized since one also finds (i) a significant result in the ca. 2012 wave but with opposite sign and (ii) a similar patter across the waves when using Gilley's legitimacy scores (table 35). Interestingly, the area 'freedom to trade internationally' becomes significantly negative when regressing legitimacy on economic freedom's areas ($r_{2001}= -0.23^{*}$, $r_{2008}= -0.31$, $r_{2012}= -0.41^{**}$). That may indicate that people are in favor of less trade freedom.[203]

203 When performing a stepwise exclusion of the most insignificant independent variables in the ca. 2001 wave, this leads to same results as above, namely that the areas 'sound money' and 'freedom to trade internationally' are highly significant (at least at the 10% level). In the ca. 2008 wave, a stepwise exclusion leads to the result that the area 'legal system and property rights' is highly significant; as well as the area 'freedom to trade internationally' when only both areas are part of the regression. In the ca. 2012 wave, a stepwise exclusion confirms that the area 'legal system and property rights' is important. In addition, the area 'freedom to trade internationally' has a negative

Table 42: Regressing Legitimacy (Norris) on Economic Freedom's Areas

Dependent: Legitimacy	Norris ca. 2001		Norris ca. 2008		Norris ca. 2012	
	(1)		(2)		(3)	
	Coeff.	p-value	Coeff.	p-value	Coeff.	p-value
Intercept	4.25***	0.000	4.52***	0.007	2.57**	0.024
Size of Government	-0.01	0.943	0.01	0.945	0.16	0.137
Legal System and Property Rights	0.13	0.218	0.52***	0.000	0.64***	0.000
Sound Money	0.28***	0.000	-0.11	0.474	-0.23*	0.072
Freedom to Trade Internationally	-0.23*	0.058	-0.31	0.164	-0.41**	0.032
Regulation	-0.11	0.55	0.05	0.799	0.36**	0.034
R^2	0.30		0.32		0.50	
Adjust. R^2	0.24		0.25		0.44	
Observations	57		53		54	

*- at 10%-level significant **- at 5%-level significant ***- at 1%-level significant

Since the area 'legal system and property rights' mainly drives the correlation between the EFW Index and legitimacy, it is not plausible to add the overall EFW Index to the basic model. However, when adding the EFW Index to the basic model, the coefficients of the EFW Index are insignificant or only significant at the 10% level ($\beta_{2001}= 0.29^{*}$, $\beta_{2008}= 0.08$, $\beta_{2012}= -0.02$) (table not stated here). These findings are similar to those in the previous sub-section (table 36). When adding only the area 'legal system and property rights' to the basic model, the results are also similar to those of the previous sub-section (table 37).

As table 43 shows, the area 'legal system and property rights' is insignificant in the ca. 2001 and the ca. 2008 waves but significant in the ca. 2012 wave ($\beta_{2001}= 0.05$, $\beta_{2008}= 0.39$, $\beta_{2012}= 0.40^{*}$). However, at the same time, the coefficients of general governance are likely to become insignificant ($\beta_{2001}= 0.56^{**}$, $\beta_{2008}= 0.63$, $\beta_{2012}= 0.27$). Since the coefficients of general governance are highly significant in the basic model (table 27), these changes indicate multicollinearity problems, which the VIFs of general governance also confirm ($VIF_{2001}^{GeneralGov}= 8.86$, $VIF_{2008}^{GeneralGov}= 15.01$, $VIF_{2012}^{GeneralGov}= 12.16$). Similar evidence is provided by the correlations between general governance and the area 'legal system and property rights', which are very strong ($r_{2001}=0.89^{***}$, $r_{2008}=0.91^{***}$, $r_{2012}=0.89^{***}$). In consequence, I add the area 'legal system and property rights' to the general governance index to obtain the 'new' general governance variable. This procedure is similar to that in the previous sub-section. When using the 'new' general governance index in the basic model, the VIFs of the 'new' general governance variable decrease to an acceptable level ($VIF_{2001}^{NewGeneralGov}= 6.78$, $VIF_{2008}^{NewGeneralGov}= 4.76$, $VIF_{2012}^{NewGeneralGov}= 2.99$).

and the area 'regulation' has a positive impact. See Appendix S for further details.

Table 43: The Basic Model Plus Legal System and Property Rights – OLS Estimates

Dependent: Legitimacy (Norris)	Norris ca. 2001			Norris ca. 2008			Norris ca. 2012		
	(1)			(2)			(3)		
	Coeff.	t-value	p-value	Coeff.	t-value	p-value	Coeff.	t-value	p-value
Intercept	7.99***	8.470	0.000	6.55***	3.168	0.002	5.88***	3.828	0.001
Input Variables									
Democracy	0.11	1.260	0.213	-0.14	-1.132	0.264	-0.13	-1.454	0.153
Democratic History	-0.09*	-1.705	0.095	0.03	0.329	0.744	0.04	0.520	0.606
Democracy*DemocraticHistory[1]	0.08***	3.582	0.001	0.01	0.432	0.668	0.02	0.713	0.480
Throughput/Output Variables									
General Governance	0.56**	2.310	0.025	0.63	1.251	0.217	0.27	0.740	0.463
HDI (absolute)	-5.97***	-4.245	0.000	-3.40**	-2.396	0.021	-2.88**	-2.096	0.042
Unemployment Rate	-0.03	-1.579	0.121	-0.00	-0.131	0.896	-0.06***	-2.844	0.007
Legal System	*0.05*	*0.501*	*0.618*	*0.26*	*1.007*	*0.319*	*0.40**	*1.948*	*0.058*
R^2		0.604			0.454			0.611	
Adjust. R^2		0.547			0.367			0.551	
Observations		57			52			53	

[1] - Interaction term is mean centered.
*- at 10%-level significant **- at 5%-level significant ***- at 1%-level significant

Now, similar to the previous sub-section, I run several regressions for each wave (tables 44-46). Again, each table states the 'new' basic model (1), the 'new' basic model plus one of the areas or sub-areas of economic freedom (models (2)-(8)), and the 'new' basic model plus all four remaining areas of economic freedom (model (9)). The results again show that the other areas of economic freedom have no or only a limited impact on legitimacy when controlling for the variables of the basic model. In this vein, the results do not differ from those when using Gilley's legitimacy scores as the dependent variable. Only the areas 'freedom to trade internationally' (since its coefficients are significant in the ca. 2001 and ca. 2012 wave) and 'sound money' (since its coefficient is significant in the ca. 2001 wave) may have little explanatory power. However, since the signs of 'freedom to trade internationally' are positive in the

Table 44: The 'New' Basic Model Plus Areas of Economic Freedom (Norris ca. 2001)

	(1)	(2)	(3)	(4)	(5)	(6)	(7)	(8)	(9)
Intercept	8.35***	8.32***	7.20***	7.74***	8.05***	7.80***	8.09***	9.21***	7.26***
Input Variables									
Democracy	0.10	0.10	0.09	0.07	0.09	0.09	0.02	0.01	0.08
Democratic History	-0.08	-0.08	-0.06	-0.08*	-0.08	-0.08*	-0.06	-0.06	-0.06
InteractionTerm[1]	0.08***	0.08***	0.07***	0.07***	0.08***	0.08***	0.06*	0.05*	0.07***
Throughput/Output Variables									
General Governance[2]	0.68***	0.68***	0.47**	0.61***	0.65***	0.60**	0.73**	0.97***	0.39
HDI (absolute)	-5.85***	-5.84***	-5.57***	-6.74***	-5.82***	-5.74***	-5.24***	-4.480**	-6.06***
Unemployment Rate	-0.03	-0.03	-0.03*	-0.03	-0.03	-0.03	-0.02	-0.03	-0.03
+ Government Size		0.00							-0.05
+ Sound Money			0.14**						0.13*
+ Freedom to Trade				0.20*					0.08
+ Regulation					0.05				0.01
+ Credit Market						0.07			
+ Labor Market							0.05		
+ Business								-0.22	
R^2	0.601	0.601	0.650	0.630	0.602	0.608	0.549	0.567	0.659
adjusted R^2	0.553	0.544	0.600	0.577	0.545	0.552	0.470	0.490	0.585
Observations	57	57	57	57	57	57	48	48	57

[1] - Interaction term is mean centered.
* - at 10%-level significant ** - at 5%-level significant *** - at 1%-level significant

ca. 2001 wave but negative in the ca. 2012 wave, no clear effect of free trade policies on legitimacy is derivable.

To sum up, the robustness check basically leads to the same results as in the previous sub-section. Some minor differences exist, which are the result of the different methodology to measure legitimacy. However, the main findings point toward the same direction, namely that the rule of law is the most important area of economic freedom to sustain legitimacy. Concerning the other areas, I find either no relationship at all ('regulation') or mixed evidence ('government size', 'sound money', and 'freedom to trade internationally'). The following chapter 6.3.3 summarizes and discusses the results in greater depth.

Table 45: The 'New' Basic Model Plus Areas of Economic Freedom (Norris ca. 2008)

	(1)	(2)	(3)	(4)	(5)	(6)	(7)	(8)	(9)
Intercept	8.23***	7.78***	8.64***	8.59***	8.19***	6.88***	8.47***	10.52***	8.18***
Input Variables									
Democracy	-0.15	-0.16	-0.13	-0.14	-0.15	-0.13	-0.15	-0.19	-0.13
Democratic History	0.02	0.02	0.02	0.02	0.02	0.02	0.03	0.03	0.02
InteractionTerm[1]	0.01	0.01	0.02	0.01	0.01	0.02	0.01	0.00	0.02
Throughput/Output Variables									
General Governance[2]	1.02***	1.07***	1.05***	1.04***	1.01***	0.94***	1.03***	1.34***	1.10***
HDI (absolute)	-3.41**	-3.41**	-3.31**	-3.32**	-3.41**	-3.84***	-3.45**	-3.78**	-3.28**
Unemployment Rate	-0.00	0.00	-0.01	-0.00	-0.00	-0.00	-0.00	0.01	-0.00
+ Government Size		0.08							0.07
+ Sound Money			-0.08						-0.06
+ Freedom to Trade				-0.07					-0.03
+ Regulation					0.01				0.02
+ Credit Market						0.18			
+ Labor Market							-0.03		
+ Business								-0.30	
R^2	0.454	0.458	0.458	0.455	0.454	0.476	0.456	0.482	0.489
adjusted R^2	0.381	0.372	0.372	0.368	0.367	0.393	0.369	0.400	0.349
Observations	52	52	52	52	52	52	52	52	52

[1] - Interaction term is mean centered.
* - at 10%-level significant ** - at 5%-level significant *** - at 1%-level significant

Table 46: The 'New' Basic Model Plus Areas of Economic Freedom (Norris ca. 2012)

	(1)	(2)	(3)	(4)	(5)	(6)	(7)	(8)	(9)
Intercept	8.55***	8.64***	9.30***	10.58***	7.50***	8.03***	8.45***	8.05***	9.29***
Input Variables									
Democracy	-0.14	-0.14	-0.14	-0.14*	-0.13	-0.15	-0.14	-0.12	-0.12
Democratic History	0.02	0.02	0.02	0.02	0.02	0.03	0.02	0.01	0.03
InteractionTerm[1]	0.02	0.02	0.02	0.01	0.02	0.02	0.02	0.02	0.02
Throughput/Output Variables									
General Governance[2]	0.88***	0.88***	0.95***	1.11***	0.79***	0.84***	0.87***	0.80***	1.06***
HDI (absolute)	-3.19**	-3.21**	-2.93**	-3.40**	-3.26**	-3.57***	-3.18**	-3.16**	-3.33**
Unemployment Rate	-0.06***	-0.06***	-0.06**	-0.06***	-0.06***	-0.06***	-0.06***	-0.07***	-0.05**
+ Government Size		-0.01							0.06
+ Sound Money			-0.12						-0.08
+ Freedom to Trade				-0.27*					-0.38**
+ Regulation					0.15				0.30*
+ Credit Market						0.10			
+ Labor Market							-0.01		
+ Business								0.13	
R^2	0.604	0.604	0.615	0.630	0.614	0.618	0.604	0.612	0.668
adjusted R^2	0.552	0.542	0.555	0.573	0.553	0.559	0.542	0.540	0.587
Observations	53	53	53	53	53	53	53	53	53

[1] - Interaction term is mean centered.
* - at 10%-level significant ** - at 5%-level significant *** - at 1%-level significant

6.3.3 Summary and Discussion of the Results

This chapter investigates the impact of economic freedom and its areas on legitimacy. According to the liberal perspective, individuals are expected to prefer economic freedom since it allows them to follow their own ends (Hayek, 1944, 1960). Although this argument suggests a positive relationship between economic freedom and legitimacy, a variety of counterarguments exist, in particular when focusing on the areas of economic freedom. To investigate which areas of economic freedom actually matter for legitimacy, I perform several multiple regressions. All these regressions include at least one area of economic freedom and the control variables of the basic model to cope with omitted variable bias (see chapter 5). Table 47 summarizes the regression results.

As table 47 shows, not all areas of economic freedom are equally important for legitimacy. Rather, the area 'legal system and property rights' has an overarching effect, whereas the other areas seem to have no or only little relevance:

Table 47: Summary of the Regression Results

	Gilley's Legitimacy Scores			Norris' Legitimacy Scores		
	ca. 2001	ca. 2008	ca. 2012	ca. 2001	ca. 2008	ca. 2012
Government Size	-- (-)	0 (0)	0 (0)	0 (0)	0 (0)	0 (0)
Legal System and Property Rights[1]	+++ (+++)	++ (++)	+++ (+++)	+++ (+++)	+++ (+++)	+++ (+++)
Sound Money	0 (0)	0 (0)	0 (0)	++ (+)	0 (0)	0 (0)
Freedom to Trade Internationally	0 (0)	0 (0)	0 (0)	+ (0)	0 (0)	- (--)
Regulation	0 (0)	0 (0)	0 (0)	0 (0)	0 (0)	0 (+)

[1] – The area 'legal system and property rights' is part of the general governance index.

Legend:
0 – No significant statistical impact.
+/- – Positive/Negative statistical impact (+/- – at 10%-level significant ++/-- – at 5%-level significant +++/--- – at 1%-level significant).

Note: The signs not in parenthesis show the impact when only one area is added to the basic model. The signs in parenthesis show the influence when all areas are included simultaneously.

- *Government Size.* Regarding the area 'government size', the results show no robust relationship. I only find a significant relationship between 'government size' and legitimacy in the ca. 2001 wave that even indicates that a larger government size leads to more legitimacy. Since states exist that show high legitimacy and a low government size (e.g. Hong Kong, Singapore, Australia, and USA), but also states with high legitimacy and a large government size (e.g. Sweden, Finland, Norway, and Denmark), the results of the regressions seem to be plausible. However, one may question why some high legitimacy states have a large government size while others have a small one. A first explanation is that not the size of the state but rather its quality matters for legitimacy. Since the regressions control for general governance (which remains significant when adding 'government size'), the results suggest that the quality of state services (or a *fair* state, in terms of no corruption) is more important than its pure size. Second, another explanation may be that individuals have different preferences toward state activities across countries. Although advocates of (substantive) economic liberalism argue that the state should only undertake a limited set of state activities, empirical individuals may prefer an expanded set of activities if this is rooted in societal consent (Wegner, 2009, 545). Which concrete activities the state should undertake depends on the preferences of the individuals which are shaped by the history and the existing norms and values of a country. Since societal consent differs among states, this may explain why some extended welfare states (e.g. the Scandinavian countries) are as legitimate as states which provide fewer welfare services (e.g. USA or Australia).
- *Legal System and Property Rights.* The area 'legal system and property rights' has – as a part of the general governance index – a significantly positive effect on legitimacy. That stresses the importance of the rule of law as Hayek (1944,

1960) also points out. Thus, to increase its legitimacy, a state should ensure important aspects of the rule of law such as an independent judiciary, impartial courts, or the enforcement of contracts (Gwartney et al., 2015, 205-207). That the rule of law enhances legitimacy is also in line with scholars who argue that the rule of law is essential for good governance (Rothstein & Teorell, 2012, 11-13). However, one should note that the other variables of the new general governance index (control of corruption and government effectiveness) are also important determinants of legitimacy. Actually, it would be interesting to extract the partial effects of the rule of law, corruption, and government effectiveness on legitimacy. However, since all three items are highly correlated, multicollinearity makes it impossible in such a small dataset to find these effects.

- *Sound Money.* When focusing on the area 'sound money', I only find a significant coefficient in the ca. 2001 wave when applying Norris' legitimacy scores. In all other cases, no significant relationship emerges, which is surprising since high inflation rates typically lead to uncertainty and cause higher costs. Several explanations for these findings exist. First, citizens may have no preference for price stability due to money illusion. In an extreme case, that means that citizens only orient themselves toward nominal sizes (e.g. nominal wage) and ignore the price level or changes in the price level. This also implies that citizens would not even recognize that their real purchasing power declines due to increasing prices. Second, citizens may accept inflation as a possibility of the state to finance government expenditures. Then, if one approved that the state prints money to finance its expenditures, inflation would be a legitimate by-product. Third, citizens may underestimate the costs of inflation or unstable prices. That may refer to the costs of correctly anticipated inflation (for example, shoe leather costs or menu costs) and to the costs of incorrectly anticipated inflation. Fourth, citizens may not even recognize that the state controls money.
- *Freedom to Trade Internationally.* The coefficients of the area 'freedom to trade internationally' are ambivalent. I find a significantly negative coefficient in one of the six regressions, which indicates that people have a preference toward less trade freedom. However, since a positive coefficient shows up in one wave (and no effect in the other four waves), the evidence is limited. Thus, it is likely that the true effect is zero, which does not support the substantive liberal perspective. Although more trade freedom should increase the possibilities of the individuals to follow their own ends, it seems to have no positive impact on the state's legitimacy. The fact that, for example, mass demonstrations in favor of open markets or free trade have never been observed in Western countries also supports these statistical findings (Wegner, 2009, 545). In contrast, empirical evidence indicates that the perceived costs of trade freedom (reduced standards, the risk of losing jobs due to foreign competition) may even outweigh the benefits (increased growth rates in the long run, more freedom to trade with foreign partners).

- *Regulation.* The coefficients of this area are not significant at all (except in the ca. 2012 wave when inserting all areas simultaneously to the regression). This indicates that the degree of 'regulation' does not matter for legitimacy. In contrast, people may simply accept regulatory activities of the state. Whether the state regulates more or less seems to be irrelevant. An explanation may be that the average citizens find (once enacted) regulations legitimate because they have always existed (status-quo bias).

In sum, only the area 'legal system and property rights' has a significant impact on legitimacy. Further, a larger government size may increase legitimacy, which contradicts the liberal perspective. Finally, the areas 'sound money', 'freedom to trade internationally', and 'regulation' seem to be irrelevant for legitimacy.

Although the coefficients indicate that some areas may be important for legitimacy and other areas are not, one should note that the results are only valid at the country level. Thus, even if the coefficients of the area 'sound money' do not differ from zero at the country level, it is possible to find significant results when focusing on the individual level. That becomes clearer when considering that the coefficients of a country-level analysis reflect the mean effect of all individuals. Thus, if 50% of the citizens favor more sound money and 50% of the citizens want less sound money, the mean effect at the country level is zero, although the individuals have clear (but diverging) preferences. In consequence, one should abstain from arguing that – for example – more price stability has no impact on individual legitimacy beliefs but rather argue that price stability is not relevant for the legitimacy belief of an average individual.

Another important point is that a zero-coefficient does not necessarily indicate that an area has no effect on legitimacy. Rather, it says that the direct effect of an area on legitimacy is zero. Since economic freedom has effects on other determinants of legitimacy (such as democracy or, in the long run, the welfare level), indirect effects could exist. For example, lower inflation rates (more 'sound money') typically increases the long-term growth rate, which impacts the welfare level and the welfare change (Berggren, 2003; Goldsmith, 1997). Unfortunately, it is not possible to extract the indirect effects of economic freedom's areas on legitimacy here due to the chosen statistical methods.

Further, statistical reasons could also be responsible for the insignificant coefficients. A first reason may be that I employ a relatively small sample size of roughly 55 observations but at least seven independent variables in each wave. It would be more likely that the coefficients turn significant when using more observations or applying fewer independent variables. However, both alternatives are not possible since the number of observations is restricted due to the WVS and the number of independent variables is determined by the basic model (see chapter 5). A second reason may be that each wave contains different countries. However, since I am looking for universals, it should be irrelevant for the results which countries are part of the sample.

6.4 Analyses at the Individual Level

As the last chapter shows, the area 'legal system and property rights' mainly drives the impact of economic freedom on legitimacy at the country level. One can find no clear evidence that the other areas of economic freedom ('government size', 'sound money', 'freedom to trade internationally', 'regulation') matter for legitimacy.
However, even if an area is statistically insignificant, this does not necessarily mean that this area is not important for legitimacy. Rather, it could mean that when focusing on the individuals (instead of the countries) each single area has an effect which simply averages to zero at the country level. In consequence, this chapter focuses on the impact of economic freedom (and its areas) on legitimacy at the individual level. Thus, I am not interested in whether more economic freedom increases the legitimacy of a whole state. Instead, I investigate whether the degree of economic freedom impacts the legitimacy beliefs of an individual of a particular state.
To approach this research question, I use four items of the WVS that reflect either (i) the degree to which an individual has a pro-market attitude (approximated by the degree to which an individual favors competition) or (ii) to what degree an individual is satisfied with the given economic situation (measured by the degree to which an individual wants more or less income inequality, government responsibility, or private ownership of businesses). Regarding the first item (i), I relate an individual's pro-market attitude to the given degree of economic freedom (EFW) in his or her country. If the degree of an individual's pro-market attitude corresponds to the degree of economic freedom, I suspect that legitimacy becomes maximized. This assumption refers to the idea of output legitimacy, according to which legitimacy increases if the actual policies reflect the interests of the citizens (Scharpf, 1970, 1999). In the same vein, legitimacy beliefs decline if the degree of economic freedom does not correspond to an individual's pro-market attitude. In other words, if the degree of economic freedom is significantly lower or higher than an individual's pro-market attitude (i.e. an *economic interest gap* exists), I expect, ceteris paribus, legitimacy to decrease. Regarding the other three items (ii), I hypothesize that legitimacy becomes maximized if the individual favors the current situation and does not want a change of it (in whatever direction). This procedure also refers to Scharpf's (1970, 1999) idea that legitimacy increases if the given situation fits with the interests of the people. More detailed, legitimacy should be maximized if the individual is satisfied with the given degree of inequality, the degree to which the government undertakes responsibility, and/or the degree to which businesses are privately owned. In other words, I expect that an individual's legitimacy belief declines if he or she wants more or less income inequality, government responsibility, or private ownership of businesses. The empirical results strongly support the hypotheses: Legitimacy becomes maximized (i) if the gap between an individual's pro-market attitude and the degree of economic freedom is zero and (ii) if an individual does not want a change of the current economic situation.
The remainder of this chapter is structured as follows. In chapter 6.4.1, I give an overview of the data and the method. In fact, I use the same data as in chapter 5.2.2 (i.e. Norris' legitimacy scores as dependent variables and both individual-level and

country-level variables as control variables) plus the items on the individual's pro-market attitudes. Regarding the method, similar to chapter 5.2.2, I use a random intercept model (multi-level analysis). Based on this, chapter 6.4.2 presents the results of the analyses. Chapter 6.4.3 summarizes the results and gives some policy advises.

6.4.1 Data and Method

To investigate whether economic freedom impacts an individual's legitimacy belief, it is necessary to use data that provide legitimacy scores at the individual level. Thus, it is only possible to use Norris' legitimacy scores as the dependent variable since Gilley's (2006a, 2012) legitimacy scores are only available at the country level.
Having defined the dependent variable, it remains necessary to deal with the independent variables. To measure the pro-market attitudes of an individual, the WVS provides several items. Table 48 gives an overview of the different items and also states in which wave each item is available.

Table 48: Items for Measuring Pro-Market Attitudes in the WVS

Item(s)	Wave(s)		
	WVS 4	WVS 5	WVS 6
Income Inequality	x	x	x
Private Ownership of Business and Industry	x	x	x
Government responsibility	x	x	x
Competition is good vs. harmful	x	x	x
Egalitarian vs. competitive society	x		
Extensive welfare vs. low taxes	x		
Regulated vs. responsible society	x		

Sources: Codebooks of the World Values Surveys (2000, 2006, 2012)

Although seven items are available for measuring an individual's pro-market attitude, I only use those four items that are available in all three waves under investigation to ensure consistency over time. In particular, that concerns the following items (WVS 4 Codebook, 2000):

- *Income Inequality.* To measure individuals' preferences toward income inequality, individuals have to state on a continuum whether they prefer that "Incomes should be more equal" (=1) or they prefer that "We need larger income differences as incentives" (=10). Actually, this item does not explicitly refer to economic freedom (i.e. economic institutions) but rather to the outcomes of economic freedom.
- *Private Ownership of Business and Industry.* The second item refers to who should own businesses and industries. On a continuum, individuals can note whether they prefer "Private ownership of businesses should be increased" (=1) or "Government ownership of businesses should be increased" (=10).

- *Government Responsibility.* The next item captures the question who should be responsible for actions. Here, respondents can decide between the statements "The government should take more responsibility" (=1) and "People should take more responsibility" (=10).
- *Competition is Good.* The fourth item measures the degree to which people favor competition. Respondents have the choice between "Competition is good" (=1) and "Competition is harmful" (=10). Since competition is a basic feature of economic freedom, I assume that people who favor competition have pro-market attitudes.

Based on these four items, I initially calculated a pro-market attitudes index (simple mean of all four items). Before calculating the index, I rescaled the items 'Private ownership of business and industry' and 'Competition is good' to ensure that higher scores reflect pro-market attitudes. Since the final pro-market attitude index ranges from one to ten, but the EFW Index (and each of its areas as well) theoretically from zero to ten, I also rescale the pro-market attitude index to range from zero to ten.[204] Unfortunately, the index of the four items is not reliable since Cronbach's alpha was too low (α_{2001}= 0.270; α_{2008}= 0.194; α_{2012}= 0.091).[205] In consequence, I decided to analyze each item separately. This is reasonable when analyzing the wording of the items in greater detail since the item 'competition is good' refers to an individual's pro-market attitude, but the other three items ('income inequality', 'private ownership of business and industry', and 'government responsibility') measure whether an individual wants more or less economic freedom (see answer possibilities of these items). For example, the answers "Incomes should be more equal" (=0) and "We need larger income differences as incentives" (=10) represent the ends of the continuum of the item 'income inequality'. In a narrow sense, the wording implies that an individual compares how he or she perceives the degree of inequality in his or her country and, then, notes whether the perceived inequality is too low or too high. Thus, if an individual finds the given degree of perceived inequality legitimate, he or she should give an answer that lies in the mid of the continuum (=5). Otherwise, if an individual evaluates the perceived degree of inequality as too low or too high, he or she should give an answer that is closer to the endpoints of the continuum (=0 or =10). Theoretically, this implies that an individual's legitimacy beliefs is highest if he or she gives an answer that belongs to the mid of the continuum (=5). Otherwise, if an individual deviates – in whatever direction – from the ideal situation, the individual's legitimacy belief should decline. In fact, the degree of economic freedom only has an indirect impact on an individual's legitimacy belief in this setting since it only shapes the perceived degree of inequality. However, since the statement only refers to the question whether income inequality should be lowered or increased, it is not possible

204 To do so, I first rescaled each item. This means that the original one to ten scale is replaced by a zero to ten scale. One became zero and ten remained ten. All other scores were equally addressed to the new scale (e.g. 2 became 1.11, 3 became 2.22, and so forth).

205 Cronbach's alpha was even too low (and showed a high variance) when calculating it for each country separately. For example, in the ca. 2001 wave (WVS 4), Cronbach's alpha for Japan was 0.407 and for South Korea it was 0.050. Similar findings could be made in the ca. 2008 and the ca. 2012 wave.

to derive what degree of inequality – and thus, also economic freedom – an individual prefers. The same thoughts apply to the items that refer to an individual's preference for private businesses and an individual's attitudes toward state responsibility. In sum, one cannot derive an individual's preference for economic freedom based on the items 'income inequality', 'private ownership of business and industry', and 'government responsibility' since these items rather reflect whether an individual wants – given the current situation in his or her country – more or less economic freedom.

Based on these considerations, I apply two different strategies to operationalize the items for the statistical investigations. On the one hand, I use the item 'competition is good' to calculate an individual's *economic interest gap* which is the squared difference between an individual's preference for competition (C_i) and the degree of economic freedom (*EFW*, measured by the EFW Index). Equation [33] expresses this mathematically.

$$Economic\ Interest\ Gap_i = (C_i - EFW)^2 \qquad [33]$$

As the equation shows, the *economic interest gap* of an individual is zero if his or her preference for competition (i.e. pro-market attitude) equals the degree of economic freedom. Otherwise, due to the squaring, the economic interest gap turns positive if the individual's preference for competition is higher or lower than the degree of economic freedom.

On the other hand, referring to the other three items ('income inequality', 'private ownership of business and industry', and 'government responsibility'), I apply a different strategy. Since an individual theoretically marks value five (i.e. the midpoint of the continuum) if he or she is satisfied with the degree of income inequality, the ownership situation, or the degree of government responsibility, any deviation from five should go along with a lower legitimacy belief. To model this, I square the term that results when calculating the attitudes of an individual minus five. This approach ensures that any deviation from the optimal value (=5) leads to a positive score. Equations [34] – [36] express all three gaps mathematically:

$$Income\ Inequality\ Gap_i = (II_i - 5)^2 \qquad [34]$$

$$Ownership\ Gap_i = (O_i - 5)^2 \qquad [35]$$

$$Responsibility\ Gap_i = (RES_i - 5)^2 \qquad [36]$$

In sum, there are four different variables to analyze, namely the *economic interest gap,* the *income-inequality gap*, the *ownership gap*, and the *responsibility gap*. In the case of the economic interest gap, I assume that legitimacy is highest when the pro-market attitude (i.e. an individual's preference for competition) equals the objective degree of economic freedom. In the cases of the other three gaps, I expect that legitimacy reaches its peak if an individual does not want more or less inequality, government ownership, or government responsibility (i.e. the individual gives an answer that lies in

the midpoint of the continuum). Further, due to the squaring (see equations [34]-[36]), any deviation from the ideal situation reduces legitimacy in a quadratic fashion.
To ensure that the estimation results are not biased (e.g. omitted variable bias), each regression also includes a variety of control variables (see chapter 5.2.2; note that the 'new' general governance index replaces the general governance index).[206] Since the control variables are both individual-level and country-level variables, it is necessary to perform multi-level analyses. Because I assume no interactions between individual-level and country-level variables, I stick to the random-intercept model (similar to chapter 5.2.2). The variables of interest (the four 'gaps') are individual-level variables since they represent either the deviation of an individual's pro-market attitude from the given degree of economic freedom in his or her country (in the case of the competition-is-good item) or the deviation from the optimal answer (in the cases of the other three items). In each regression, I include the gap plus control variables. Equation [37] shows this mathematically,

$$L = \beta_{0,j} + \boldsymbol{\beta} X + \alpha_1 Gap + r \qquad [37]$$

where $\beta_{0,j}$ is the intercept for all individuals of the same country (country-level variables explain the variation of the intercepts across countries; see equation [21]), $\boldsymbol{\beta}$ is the vector of coefficients of the individual-level control variables, $\boldsymbol{X}$ represent the vector of individual-level control variables, α_1 is the coefficient of the particular gap, and r reflects the error term. According to the theoretical considerations, I expect that α_1 will be significantly negative.
Since the data are the same as in chapter 5.2.2, the intra-class correlation coefficients have the same values as above ($ICC_{2001}=0.289$, $ICC_{2008}=0.351$, $ICC_{2012}=0.264$, see chapter 5.2.2), indicating that one should prefer a multi-level analysis to a fixed-effect OLS model. Regarding the centering of variables, I again use raw data. This is not problematic since I model no cross-level interaction terms, which would require grand mean centering of the data to avoid multicollinearity. Thus, the intercepts can be interpreted as the average legitimacy belief of an individual when all independent variables at the individual level are zero.

6.4.2 Results

Economic Interest Gap

The inclusion of the *economic interest gap* leads to the expected results (table 49 below). The coefficients of the economic interest gap show the expected signs in all three waves ($\alpha_1^{2001}= -0.007^{***}$, $\alpha_1^{2008}= -0.007^{***}$, $\alpha_1^{2012}= -0.003^{***}$). The negative sign indicates that any deviation from the theoretically ideal situation (i.e. the pro-market attitude of an individual equals the degree of economic freedom) leads to a reduction of an individual's legitimacy beliefs. In this vein, the coefficients indicate that an increase of economic freedom is only beneficial if the gap between an individual's pro-

206 The 'new' general governance index consist of the Government Effectiveness Index, the Control of Corruption Index, and the area 'legal system and property rights' (reflecting the rule of law).

Table 49: Economic Interest Gap

Model	(1) Norris ca. 2001		(2) Norris ca. 2008		(3) Norris ca. 2012	
	Coeff.	p-value	Coeff.	p-value	Coeff.	p-value
Individual-Level Variables						
Intercept	7.312***	0.000	6.184***	0.000	7.586***	0.000
Age	-0.011***	0.010	-0.004	0.136	-0.011***	0.000
Age^2	0.0001***	0.003	0.0001***	0.004	0.0002***	0.000
Male	0.074***	0.003	-0.003	0.840	-0.037**	0.011
Compl. primary school[a]	-0.244***	0.000	-0.261***	0.000	-0.070**	0.019
Compl. secondary school[a]	-0.377***	0.000	-0.320***	0.000	-0.177***	0.000
Compl. college[a]	-0.388***	0.000	-0.349***	0.000	-0.188***	0.000
Compl. university[a]	-0.361***	0.000	-0.446***	0.000	-0.333***	0.000
Income (continuous)	-0.038***	0.000	0.036***	0.000	0.055***	0.000
Religious Person[b]	0.275***	0.000	0.281***	0.000	0.245***	0.000
Atheist Person[b]	-0.176***	0.005	-0.243***	0.000	-0.177***	0.000
Media Contact	-	-	0.064***	0.000	0.118***	0.000
Political Interest	0.604***	0.000	0.375***	0.000	0.406***	0.000
Interpersonal Trust	-	-	0.479***	0.000	0.417***	0.000
Life Satisfaction	0.070***	0.000	0.113***	0.000	0.110***	0.000
Victim of Crime	-	-	-	-	-0.176***	0.000
Feels Unsafe	-	-	-	-	-0.064***	0.000
Economic Interest Gap	*-0.007****	*0.000*	*-0.007****	*0.000*	*-0.003****	*0.000*
Country-Level Variables						
Democracy	0.11	0.559	-0.196	0.152	-0.141*	0.072
Democratic History	-0.074	0.486	0.052	0.527	-0.002	0.969
Democracy*DemocraticHistory[1]	0.095*	0.086	-0.004	0.916	0.020	0.275
New General Governance	0.336	0.471	0.762**	0.025	0.837***	0.000
HDI (absolute)	-5.179**	0.038	-1.563	0.334	-3.638***	0.004
Unemployment Rate	-0.004	0.913	-0.017	0.684	-0.056**	0.010
-2LL	85263		191204		249184	
AIC/BIC	85267/85283		191208/191226		249188/249207	
Pseudo-R^2	0.1538		0.1717		0.2191	
Observations (individual level)	21346		49451		62105	
Observations (country level)	19		41		50	

[1] - Interaction term is mean centered.
* - at 10%-level significant ** - at 5%-level significant *** - at 1%-level significant
[a] - reference category: no primary school completed [b] - reference category: no religious person

market attitude and economic freedom narrows. If an individual has an anti-market attitude, an increase of economic freedom reduces legitimacy.
To illustrate this, one may look at equation [38], which expresses an individual's legitimacy belief as a function of the gap (suppressing all other explanatory variables).

$$L=\beta_0+\alpha_1 Gap \quad [38]$$

For the gap, one can plug in an individual's pro-market attitude (in terms of the item 'Competition is good'; C_i) minus the degree of economic freedom (*EFW*) as expressed in equation [39].

$$L=\beta_0+\alpha_1 (C_i-EFW)^2 \quad [39]$$

Finally, to illustrate the dependency between an individual's pro-market attitude and the degree of economic freedom, I use the value of the coefficient of the ca. 2001 wave (α_1^{2012}= -0.007***) and assume three cases, namely when an individual's pro-market attitudes are three, five, and seven ($C_i^{Case1}=3$, $C_i^{Case2}=5$, $C_i^{Case3}=7$). Then, I vary the degree of economic freedom from zero to ten and show how legitimacy develops. For reasons of illustration, the intercept is set to five ($\beta_0=5$). Figure 16 shows the results.

Figure 16: Legitimacy, EFW, and Pro-Market Attitude

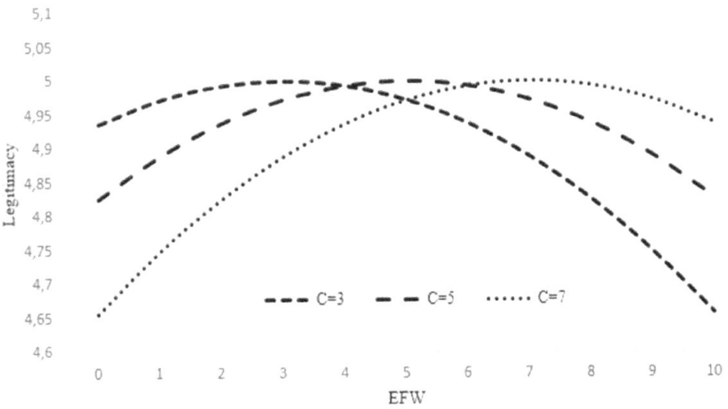

Source: Own representation

Inequality Gap, Ownership Gap, and Responsibility Gap

The results above show that the *economic interest gap* helps to explain an individual's legitimacy belief. In addition to this, I also define three further gaps, namely the income-inequality gap, the ownership gap, and the responsibility gap (see chapter 6.4.1). Table 50 states the results when including each of these gaps separately in a regression (while suppressing all other control variables in the table for reasons of space; full tables are provided in Appendix T).[207]

Table 50: Inequality Gap, Ownership Gap, and Responsibility Gap

Dependent: Legitimacy	(1) Norris ca. 2001		(2) Norris ca. 2008		(3) Norris ca. 2012	
	Coeff.	p-value	Coeff.	p-value	Coeff.	p-value
Income-Inequality Gap (+Control Variables)						
Income-Inequality Gap	-0.005***	0.000	-0.003***	0.000	-0.007***	0.000
Ownership Gap (+Control Variables)						
Ownership Gap	-0.004***	0.000	-0.003***	0.003	-0.006***	0.000
Responsibility Gap (+Control Variables)						
Responsibility Gap	-0.007***	0.000	-0.006***	0.000	-0.009***	0.000

*- at 10%-level significant **- at 5%-level significant ***- at 1%-level significant

Note: All other control variables (both at the individual level and at the country level) are part of the regressions but suppressed here. Full tables can be found in Appendix T.

Again, the results fit with the theoretical expectations since all coefficients are significantly negative (income-inequality gap: α_1^{2001}= -0.005***, α_1^{2008}= -0.003***, α_1^{2012}= -0.007***; ownership gap: α_2^{2001}= -0.004***, α_2^{2008}= -0.003***, α_2^{2012}= -0.006***; responsibility gap: α_2^{2001}= -0.007***, α_2^{2008}= -0.006***, α_2^{2012}= -0.009***). This indicates that individuals who prefer to change the current situation (for example, more or less income inequality) show lower legitimacy beliefs than individuals who are satisfied with the current situation. In this sense, the results also confirm the theoretical considerations of Scharpf's (1970, 1999) output dimension, namely that legitimacy depends on the degree to which policies are in line with the preferences of the people.

6.4.3 Summary and Discussion

This chapter investigates the legitimacy beliefs at the individual level concerning economic freedom. I assume that – applying Scharpf's (1970, 1999) input-output scheme – economic freedom refers to the output dimension of legitimacy. Thus, one can derive that an individual's legitimacy belief becomes maximized if the degree of

207 Overall, I perform nine regressions (three distinct gaps times three waves).

economic freedom fits with the market attitudes of that individual. In consequence, I use an individual's attitude toward competition (as a proxy for its market attitude) and relate it to economic freedom. According to theory, if the given situation of economic freedom deviates from an individual's pro-market attitude (*economic interest gap*), legitimacy is expected to decline. In addition, I also define three further gaps that indicate whether an individual prefers to change the given economic situation in his or her country (income-inequality gap, ownership gap, and responsibility gap).

The results strongly support the theoretical considerations since all gaps – in whatever specification – show negative coefficients that are highly significant. Thus, legitimacy becomes maximized if the degree of economic freedom fits with the pro-market attitude of an individual. The results further indicate that more economic freedom only leads to more legitimacy if the gap between an individual's pro-market attitude and economic freedom narrows. Finally, I find that individuals who do not want to change the current economic situation in their country show higher legitimacy beliefs than individuals who favor changing the situation.

The findings also indicate that individuals do not necessarily accept market freedom. Thus, one may ask what a policy planner – who favors liberalism and free markets – can do to enact liberal policies while maintaining legitimacy. According to the empirical results, the only possibility is to shape the market attitudes of the individuals in such a way that the individuals favor market-friendly policies. To give only one example, a strategy is to shape the attitudes of young students during school. However, according to a study of Slomcyznski and Shabad (1998, 749) in post-communist Poland, the support for the market can only be learned to a limited degree since students who participated in market simulation games "were less likely to take [...] extreme anti-market positions, and they were less likely to take [...] extreme pro-market positions." That already indicates that teaching about the market does not necessarily lead to pro-market attitudes since students also get to know the disadvantages of the market.

7 Final Summary and Conclusion

This thesis deals with the concept, the measurement, and the determinants of legitimacy with a specific focus on economic freedom. In this vein, the main research purpose is to investigate the impact of economic institutions (i.e. the degree of economic freedom) on state legitimacy. To approach this question, chapter 2 initially reviews the concept of legitimacy in greater detail. This review shows that legitimacy is a multidimensional concept that can be analyzed from the macro perspective (i.e. according to normative criteria proposed and evaluated by the researcher) or the micro perspective (i.e. according to the beliefs and the actions of the citizens).

Since this thesis follows the micro perspective, chapter 3 reviews different approaches to measuring legitimacy. The review shows that a variety of both unidimensional and multidimensional approaches exist that use individuals' attitudes (such as confidence in the police, the courts, or the civil service) and/or individuals' behaviors (such as voter turnout) to measure legitimacy. Since legitimacy is a multidimensional concept, it further turns out that the measurement approaches of Gilley (2006a, 2012) and Norris (1999) are most appropriate for my research question. Although these approaches differ in the method to derive legitimacy's dimensions (theory-driven vs. correlation-based) and in the choice of the items (attitudinal items vs. behavioral items), both approaches are largely comparable. In consequence, I use both legitimacy scores throughout the thesis. Norris' legitimacy scores mainly serve (i) to check the robustness of the results when using Gilley's legitimacy scores as the dependent variable and (ii) to perform individual-level analyses.

To ensure that the impact of economic freedom on legitimacy is correctly estimated (for example, to cope with omitted variable bias), chapter 4 reviews the literature on the determinants of legitimacy. Using an extended version of Scharpf's (1970, 1999) input-output methodology (i.e. plus throughput legitimacy), the overview suggests a variety of variables that are statistically relevant for explaining legitimacy. First, concerning the input dimension, scholars find that the degree of democracy, a country's regime tradition, and the degree of fractionalization may explain legitimacy (Booth & Seligson, 2009a; Gilley, 2006b; Gjefsen, 2012; Power & Cyr, 2009). Focusing on the throughput dimension, the degree of corruption, the rule of law, and the degree of impartiality are strong predictors of legitimacy (Gilley, 2006b; Gjefsen, 2012; Power & Cyr, 2009). Finally, regarding the output dimension, the results of several studies show that the welfare level and its change (such as GDP per capita or the HDI), the effectiveness of the government, the economic distribution, and the unemployment rate are relevant for explaining legitimacy (Booth & Seligson, 2009a; Domański, 2005; Gilley, 2006b; Gjefsen, 2012; Levi & Sacks, 2009; Power & Cyr, 2009). In addition, besides these country-level variables, a variety of further variables helps to explain legitimacy at the individual level.

Chapter 5 sets up a basic model of legitimacy based on the determinants suggested in the previous chapter. This is necessary since the determinants of legitimacy that have been extracted in various studies differ regarding (i) the applied legitimacy measure, (ii) the spatial scope, (iii) the set of control variables, and (iv) the applied (statistical) method. Using Gilley's legitimacy scores as the dependent variable, an initial all-in

C. M. Hindermann, *The Impact of Economic Freedom on State Legitimacy*,
Wirtschaft und Politik, https://doi.org/10.1007/978-3-658-23195-8_7

approach (kitchen-sink approach) shows that not all determinants are relevant when applying the OLS method. In consequence, I use both the backward regression technique and the Bayesian model averaging (BMA) approach to filter the most relevant determinants. As it turns out, the degree of democracy, an interaction term (democracy * democratic history), general governance (an index that consists of government effectiveness and the degree of corruption), the unemployment rate, and the HDI (in absolute terms) are most relevant. I next use the OLS method to estimate the impact of these variables on legitimacy. Several robustness checks (different methods such as ordered logit estimates or multi-level analysis and a different legitimacy measure) lead to similar results, indicating that the basic model seems to be appropriate.

After that, chapter 6 analyzes the impact of economic freedom on legitimacy. In a first sub-section, I give arguments why more (or less) economic freedom should lead to more legitimacy. In this vein, I present the arguments of Hayek (1944) and Friedman (1969). Since I use the Fraser-Index (EFW) as the measure for economic freedom, I also present how Gwartney et al. (2015) measure economic freedom and its five areas ('government size', 'legal system and property rights', 'sound money', 'freedom to trade internationally' and 'regulation'). The theoretical discussion already shows that a variety of arguments for and against economic freedom exist such that the theoretical effect of economic freedom on legitimacy is not clearly identifiable in advance. In particular, this becomes apparent when theoretically analyzing the areas of economic freedom separately. In consequence, it is more reasonable to analyze each area separately instead of the overall EFW Index.

Consequently, the next sub-section empirically investigates the impact of economic freedom (and its areas) on legitimacy at the country level. Although the correlation between the EFW Index and legitimacy is positive, initial analyses already suggest that this effect is mainly driven by the area 'legal system and property rights', indicating the importance of the rule of law. The OLS results confirm this first impression since the other four areas of economic freedom ('government size', 'sound money', 'freedom to trade internationally', 'regulation') have no or only a very weak (and partly negative) impact on legitimacy, irrespective of using Gilley's or Norris' legitimacy scores. Based on these results, the question arose why there is no relationship between the areas of economic freedom (except 'legal system and property rights') and legitimacy. One potential explanation is that the zero-coefficients reflect the average impact of economic freedom on legitimacy at the country level. If that is the case, one should find some evidence at the individual level.

In consequence, the next sub-section of chapter 6 focuses on the relationship between economic freedom and legitimacy at the individual level. Since economic freedom belongs to the output dimension of legitimacy (Scharpf, 1970, 1999), the idea is to identify whether an individual's legitimacy belief decreases if the degree of economic freedom is significantly higher or lower than the individual's attitude towards the market (approximated by the degree to which an individual states that competition is good). Besides this, I also investigate whether people show lower legitimacy beliefs if they prefer to change the current economic situation in his or her country. The empirical results support both hypotheses. Thus, although it is not possible to find an

effect of economic freedom (except for the rule of law) at the country level, there is evidence that economic freedom matters to the individuals.
This thesis largely refers to the existing literature. Nonetheless, a variety of findings either challenge the results of the literature or lead to new insights. In consequence, the following list enumerates the main achievements and (empirical) results of this thesis:

1. *Updating Gilley's (2006a, 2012) Legitimacy Scores for ca. 2012 and Creating a New Legitimacy Measure Following Norris (1999, 2011).* Based on Gilley's (2006a, 2012) approach to measure legitimacy, I compile legitimacy scores for 59 countries in ca. 2012 (based on the WVS 6). In addition to Gilley's legitimacy scores, I also measure legitimacy based on Norris (1999, 2011) approach, in particular to have an alternative legitimacy measure for the empirical part (to perform robustness checks). Here, I define legitimacy as the geometric average of two (out of five) dimensions of political support, namely 'confidence in regime institutions' and 'support for regime performance'. The main difference between both measures is that Gilley's measure contains attitudinal and behavioral items, whereas the Norris' measure solely contains attitudinal items.
2. *Challenging Gilley's (2006b, 2009) Results Regarding the Determinants of Legitimacy.* Although the determinants of the basic model (chapter 5) are basically congruent with those of Gilley (2006b, 2009) (welfare gains, democracy, general governance), I come to different conclusions regarding the role of democracy and welfare gains (using both Gilley's and Norris' legitimacy scores as dependent variables). According to Gilley (2006b, 2009), both democracy and welfare gains contribute positively to state legitimacy (based on bivariate correlation analyses). In contrast, using different multiple regression techniques (OLS, ordered logit estimates, multi-level analysis), my findings suggest (i) that the impact of democracy on legitimacy is not necessarily positive since it seems to depend on a country's democratic history (but the robustness of this relationship is limited) and (ii) that the welfare level of a country has a negative effect on legitimacy in multiple regressions. In fact, concerning democracy, this result can be seen as controversial since various scholars argue that democracy is necessary or at least important for legitimacy (consider Scharpf (1970, 1999) or the results of Gilley (2006b); see also Rawls (1993) for theoretical arguments), whereas other scholars come to similar results as in my empirical research (see Rothstein (2009) for theoretical arguments and Gjefsen (2012) for empirical evidence). Second, regarding the welfare level, most scholars find that the welfare level is positively related to legitimacy (Gilley, 2006b; Power & Cyr, 2009). However, one has to notice that these scholars' results are based on simple correlations. Since the positive correlation turns into a negative one when using multiple regression techniques, bivariate correlations are likely to produce spurious results. Regarding the interpretation, a negative relationship between the welfare level and legitimacy is highly plausible when assuming that people have higher aspirations toward the state in more developed countries. Another explanation may be that highly

developed states have a higher degree of value pluralism. In sum, highly developed states have to provide better services in terms of general governance to maintain legitimacy.

3. *The Rule of Law as the Only Area of Economic Freedom that Significantly Drives Legitimacy at the Country Level.* An extensive investigation of the impact of economic freedom on legitimacy shows that – among the five areas of economic freedom according to the EFW Index – the rule of law has the most explanatory power. Thus, in states where the rule of law governs, legitimacy scores are higher (ceteris paribus). Since the other four areas of economic freedom ('government size', 'sound money', 'freedom to trade internationally', and 'regulation') show no robust relationship to legitimacy, one can also derive that the area 'legal system and property rights' mainly drives the relationship between the overall EFW Index and legitimacy. Also other studies find that the rule of law is an important determinant of legitimacy (Gilley, 2006b; Power & Cyr, 2009).
4. *Explaining Individual Legitimacy Beliefs by the Gap Between an Individual's Market Attitude and the Degree of Economic Freedom.* Based on the Scharpfian (1970, 1999) idea that output legitimacy increases if state activities and policies are in line with the preferences of the people, I define an economic interest gap that measures an individual's pro-market attitude (approximated by the degree to which an individual favors competition) minus the degree of economic freedom. The results strongly suggest that any gap (i.e. too much or too little economic freedom in comparison to an individual's pro-market attitude) leads to a reduction of an individual's legitimacy belief. Based on this finding, one can derive that an increase of economic freedom is legitimacy-enhancing if the gap between an individual's pro-market attitude and economic freedom becomes smaller. Thus, to enhance legitimacy via more economic freedom, it is necessary to promote pro-market attitudes of citizens in advance.
5. *A Contribution to Output Legitimacy at the Individual Level – Showing that Citizens who Want an Economic Change Have Lower Legitimacy Beliefs.* Applying the same idea as above, I also find that the legitimacy beliefs are lower among those individuals who want to change the current economic situation (regarding the degree of inequality, government ownership of businesses, and government responsibility). Thus, if an individual has a preference to change the situation (i.e. the given situation is, for whatever reason, not congruent with its interests), he or she shows lower legitimacy beliefs than an individual who does not want a change. These findings strongly support the theoretical consideration that economic issues affect legitimacy via the output dimension.

To conclude, this thesis helps to understand what determines legitimacy. This is of particular importance for policymakers since legitimacy is a central pillar of system stability. Thus, policy-makers can derive clear recommendations from this thesis to build a legitimate (and, thus, stable) state. First, legitimacy depends on the form of government. Although it is widely believed that only democracy leads to legitimacy, policymakers should always consider the democratic history of a country. In countries with a long autocratic history, the rapid implementation of democracy seems to be problematic since it may trigger a legitimacy crisis. Instead, the empirical results suggest implementing a democratic system incrementally. Then, citizens can slowly adapt to the new democratic value system. Second, policymakers should also consider that a growing welfare level does not lead per se to more legitimacy. Instead, when the country's welfare level rises, legitimacy, ceteris paribus, declines due to rising aspirations of the citizens. Thus, when the welfare level rises, the state has to provide better services (in terms of a higher quality of public goods, fighting corruption, or reducing the unemployment rate) to maintain legitimacy at a high level. Third, when it comes to economic institutions, the most important task of policymakers is to provide a functioning rule of law, including a strong legal system, the availability of property rights, and freedom of contract. In contrast, regarding the other areas of economic freedom ('government size', 'freedom of trade internationally', 'sound money', and 'regulation'), there is no clear evidence which economic institutions are legitimacy-enhancing. Rather, policymakers need to know the citizens' preferences, which, however, vary across countries and across time. This becomes apparent when noting that economic institutions other than the legal system affect the legitimacy beliefs at the individual level, but these effects sum up to zero at the country level. For example, trade freedom may matter for an individual, but since some individuals want more but others less trade, it is possible that the net effect averages to zero at the country level. Altogether, policymakers should always consider that economic liberalism is legitimacy-enhancing in terms of the rule of law. Regarding the other areas of economic freedom, no universal recommendation can be given.

In sum, all those recommendations help policymakers to understand why some states are more legitimate than others. To give a first example, when comparing the USA with Norway or Denmark, the legitimacy scores indicate that the Scandinavian countries are slightly more legitimate than the USA, although the welfare standard and the degree of democracy are similar. The difference between both is caused by better governance (fighting corruption and providing more public goods with higher quality) in the Scandinavian countries. To give a second example, when focusing on very low legitimacy countries like Macedonia, Lithuania, or Armenia, is seems problematic that those countries had – among other reasons – a too rapid implementation of democracy. And to give a final example, the very bad legitimacy values of the Russian state may be attributed to its very bad governance activities (high corruption, bad quality of public goods). However, although it is possible to understand what determines different legitimacy levels across countries, one should note that these insights are based on cross-country analyses that cover countries all over world, which can only provide general findings. In turn, since the value systems differ among but also within states, there may be further factors or determinants that are not captured in this thesis that impact the legitimacy of each single state. Thus, an insignificant determinant, such as inequality, just tells us that it has on average no effect on legitimacy, but it could have an impact in some single states. Thus, policy- makers should not only consider the general findings of this thesis (which apply to the average state) but also treat their country as an individual case. In fact, it is possible that in some states other determinants are equally or even more important than those extracted in this thesis, simply because the models cannot explain the whole variance of legitimacy. To cope with this shortcoming, policymakers should ideally monitor citizens' preferences by creating new surveys especially designed for legitimacy research. Such a survey should contain not only items for measuring legitimacy but also individual-level items that measure attitudes toward economic, political, religious, social, ecological, and other topics. Based on these information, legitimacy-enhancing policies can be enacted that fit with the citizens' value system in each country.

Appendices

Appendix A – Legitimacy and System Stability

As mentioned above, legitimacy is one of the main pillars of system stability, as stressed by Easton (1965, 1975), Lipset (1959), Hurd (1990), and Gerschewski (2013). To be more detailed, I briefly present the considerations of each author in the following:

- *Easton (1965, 1975).* David Easton (1975, 436) argues that legitimacy is a dimension of overall political support, which he defines "as an attitude by which a person orients himself to an object either favorably or unfavorably, positively or negatively". The object of political support is the state as a whole, including institutions, norms, and rules, but also every-day politics. Based on this consideration, he further distinguishes between diffuse and specific support. Specific support expresses the perception of the performance of political authorities in an everyday context. The idea is that daily decisions, policies, actions, utterances, as well as the general style of the authorities have to meet the articulated demands of the citizens. However, it is important to notice that the actual performance of the political authorities does not matter but rather the perception of the performance.
  In contrast, diffuse support refers to "evaluations of what an object is or represents – to the general meaning it has for a person – not of what it does" (Easton, 1975, 444). Further "it consists of a reservoir of favorable attitudes or good will that helps members to accept or tolerate outputs to which they are opposed or the effects of which they see as damaging to their wants" (Easton, 1975, 444). Hence, diffuse support is more stable than specific support. The reason is that diffuse support is more difficult to strengthen if it is weak but also more difficult to weaken if it is strong. Furthermore, diffuse support is more or less independent of the actual and perceived performance of the authorities in the short-run but "if discontent with perceived performance continues over a long enough time, it may gradually erode even the strongest underlying bonds of attachment" (Easton, 1975, 445). Altogether, diffuse support reflects a more basic, fundamental support for political authorities and the regime. It has two dimensions, namely trust and legitimacy.
  Easton (1975, 451) defines legitimacy, as "the conviction [...] that it is right and proper [...] to accept and obey the authorities and to abide by the requirements of the regime. It reflects the fact that in some vague or explicit way he [a person, author's note] sees these objects as conforming to his own moral principles, his own sense of what is right and proper in the political sphere". According to Easton, there are three different sources of legitimacy. These are ideology, structure, and personal qualities. The objects of all three sources are either the regime or the authorities (for more details, see Easton, 1975, 452).
  To sum up, Easton (1965, 1975) argues that overall political support is dependent on specific and diffuse support. Specific support refers to the

C. M. Hindermann, *The Impact of Economic Freedom on State Legitimacy*,
Wirtschaft und Politik, https://doi.org/10.1007/978-3-658-23195-8

perceived performance of political decisions and may be highly volatile in the short run. In contrast, diffuse support (reflecting trust and legitimacy) is stable in the short-run and changes only slowly over time.

- *Lipset (1959).* According to Lipset (1959), overall political support depends on legitimacy and effectiveness. Effectiveness is defined as "the actual performance of a political system, the extent to which it satisfies the basic functions of government as defined by the expectations of most members of a society, and the expectations of powerful groups within it which might threaten the system, such as the armed forces" (Lipset, 1959, 86). On the other hand, legitimacy "involves the capacity of a political system to engender and maintain the belief that existing political institutions are the most appropriate or proper ones for the society" (Lipset, 1959, 86). Both legitimacy and effectiveness are two dimensions contributing to system stability (the "Lispet-Matrix", Lipset, 1959, 90).

Figure 17: The Lipset-Matrix

		Effectiveness +	Effectiveness -
Legitimacy	+	A	B
	-	C	D

Source: Adopted from Lipset (1959, 90)

Lipset assumes that legitimacy and effectiveness are independent in the short run. Thus, a system that lacks either legitimacy (C) or effectiveness (B) may remain stable in the short run. However, in the long-run, legitimacy and effectiveness are interdependent. A system that structurally lacks effectiveness, may lose legitimacy (which leads from B to D). In the same vein, Lipset (1959, 91) notes that "prolonged effectiveness of the system as a whole may, as in the cases of the United States and Switzerland, eventually legitimate the democratic political system." A more detailed discussion is provided by Lipset (1959).

- *Hurd (1999).* Hurd (1999) argues that system stability (in terms of compliance with the rules) depends on the three ideal types of social control, namely coercion, self-interest, and legitimacy. First, *coercion* operates through fear. The basic principle of coercion is that people obey a rule or an executive power because they have to fear punishment from a stronger power if they do not follow the rule or the person in question. If a society is based on coercion, voluntary compliance is low such that the regime has to use enormous resources to enforce the rules.

  A second reason to obey a particular rule is *self-interest.* Assuming rationality, that means that the actor's net benefits of compliance are higher than the net benefits of non-compliance. In this vein, self-interest and coercion refer to the same logic. In both cases, a risk neutral agent would come to the same result since compliance leads to non-punishment (which is a benefit) and non-compliance leads to punishment (which symbolizes the costs). The main difference between both concepts is that coercion operates through an external restraint, whereas an internal restraint determines self-interest (Hurd, 1999, 386).

Legitimacy – understood as a normative belief – also contributes to compliance with the rules since it creates some internal reason to follow the rule. In this case, compliance is not achieved through fear or self-interest but through "an internal sense of obligation" (Hurd, 1999, 387). This "internal sense of obligation" is the result of internalizing an external rule. Although a given rule may not fit with the interest of the people, the internalization process of the rule alters the definition of one's own interests such that particular citizens no longer perceive a gap between the rule and their interests. Based on these considerations, legitimacy is the derivative of coercion. If the executive power imposed a rule that citizens only obey because of coercion, people may internalize the new rule over time such that a new social consensus emerges. Hurd (1999, 389) argues that many regimes and government relations that are today seen as legitimate originally used coercion. In particular, he refers to almost all of the modern liberal democratic states, which had times in history where system stability could only be achieved through coercion.

- *Gerschewski (2013).* Gerschweski (2013) is particularly interested in the stability of autocratic regimes. According to him, system stability of autocratic regimes depends on three pillars, namely legitimacy, repression, and co-optation.

  At first, Gerschewski (2013) argues that legitimization – or legitimacy – is a central pillar of system stability, in particular in the long-run. He argues that legitimacy not only increases the rate of compliance of citizens but also reduces the costs of maintaining a stable political and social order. In autocratic systems, it can be achieved via ideological indoctrination and through a good performance of the regime.

  The second pillar is *repression.* It is defined as "actual or threatened use of physical sanctions against an individual or organization, within the territorial jurisdiction of the state, for the purpose of imposing a cost on the target as well as deterring specific activities" (Gerschewski, 2013, 21 qt. in Davenport, 2007). One can distinguish between different types of repression intensities. High repression intensity is defined as visible acts (of violence) that target well-known individuals, a large number of people, or major oppositional organizations. In contrast, low repression intensity can be described as targeting groups of lesser importance, being less visible, and using more subtle ways of execution. From the perspective of an autocratic regime, repression is an effective way to sustain system stability, especially in the short run. In contrast, a regime should avoid using repression in the long-run since it is – in contrast to other pillars like legitimacy – too costly.

  The third pillar of system stability is *co-optation.* It refers to the ability of the regime or the regime's elites to bind strategically-relevant actors, such as business elites and military personnel, to themselves such that they use their power to support the regime rather than to obstruct it. At the same time, the regime needs not only to tie relevant actors but also to ensure that particular actors do not become too strong. Typically, co-optation operates through formal (e.g. parliament, parties, elections, or other democratic institutions) and informal (mostly patronage, clientelism, and corruption) channels (Gerschewski, 2013, 22).

Appendix B – Legitimacy Definitions

The following list offers an overview of selected legitimacy definitions by different scholars:

- Legitimacy is "the belief in a political or social order." (Weber, 1968, qt. in Bensman, 1979, 360)
- Legitimacy is "a justification for an existing form of political domination." (Weber, 1968, qt. in Bensman, 1979, 360)
- Legitimacy is "the belief that existing political institutions are most appropriate or proper ones for the society." (Lipset, 1959, 86)
- Legitimacy is "the conviction […] that it is right and proper […] to accept and obey the authorities and to abide by the requirements of the regime. It reflects the fact that in some vague or explicit way he [a person, author's note] sees these objects as conforming to his own moral principles, his own sense of what is right and proper in the political sphere." (Easton, 1965, 278)
- Legitimacy is "the belief that in spite of shortcomings and failures, the political institutions are better than any other that might be established, and therefore can demand obedience." (Linz, 1988, 65)
- "Political power is legitimate, we can say, to the extent that:
    - it is acquired and exercised in accordance with the rules or the laws; and
    - the rules or laws embody an acknowledged principle of political authority, in terms of which they can be justified; and
    - there is evidence of express consent to authority on the part of those qualified to give it." (Beetham, 1991, 42)
- "A state is more legitimate the more that its citizens treat it as holding and exercising power rightfully, meaning in a manner that is consistent with rules and laws (legality), that is morally justified (justification), and to which they have actively consented (consent), where justification is roughly twice as important as legality and consent." (Gilley, 2012, 694)
- "Legitimacy […] refers to the normative belief by an actor that a rule or institution ought to be obeyed." (Hurd, 1999, 381)
- "Legitimacy is a psychological property of an authority, institution, or social arrangement that leads those connected to it to believe that it is appropriate, proper, and just." (Tyler, 2006, 375)
- "Legitimacy derives from the beliefs citizens hold about the normative appropriateness of government structures, officials, and processes. Of central

importance is the belief that rules and regulations are entitled to be obeyed by virtue of who made the decision or how it was made." (Levi et al., 2009, 354)
- Legitimacy is "citizen support for government."(Booth & Seligson, 2009, 1)
- "Legitimacy is defined as popular compliance with and acceptance of political authority […] and will be analysed comparatively as a systemic outcome of variations in the democratic performance of political parties in parliament and government within its institutional fabric […]." (Keman, 2014, 310)

Appendix C – Items to Measure Legitimacy

Table 51: Items to Measure the Three Dimensions of Legitimacy (Beetham)

	Views of Legality	Views of Justification	Acts of Consent
Attitudes	Attitude surveys about legality	Surveys of political system support, political trust, alienation etc.	N/A
	Attitude surveys about corruption	Views of effectiveness of political institutions	
	Acceptance of electoral or revolutionary mandates	Popularity of embedded polity (authoritarian leaders or parties)	
	Views of police, judges, and civil servants		
Actions	Demonstrations or social movements over legal or constitutional issues	Political violence	Election turnout, voter registration
	Importance of laws or constitution in political life	Size of internal secret police	Military recruitment, use of mercenary soldiers
	Dissonance over election results	Political prisoners	Tax payments/reliance on foreign loans or resource export taxes
		Anti-system movements/ secessionism/ civil war	Popular mobilization in authoritarian systems
		Mass emigration	
		Crime levels	

Source: Adopted from Gilley (2006a, 505)

Appendix D – Gilley's Legitimacy Scores

Table 52: Gilley's Legitimacy Scores

		Scores	
Country	*ca. 2001*	*ca. 2008*	*ca. 2012*
Albania	3.27	-	-
Algeria	4.48	-	3.11
Argentina	4.03	4.47	5.61
Armenia	2.83	-	3.54
Australia	6.38	7.18	7.58
Austria	7.00	-	-
Azerbaijan	6.78	-	4.77
Bangladesh	5.58	-	-
Belarus	4.41	-	5.35
Belgium	6.64	-	-
Bosnia Herzegovina	3.54	-	-
Bulgaria	4.07	3.21	-
Burkina Faso	-	4.32	-
Brazil	5.19	4.68	4.89
Britain	6.28	6.21	-
Canada	7.03	7.26	-
Chile	5.81	5.05	5.10
China	6.58	5.36	5.30
Colombia	2.95	2.35	-
Croatia	4.62	-	-
Cyprus	-	5.26	-
Czech Republic	5.28	-	-
Denmark	7.62	-	-
Dominican Republic	2.86	-	-
Ecuador	-	-	6.18
Egypt	5.01	-	2.28
El Salvador	4.27	-	-
Estonia	4.88	-	6.15
Ethopia	-	1.82	-
Finland	6.98	7.40	-
France	5.24	5.03	-

Table 52: Gilley's Legitimacy Scores (cont.)

	Scores		
Country	*ca. 2001*	*ca. 2008*	*ca. 2012*
Georgia	2.90	2.42	4.04
Germany	6.68	5.84	7.63
Ghana	6.00	-	6.84
Greece	5.22	-	-
Hungary	5.21	-	-
India	4.46	5.21	5.92
Indonesia	5.05	6.03	-
Iraq	-	-	3.43
Iran	4.72	2.04	-
Ireland	6.48	-	-
Italy	5.90	6.15	-
Japan	5.62	6.13	6.48
Jordan	4.99	5.17	4.83
Kazakhstan	-	-	5.45
Kuwait	-	-	5.71
Kyrgyzstan	-	-	4.32
Latvia	4.16	-	-
Lebanon	-	-	3.74
Lithuania	3.22	-	-
Libya	-	-	1.78
Macedonia	2.97	-	-
Malaysia	-	-	5.98
Mali	-	5.91	-
Mexico	3.55	3.50	3.44
Moldova	4.33	0.98	-
Morocco	5.25	4.58	4.31
Netherlands	7.13	5.74	6.85
New Zealand	5.69	6.78	7.71
Nigeria	5.56	-	3.33
Norway	7.61	7.97	-
Pakistan	2.41	-	3.43
Peru	3.13	3.44	4.43

Table 52: Gilley's Legitimacy Scores (cont.)

	Scores		
Country	*ca. 2001*	*ca. 2008*	*ca. 2012*
Philippines	5.66	-	6.58
Poland	5.23	4.37	4.99
Portugal	6.39	-	-
Romania	3.92	2.44	2.65
Russia	2.27	3.18	3.08
Rwanda	-	6.13	6.09
Serbia/Yugoslavia	3.89	2.69	-
Singapore	-	-	7.01
Slovakia	4.62	-	-
Slovenia	4.93	4.33	3.73
South Africa	6.24	5.45	5.09
South Korea	5.45	5.87	6.53
Spain	6.28	6.64	5.74
Sweden	6.93	7.33	7.51
Switzerland	5.68	6.50	-
Taiwan	6.62	-	6.89
Tanzania	5.67	-	-
Thailand	-	5.89	5.78
Trinidad & Tobago	-	4.70	5.16
Tunisia	-	-	4.22
Turkey	3.39	3.96	5.36
Uganda	5.05	-	-
Ukraine	4.02	2.99	2.00
United States	6.82	5.83	5.93
Uruguay	5.94	6.66	6.62
Venezuela	4.66	-	-
Vietnam	-	7.07	-
Yemen	-	-	2.53
Zambia	-	4.17	-
Zimbabwe	3.82	-	3.67

Sources: Gilley (2006a, 2012), own computation

I compile the legitimacy scores for ca. 2012, following the procedure of Gilley (2012). Regarding the dimension 'acts of consent', no data on voter turn-out are available for China; and no data on quasi-voluntary taxes are available for Algeria, Argentina, Ecuador, Iraq, Kuwait, Kyrgyzstan, Lebanon, Libya, Malaysia, Mexico, Nigeria, Philippines, Taiwan, Yemen, and Zimbabwe. In these cases, the sub-score for 'acts of consent' solely consists of one indicator (either voter-turnout or quasi-voluntary taxes). Data are available on request.

Appendix E – Substitutive and Constitutive Indicators

To evaluate the internal consistency correctly, it is important to know the indicator types. Referring to Bollen and Lennox (1991), there are two types of indicators to measure a latent concept (as it is the legitimacy of the state). Those are (i) substitutive (or causal) and (ii) constitutive (or effect) indicators (see also Lamb, 2014):

- *Substitutive Indicators.* Substitutive (or originally named effect or proxy) indicators depend on the latent variable. Equation [40] expresses this in a formalized fashion,

$$Y = \lambda L_i + \epsilon \qquad [40]$$

where Y is the substitutive indicator, L_i the latent variable (in this thesis legitimacy), ε the measurement error, and λ the coefficient that shows the impact of the latent variable L_i on the substitutive indicator Y (Bollen & Lennox, 1991, 305; Lamb, 2014, 33). Referring to Gilley (2006a), he uses the items "Confidence in the police", "Confidence in the civil service", and "Use of violence in civil protest" as substitutive indicators. Then, for means of internal consistency, Bollen and Lennox (1991, 307) show that substitutive indicators should be highly correlated to be internally consistent. They (1991, 307) conclude that "for effect indicators of a single latent variable [...] we find high correlations superior to moderate or low ones."
- *Constitutive Indicators.* Constitutive (or originally named causal or composite) indicators determine the latent variable or, in other words, theoretically define the higher order concept (Gilley, 2009b, 2). Equation [41] formalizes this relation,

$$L_i = \gamma_1 X_1 + \gamma_2 X_2 + \ldots + \gamma_n X_n + \epsilon \qquad [41]$$

where L_i is the latent variable, X reflects one of the n different constitutive indicators, γ expresses one of the n different coefficients, and ε signals the measurement error term (Bollen & Lennox, 1991, 306; Lamb, 2014, 33). Again, Gilley (2006a) notes that the "Provision of human rights", "Satisfaction with democratic development", "Evaluation of current political system", "Satisfaction with operation of democracy", "Voter turnout", and "Quasi-voluntary taxes" are constitutive indicators.

> In contrast to substitutive indicators, Bollen and Lennox (1991) show that constitutive indicators do not need to be positively correlated to be internally consistent. Rather, they (1991, 307) note that constitutive or "causal indicators of the same concept can have positive, negative, or no correlation". Further, they conclude that "we have no recommendations of correlations for causal [or constitutive, author's note] indicators, because these correlations are explained by factors outside the model."

To sum up, the distinction between substitutive and constitutive indicators are important when interpreting measures of internal consistency such as Cronbach's alpha. Inter-item correlations are only a useful measure of the internal consistency if all indicators are substitutive. In contrast, if a dimension consists of only constitutive indicators or an admixture of substitutive and constitutive indicators, inter-item correlations are not useful for measuring reliability. (Gilley, 2009b, 5)

Appendix F – Norris‘ Legitimacy Scores

Table 53: Norris' Legitimacy Scores

	Scores		
Country	*ca. 2001*	*ca. 2008*	*ca. 2012*
Albania	4.19	-	-
Algeria	4.18	-	4.74
Andorra	-	4.70	-
Argentina	3.02	3.64	4.00
Armenia	-	-	3.62
Australia	-	5.72	5.61
Austria	5.42	-	-
Azerbaijan	-	-	5.64
Bahrain	-	-	5.54
Bangladesh	6.49	-	-
Belarus	4.05	-	5.10
Belgium	4.50	-	-
Bosnia Herzegovina	3.90	-	-
Brazil	-	-	3.94
Britain	5.29	5.43	-
Bulgaria	3.96	3.77	-
Burkina Faso	-	4.84	-
Canada	5.46	5.90	-
Chile	4.59	4.79	4.54
China	6.94	6.95	6.71
Colombia	-	4.40	4.02
Croatia	3.97	-	-
Cyprus	-	5.51	4.69
Czech Republic	3.99	-	-
Denmark	5.88	-	-
Ecuador	-	-	4.85
Egypt	6.45	-	3.27
Ethiopia	-	3.82	-
Estonia	4.22	-	5.19
Finland	5.96	6.60	-
France	4.72	5.17	-

Table 53: Norris' Legitimacy Scores (cont.)

	Scores		
Country	*ca. 2001*	*ca. 2008*	*ca. 2012*
Georgia	-	3.95	-
Germany	5.27	4.84	6.06
Ghana	-	6.59	6.30
Greece	4.33	-	-
Guatemala	-	3.07	-
Hungary	4.20	3.76	-
Iceland	5.84	-	-
India	5.29	6.07	5.57
Indonesia	4.94	5.57	-
Iran	5.49	4.73	-
Iraq	3.38	3.66	4.04
Ireland	5.75	-	-
Italy	4.56	4.85	-
Japan	4.41	4.99	5.30
Jordan	6.40	6.95	5.83
Kazakhstan	-	-	5.75
Kuwait	-	-	6.47
Kyrgyzstan	3.53	-	5.38
Latvia	4.19	-	-
Lebanon	-	-	4.00
Libya	-	-	3.69
Lithuania	3.26	-	-
Luxembourg	5.85	-	-
Macedonia	2.80	-	-
Malaysia	-	6.37	6.22
Mali	-	6.33	-
Malta	5.75	-	-
Mexico	3.58	4.48	4.17
Moldova	3.57	3.49	-
Morocco	4.46	4.81	4.29
Netherlands	5.52	4.99	5.33
New Zealand	-	5.60	6.18

Table 53: Norris' Legitimacy Scores (cont.)

	Scores		
Country	*ca. 2001*	*ca. 2008*	*ca. 2012*
Nigeria	4.98	-	4.82
Norway	-	6.33	-
Pakistan	4.25	-	4.92
Peru	3.66	2.98	3.19
Philippines	5.62	-	6.41
Poland	4.49	4.41	4.56
Portugal	5.52	-	-
Qatar	-	-	8.70
Romania	3.82	4.17	3.64
Russia	2.82	3.99	4.19
Rwanda	-	-	6.44
Saudi Arabia	6.09	-	-
Serbia/ Yugoslavia	4.19	3.52	-
Singapore	-	-	6.65
Slovakia	4.28	-	-
Slovenia	4.17	4.13	3.46
South Africa	4.76	5.91	4.93
South Korea	4.17	5.13	5.12
Spain	4.99	5.38	4.74
Sweden	5.28	5.90	6.10
Switzerland	-	6.22	-
Taiwan	-	4.57	5.39
Tanzania	6.66	-	-
Thailand	-	5.42	5.69
Trinidad & Tobago	-	4.03	4.28
Tunisia	-	-	3.69
Turkey	3.61	5.11	5.60
Uganda	5.88	-	-
United States	5.35	5.39	5.28
Ukraine	3.36	3.66	3.64
Uruguay	-	5.39	5.06
Venezuela	4.39	-	-

Table 53: Norris' Legitimacy Scores (cont.)

	Scores		
Country	*ca. 2001*	*ca. 2008*	*ca. 2012*
Vietnam	8.51	8.27	-
Yemen	-	-	3.51
Zambia	-	4.89	-
Zimbabwe	3.84	-	5.18

Source: Own computation

Appendix G – Legitimacy and GDP per Capita

Figure 18: Legitimacy and GDP per Capita (Norris and Gilley)

Gilley ca. 2008:

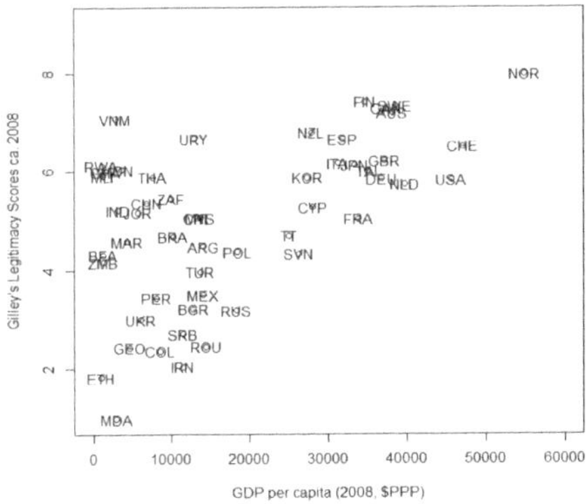

Gilley ca. 2012:

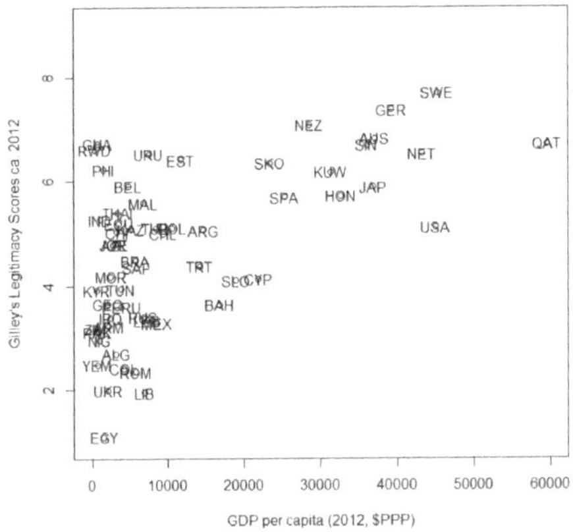

Figure 18: Legitimacy and GDP per Capita (Norris and Gilley) (cont.)

Norris ca. 2001:

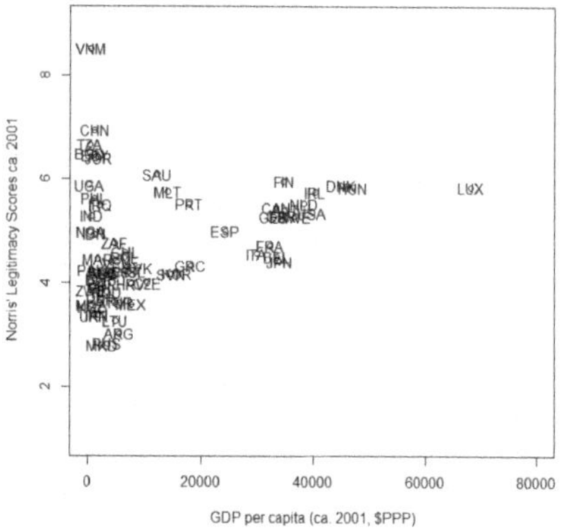

Norris ca. 2006:

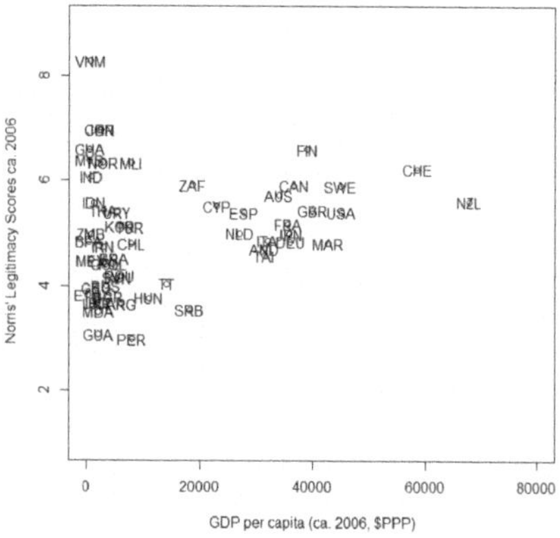

Norris ca. 2012:

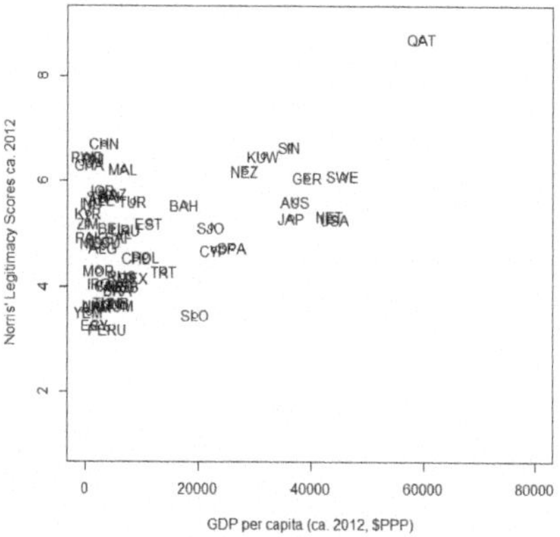

Appendix H – Legitimacy and HDI

Figure 19: Legitimacy and HDI (Norris and Gilley)

Gilley ca. 2001:

Gilley ca. 2006:

Gilley ca. 2012:

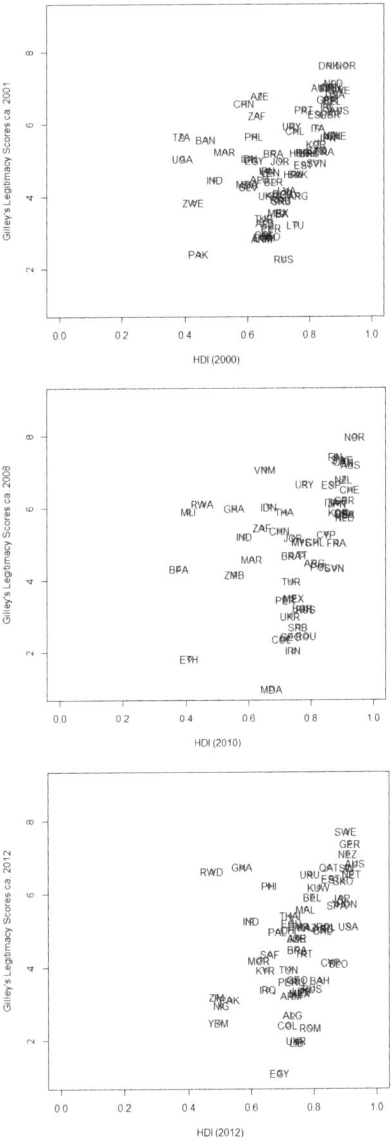

Figure 19: Legitimacy and HDI (Norris and Gilley) (cont.)

Norris ca. 2001:

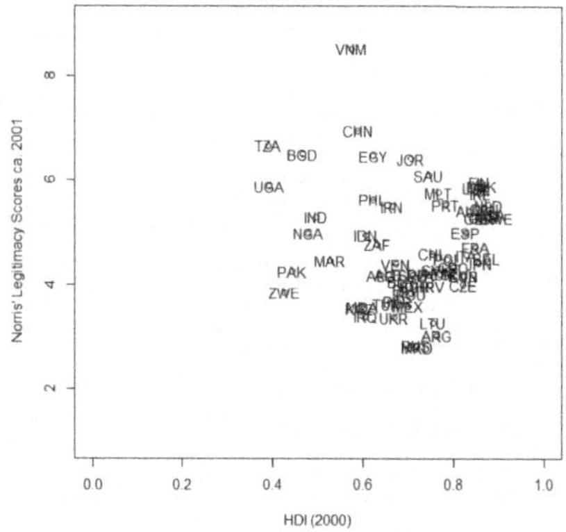

Norris ca. 2006:

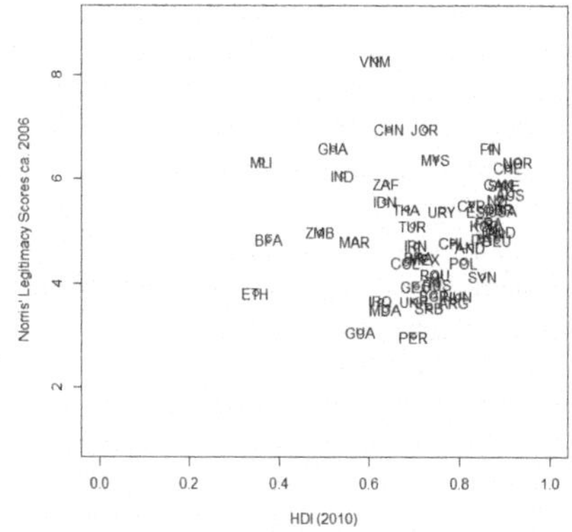

Norris ca. 2012:

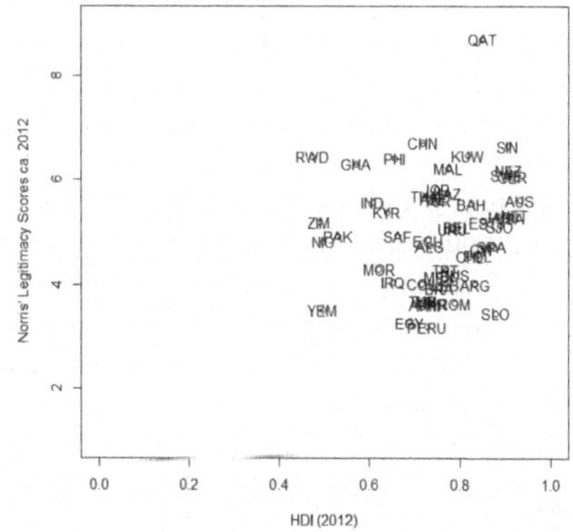

Appendix I – Legitimacy and the Growth Rate

As mentioned above, Berggren et al. (2015) argue that legitimacy has an impact on the growth rate through five different channels. First, they argue that legitimacy increases the willingness of the people to obey and defer to the government. On the one hand, this has the advantage that the government needs to spend fewer resources on the enforcement of its policies and the maintenance of the social order. On the other hand, people are more prone to pay their taxes (Levi & Sachs, 2009; Levi et al., 2009). In sum, the government has more resources available which can be used to increase expenditures on public goods and public investments or to lower the tax level. The net effect on growth, however, remains unclear since it depends on the actual usage of the available resources. Government expenditures on public investments (such as infrastructure) should have a positive effect on the growth rate, whereas an increase of the pensions is more likely to lower the growth rate.

Second, legitimacy itself has an impact on policies that affect growth. For example, it is easier for a legitimate government to cut taxes or to increase expenditures. In contrast, if legitimacy is low, people distrust the ability of the government to solve economic problems such that the demand for government intervention is rather low.

Third, a legitimate government has more possibilities to impose policies they want without a reduction of popularity. As long as the government is legitimate, legitimacy provides a "reservoir of support" that reduces the importance of even negative outcomes in the form of reduced growth rates caused by bad governance. A reason for this phenomenon may be that citizens have fewer incentives to acquire information about the outcomes – in particular economic growth – of government activities as long as they believe in governmental legitimacy. The net effects on growth are likely to be negative. On the one hand, politicians may use their governmental legitimacy to implement policies that are only beneficial to specific interest groups such as tax reduction or other economic or political benefits. On the other hand, politicians may implement policies in exchange for votes. In this case, there are negative effects on growth rates, although it may be rational for the government in the short-run to act like this to become reelected. To sum up, one should expect a negative impact on the growth rates in both cases (policies for interest groups or populism).

Fourth, legitimacy affects not only the usage of the resources of the government but also the usage of people's own resources. Here, the argument runs that, in a system with high legitimacy, people use fewer resources to protect their incomes and wealth. As a consequence, people spend less time in rent-seeking activities and engage less in the shadow economy. This leads to a positive effect on the growth rate.

Eventually, if legitimacy is high, a given tax level is typically perceived as less encumbering. The reason is that people have more confidence in the appropriate use of the taxes by the government if it is legitimate. Thus, people work and invest more in comparison to a situation where governmental legitimacy is low. To speak economically, Berggren et al. (2015, 7) argue that "legitimacy may reduce the negative labor-supply effects of high marginal tax rates and therefore limit the negative growth effects of a given heavy tax burden." Thus, it is expected that legitimacy has a positive effect on the growth rate through this channel.

Appendix J – Marginal Effect of Democracy

To illustrate the marginal effect of democracy, I use the coefficients of the first wave (see table 16) and vary the values of democracy holding democratic history and all other regressors constant. Equation [42] shows the simplified model of the first wave,

$$Legitimacy = \beta_0 + \boldsymbol{\beta} X + \alpha_1 D + \alpha_1 DH + \alpha_3 (D - \overline{D})(DH - \overline{DH}) + \epsilon \qquad [42]$$

where β_0 is the intercept, $\boldsymbol{\beta}$ the vector of the coefficients (except democracy, democratic history and the interaction term), α_1 the coefficient of democracy, α_2 the coefficient of democratic history, α_3 the coefficient of the interaction term, and ε the error term. Inserting the coefficients and the mean values of democracy and democratic history yields equation [43].

$$Legitimacy = \beta_0 + \boldsymbol{\beta} X + \%0.21\, D - 0.08\, DH + \%0.08 (D - 7.66)(DH - 5.35) + \epsilon \qquad [43]$$

To show the marginal effect of democracy on legitimacy, one has to take the first derivative with respect to democracy as expressed in equation [44].

$$\frac{\partial\, Legitimacy}{\partial\, Demo} = 0.21 + 0.08 (DemoH - 5.35) \qquad [44]$$

Thus, the equation shows that the effect of democracy on legitimacy can be positive, null, or negative, depending on a country's democratic history. Varying the values of democratic history from zero to ten, figure 20 illustrates this graphically.

Figure 20: Marginal Effect of Democracy

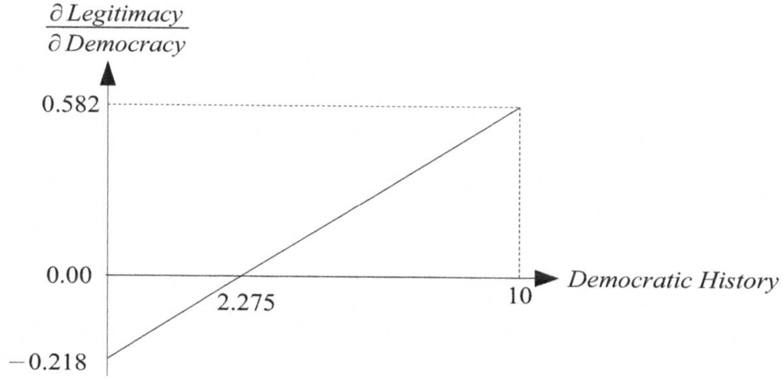

Source: Own representation

Appendix K – Predicted and Actual Legitimacy Scores (Gilley)

Figure 21: Predicted and Actual Legitimacy Scores (Gilley)

Gilley ca. 2001:

Gilley ca. 2008:

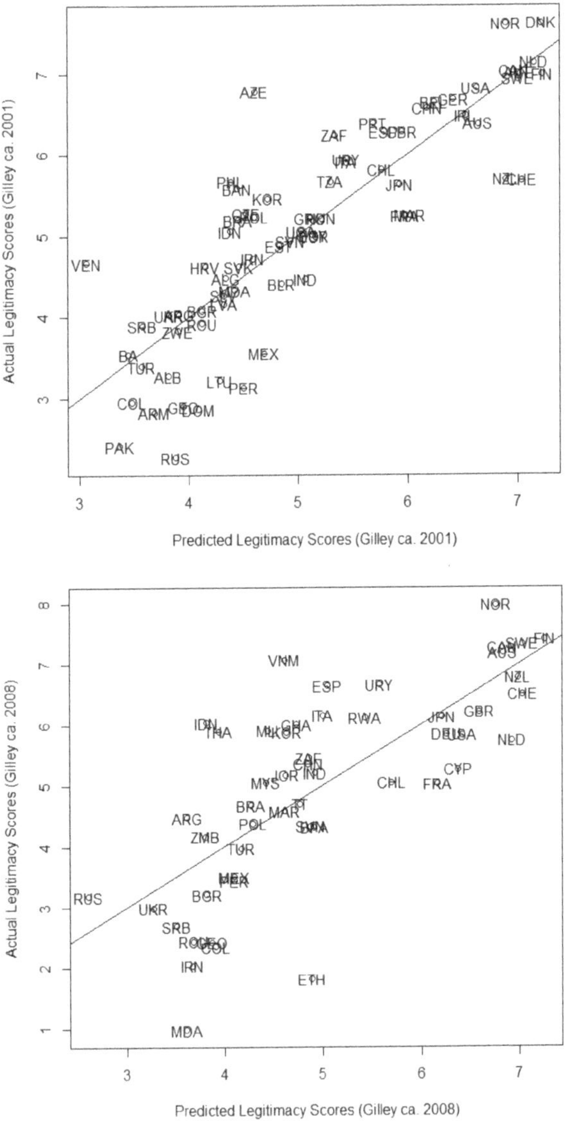

Figure 21: Predicted and Actual Legitimacy Scores (Gilley) (cont.)

Gilley ca. 2012:

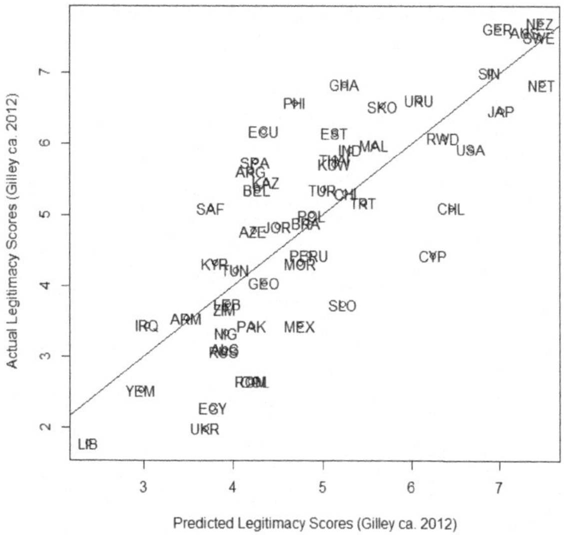

Appendix L – Low-Income and High-Income Countries (Gilley)

Table 54: OLS Estimates Based on Gilley's Legitimacy Scores – The Basic Model – Only Low-Income Countries (< 14000 $ GDP per Capita)

Dependent: Legitimacy	Gilley ca. 2001			Gilley ca. 2008			Gilley ca. 2012		
	(1)			(2)			(3)		
	Coeff.	t-value	p-value	Coeff.	t-value	p-value	Coeff.	t-value	p-value
Intercept	7.23***	6.31	0.000	6.82***	3.17	0.005	7.02***	4.44	0.000
Input Variables									
Democracy	0.05	0.69	0.495	0.15	0.71	0.488	0.08	0.56	0.581
Democratic History	-0.15*	-1.99	0.054	-0.10	-0.47	0.642	-0.11	-0.83	0.411
Democracy*DemocraticHistory[1]	0.12***	4.09	0.000	0.10	1.29	0.212	0.10**	2.16	0.039
Throughput/Output Variables									
General Governance	0.99***	3.26	0.002	1.59*	1.94	0.067	1.27***	3.34	0.002
HDI (absolute)	-3.64*	-2.01	0.052	-4.03	-1.50	0.148	-2.89	-1.45	0.156
Unemployment Rate	-0.02	-0.90	0.374	-0.07	-1.21	0.242	-0.10***	-3.05	0.004
R^2		0.526			0.360			0.559	
Adjust. R^2		0.452			0.168			0.477	
Observations		45			27			39	

[1] - Interaction term is mean centered.
* - at 10%-level significant ** - at 5%-level significant *** - at 1%-level significant

Table 55: OLS Estimates Based on Gilley's Legitimacy Scores – The Basic Model – Only High-Income Countries (> 14000 $ GDP per Capita)

Dependent: Legitimacy	Gilley ca. 2001			Gilley ca. 2008			Gilley ca. 2012		
	(1)			(2)			(3)		
	Coeff.	t-value	p-value	Coeff.	t-value	p-value	Coeff.	t-value	p-value
Intercept	4.78	0.84	0.412	2.94	0.28	0.779	-7.21	-0.59	0.570
Input Variables									
Democracy	0.32	1.06	0.304	-0.99	-0.94	0.358	-0.09	-0.20	0.842
Democratic History	0.03	0.33	0.748	0.20**	2.15	0.047	0.04	0.17	0.872
Democracy*DemocraticHistory[1]	0.06	0.44	0.669	-0.25	-1.14	0.272	-0.00	-0.01	0.990
Throughput/Output Variables									
General Governance	0.88*	2.54	0.021	0.75	1.22	0.239	0.21	0.23	0.822
HDI (absolute)	-3.61	-0.57	0.573	11.23*	1.76	0.096	15.40	1.00	0.343
Unemployment Rate	-0.03	-0.53	0.602	0.05	0.937	0.362	-0.03	-0.49	0.632
R^2		0.598			0.791			0.459	
Adjust. R^2		0.456			0.717			0.134	
Observations		24			24			17	

[1] - Interaction term is mean centered.
* - at 10%-level significant ** - at 5%-level significant *** - at 1%-level significant

Note: Model (2) is overspecified since the VIFs indicate strong multicollinearity ($VIF_{Democracy}$= 55.23; $VIF_{GeneralGov}$= 11.82; $VIF_{Interaction\ Term}$= 40.57).

Note: Model (3) is not significant at all according to the F-statistics (p-value= 0.30). Further, the VIFs indicate strong multicollinearity ($VIF_{Democracy}$= 24.83; $VIF_{DemocraticHistory}$= 10.43).

Appendix M – Predicted and Actual Legitimacy Scores (Norris)

Figure 22: Predicted and Actual Legitimacy Scores (Norris)

Norris ca. 2001:

Norris ca. 2008:

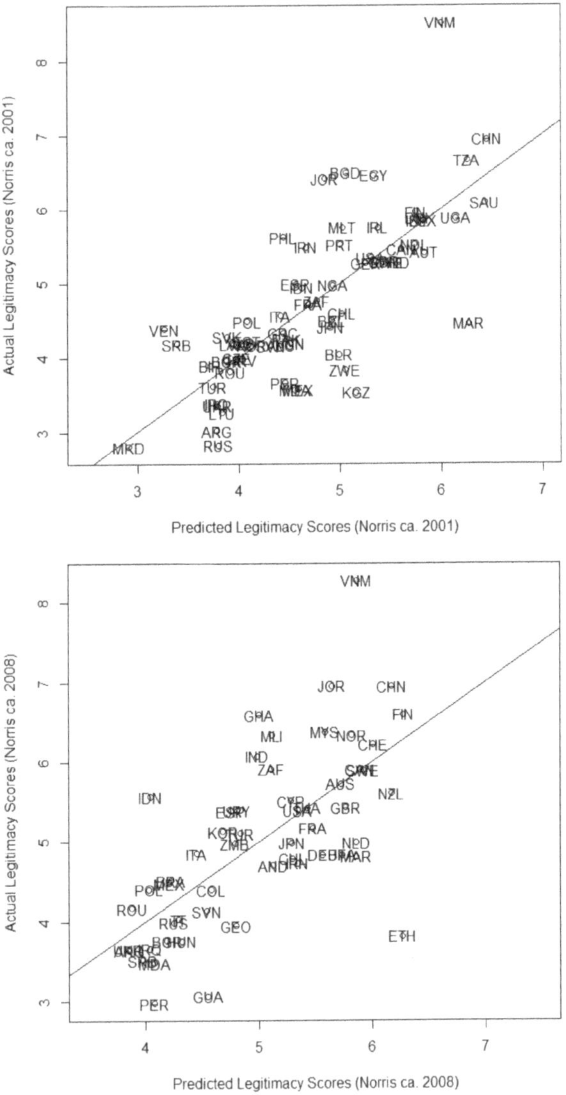

Figure 22: Predicted and Actual Legitimacy Scores (Norris) (cont.)

Norris ca. 2012:

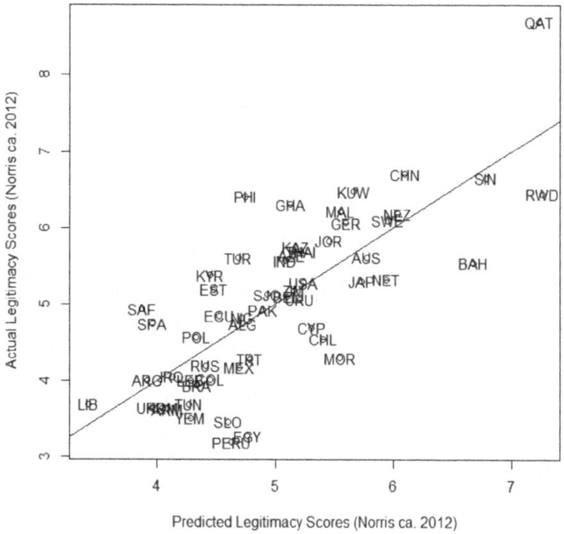

Appendix N – Low-Income and High-Income Countries (Norris)

Table 56: Robustness of the Basic Model: Alternative Legitimacy Measure – OLS Estimates – Only Low-Income Countries (< 14000 $ GDP per Capita)

Dependent: Legitimacy (Norris)	Norris ca. 2001			Norris ca. 2006			Norris ca. 2012		
	(1)			(2)			(3)		
	Coeff.	t-value	p-value	Coeff.	t-value	p-value	Coeff.	t-value	p-value
Intercept	9.35***	7.29	0.000	8.61***	6.19	0.000	8.29***	7.506	0.000
Input Variables									
Democracy	-0.01	-0.18	0.860	-0.19	-1.67	0.106	-0.14	-1.42	0.165
Democratic History	-0.16*	-1.76	0.087	-0.00	-0.03	0.976	0.04	0.412	0.681
Democracy*DemocraticHistory[1]	0.08***	2.96	0.005	0.04	1.03	0.311	0.03	0.93	0.358
Throughput/Output Variables									
General Governance	0.68**	2.05	0.048	1.25***	2.92	0.007	0.81***	3.06	0.004
HDI (absolute)	-5.64***	-2.78	0.008	-3.42*	-1.94	0.063	-3.04**	-2.14	0.040
Unemployment Rate	-0.04*	-1.83	0.076	-0.02	-0.37	0.717	-0.07**	-2.58	0.015
R^2		0.519			0.452			0.758	
Adjust. R^2		0.441			0.330			0.397	
Observations		44			34			39	

[1] - Interaction term is mean centered.
* - at 10%-level significant ** - at 5%-level significant *** - at 1%-level significant

Table 57: Robustness of the Basic Model: Alternative Legitimacy Measure – OLS Estimates – Only High-Income Counries (>14000 $ GDP per Capita)

Dependent: Legitimacy (Norris)	Norris ca. 2001			Norris ca. 2006			Norris ca. 2012		
	(1)			(2)			(3)		
	Coeff.	t-value	p-value	Coeff.	t-value	p-value	Coeff.	t-value	p-value
Intercept	2.77***	0.65	0.527	3.46	0.69	0.506	4.52	0.50	0.627
Input Variables									
Democracy	0.69**	2.18	0.046	1.03	1.60	0.135	-0.04	-0.14	0.890
Democratic History	0.05	1.15	0.267	-0.01	-0.09	0.928	-0.04	-0.20	0.846
Democracy*DemocraticHistory[1]	0.09*	1.99	0.065	0.11	1.36	0.200	0.04	1.07	0.313
Throughput/Output Variables									
General Governance	0.73***	3.43	0.004	1.04***	4.04	0.002	0.86	1.15	0.279
HDI (absolute)	-6.96*	-2.03	0.060	-11.31**	-2.90	0.013	0.40	0.03	0.973
Unemployment Rate	-0.02	-0.77	0.455	-0.01	-0.211	0.836	-0.04	-0.60	0.560
R^2		0.903			0.780			0.691	
Adjust. R^2		0.864			0.670			0.484	
Observations		22			19			16	

[1] - Interaction term is mean centered.
* - at 10%-level significant ** - at 5%-level significant *** - at 1%-level significant

Note: Model (1) is overspecified due to multicollinearity ($VIF_{Democracy}$= 15.35). The same applies to model (2) ($VIF_{Democracy}$= 112.72; VIF_{HDI} = 14.19; $VIF_{InteractionTerm}$= 70.12) and model (3) ($VIF_{Democracy}$= 25.95).

Appendix O – Multi-Level Analysis (Further Specifications)

Table 58: Multi-Level Analysis (Plus Further Dummies)

Model	Norris ca. 2001		Norris ca. 2008		Norris ca. 2012	
	(1)		(2)		(3)	
	Coeff.	p-value	Coeff.	p-value	Coeff.	p-value
Individual-Level Variables						
...	...	...	...	...	...	...
Residence (town)[c]	-0.266***	0.000	-0.009	0.804	-0.078**	0.016
Residence (medium city)[c]	-0.147***	0.005	0.040	0.297	-0.171***	0.000
Residence (large city)[c]	-0.267***	0.000	-0.106**	0.010	-0.242***	0.000
Residence (metro)[c]	-0.238***	0.000	-0.152***	0.000	-0.450***	0.000
Political Positioning (left)[d]	-0.104***	0.008	-0.143***	0.000	-0.239***	0.000
Political Positioning (right)[d]	0.136***	0.000	0.105***	0.000	0.293***	0.000
Employment (full-time)[e]	-0.012	0.886	0.025	0.686	-0.173**	0.039
Employment (part-time)[e]	-0.069	0.450	0.092	0.193	-0.165*	0.057
Employment (self-employed)[e]	-0.133	0.112	-0.086	0.189	-0.132	0.125
Employment (retired)[e]	-0.039	0.677	-0.039	0.577	-0.161*	0.072
Employment (housewife)[e]	0.154*	0.073	0.078	0.266	0.124	0.150
Employment (students)[e]	-0.125	0.179	0.031	0.680	-0.102	0.255
Employment (unemployed)[e]	-0.086	0.322	-0.161**	0.019	-0.179**	0.039
...	...	...	...	...	...	...
-2LL	71419		106259		169769	
AIC/BIC	71421/71436		106263/106280		169773/169791	
Pseudo-R^2	0.1189		0.1306		0.1560	
Observations (individual level)	17792		27695		42197	
Observations (country level)	21		31		40	

* - at 10%-level significant ** - at 5%-level significant *** - at 1%-level significant
[c] - reference category: Residence (village) [d] - reference category: Political Positioning (center)
[e] - reference category: Employment (other)

Note: All regressions contain the standard control variables at the individual level (age, age squared, male, educational dummies, income (continuous), religion dummies, political interest, life satisfaction, media contact, interpersonal trust, victim of crime, and feeling of safety) and at the country level (democracy, democratic history, interaction term, general governance, unemployment rate, and the HDI) as far as available.

Table 59: Multi-Level Analysis (Plus Employment Sector)

Model	Norris ca. 2008		Norris ca. 2012	
	Coeff.	p-value	Coeff.	p-value
Individual-Level Variables				
...	...	...	...	...
Employment Sector (government or public institution)[c]	*0.110****[***]*	*0.000*	*0.135*[***]	*0.000*
Employment Sector (private non-profit organization)[c]	*0.000*	*0.994*	*0.036*	*0.238*
Employment Sector (self-employed, informal sector)[c]	*0.154*[**]	*0.013*	*0.061*	*0.119*
...	...	...	...	...
-2LL	133757		210398	
AIC/BIC	133761/133778		210402/210420	
Pseudo-R^2	0.181		0.220	
Observations (individual level)	34879		52663	
Observations (country level)	43		52	

[1] - Interaction term is mean centered.
[*] - at 10%-level significant [**] - at 5%-level significant [***] - at 1%-level significant
[c] - reference category: employment sector (private business or industry)

Note: All regressions contain the standard control variables at the individual level (age, age squared, male, educational dummies, income (continuous), religion dummies, political interest, life satisfaction, media contact, interpersonal trust, victim of crime, and feeling of safety) and at the country level (democracy, democratic history, interaction term, general governance, unemployment rate, and the HDI) as far as available.

Appendix P – Stepwise Regression of the Areas of Economic Freedom (Gilley)

Table 60: Stepwise Regressions of the Areas of Economic Freedom (Gilley ca. 2001)

	(1)	(2)	*(3)*	(4)	(5)	(6)	(7)	*(8)*
Intercept	3.02***	2.98***	*2.81****	3.48***	3.41***	3.35***	2.98***	*2.81****
Areas of Economic Freedom								
Government Size	-0.15*	-0.15*	*-0.15**	-0.12	-0.11	-0.12	-0.15*	*-0.15**
Legal System and Property Rights	0.37***	0.36***	*0.35****	0.44***	0.44***	0.41***	0.36***	*0.35****
Sound Money	0.17*	0.17*	*0.14**	0.22**	0.22**	0.21**	0.17*	*0.14**
Freedom to Trade Internationally	-0.06	-0.06		-0.23	-0.24	-0.24	-0.06	
Regulation	-0.02							
Credit Market				-0.03				
Labor Market				0.06	0.05	0.06		
Business				-0.05	-0.05			
R^2	0.602	0.602	*0.601*	0.607	0.607	0.606	0.602	*0.601*
adjusted R^2	0.568	0.575	*0.581*	0.552	0.561	0.568	0.575	*0.581*
Observations	64	64	*64*	58	58	58	64	*64*

*- at 10%-level significant **- at 5%-level significant ***- at 1%-level significant

Table 61: Stepwise Regressions of the Areas of Economic Freedom (Gilley ca. 2008)

	(1)	(2)	(3)	(4)	*(5)*	(6)	(7)	(8)	*(9)*
Intercept	0.11	0.01	0.19	-0.12	*0.21*	0.26	-0.06	-0.72	*0.21*
Areas of Economic Freedom									
Government Size	-0.01					-0.01			
Legal System and Property Rights	0.70***	0.71***	0.72***	0.71***	*0.76****	0.72***	0.74***	0.69***	*0.76****
Sound Money	0.12	0.12	0.12	0.08		0.15			
Freedom to Trade Internationally	-0.11	-0.11	-0.09			0.23			
Regulation	0.05	0.05							
Credit Market						0.22	0.19	0.16	
Labor Market						0.04			
Business						-0.24	-0.19		
R^2	0.369	0.369	0.369	0.367	*0.365*	0.390	0.381	0.374	*0.365*
adjusted R^2	0.301	0.316	0.329	0.342	*0.352*	0.293	0.342	0.349	*0.352*
Observations	52	52	52	52	*52*	52	52	52	*52*

*- at 10%-level significant **- at 5%-level significant ***- at 1%-level significant

Note: Due to reasons of space, I exclude the areas 'government size', 'sound money', 'freedom to trade internationally', and 'labor market regulation' when comparing model (6) and (7) (all coefficients of the particular areas show p-values close to or larger than 0.50 in model (6)).

Table 62: Stepwise Regressions of the Areas of Economic Freedom (Gilley ca. 2012)

	(1)	(2)	(3)	(4)	*(5)*	(6)	(7)	(8)	*(9)*
Intercept	0.66	0.73	0.41	0.91	*0.21*	1.18	0.88	1.23	*0.21*
Areas of Economic Freedom									
Government Size	0.09	0.09	0.08			0.15			
Legal System and Property Rights	0.97***	0.98***	0.93***	0.90***	*0.83****	1.09***	0.91***	0.93***	*0.83****
Sound Money	-0.11	-0.11	-0.16	-0.13		-0.09			
Freedom to Trade Internationally	-0.17	-0.16				-0.23			
Regulation	0.04								
Credit Market						0.17	0.10		
Labor Market						-0.09			
Business						-0.29	-0.31	-0.26	
R^2	0.528	0.528	0.524	0.521	*0.512*	0.556	0.530	0.523	*0.512*
adjusted R^2	0.477	0.488	0.494	0.502	*0.503*	0.485	0.501	0.504	*0.503*
Observations	52	52	52	52	*52*	52	52	52	*52*

* - at 10%-level significant ** - at 5%-level significant *** - at 1%-level significant

Note: Due to reasons of space, I exclude the areas 'government size', 'sound money', 'freedom to trade internationally', and 'labor market regulation' when comparing model (6) and (7) (all coefficients of the particular areas show p-values larger than 0.30 in model (6)).

Appendix Q – The Basic Model Plus (Squared) Areas of EFW (Gilley)

Table 63: The 'New' Basic Model Plus (Squared) Areas of EFW (Gilley ca. 2001)

	(1)	(2)	(3)	(4)	(5)	(6)	(7)	(8)
Intercept	6.01***	6.97***	6.15***	5.48***	5.69***	6.69***	7.62***	6.13***
Input Variables								
Democracy	0.17*	0.20**	0.21**	0.15*	0.15	0.12	0.17*	0.17*
Democratic History	-0.05	-0.03	-0.03	-0.04	-0.04	-0.03	-0.04	-0.04
Interaction Term[1]	0.07***	0.07***	0.08***	0.07***	0.07***	0.06***	0.07***	0.07***
Throughput/Output Variables								
New General Governance	1.05***	0.93***	0.90***	0.99***	1.04***	1.17***	1.27***	1.27***
HDI (absolute)	-3.45**	-3.94**	-4.00***	-3.42**	-3.76**	-3.80**	-3.83***	-3.69**
Unemployment Rate	-0.01	-0.01	-0.01	-0.01	-0.01	-0.01	-0.01	-0.01
+ Government Size		-0.15**	-0.16**					
+ (Government Size)^2			-0.02					
+ Sound Money				0.08				
+ Freedom to Trade					0.08	-0.02		
+ (Freedom to Trade)^2						-0.05		
+ Regulation							-0.24	-0.24
+ (Regulation)^2								-0.04
R^2	0.738	0.758	0.760	0.744	0.740	0.746	0.750	0.751
adjusted R^2	0.709	0.727	0.724	0.711	0.707	0.708	0.717	0.713
Observations	62	62	62	62	62	62	62	62

[1] - Interaction term is mean centered.
* - at 10%-level significant ** - at 5%-level significant *** - at 1%-level significant

Note: When including both the area and its squared term, I use the mean centered version of these variables to limit multicollinearity.

Table 64: The 'New' Basic Model Plus (Squared) Areas of EFW (Gilley ca. 2008)

	(1)	(2)	(3)	(4)	(5)	(6)	(7)	(8)
Intercept	4.66**	4.13*	4.71**	4.53**	5.91**	4.85**	6.39**	4.96**
Input Variables								
Democracy	0.23	0.22	0.21	0.22	0.28	0.24	0.19	0.19
Democratic History	0.07	0.07	0.07	0.07	0.05	0.06	0.08	0.08
Interaction Term[1]	0.07	0.07	0.07	0.07	0.07	0.10**	0.06	0.06
Throughput/Output Variables								
New General Governance	0.91**	0.94**	0.96**	0.90**	0.99**	1.07***	1.06**	1.06**
HDI (absolute)	-3.15	-3.17	-3.19	-3.28	-2.70	-3.34*	-3.39*	-3.37*
Unemployment Rate	-0.02	-0.02	-0.02	-0.03	-0.03	-0.00	-0.03	-0.02
+ Government Size		0.08	0.12					
+ (Government Size)^2			0.06					
+ Sound Money				0.03				
+ Freedom to Trade					-0.26	-0.37		
+ (Freedom to Trade)^2						-0.57***		
+ Regulation							-0.20	-0.19
+ (Regulation)^2								0.11
R^2	0.526	0.528	0.530	0.526	0.534	0.629	0.532	0.535
adjusted R^2	0.461	0.451	0.440	0.449	0.458	0.558	0.456	0.447
Observations	51	51	51	51	51	51	51	51

[1] - Interaction term is mean centered.
* - at 10%-level significant ** - at 5%-level significant *** - at 1%-level significant

Note: When including both the area and its squared term, I use the mean centered version of these variables to limit multicollinearity.

Table 65: The 'New' Basic Model Plus (Squared) Areas of EFW (Gilley ca. 2012)

	(1)	(2)	(3)	(4)	(5)	(6)	(7)	(8)
Intercept	6.68***	6.76***	6.77***	7.57***	9.23***	6.97***	6.62***	7.16***
Input Variables								
Democracy	0.07	0.07	0.07	0.08	0.07	0.08	0.07	0.03
Democratic History	0.05	0.05	0.05	0.04	0.05	0.04	0.05	0.07
Interaction Term	0.03	0.03	0.03	0.03	0.02	0.02	0.03	0.02
Throughput/Output Variables								
New General Governance	1.17***	1.17***	1.18***	1.26***	1.45***	1.41***	1.17***	1.28***
HDI (absolute)	-2.84	-2.86	-2.84	-2.59	-3.14*	-3.33*	-2.84	-3.07
Unemployment Rate	-0.08***	-0.08***	-0.08***	-0.07**	-0.07**	-0.07**	-0.08***	-0.08***
+ Government Size		-0.01	-0.04					
+ (Government Size)^2			-0.04					
+ Sound Money				-0.14				
+ Freedom to Trade					-0.32	-0.24		
+ (Freedom to Trade)^2						0.05		
+ Regulation							0.01	0.10
+ (Regulation)^2								-0.09
R^2	0.645	0.645	0.647	0.653	0.664	0.666	0.645	0.650
adjusted R^2	0.596	0.587	0.580	0.597	0.610	0.603	0.587	0.583
Observations	51	51	51	51	51	51	51	51

[1] - Interaction term is mean centered.
* - at 10%-level significant ** - at 5%-level significant *** - at 1%-level significant

Note: When including both the area and its squared term, I use the mean centered version of these variables to limit multicollinearity.

Appendix R – Legitimacy and Government Size

Figure 23: Legitimacy and Government Size

Gilley ca. 2001:

Gilley ca. 2008:

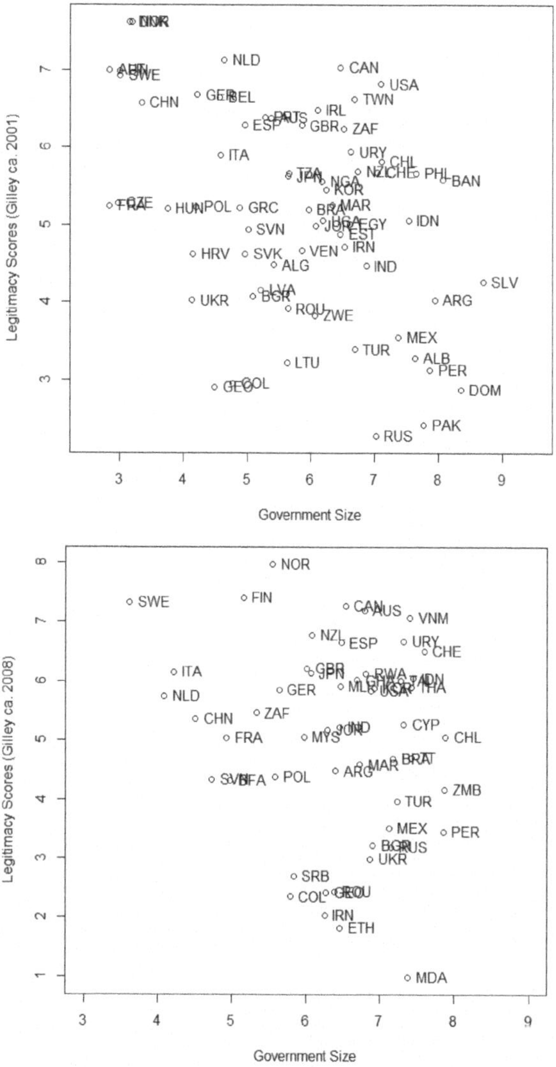

Figure 23: Legitimacy and Government Size (cont.)

Gilley ca. 2012:

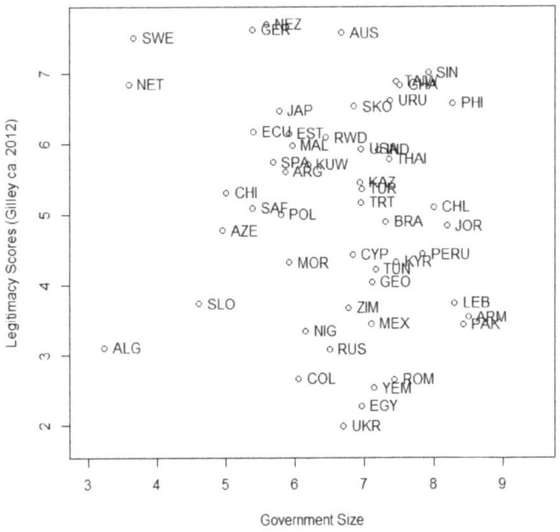

Appendix S – Stepwise Regression of the Areas of Economic Freedom (Norris)

Table 66: Stepwise Regressions of the Areas of Economic Freedom (Norris ca. 2001)

	(1)	(2)	*(3)*	(4)	(5)	(6)	*(7)*	(8)	*(9)*
Intercept	4.25***	*3.84****	3.75***	4.68***	4.74***	5.14***	*4.54****	3.84***	3.75***
Areas of Economic Freedom									
Government Size	-0.01			-0.15	-0.15	-0.08			
Legal System and Property Rights	0.13	*0.11*		0.18	0.18	0.23	*0.26**	0.11	
Sound Money	0.28***	*0.27****	0.30***	0.28***	0.29**	0.29***	*0.27****	0.27***	0.30***
Freedom to Trade Internationally	-0.23*	*-0.25***	-0.17*	-0.26	-0.25	-0.29	*-0.28**	-0.25**	-0.17*
Regulation	-0.11								
Credit Market				0.03					
Labor Market				0.15	0.15				
Business				-0.24	-0.24	-0.24	*-0.24*		
R^2	0.305	*0.298*	0.272	0.377	0.376	0.355	*0.346*	0.298	0.272
adjusted R^2	0.237	*0.259*	0.245	0.268	0.284	0.278	*0.285*	0.259	0.245
Observations	57	*57*	57	48	48	48	*48*	57	57

*- at 10%-level significant **- at 5%-level significant ***- at 1%-level significant

Note: Due to reasons of space, I exclude the areas 'government size' and 'regulation' when comparing model (1) and (2) (all coefficients of the particular areas show p-values larger than 0.50 in model (1)).

Table 67: Stepwise Regression of the Areas of Economic Freedom (Norris ca. 2008)

	(1)	(2)	(3)	(4)	(5)	(6)	(7)	(8)
Intercept	4.52***	4.74***	4.68	4.45**	4.59	4.50***	4.74***	4.68
Areas of Economic Freedom								
Government Size	0.01			0.01				
Legal System and Property Rights	0.52***	0.53***	0.49***	0.53***	0.53***	0.52***	0.53***	0.49***
Sound Money	-0.11	-0.11		-0.10	-0.10	-0.10	-0.11	
Freedom to Trade Internationally	-0.31	-0.29	-0.37**	-0.31	-0.31	0.32	-0.29	-0.37**
Regulation	0.05							
Credit Market				0.06	0.06	0.06		
Labor Market				0.01				
Business				-0.05	-0.04			
R^2	0.319	0.318	0.311	0.322	0.322	0.321	0.318	0.311
adjusted R^2	0.247	0.277	0.283	0.217	0.250	0.265	0.277	0.283
Observations	53	53	53	53	53	53	53	53

* - at 10%-level significant ** - at 5%-level significant *** - at 1%-level significant

Note: Due to reasons of space, I exclude the areas 'government size' and 'regulation' when comparing model (1) and (2) (all coefficients of the particular areas show p-values close to or larger than 0.80 in model (1)). Similarly, I also exclude the areas 'government size' and 'labor market regulation' when comparing model (4) and (5) (all coefficients of the particular areas show p-values close to or larger than 0.90 in model (4)).

Table 68: Stepwise Regression of the Areas of Economic Freedom (Norris ca. 2012)

	(1)	(2)	(3)	(4)	(5)	(6)	(7)
Intercept	2.57**	3.30***	2.84	2.27**	2.50**	2.82***	3.13***
Areas of Economic Freedom							
Government Size	0.15			0.10	0.09		
Legal System and Property Rights	0.64***	0.57***	0.53***	0.53***	0.54***	0.47***	0.49***
Sound Money	-0.23*	-0.21		-0.24*	-0.25*	-0.24*	-0.23*
Freedom to Trade Internationally	-0.41**	-0.36*	-0.49***	-0.40**	-0.35*	-0.32*	-0.30*
Regulation	0.36**	0.39**	0.38**				
Credit Market				0.07			
Labor Market				0.11	0.12	0.13	
Business				0.40**	0.40**	0.45**	0.49**
R^2	0.496	0.472	0.443	0.520	0.512	0.504	0.486
adjusted R^2	0.443	0.429	0.409	0.447	0.450	0.452	0.444
Observations	54	54	54	54	54	54	54

* - at 10%-level significant ** - at 5%-level significant *** - at 1%-level significant

Appendix T – Income-Inequality Gap, Ownership Gap, and Responsibility Gap

Table 69: Income-Inequality Gap

Model	(1) Norris ca. 2001		(2) Norris ca. 2008		(3) Norris ca. 2012	
	Coeff.	p-value	Coeff.	p-value	Coeff.	p-value
Individual-Level Variables						
Intercept	7.639***	0.000	6.145***	0.000	7.632***	0.000
Age	-0.121***	0.000	-0.004	0.194	-0.011***	0.000
Age^2	0.0001***	0.003	0.00001***	0.005	0.0002***	0.000
Male	0.021	0.292	-0.004	0.801	-0.038**	0.011
Compl. primary school[a]	-0.224***	0.000	-0.255***	0.000	-0.074**	0.013
Compl. secondary school[a]	-0.346***	0.000	-0.308***	0.000	-0.175***	0.000
Compl. college[a]	-0.443***	0.000	-0.333***	0.000	-0.186***	0.000
Compl. university[a]	-0.474***	0.000	-0.429***	0.000	-0.330***	0.000
Income (continuous)	-0.026***	0.000	0.036***	0.000	0.052***	0.000
Religious Person[b]	0.304***	0.000	0.281***	0.000	0.245***	0.000
Atheist Person[b]	-0.252***	0.000	-0.230***	0.000	-0.179***	0.000
Media Contact	-	-	0.068***	0.000	0.116***	0.000
Political Interest	0.508***	0.000	0.378***	0.000	0.402***	0.000
Interpersonal Trust	-	-	0.486***	0.000	0.416***	0.000
Life Satisfaction	0.075***	0.000	0.115***	0.000	0.111***	0.000
Victim of Crime	-	-	-	-	-0.179***	0.000
Feels Unsafe	-	-	-	-	-0.069***	0.000
Income-Inequality Gap	*-0.005****	*0.000*	*-0.003****	*0.000*	*-0.007****	*0.000*
Country-Level Variables						
Democracy	0.087	0.838	-0.198	0.152	-0.139*	0.078
Democratic History	-0.106	0.154	0.049	0.550	-0.004	0.945
Democracy*DemocraticHistory[1]	0.091***	0.007	-0.003	0.923	0.020	0.277
New General Governance	0.472	0.170	0.767**	0.025	0.827***	0.000
HDI (absolute)	-4.981**	0.010	-1.567	0.336	-3.623***	0.004
Unemployment Rate	-0.019	0.433	-0.017	0.681	-0.056**	0.010
-2LL	137265		192736		249878	
AIC/BIC	137269/137286		192740/192757		249882/2499001	
Pseudo-R^2	0.1579		0.1694		0.2186	
Observations (individual level)	34270		49788		62288	
Observations (country level)	27		45		50	

[1] - Interaction term is mean centered.
* - at 10%-level significant ** - at 5%-level significant *** - at 1%-level significant
[a] - reference category: no primary school completed [b] - reference category: no religious person

Table 70: Ownership Gap

Model	(1) Norris ca. 2001		(2) Norris ca. 2008		(3) Norris ca. 2012	
	Coeff.	p-value	Coeff.	p-value	Coeff.	p-value
Individual-Level Variables						
Intercept	7.708***	0.000	5.954***	0.000	7.618***	0.000
Age	-0.012***	0.001	-0.002	0.387	-0.011***	0.000
Age²	0.0002***	0.000	0.00001**	0.022	0.0002***	0.000
Male	0.004	0.845	0.003	0.849	-0.034**	0.024
Compl. primary school[a]	-0.202***	0.000	-0.268***	0.000	-0.059*	0.051
Compl. secondary school[a]	-0.342***	0.000	-0.344***	0.000	-0.169***	0.000
Compl. college[a]	-0.406***	0.000	-0.377***	0.000	-0.185***	0.000
Compl. university[a]	-0.458***	0.000	-0.465***	0.000	-0.327***	0.000
Income (continuous)	-0.032***	0.000	0.038***	0.000	0.053***	0.000
Religious Person[b]	0.297***	0.000	0.281***	0.000	0.247***	0.000
Atheist Person[b]	-0.251***	0.000	-0.215***	0.000	-0.164***	0.000
Media Contact	-	-	0.068***	0.000	0.116***	0.000
Political Interest	0.438***	0.000	0.378***	0.000	0.397***	0.000
Interpersonal Trust	-	-	0.464***	0.000	0.416***	0.000
Life Satisfaction	0.072***	0.000	0.114***	0.000	0.111***	0.000
Victim of Crime	-	-	-	-	-0.174***	0.000
Feels Unsafe	-	-	-	-	-0.070***	0.000
Ownership Gap	*-0.004****	*0.000*	*-0.003****	*0.003*	*-0.006****	*0.000*
Country-Level Variables						
Democracy	0.095	0.874	-0.199	0.171	-0.141*	0.072
Democratic History	-0.106	0.164	0.053	0.540	-0.002	0.977
Democracy*DemocraticHistory[1]	0.093***	0.008	-0.002	0.962	0.020	0.268
New General Governance	0.451	0.204	0.753**	0.038	0.829***	0.000
HDI (absolute)	-5.081**	0.011	-1.242	0.478	-3.658***	0.003
Unemployment Rate	-0.020	0.427	-0.021	0.636	-0.055**	0.011
-2LL	123977		174232		244853	
AIC/BIC	123979/123996		174236/174253		244857/244875	
Pseudo-R²	0.1600		0.1753		0.2186	
Observations (individual level)	31247		45072		61058	
Observations (country level)	26		42		50	

[1] - Interaction term is mean centered.
* - at 10%-level significant ** - at 5%-level significant *** - at 1%-level significant
[a] - reference category: no primary school completed [b] - reference category: no religious person

Table 71: Responsibility Gap

Model	(1) Norris ca. 2001		(2) Norris ca. 2008		(3) Norris ca. 2012	
	Coeff.	p-value	Coeff.	p-value	Coeff.	p-value
Individual-Level Variables						
Intercept	7.643***	0.000	6.185***	0.000	7.671***	0.000
Age	-0.012***	0.000	-0.003	0.187	-0.011***	0.000
Age^2	0.0002***	0.000	0.00001***	0.004	0.0002***	0.000
Male	0.024	0.217	-0.001	0.950	-0.036**	0.013
Compl. primary school[a]	-0.218***	0.000	-0.265***	0.000	-0.072**	0.015
Compl. secondary school[a]	-0.346***	0.000	-0.315***	0.000	-0.176***	0.000
Compl. college[a]	-0.441***	0.000	-0.342***	0.000	-0.186***	0.000
Compl. university[a]	-0.481***	0.000	-0.435***	0.000	-0.331***	0.000
Income (continuous)	-0.027***	0.000	0.034***	0.000	0.052***	0.000
Religious Person[b]	0.302***	0.000	0.281***	0.000	0.247***	0.000
Atheist Person[b]	-0.236***	0.000	-0.238***	0.000	-0.177***	0.000
Media Contact	-	-	0.068***	0.000	0.117***	0.000
Political Interest	0.507***	0.000	0.374***	0.000	0.400***	0.000
Interpersonal Trust	-	-	0.480***	0.000	0.412***	0.000
Life Satisfaction	0.075***	0.000	0.115***	0.000	0.111***	0.000
Victim of Crime	-	-	-	-	-0.177***	0.000
Feels Unsafe	-	-	-	-	-0.070***	0.000
Responsibility Gap	*-0.007****	*0.000*	*-0.006****	*0.000*	*-0.009****	*0.000*
Country-Level Variables						
Democracy	0.093	0.382	-0.198	0.153	-0.139*	0.077
Democratic History	-0.107	0.151	0.051	0.535	-0.004	0.947
Democracy*DemocraticHistory[1]	0.092***	0.007	-0.003	0.929	0.020	0.269
New General Governance	0.463	0.180	0.758**	0.027	0.823***	0.000
HDI (absolute)	-5.008**	0.010	-1.572	0.336	-3.631***	0.004
Unemployment Rate	-0.020	0.415	-0.016	0.691	-0.056**	0.010
-2LL	138046		193183		251086	
AIC/BIC	138050/138067		193187/193204		251090/251108	
Pseudo-R^2	0.1593		0.1695		0.2210	
Observations (individual level)	34482		49936		62581	
Observations (country level)	27		46		50	

[1] - Interaction term is mean centered.
* - at 10%-level significant ** - at 5%-level significant *** - at 1%-level significant
[a] - reference category: no primary school completed [b] - reference category: no religious person

References

Aghion, P., Alesina, A., & Trebbi, F. (2004). Endogenous Political Institutions. *The Quarterly Journal of Economics*, *119*(2), 565-611.

Alesina, A., Devleeschauwer, A., Easterly, W., Kurlat, S., & Wacziarg, R. (2003). Fractionalization. *Journal of Economic Growth*, *8*(2), 155-194.

Alesina, A., & Spolaore, E. (2005). *The Size of Nations*. MIT Press.

Anderson, C. (2005). *Losers' Consent: Elections and Democratic Legitimacy*. Oxford University Press on Demand.

Anderson, C. J., & Guillory, C. A. (1997). Political Institutions and Satisfaction with Democracy: A Cross-National Analysis of Consensus and Majoritarian Systems. *American Political Science Review*, *91*(01), 66-81.

Ansell, C.K. (2001). Legitimacy: Political. In Smelser, N.J., Wright, James & Baltes. P.B. (ed.), *International Encyclopedia of the Social and Behavioural Sciences*. (pp. 8704-8706). Elsevier Sciences Ltd.

Baier, S. L., & Bergstrand, J. H. (2001). The Growth of World Trade: Tariffs, Transport Costs, and Income Similarity. *Journal of International Economics*, *53*(1), 1-27.

Baltes-Götz, B. (2013). Analyse von hierarchischen linearen Modellen mit der SPSS-Prozedur MIXED. *Zentrum für Informations-, Medien- und Kommunikations-technologie, Trier*.

Barro, R. J. (1995). Inflation and Economic Growth. *Bank of England Quarterly Bulletin, 35 (May 1995)*, 166–176.

Barro, R. J. (1997). *Determinants of Economic Growth: A Cross-Country Empirical Study*. Cambridge, MA: MIT Press.

Beetham, D. (1991). Max Weber and the Legitimacy of the Modern State. *Analyse & Kritik*, *13*(1), 34-45.

Beetham, D. (1993). In Defence of Legitimacy. *Political Studies*, *41*(3), 488-491.

Bensman, J. (1979). Max Weber's Concept of Legitimacy: An Evaluation. In A. Vidich & R. Glassman (eds), *Conflict and Control*. Thousand Oaks, CA: Sage.

Berggren, N. (1999). Economic Freedom and Equality: Friends or Foes?. *Public Choice*, *100*(3), 203-223.

C. M. Hindermann, *The Impact of Economic Freedom on State Legitimacy*,
Wirtschaft und Politik, https://doi.org/10.1007/978-3-658-23195-8

Berggren, N. (2003). The Benefits of Economic Freedom: A Survey. *The Independent Review*, *8*(2), 193-211.

Berggren, N., & Jordahl, H. (2005). Does Free Trade Really Reduce Growth? Further Testing Using the Economic Freedom Index. *Public Choice*, *122*(1-2), 99-114.

Berggren, N., Bjørnskov, C., & Lipka, D. (2015). Legitimacy and the Cost of Government. *Public Choice*, *162*(3-4), 307-328.

Bickel, R. (2007). *Multilevel Analysis for Applied Research: It's Just Regression!*. Guilford Press.

Blais, A. (2006). What Affects Voter Turnout?. *Annual Review of Political Science*, *9*, 111-125.

Blanchard, O. J., Das, M., & Faruqee, H. (2010). The Initial Impact of the Crisis on Emerging Market Countries. *Brookings Papers on Economic Activity*, *2010*(1), 263-307.

Bolaky, B., & Freund, C. L. (2004). Trade, Regulations, and Growth. *World Bank Policy Research Working Paper*, (3255).

Bollen, K., & Lennox, R. (1991). Conventional Wisdom on Measurement: A Structural Equation Perspective. *Psychological Bulletin*, *110*(2), 305.

Booth, J. A., & Seligson, M. A. (2005). Political Legitimacy and Participation in Costa Rica: Evidence of Arena Shopping. *Political Research Quarterly*, *58*(4), 537-550.

Booth, J. A., & Seligson, M. A. (2009a). *The Legitimacy Puzzle in Latin America: Political Support and Democracy in Eight Nations*. Cambridge University Press.

Booth, J. A., & Seligson, M. A. (2009b). Legitimacy and Political Participation in Eight Latin American Nations. In *Midwest Political Science Meeting, Chicago, IL*.

Bornschier, V. (1989). Legitimacy and Comparative Economic Success at the Core of the World System: An Exploratory Study. *European Sociological Review*, *5*(3), 215-230.

Brady, A. M. (2009). Mass Persuasion as a Means of Legitimation and China's Popular Authoritarianism. *American Behavioral Scientist*, *53*(3), 434-457.

Bruno, M., & Easterly, W. (1998). Inflation Crises and Long-Run Growth. *Journal of Monetary Economics*, *41*(1), 3-26.

Buchanan, J. M. (1992). *Markt, Freiheit und Demokratie*. Sankt Augustin: Comdok.

Büchs, M. (2008). How Legitimate is the Open Method of Coordination?. *Journal of Common Market Studies*, *46*(4), 765-786.

Cambridge Online Dictionary (2016, October 25). *Legitimacy*. Retrieved from http://dictionary.cambridge.org/dictionary/english/legitimacy

Caplan, B. (2007). *The Myth of the Rational Voter.* Princton: Princton University Press.

Carlsson, F., & Lundström, S. (2002). Economic Freedom and Growth: Decomposing the Effects. *Public Choice*, *112*(3-4), 335-344.

Catlaw, T. J., & Hu, Q. (2009). Legitimacy and Public Administration Constructing the American Bureaucratic Fields. *American Behavioral Scientist*, *53*(3), 458-481.

Cauchy, A. L. (1821). *Cours d'analyse de l'École Royale Polytechnique* (Vol. 1). Imprimerie royale.

Cebula, R. J. (2013). Which Economic Freedoms Influence per Capita Real Income?. *Applied Economics Letters*, *20*(4), 368-372.

Chamlin, M. B., & Cochran, J. K. (2006). Economic Inequality, Legitimacy, and Cross-National Homicide Rates. *Homicide Studies*, *10*(4), 231-252.

Chen, M. X., Otsuki, T., & Wilson, J. S. (2006). Do Standards Matter for Export Success?. *World Bank Policy Research Working Paper*, (3809).

Clarke, H., Ditt, N. & Kornberg, A. (1993). The Political Economy of Attitudes Toward Polity and Society in Western European Democracies, *Journal of Politics, 55*, 998–1021.

Costa-Lopes, R., Dovidio, J. F., Pereira, C. R., & Jost, J. T. (2013). Social Psychological Perspectives on the Legitimation of Social Inequality: Past, Present and Future. *European Journal of Social Psychology*, *43*(4), 229-237.

Crespo, F. (2006). Institutional Legitimacy and Crime in Venezuela. *Journal of Contemporary Criminal Justice*, *22*(4), 347-367.

Dahl, R. A. (1973). *Polyarchy: Participation and Opposition*. Yale University Press.

Dahl, R. A. (2006). *On Political Equality*. Yale University Press.

Dalton, R. J. (1999). Political Support in Advanced Industrial Societies. In P. Norris (ed.), *Critical Citizens. Global Support for Democratic Governance.* Oxford: Oxford University Press.

Dalton, R. J. (2004). *Democratic Challenges, Democratic Choices: The Erosion of Political Support in Advanced Industrial Democracies.* OUP Oxford.

Davenport, C. (2007). State Repression and Political Order. *Annual Review of Political Science, 10*, 1–23.

De Haan, J., & Sturm, J. E. (2000). On the Relationship Between Economic Freedom and Economic Growth. *European Journal of Political Economy, 16*(2), 215-241.

De Soysa, I., & Vadlammanati, K. C. (2013). Do Pro-Market Economic Reforms Drive Human Rights Violations? An Empirical Assessment, 1981–2006. *Public Choice, 155*(1-2), 163-187.

Disdier, A. C., Fontagné, L., & Mimouni, M. (2008). The Impact of Regulations on Agricultural Trade: Evidence from the SPS and TBT Agreements. *American Journal of Agricultural Economics, 90*(2), 336-350.

Di Tella, R., MacCulloch, R. J., & Oswald, A. J. (2001). Preferences over Inflation and Unemployment: Evidence from Surveys of Happiness. *The American Economic Review, 91*(1), 335-341.

Djankov, S., Freund, C., & Pham, C. S. (2010). Trading on Time. *The Review of Economics and Statistics, 92*(1), 166-173.

Dogan, M. (2003). Conceptions of Legitimacy. In *Encyclopedia of Government and Politics. Volume 1*, 116-128.

Dogan, M. (2009). Political Legitimacy: New Criteria and Anachronistic Theories. *International Social Science Journal, 60*(196), 195-210.

Domański, H. (2005). Determinants of Legitimization in Europe: An Empirical Analysis for 21 Countries. *Empiria. Revista de Metodología de Ciencias Sociales,* (9), 61-88.

Doyle, D. (2011). The Legitimacy of Political Institutions Explaining Contemporary Populism in Latin America. *Comparative Political Studies, 44*(11), 1447-1473.

Easterlin, R. A. (2001). Income and Happiness: Towards a Unified Theory. *The Economic Journal, 111*(473), 465-484.

Easterly, W., & Levine, R. (1997). Africa's Growth Tragedy: Policies and Ethnic Divisions. *The Quarterly Journal of Economics, 112*(4), 1203-1250.

Easton, D. (1965). *A Framework for Political Analysis* (Vol. 25). Englewood Cliffs, NJ: Prentice-Hall.

Easton, D. (1975). A Re-Assessment of the Concept of Political Support. *British Journal of Political Science* 5(4). 435-457.

Eriksen, E. O., & Fossum, J. E. (2000). Legitimation Through Deliberation. *Democracy in the EU: Integration Through Deliberation*, 256-269.

Fearon, J. D. (2003). Ethnic and Cultural Diversity by Country. *Journal of Economic Growth*, *8*(2), 195-222.

Farr, W. K., Lord, R. A., & Wolfenbarger, J. L. (1998). Economic Freedom, Political Freedom, and Economic Well-Being: A Causality Analysis. *Cato J.*, *18*, 247.

Feld, L. P., & Voigt, S. (2003). Economic Growth and Judicial Independence: Cross-Country Evidence Using a New Set of Indicators. *European Journal of Political Economy*, *19*(3), 497-527.

Feldmann, M. & Mazepus H. (2014). Social Contract and Legitimacy: The Case of Putin's Russia. Prepared for Workshop on 'Regime Legitimisation Through Institutional Reform: Analysing its Dimensions and Effectiveness' at the ECPR Joint Sessions in Salamanca, 10-15 April 2014.

Finkel, S.E., Muller, E.N. & Seligson, M.A. (1989). Economic Crisis, Incumbent Performance and Regime Support: A Comparison of Longitudinal Data from West Germany and Costa Rica, *British Journal of Political Science 19(3)*, 329–51.

Fischer, S. (1993). The Role of Macroeconomic Factors in Growth. *Journal of Monetary Economics*, *32*(3), 485-512.

Follesdal, A., & Hix, S. (2006). Why There is a Democratic Deficit in the EU: A Response to Majone and Moravcsik. *Journal of Common Market Studies*, *44*(3), 533-562.

Freedom House (2015). Freedom in the World 2015: Discarding Democracy: A Return to the Iron Fist. *Washington, DC: Freedom House.*

Frey, B. S., & Stutzer, A. (2002). What Can Economists Learn from Happiness Research?. *Journal of Economic Literature*, *40*(2), 402-435.

Friedman, M. (1969). *Capitalism and Freedom*. University of Chicago Press.

Friedrich, C. J. (1961). Political Leadership and the Problem of the Charismatic Power. *The Journal of Politics*, *23*(01), 3-24.

Gaus, D. (2011). *The Dynamics of Legitimation. Why the Study of Political Legitimacy Needs More Realism* (No. p0336). ARENA.

Gerschewski, J. (2013). The Three Pillars of Stability: Legitimation, Repression, and Co-Optation in Autocratic Regimes. *Democratization*, *20*(1), 13-38.

Gibson, J. L., Caldeira, G. A., & Baird, V. A. (1998). On the Legitimacy of National High Courts. *American Political Science Review*, *92*(02), 343-358.

Gill, G. (1982). Personal Dominance and the Collective Principle: Individual Legitimacy in Marxist—Leninist Systems. In *Political Legitimation in Communist States*, 94-110. Palgrave Macmillan UK.

Gilley, B. (2006a). The Meaning and Measure of State Legitimacy: Results for 72 Countries. *European Journal of Political Research*, *45*(3), 499-525.

Gilley, B. (2006b). The Determinants of State Legitimacy: Results for 72 Countries. *International Political Science Review*, *27*(1), 47-71.

Gilley, B. (2009a). *The Right to Rule. How States Win and Lose Legitimacy*. New York: Columbia University Press.

Gilley, B. (2009b). *The Right to Rule: How States Win and Lose Legitimacy. Online Appendices.* Retrieved from http://www.web.pdx.edu/~gilleyb/RighttoRule_Appendices.pdf

Gilley, B. (2012). State Legitimacy: An Updated Dataset for 52 Countries. *European Journal of Political Research*, *51*(5), 693-699.

Gjefsen, T. (2012). Sources of Regime Legitimacy: Quality of Government and Electoral Democracy.

Goel, R. K., & Nelson, M. A. (2005). Economic Freedom Versus Political Freedom: Cross-Country Influences on Corruption. *Australian Economic Papers*, *44*(2), 121-133.

Goldsmith, A. A. (1997). Economic Rights and Government in Developing Countries: Cross-National Evidence on Growth and Development. *Studies in Comparative International Development, 32(2)*, 29-44.

Graham, C. (2005). The Economics of Happiness. *World Economics*, *6*(3), 41-55.

Grauvogel, J. & von Soest, C. (2013). *Claims to Legitimacy Matter: Why Sanctions Fail to Instigate Democratization in Authoritarian Regimes*. GIGA Working Papers 235.

Gwartney, J. D., Lawson, R., & Block, W. (1996). *Economic Freedom of the World, 1975-1995*. Fraser Institute.

Gwartney, J., Holcombe, R., & Lawson, R. (1998). Scope of Government and the Wealth of Nations, *Cato J.*, *18*, 163.

Gwartney, J, Lawson, R. & Hall, J. (2014). *Economic Freedom of the World: 2014 Annual Report.* Fraser Institute.

Gwartney, J, Lawson, R. & Hall, J. (2015). *Economic Freedom of the World: 2015 Annual Report.* Fraser Institute.

Habermas, J. (1975). *Legitimation Crisis* (Vol. 519). Beacon Press.

Habermas, J. (1996). *Between Facts and Norms: Contribution to a Discourse Theory of Law and Democracy.* Cambridge, MA: MIT Press.

Habermas, J. (1998). Remarks on Legitimation Through Human Rights. *The Modern Schoolman*, *75*(2), 87-100.

Hachez, N., & Wouters, J. (2013). *Promoting the Rule of Law: A Benchmarks Approach.* Available at SSRN https://ssrn.com/abstract=2258331 or http://dx.doi.org/10.2139/ssrn.2258331

Hadenius, A., & Teorell, J. (2005). Assessing Alternative Indices of Democracy. Retrieved from http://lup.lub.lu.se/record/740759

Hayek, F. A. (1944). *The Road to Serfdom, London.* George Routledge & Sons.

Hayek, F. A. (1960). *The Constitution of Liberty.* Chicago: University of Chicago.

Hayek, F. A. (1976). *Denationalisation of Money*. London: Institute of Economic Affairs.

Hayek, F. A. (1993). *Law, Legistlation and Liberty: A New Statement of the Liberal Principles of Justice and Political Economy*. London: Routledge.

Hayes, A. F. (2006). A Primer on Multilevel Modeling. *Human Communication Research*, *32*(4), 385-410.

Hechter, M. (2009). Introduction: Legitimacy in the Modern World. *American Behavioral Scientist, 53*(3), 279-288.

Heck, R. H., & Thomas, S. L. (2015). *An Introduction to Multilevel Modeling Techniques: MLM and SEM Approaches Using Mplus*. Routledge.

Heckelman, J. C., & Stroup, M. D. (2005). A Comparison of Aggregation Methods for Measures of Economic Freedom. *European Journal of Political Economy, 21*(4), 953-966.

Hegtvedt, K. A., & Johnson, C. (2009). Power and Justice Toward an Understanding of Legitimacy. *American Behavioral Scientist*, *53*(3), 376-399.

Heinemann, F. (2001). After the Death of Inflation: Will Fiscal Drag Survive?. *Fiscal Studies*, *22*(4), 527-546.

Höreth, M. (2001). *The European Commission's White Paper on Governance: A "tool-kit" for Closing the Legitimacy Gap of EU Policy-making*. Zentrum für Europäische Integrationsforschung.

Horne, C. (2009). A Social Norms Approach to Legitimacy. *American Behavioral Scientist*, *53*(3), 400-415.

Hough, M., Jackson, J., Bradford, B., Myhill, A., & Quinton, P. (2010). Procedural Justice, Trust, and Institutional Legitimacy. *Policing: A Journal of Policy and Practice*, *4*(3), 203-210.

Hox, J. J. (2002). *Multilevel Analysis: Techniques and Applications*. Mahwah, NJ: LawrenceErlbaum.

Huang, M. H., Chang, Y. T., & Chu, Y. H. (2008). Identifying Sources of Democratic Legitimacy: A Multilevel Analysis. *Electoral Studies*, *27*(1), 45-62.

Hurd, I. (1999). Legitimacy and Authority in International Politics. *International Organization*, *53*(02), 379-408.

Hurrelmann, A., Schneider, S., & Steffek, J. (2007). Introduction: Legitimacy in an Age of Global Politics. In *Legitimacy in an Age of Global Politics,* 1-16. Palgrave Macmillan UK.

Hurrelmann, A., Krell-Laluhová, Z., Nullmeier, F., Schneider, S., & Wiesner, A. (2009). Why the Democratic Nation-State Is Still Legitimate: A Study of Media Discourses. *European Journal of Political Research*, *48*(4), 483-515.

Hurrelmann, A., Gora, A., & Wagner, A. (2013). The Legitimation of the European Union in the News Media: Three Treaty Reform Debates. *Journal of European Public Policy*, *20*(4), 515-534.

Immervoll, H. (2005). Falling Up the Stairs: The Effects of 'Bracket Creep' on Household Income. *Review of Income and Wealth*, *51*(1), 37-62.

Inglehart, R., & Baker, W. E. (2000). Modernization, Cultural Change, and the Persistence of Traditional Values. *American Sociological Review*, 19-51.

Jahan, S. (2015). Human Development Report 2015. *Work for Human Development. New York: United Nations Development Programme.*

Jarausch, K. H. (2012). Realer Sozialismus als Fürsorgediktatur: zur begrifflichen Einordnung der DDR. *Historical Social Research, Supplement, 24*, 249-272.

Jost, J. T., & Hunyady, O. (2005). Antecedents and Consequences of System-Justifying Ideologies. *Current Directions in Psychological Science*, *14*(5), 260-265.

Jost, J. T., & Major, B. (2001). *The Psychology of Legitimacy: Emerging Perspectives on Ideology, Justice, and Intergroup Relations*. Cambridge University Press.

Katz, R. S., & Wessels, B. (1999). *The European Parliament, the National Parliaments, and European Integration*. Oxford University Press.

Kaufman, A. (1997). Reason, Self-legislation and Legitimacy: Conceptions of Freedom in the Political Thought of Rousseau and Kant. *The Review of Politics*, *59*(01), 25-52.

Kaufmann, D., Kraay, A., & Mastruzzi, M. (2009). Governance Matters VIII: Aggregate and Individual Governance Indicators, 1996-2008. *World Bank Policy Research Working Paper*, (4978).

Keman, H. (2014). Democratic Performance of Parties and Legitimacy in Europe. *West European Politics*, *37*(2), 309-330.

Kim, J. (2003). *Effekte und Grenzen der politischen Legitimität und die Regimestabilität der autoritären Herrschaft* (Doctoral dissertation, Freie Universität Berlin).

Klingemann, H. D. (1999). Mapping Political Support in the 1990s: A Global Analysis. In P. Norris (ed.), *Critical Citizens: Global Support for Democratic Government*, 31-56. Oxford: Oxford University Press.

Klodt, H. (2015). *TTIP: Chance Handel-Risiko Investorenschutz* (No. 84). Kiel Policy Brief.

Kluegel, J. R., Mason, D. S., & Wegener, B. (1999). The Legitimation of Capitalism in the Postcommunist Transition Public Opinion about Market Justice, 1991—1996. *European Sociological Review, 15*(3), 251-283.

Kornberg, A., & Clarke, H. D. (1992). *Citizens and Community: Political Support in a Representative Democracy*. Cambridge University Press.

Kostadinova, T., & Power, T. J. (2007). Does Democratization Depress Participation? Voter Turnout in the Latin American and Eastern European Transitional Democracies. *Political Research Quarterly, 60*(3), 363-377.

Krueger, A. (2012). The Rise and Consequences of Inequality. *Presentation Made to the Center for American Progress, January 12th. Available at http://www. americanprogress. org/events/2012/01/12/17181/the-rise-and-consequences-of-inequality.*

Kvanli, A., Pavur, R., & Keeling, K. (2005). *Concise Managerial Statistics*. Cengage Learning.

Lake, D. A. (2009). Relational Authority and Legitimacy in International Relations. *American Behavioral Scientist, 53*(3), 331-353.

Lamb, R. D. (2005). Measuring Legitimacy in Weak States. In *Graduate Student Conference on Security, Georgetown University, Washington, DC.*

Lamb, R. D. (2014). *Rethinking Legitimacy and Illegitimacy: A New Approach to Assessing Support and Opposition across Disciplines*. Rowman & Littlefield.

Lane, C. (1984). Legitimacy and Power in the Soviet Union Through Socialist Ritual. *British Journal of Political Science, 14*(02), 207-217.

Lawson, R. A., & Clark, J. R. (2010). Examining the Hayek–Friedman Hypothesis on Economic and Political Freedom. *Journal of Economic Behavior & Organization, 74*(3), 230-239.

Levi, M., Sacks, A., & Tyler, T. (2009). Conceptualizing Legitimacy, Measuring Legitimating Beliefs. *American Behavioral Scientist, 53*(3), 354-375.

Levi, M., & Sacks, A. (2009). Legitimating Beliefs: Sources and Indicators. *Regulation & Governance, 3*(4), 311-333.

Lijphart, A. (1984). *Democracies: Patterns of Majoritarian and Consensus Government in Twenty-One Countries*. Yale University Press.

Lindgren, K. O., & Persson, T. (2010). Input and Output Legitimacy: Synergy or Trade-Off? Empirical Evidence from an EU Survey. *Journal of European Public Policy*, *17*(4), 449-467.

Linz, J. J. (1988). Legitimacy of Democracy and the Socioeconomic System. *Comparing Pluralist Democracies*, 65-113.

Lipset, S. M. (1959). Some Social Requisites of Democracy: Economic Development and Political Legitimacy. *American Political Science Review*, *53*(01), 69-105.

Loayza, N., Oviedo, A. M., & Servén, L. (2005). The Impact of Regulation on Growth and Informality Cross-Country Evidence. *World Bank Policy Research Working Paper*, (3623).

Luhmann, N. (1969). *Legitimation durch Verfahren*. Frankfurt a.M.: Suhrkamp.

Mainwaring, S., Brinks, D. & Pérez-Liñán, A. (2007). Classifying Political Regimes in Latin America, 1945–2004. In Munck, G. (ed.), *Regimes and Democracy in Latin America: Theories and Methods*, 123-162. New York: Oxford University Press.

Majone, G. (1998). Europe's 'Democratic Deficit': The Question of Standards. *European Law Journal*, *4*(1), 5-28.

Marshall, M. G. & Jaggers, K. (2007). *Polity IV Project. Political Regime Characteristics and Transitions, 1800-2006. Users Manual*. Center for Systemic Peace. Retrieved from http://www.systemicpeace.org/polity4

Maskus, K. E., Otsuki, T., & Wilson, J. S. (2005). The Cost of Compliance with Product Standards for Firms in Developing Countries: An Econometric Study. *World Bank Policy Research Working Paper*, (3590).

Mehlkop, G. (2002). *Wirtschaftliche Freiheit, Einkommensungleichheit und physische Lebensqualität*. VS Verlag für Sozialwissenschaften.

Miller, T. & Kim, A. B. (2016). *2016 Index of Economic Freedom*. The Heritage Foundation.

Montgomery, D. C., Peck, E. A., & Vining, G. G. (2012). *Introduction to Linear Regression Analysis* (Vol. 821). John Wiley & Sons.

Munck, G. L. (2009). *Measuring Democracy: A Bridge Between Scholarship and Politics*. JHU Press.

Møller, F. S. (2016). Legitimitet og Borgerkriges Opståen: Befolkningens Oversete Motiver. *Politica, 48*(1), 30-48.

Nivette, A. E., & Eisner, M. (2013). Do Legitimate Polities Have Fewer Homicides? A Cross-National Analysis. *Homicide Studies, 17*(1), 3-26.

Nordås, H., Pinali, E., & Grosso, M. G. (2006). *Logistics and Time as a Trade Barrier* (No. 35). OECD Publishing.

North, D. C., Wallis, J. J., & Weingast, B. R. (2009). *Violence and Social Orders: A Conceptual Framework for Interpreting Recorded Human History*. Cambridge University Press.

Norris, P. (1999). *Critical Citizens: Global Support for Democratic Government*. OUP Oxford.

Norris, P. (2011). *Democratic Deficit: Critical Citizens Revisited*. Cambridge University Press.

Nullmeier, F. (2013). Die Legitimation der Marktwirtschaft. *Wirtschaftsdienst*, *93*(1), 34-40.

Ochsner, M. (2016). *Die soziale Verantwortung des Staates: Wie sich Wohlfahrtsleistungen auf die Legitimität des Staates auswirken*. Springer-Verlag.

Olson, M. (1982). The Rise and Decline of Nations: Economic Growth, Stagnation, and Social Rigidities. *New Heaven*.

O'Sullivan, M. (1989). Failing Gym Is Like Failing Lunch or Recess: Two Beginning Teachers' Struggle for Legitimacy. *Journal of Teaching in Physical Education*, *8*(3), 227-242.

O'Sullivan, S., Healy, A. E., & Breen, M. J. (2014). Political Legitimacy in Ireland During Economic Crisis: Insights from the European Social Survey. *Irish Political Studies*, *29*(4), 547-572.

Ostry, J. D., Ghosh, A. R., Habermeier, K., Chamon, M., Qureshi, M. S., & Reinhardt, D. (2010). Capital Inflows: The Role of Controls. *Revista de Economia Institucional*, *12*(23), 135-164.

Partzsch, L. (2011). The Legitimacy of Biofuel Certification. *Agriculture and Human Values*, *28*(3), 413-425.

Pierre, J., Røiseland, A., & Gustavsen, A. (2011). Legitimacy by Performance in Democratic Systems? Preparing for Empirical Analysis. *Nordisk Kommuneforskerkonferanse*, 24-25.

Power, T. J. & Cyr, J.M. (2009). Mapping Political Legitimacy in Latin America. *International Social Science Journal 60*(196). 253-272.

Rawls, J. (1971). *A Theory of Justice*. Cambridge: Harvard University Press.

Rawls, J. (1993). *Political Liberalism*. New York: Columbia University Press.

Rawls, J. (2001). *Justice as Fairness: A Restatement*. Cambridge: Harvard University Press.

Rigby, T. H. (1982). Introduction: Political Legitimacy, Weber and Communist Mono-Organisational Systems. In *Political Legitimation in Communist States*,1-26. Palgrave Macmillan UK.

Risse, T. (2006). Transnational Governance and Legitimacy. In A. Benz & I. Papadopoulos (eds.), *Governance and Democracy: Comparing National, European and International Experiences*, Routledge.

Rohwer, A. (2009). Measuring Corruption: A Comparison Between the Transparency International's Corruption Perceptions Index and the World Bank's Worldwide Governance Indicators. *CESifo DICE Report*, *7*(3), 42-52.

Roller, E. (1994). Ideological Basis of the Market Economy: Attitudes Toward Distribution Principles and the Role of Government in Western and Eastern Germany. *European Sociological Review*, *10*(2), 105-117.

Rothschild, J. (1977). Observations on Political Legitimacy in Contemporary Europe. *Political Science Quarterly*, *92*(3), 487-501.

Rothstein, B. (2009). Creating Political Legitimacy: Electoral Democracy Versus Quality of Government. *American Behavioral Scientist*, *53*(3), 311-330.

Rothstein, B. & Teorell, J. (2008). What Is Quality of Government: A Theory of Impartial Political
Institutions. *Governance, 21(2),* 165-190.

Rothstein, B., & Teorell, J. (2012). Defining and Measuring Quality of Government. *Good Government: The Relevance of Political Science*, 6-26.

Rousseau, J. J. (1920). *The Social Contract and Discourses* (No. 660). JM Dent & Sons.

Sala-i-Martin, X., Doppelhofer, G., & Miller, R. I. (2004). Determinants of Long-Term Growth: A Bayesian Averaging of Classical Estimates (BACE) Approach. *The American Economic Review, 94*(4), 813-835.

Schaar, J. H. (1981). *Legitimacy in the Modern State*. Transaction Publishers.

Scharpf, F. W. (1970). *Demokratietheorie zwischen Utopie und Anpassung* (Vol. 25). Druckerei u. Verlagsanst. Universitätsverl..

Scharpf, F. W. (1998). *Interdependence and Democratic Legitimation* (No. 98/2). Max Planck Institute for the Study of Societies.

Scharpf, F. W. (1999). *Governing in Europe: Effective and Democratic?*. Oxford University Press.

Scharpf, F. W. (2015). Political Legitimacy in a Non-Optimal Currency Area. *Democratic Politics in a European Union Under Stress*, 20-44.

Schivardi, F., & Viviano, E. (2011). Entry Barriers in Retail Trade. *The Economic Journal, 121*(551), 145-170.

Schmidt, M. G. (2008). *Demokratietheorien. Eine Einführung, 4. überarbeitete und erweiterte Auflage*. Springer-Verlag.

Schmidt, V. A. (2013). Democracy and Legitimacy in the European Union Revisited: Input, Output and 'Throughput'. *Political Studies, 61*(1), 2-22.

Schmidtke, H., & Schneider, S. (2012). Methoden der empirischen Legitimationsforschung: Legitimität als mehrdimensionales Konzept. *Leviathan, 40(27)*, 225-242.

Schnabl, G., & Hoffmann, A. (2008). Monetary Policy, Vagabonding Liquidity and Bursting Bubbles in New and Emerging Markets: An Overinvestment View. *The World Economy, 31*(9), 1226-1252.

Schoon, E. W. (2014). The Asymmetry of Legitimacy: Analyzing the Legitimation of Violence in 30 Cases of Insurgent Revolution. *Social Forces, 93*(2), 779-801.

Seligson, M. A. (2002). The Impact of Corruption on Regime Legitimacy: A Comparative Study of Four Latin American Countries. *Journal of Politics, 64*(2), 408-433.

Seligson, M. A. (2007). The Rise of Populism and the Left in Latin America. *Journal of Democracy, 18*(3), 81-95.

Seron, C., Pereira, J., & Kovath, J. (2004). Judging Police Misconduct: "Street-Level" Versus Professional Policing. *Law & Society Review*, *38*(4), 665-710.

Slomcyznski, K. M., & Shabad, G. (1998). Can Support for Democracy and the Market Be Learned in School? A Natural Experiment in Post-Communist Poland. *Political Psychology*, *19*(4), 749-779.

Spector, H. (2010). Four Conceptions of Freedom. *Political Theory*, *38*(6), 780-808.

Spicer, M. W. (1995). On Friedrich Hayek and Taxation: Rationality, Rules, and Majority Rule. *National Tax Journal*, 103-112.

Stanford Encyclopedia (2016, October 26). *Political Legitimacy*. Retrieved from http://stanford.library.sydney.edu.au/entries/legitimacy/

Stroup, M. D. (2007). Economic Freedom, Democracy, and the Quality of Life. *World Development*, *35*(1), 52-66.

Stroup, M. D. (2008). Separating the Influence of Capitalism and Democracy on Women's Well-Being. *Journal of Economic Behavior & Organization*, *67*(3), 560-572.

Suchman, M. C. (1995). Managing Legitimacy: Strategic and Institutional Approaches. *Academy of Management Review*, *20*(3), 571-610.

Sunshine, J., & Tyler, T. R. (2003). The Role of Procedural Justice and Legitimacy in Shaping Public Support for Policing. *Law & Society Review*, *37*(3), 513-548.

Tajfel, H. & Turner, J. C. (1986). The Social Identity Theory of Intergroup Behavior. In S. Worchel & W. G. Austin (Eds.), *Psychology of Intergroup Relations,* 7–24. Chicago: Nelson-Hall.

Tamirisa, N. T. (1999). Exchange and Capital Controls as Barriers to Trade. *IMF Staff Papers*, *46*(1), 69-88.

Teorell, J., Charron, N., Dahlberg, S., Holmberg, S., Rothstein, B., Sundin, P. & Svensson, R. (2013). *The Quality of Government Dataset, Version May13*. University of Gothenburg: The Quality of Government Institute.

Teorell, J., Dahlberg, S., Holmberg, S., Rothstein, B., Hartmann, F., & Svensson, R. (2015). *The Quality of Government Standard Dataset, Version January15*. University of Gothenburg: The Quality of Government Institute.

Train, K. E. (2009). *Discrete Choice Methods with Simulation*. Cambridge University Press.

Transparency International (2015). *Corruption Perceptions Index: Data and Methodology*. Retrieved from http://files.transparency.org/content/download/1950/12812/file/2015_CPI_DataMethodologyZIP.zip

Transparency International (2016, December 21). *What is Corruption?*. Retrieved from http://www.transparency.org/what-is-corruption

Tyler, T. R. (2001). A Psychological Perspective on the Legitimacy of Institutions and Authorities. In J. T. Jost & B. Major (Eds.), *The Psychology of Legitimacy: Emerging Perspectives on Ideology, Justice, and Intergroup Relations*, 416-436. Cambridge, UK: Cambridge University Press.

Tyler, T. R. (2006). Psychological Perspectives on Legitimacy and Legitimation. *Annu. Rev. Psychol.*, *57*, 375-400.

Tyler, T. R., & Wakslak, C. J. (2004). Profiling and Police Legitimacy: Procedural Justice, Attributions of Motive, and Acceptance of Police Authority. *Criminology*, *42*(2), 253-282.

von Haldenwang, C. (2016). *Measuring Legitimacy – New Trends, Old Shortcomings?*. DIE Discussion Paper 18/2016.

Wacziarg, R., & Welch, K. H. (2008). Trade Liberalization and Growth: New Evidence. *The World Bank Economic Review*, *22*(2), 187-231.

Weatherford, M. S. (1992). Measuring Political Legitimacy. *American Political Science Review*, *86*(01), 149-166.

Weber, M. (1922). Die drei reinen Typen der legitimen Herrschaft. *Preußische Jahrbücher*, *187*, 1-12.

Weber, M. (1972). *Wirtschaft und Gesellschaft*. Tübingen: JCB Mohr.

Weede, E. (1996). Legitimacy, Democracy, and Comparative Economic Growth Reconsidered. *European Sociological Review*, *12*(3), 217-225.

Wegner, G. (2009). Substantive Versus Procedural Liberalism: Exploring a Dilemma of Contemporary Liberal Thought. *Journal of Institutional and Theoretical Economics JITE*, *165*(3), 535-557.

Wegner, G. (2012). *Ökonomischer Liberalismus als politische Theorie: Befund, Kritik, Rekonstruktion* (Vol. 62). Mohr Siebeck.

Wong, B., & Huang, X. (2010). Political Legitimacy in Singapore. *Politics & Policy, 38*(3), 523-543.

World Bank (2017, January 1). *General Government Final Consumption Expenditure.* Retrieved from http://worldbank.270a.info/classification/indicator/NE.CON.GOVT.CD.html

World Bank (2016, December 21). *Using the WGI data: Over Time Comparisons.* Retrieved from http://info.worldbank.org/governance/wgi/index.aspx#doc-over

World Values Survey – Third Wave (1995). *Codebook.* Retrieved from http://www.worldvaluessurvey.org/WVSDocumentationWV3.jsp

World Values Survey – Fourth Wave (1999). *Codebook.* Retrieved from http://www.worldvaluessurvey.org/WVSDocumentationWV4.jsp

World Values Survey – Fifth Wave (2005). *Codebook.* Retrieved from http://www.worldvaluessurvey.org/WVSDocumentationWV5.jsp

World Values Survey – Sixth Wave (2012). *Codebook.* Retrieved from http://www.worldvaluessurvey.org/WVSDocumentationWV6.jsp

Zelditch, M., Jr. (2001). Theories of Legitimacy. In J. T. Jost & B. Major (Eds.), *The Psychology of Legitimacy: Emerging Perspectives on Ideology, Justice, and Intergroup Relations*, 33–53. Cambridge, UK: Cambridge University Press.

Zeugner, S. (2011). Bayesian Model Averaging with BMS. *Tutorial to the R-package BMS 1e30.*

Zhao, D. (2009). The Mandate of Heaven and Performance Legitimation in Historical and Contemporary China. *American Behavioral Scientist, 53*(3), 416-433.

The manufacturer's authorised representative in the EU is Springer Nature Customer Service Centre GmbH, Europaplatz 3, 69115 Heidelberg, Germany. If you have any concerns regarding our products, please contact ProductSafety@springernature.com

Printed and bound by CPI Group (UK) Ltd, Croydon, CR0 4YY
05/10/2026
02228128-0007